WHEN YOU FREEZE VE...
HOW MUCH WILL IT MAKE?

Fresh	Frozen Pints	Fresh	Frozen Pints
ASPARAGUS		**EGGPLANT**	
1 crate (12 2-lb. bunches)	15 to 22	1 lb.	1
1 to 1½ lbs.	1		
		GREENS	
BEANS, LIMA, IN PODS		BEET GREENS	
1 bu. (32 lbs.)	12 to 16	15 lbs.	10 to 15
2 to 2½ lbs.	1	1 to 1½ lbs.	1
BEANS, SNAP, GREEN AND WAX		CHARD, COLLARDS,	
1 bu. (30 lbs.)	30 to 45	MUSTARD GREENS	
⅔ to 1 lb.	1	1 bu. (12 lbs.)	8 to 12
		1 to 1½ lbs.	1
BEETS, WITHOUT TOPS		KALE	
1 bu. (52 lbs.)	35 to 42	1 bu. (18 lbs.)	12 to 18
1¼ to 1½ lbs.	1	1 to 1½ lbs.	1
BROCCOLI		**PEAS**	
1 crate (25 lbs.)	24	1 bu. (30 lbs.)	12 to 15
1 lb.	1	2 to 2½ lbs.	1
BRUSSELS SPROUTS		**PEPPERS, GREEN**	
4 qt. boxes	6	⅔ lb. (3 peppers)	1
1 lb.	1		
		PUMPKIN, WINTER SQUASH	
CARROTS, WITHOUT TOPS		3 lbs.	2
1 bu. (50 lbs.)	32 to 40	**SPINACH**	
1¼ to 1½ lbs.	1	1 bu. (18 lbs.)	12 to 18
		1 to 1½ lbs.	1
CAULIFLOWER		**SQUASH, SUMMER**	
2 medium heads	3	1 bu. (40 lbs.)	32 to 40
1⅓ lbs.	1	1 to 1¼ lbs.	1
CORN, SWEET, IN HUSKS		**SWEET POTATOES**	
1 bu. (35 lbs.)	14 to 17	⅔ lb.	1
2 to 2½ lbs.	1		

Freezing & Canning
COOKBOOK

REVISED EDITION

Prized Recipes from the Farms of America

EDITED BY

NELL B. NICHOLS

FIELD FOOD EDITOR

FARM JOURNAL

DOUBLEDAY & COMPANY, INC.
GARDEN CITY, NEW YORK

ISBN: 0-385-00487-7
Library of Congress Catalog Card Number 72–91947

CONTENTS

COLOR ILLUSTRATIONS

All photographs created by Farm Journal Food and Art Staffs
Jacket design by Al Reagan, Farm Journal Art Department

Color Photographs by: Peter Dant Studios, George Faraghan Studios, Hoedt Studios, Tom Meehan, Mel Richman, Inc.

WHAT YOU WILL FIND
IN THIS COOKBOOK

This is a revised edition of the widely used FREEZING & CANNING COOKBOOK produced by the Food Editors of FARM JOURNAL in our Countryside Test Kitchens. Since 1963, when the book appeared, home freezing and canning have become extremely popular.

The interest in countryside living and the good things of the earth has brought with it a revival of the "home arts" practiced by earlier generations out of necessity. Gardening and the preparation and preserving of home-grown foods are today among the popular do-it-yourself occupations.

Of course, it's thrifty—and in an era of high food prices, that is a popular incentive. But the trend to simple living—especially among young people—is accompanied by the yearning to capture the tastes and smells of country kitchens, origin of such treats as jellies and jams, pickled peaches, ketchup, tomato preserves, mincemeat. Along with other old-time arts like baking yeast breads, cooking whole grain cereal, quilting, weaving, crocheting and home sewing, home food preservation is the "in thing." Young people also like to gather the native berries and fruits that nature provides and to prolong their use by freezing and canning.

With many women freezing and canning for the first time, a major purpose of this revised edition is to emphasize the basic methods, both old and new, that yield superior food with excellent keeping qualities.

To reduce spoilage problems in canning and to determine its causes, we analyzed our correspondence with home canners and found that tomatoes cause the most trouble. While some of the difficulty arises from the recent development of new varieties containing less acid than old-time varieties, the largest number of home canners who have spoilage with this favorite vegetable-fruit cling to the open-kettle method. In this revised edition, we recommend that it be abolished completely and that the processing time be increased.

Another canning failure results from fruit juices sometimes overflowing jars and interfering with the lid forming a tight seal. We discussed this problem with home economists employed by manufacturers of glass jars and self-sealing lids and also with Extension Service Home Economists who help homemakers with food preservation problems. From them, as well as from farm women who do a great deal of canning, we learned that this is a difficulty with raw-pack fruits. For this reason, in this edition, we recommend leaving from 1 to 1½" head space instead of ½ to 1" in jars of fruit canned by the raw-pack method. These are small changes but they are important in canning.

Country women are a great source of recipes for "putting up" foods, whether canned or frozen. With vegetables harvested at top succulence, fruits ripened by the sun, and barnyard animals fed until sleek and prime, good food is at home on country tables. The pioneer's need to extend summer's fullness throughout the year is an inherited instinct with farm women—not merely a means to salvage surpluses.

This cookbook, filled with long-time country favorite recipes—many of them consistently blue ribbon winners at fairs—is a testimonial to farm women.

The first chapter has original slick freezing tricks from country homemakers, for instance. See how gourmet cooks freeze the herbs they grow, fresh ginger root they buy. Notice how busy women put just-ripe apples in their freezers for making springtime applesauce with that wonderful, late-summer taste—how they buy or bake several kinds of bread, wrap a variety of slices together to freeze for mealtime choices.

Making jellies, jams, preserves and pickles for canning and freezing is important in country cooking. Farm homemakers still treasure and use heirloom recipes. This cookbook contains a carefully selected collection of these recipes, hundreds of them prize and praise winners. Exhibits at county and state fairs and their own family table are the farm cooks' display showcases. But they constantly refine and adapt recipes to new ingredients, such as powdered and liquid fruit pectins, vinegars with standardized acid content and new utensils and appliances. When the first edition of FREEZING & CANNING COOKBOOK went to press, the plastic bags for use in freezing and cooking foods didn't exist, for example.

Even if you live in town and have no garden, orchard, berry patch or livestock—no fisherman or hunter in your family—you can use the recipes in this book with frozen and canned foods you buy. You will find ways to use home and commercially preserved foods the year round.

How did the first cookbook come to be? It started with FARM JOURNAL readers. Whenever we print recipes for jams, jellies and relishes, for instance, thoughtful readers will write to share with us some of the traditional sweets and sours they make. Their letters inspired us to invite all our readers to share their best jelly, jam and pickle recipes. We received more than 30,000!

At the same time, most of the letter writers paid tribute to home freezers, telling us how they dovetail their freezing and canning operations for maximum results.

We sorted and tested recipes and then sent them to homemakers trained in home economics, from Washington to California, Virginia to Maine, to try in their kitchens with fruits and vegetables in their different parts of the country. We taste-tested samples they sent back to us and compared reactions with our own Test Kitchen results. In the meantime, we collected the most popular dishes to freeze from the state food specialists at the universities and colleges and added them to recipes developed in our Countryside Test Kitchens.

A cookbook with splendid recipes is valuable, but not complete when freezing and canning are involved—which is why we took a good look at the most prevalent problems today. So this revised cookbook is also a "refresher course" for homemakers already experienced in storing food, and a guide to brides and to women who have moved from city to country and have the new delight of home-grown food.

We relied also on freezing and canning research that has been done by the Department of Agriculture and the state Land Grant colleges. Special recognition must go to Shirley Trantanella Munson, Institute of Agriculture, University of Minnesota, who consulted with us on the freezing chapters. Home economists at the U. S. Department of Agriculture also reviewed the manuscript for this revised edition. The extra-good recipes from farm homemakers, from home economists who work with country women and from the FARM JOURNAL food staff make this cookbook an exciting one. Good luck with your freezing and canning!

NELL B. NICHOLS
Field Food Editor

FREEZING & CANNING COOKBOOK

Prized Recipes from the Farms of America

Freezing Foods at Home

Freezer Management · Steps to Successful Freezing · Packaging
Materials · Correct Packaging · Nutritive Value of Frozen Foods ·
Storage Temperature Is Important · Quantity Freezers Will Hold ·
Freezing Costs · Defrosting Nonautomatics

Country cooking never was so good as it is today. That's what people
who sit down to farm meals say. Ask the cooks why and they agree that
fresh-tasting frozen foods have much to do with it. They also like the
dollars-and-cents savings—freezers take farm products when they're most
plentiful and at their best and keep them fresh for months. And busy
women find it's less work to freeze than to can, and to freeze meats
rather than to cure them.

The four farm-to-freezer favorites of FARM JOURNAL readers are
fruits, vegetables, meats and poultry. And the two greatest from-super-
market-to-freezer favorites on the farm are ice cream and bread. With
such a stockpile, farm kitchens today are miniature markets; shopping
trips to town can be less frequent.

Frozen foods add variety to meals because just about everything is
available around the calendar—fresh meats in July; young, tender chickens to fry in January. Combining foods seasonal at different times is
cooking adventure our grandmothers could not enjoy. "You get some
wonderful flavor blends," one farm woman says. "It's like discovering a
brand-new food no one ever tasted before."

Smart homemakers cook, bake and shop for their freezers on less busy
days to distribute their work loads. Dishes to heat or thaw-and-serve
make no-watch meals when there's little time to stay in the kitchen. And
they help women to feed unexpected people without fuss and worry, to
entertain graciously and to take the right food to church bazaars, community suppers and home economics extension club teas.

Thumb through the pages on freezing that follow for up-to-date directions. Don't miss the clever slick tricks of smart farm women. And do try
the recipes using the freezer and its contents if you like compliments
on your cooking.

Manage Your Freezer—Make It Work

What's in the freezer? That's your first thought when your husband comes to the kitchen to tell you he has a steer in prime condition for slaughtering . . . when you see some good supermarket bargains in frozen foods . . . when a letter arrives with news of visitors on the way . . . when a bumper strawberry crop piles up. You can answer that question quickly if you're a good freezer operator. You'll look at your records.

The first rule for superior freezer management is to keep foods going in and coming out and to keep track of the flow. The second rule is to make the freezer do part of your work.

If your load is especially heavy at mealtime, cooking and freezing ahead will ease the situation. If you occasionally are away from home at dinnertime, foods from the freezer, heating in the oven or thawing on the counter top while you're gone, make the men expert chefs. You give them fine meals whether you're there or not. And if you entertain a large group—have a family reunion at Christmas, for instance—you'll have better food and enjoy your guests more if you fix and freeze much of the food.

Every homemaker needs to manage her freezer so it will take over part of her work. One farm woman adds: "I also see that my freezer takes care of plentiful foods when they're priced low. My freezer must cut down on our food bills."

Steps to Successful Freezing

Although detailed directions for preparing, handling and freezing the different foods follow in this cookbook, here are the rules, in a nutshell.

Select foods of top quality. The freezer is not a magician—it does not improve food. Its function is to preserve quality and food values and to prevent spoilage.

Choose vegetables and fruits suitable for freezing and the best varieties for freezing. Growing conditions and the varieties available vary greatly across the country. Check with your County Extension Home Economist or write to your State Agricultural Experiment Station to find out which are best.

Freeze fruits and vegetables when they are at their best for table use. Fruits should be ripe, but firm, and if possible, freeze those that are tree-, vine- or bush-ripened. Freeze garden-fresh, young, tender vegetables in their prime. Some of them, like asparagus, corn, peas, snap beans, lima beans and soybeans, change rapidly in the garden. A delay of a day or two in harvesting them may give you a tough frozen product.

Do not let fruits and vegetables wait in the kitchen any longer than necessary. Hurry them into the freezer to retain their flavors. Many of them lose from one third to two thirds of their vitamin C if allowed to wait a day after picking.

Chill meats, poultry and fish immediately after killing. If you want to age beef or lamb, hang it a shorter time than when you plan to use the meat without freezing. Overaging shortens freezer storage time.

Observe cleanliness to avoid contamination of foods.

Heed the directions for the different foods that follow in this book. Do not slight any of the steps outlined. Even if you know a woman who has frozen peas or corn without scalding, don't try it. Scalding destroys enzymes that continue to change the taste and texture of foods when frozen.

Use Good Packaging Materials

It is false economy to skimp on wrappings and containers. They should protect the food from cold air, which is dry, and retain the moisture in foods. Among the best materials for freezing are heavy-duty aluminum foil, heavyweight plastic wrap (or film) and freezer bags and containers.

Freeze-and-cook bags are available. Follow package directions in using them. Such bags are excellent for freezing and reheating cooked foods, such as stews, chow mein, sauces and gravies, and for cooking foods you ordinarily cook in boiling water, such as corn on the cob, other vegetables and shrimp. The bags endure the 0° or below temperatures of the freezer to 240°F. without change. This makes it possible to freeze and reheat or cook food in the same pouch. Usually the foods reheat or cook in 15 to 20 minutes, or in less time.

Most of the freezer containers on the market today give satisfactory results. Rigid plastic containers with wide tops are favorites with farm women. Do not use lightly waxed cartons, like those in which you buy ice cream, cottage cheese or milk. They are not moisture-vaporproof. Instead use waxed cartons made especially for freezing foods. Clean tin cans with tight-fitting lids, glass canning jars and plastic containers are excellent for liquids and semiliquids. They are moisture-vaporproof, easy to fill and clean. If cared for properly, they are long-lasting. Consider the possibility of reusing freezer containers when comparing the costs of different kinds.

Standard glass canning jars make good containers. Be sure to allow head space in them to permit expansion of food.

Select the containers you like, but keep in mind their convenience and their economical use of freezer space. Tub-type containers take up more room than rectangular and cube-shaped ones, for instance.

Avoid air pockets by making tight packages. Pack food in containers as solidly as possible, *leaving the necessary head space for expansion.*

Seal containers to exclude the air. Usually you seal rigid containers by pressing down or screwing on lids. Some of them should be sealed with freezer tape to make them airtight and to prevent leakage. Cover glass jars with tight-fitting lids.

Most plastic bags for freezing are sealed, after as much air as possible is pressed out with the hands, by twisting open end, folding it over and fastening with a twist-seal, like that the florists and commercial gardeners use. String is also satisfactory for sealing bags. Use heavy plastic bags.

Label packages clearly and carefully; use a wax pencil or crayon for writing on cans. Sharpened waxed crayons give easily read labels on waxed surfaces or freezer tape. Give name of product, date when frozen and any information that will help you identify it. Some women like to indicate number of servings on labels.

Spread out packages of food to freeze, allowing at least 1″ between them for the circulation of the cold air in the freezer, which removes the heat more quickly. Freeze only the number of packages that can be spread against the sides of chest freezers and on the refrigerator shelves of upright models. From 2 to 3 lbs. food to 1 cubic ft. storage space may be frozen at a time in most freezers—30 to 45 lbs. in a 15-ft. freezer. It should freeze in 10 to 12 hours or less.

You need not change the cold control when freezing a few pounds of food, but with larger quantities, it is a good idea to set it at −10°F. *24 hours in advance.* The speed of freezing will not increase if you set the temperature control lower when you place unfrozen food in freezer. Leave packages in freezing position for 24 hours before stacking them close together. If you need to freeze more than 5% of your freezer's capacity at one time, take the food to a locker plant or other commercial establishment for quick freezing. Then bring it home. Stack the packages when the food in them is frozen. *Keep the freezer temperature at 0°F. or lower.* You can use a freezer thermometer to check the temperature of your freezer. *Recommended storage times in this cookbook are based on maintaining freezer temperature at 0°F. or lower. They are not for the maximum time you can keep food in the freezer, but for the period in which top quality is maintained. No frozen food is improved by long storage.*

When the Freezer Stops: Every freezer owner needs to know what to do when the power fails or a mechanical breakdown occurs. The first step is to keep the freezer door closed. Little thawing takes place the first 12 to 20 hours if the freezer is fairly full of food that has been stored at 0°F.

If the freezer will be off longer than a day, move the food, if possible, to some place where low storage temperature is available. In case the freezer is full, it might be unable to refreeze the large quantity of food before spoilage starts.

Dry ice may be used to check thawing. A 50-lb. cake of dry ice, if placed in the freezer soon after it stops operating, prevents thawing for

2 to 3 days. Wear gloves when you handle dry ice to avoid freezer burn. Place pieces of it on cardboard or a board, not directly on food packages.

Refreezing Foods: You may safely refreeze frozen foods that have thawed if they still contain ice crystals or if they are still cold, about 40°F., and have been held no longer than 1 or 2 days at refrigerator temperature after thawing. If frozen foods have gone through slow temperature changes and reached a temperature higher than refrigerator temperatures (about 40°F.), do not refreeze or eat them. Thawed ground meats, poultry or fish that have any off-odor or off-color should not be refrozen and should not be eaten. Thawed ice cream should be discarded. If the odor or color of any food is poor or questionable, do not use it. There is nothing harmful about the refreezing process. The danger is that the more rapid spoilage of thawed than fresh foods has resulted in spoilage before you can refreeze them. Partial thawing and refreezing reduce the eating quality of foods, particularly fruits, vegetables and prepared foods. The eating quality of red meats is affected less than that of many other foods. Use refrozen foods as soon as possible.

Meats and Poultry: If their temperature has not reached above 45°F., they are still in good condition. You can detect the beginning of spoilage by the odor and color. Both thawed meats and poultry do lose juices.

Shellfish: It is unwise to refreeze them because they spoil so easily and there is no way to detect whether early deterioration has started.

Fruits: When thawed, they may be refrozen. Even though fruits ferment, they are not a risk, but some of their flavor is lost. And they may shrink and become mushy.

Fruit Juices: Some deterioration occurs when you refreeze thawed concentrated juices. Sometimes it is difficult to reconstitute juices that have been refrozen. There is little change in other frozen juices.

Ice Cream: Do not use if melted.

Vegetables: Thawed vegetables will spoil more quickly than fruits. It is best not to refreeze them. Also, they often become tough when refrozen.

Cooked Foods: Do not refreeze dishes that contain meats and poultry, such as stews, casseroles and pies.

You usually lose quality when foods are refrozen. The texture especially is likely to be less desirable.

Nutritive Value of Frozen Foods

Meat, fish, poultry and eggs are equal in food value to the fresh products. The retention of the vitamins and other nutrients in fruits and vegetables depends on how they are handled before freezing, on the storage temperature in the freezer and on how you cook them. This is one good reason for following the directions given in this book. Foods that taste delicious almost always are those that have kept their food values.

Storage Temperature Is Important

The freezer should maintain a temperature of at least 0°F. Some freezers operate −5 to −10°F., which is even better. The deterioration in quality when temperatures are high is due to enzyme activity, not to the development of bacteria. Enzyme activity speeds up chemical changes which produce unpleasant flavors, loss of vitamin C and unattractive color. Some people believe that foods will keep indefinitely if they are "frozen hard." This is not true. Frozen foods should not be stored in an open-end ice cube compartment of a household refrigerator. The temperature is not low enough and it is not adequately controlled. A loss of quality may take place, even though the freezer is cold enough, if the frozen foods are stored too long or were not handled properly before freezing, or if they were not packaged correctly. Follow the directions in this cookbook. (Another fallacy is that foods must be frozen fast. "Quick freezing" means getting foods frozen before they start to deteriorate.)

You can check the operating temperature of your freezer by placing an accurate freezer thermometer on top of the food packages.

Quantity Freezers Will Hold

A good estimate is 35 lbs. per cubic foot of usable space. The amount varies with different foods—from 30 to 42 lbs. meat, 20 to 50 lbs. fruit, 15 to 25 lbs. vegetables. Bulky foods, like chicken, take more space.

SIZE OF FREEZER (CUBIC FEET)	APPROXIMATE POUNDS OF FOOD
9	315
11	385
15	525
22	770

Note: During a year 2½ to 3 times this amount of frozen food can be stored in freezers, of course, because of turnover through use.

Cost of Electricity for Operating Freezers

The average estimate is 140 kilowatt-hours per month for a 15-ft. automatic freezer. To determine the approximate cost in your home, multiply 140 by the cost of electricity per kilowatt-hour. Nonautomatic freezers use somewhat less electric current.

Defrost Your Freezer

Many freezers now defrost automatically. If you have a nonautomatic chest-type model, scrape the frost when it is ⅓ " thick. Turn off the electricity. Move as much food as possible to one part of the chest or take it out and wrap it in a blanket or newspapers. Spread towels on the bottom to absorb the moisture. Scrape off the frost with a wooden or plastic scraper, not metal.

With an upright model, complete defrosting may be necessary. This should be done with all nonautomatic defrosting freezers when food is spilled and a scraper will not remove it. Turn off the electricity. Remove the food and wrap it in blankets. Place towels in bottom of freezer to absorb moisture. Place pans of hot water in freezer; close door or lid.

After thawing, wash inside of freezer with a soda solution, 3 tblsp. baking soda to 1 qt. water, or use water with synthetic detergent added. Rinse, wipe dry and turn on the electricity. When the moisture in the freezer is frozen, return the food.

CHAPTER 1

SLICK FREEZING TRICKS

Imagination in the Kitchen · Original Short Cuts · Recipes from
Country Cooks · Time-savers · Garnishing Ideas · Thrift Tips

We take off our hats to farm women, the greatest of all cooks and experimenters. And we want to acknowledge right off that they send our Food Department many original recipes and ideas. Take a look at the collection of their slick freezing tricks in this chapter—see if you don't think it's different and fascinating.

We put this chapter first because we think it will be an interesting introduction to the other 14 chapters of wonderful, tested recipes and latest up-to-date directions for freezing and canning. This chapter gives you glimpses of imagination in the kitchen, which we hope will tempt you to experiment. Easy—here are two examples of how it works.

Your neighbor's daughter soon will be a bride. This cookbook has recipes for punch and cookies from the freezer, but you want to add your own individuality. While you are dusting the window sill, you notice a rosebush covered with dainty pink buds. You get the idea of freezing tiny flowers-in-bud in ice cubes to decorate the punch bowl. You try and it works!

Or you're putting asparagus tips in the freezer and feel guilty about wasting so much of the long tender stalks. So you cook some of them in your pressure saucepan, put them through your food mill and come up with a purée to freeze. This delicate-flavored vegetable, reheated and lovingly seasoned, becomes the talk of the table when you have guests. Friends ask for your "recipe"! You can find many such ways to add your own touch of genius to your freezer.

Imagination at Work in Country Kitchens

You will notice that some of these slick tricks are short cuts—proof that farm homemakers are not only creative but also smart time and money managers. Some of their ideas salvage food that would otherwise be wasted. Some of the short cuts bring variety and real country tastiness to meals. This chapter tells how women team mulberries and gooseberries in a freezer container, ready for pie baking; how they put sassafras roots away in spring for that refreshing apricot-colored tea the year round. Wild persimmon pulp, frozen after the fruit has been sweetened by nature's frost, makes tasty out-of-season pudding.

But let farm women themselves tell you about their ingenious tricks in their own words.

From the Woods

WILD PERSIMMONS: After the frost touches the little persimmons on the trees in the woods or fence rows, I gather the ripe fruit, pick over, wash and drain it. Then I put it through a food mill or colander and package the purée in moistureproof containers, usually glass jars, and freeze. We can enjoy the wonderful Hoosier, Tennessee or North Carolina persimmon puddings the year round. Here is one of our easy-to-fix favorites.

HOOSIER PERSIMMON ROLL

Fix it when frost is on the pumpkins

2 c. frozen persimmon purée
2 c. sugar
1 c. brown sugar, firmly packed
1 lb. crushed graham crackers
1 c. chopped pecans
1 lb. miniature marshmallows

• Thaw persimmon purée. Combine ingredients in order listed and mix together. Spoon about one third of mixture on a sheet of waxed paper; shape in a roll. Wrap in aluminum foil or plastic wrap and freeze. Repeat until all mixture is used.
• To serve, cut the slightly thawed roll in slices for individual servings. Top with whipped cream or vanilla ice cream. Makes about 24 servings.

Note: Shape the rolls about 4" in diameter. If you plan to serve this dessert at an afternoon club meeting or other social gathering, you may wish to make the rolls smaller, about 3" in diameter. If topped with whipped cream, the dessert is quite rich.

GOOSEBERRIES AND MULBERRIES: I combine these berries, half and half, and freeze them unsweetened, in quart jars. The two kinds of berries complement each other in pies.

MULBERRY DESSERT: I freeze mulberries, after washing and drying, in moistureproof containers with tight lids.

About 45 minutes or an hour before I wish to serve them, I stir them into sweetened whipped cream which coats the berries. When it's time to serve them, I pile the berries in dessert dishes and carry the dessert to the table.

SASSAFRAS ROOTS: Dig the roots in the spring, wash and remove the bark. Dry and store in tightly covered glass jars in your freezer. You can make the pretty pink tea, iced or piping hot, all year. I also like to add a bit of the root to the sieved fruit when cooking apple butter. Remove it before storing the spicy butter.

Meats and Poultry

DUCK: Use absorbent paper towels to dry out the body cavity and the outside of bird before roasting a thawed duck.

MEAT: Save and freeze small leftover bits of meat until you have enough to make a meat pie.

MEAT PORTIONS: When there's a special sale on pork, veal or lamb chops, frankfurters or cold cuts, I separate the chops, hot dogs or slices of cold cuts and spread them on baking sheets so they do not touch one another and freeze them quickly. When frozen, I put them in moisture-vapor-proof containers and seal. The meats do not adhere to each other, and I can quickly cook (or thaw the cold cuts) in the quantity I want.

HAMBURGERS AND MEAT LOAVES: I shape ground beef into patties, place them on baking sheets so they do not touch, and freeze overnight. In the morning, I place them in coffee cans with tight-fitting lids and seal. Then I can take out as many as I need for a meal. Frozen in this way, they do not stick together. I find that several patties, used to make a meat loaf, will thaw much faster than a solid piece of ground beef.

SPUR-OF-THE-MOMENT HAMBURGERS: Scoop out centers of split hamburger buns. (Freeze crumbs from the centers in a plastic freezer bag.) Fill buns with raw ground beef seasoned as you like it and package each bun in foil. Freeze. To serve, bake bun packages, opened, without thawing, in a slow oven (325°F.) 1 hour. I tried using a warmer oven, but the buns browned too much. Sometimes I cook the filling and cool it before putting it in the buns. Then I do not open the individual sandwich packages but bake them in a moderate oven (350°F.) 30 to 40 minutes.

HAM: Chop or cube baked ham left near the bone; freeze in 1½ c. portions. If unexpected company comes, mix ham with 1 can condensed cream of mushroom soup and 2 sliced, hard-cooked eggs; serve over rice, potatoes, or in toast cups.

LARD: If you render your own lard, don't store it in jars. While it is in liquid form, pour it into square layer cake pans and cool it. When cold, cut in blocks. Wrap each block in moistureproof packaging material; freeze. It saves a lot of digging fat out of jars.

Another country cook packages home-rendered lard in recipe-measured amounts and seals them in labeled containers with tight lids. She says its wonderful not to have to measure the lard when baking pies and other foods.

PORK TENDERLOIN: I pound and flatten rather thick slices of tenderloin before freezing. Then they may be dipped in flour and put on to cook without thawing. I freeze the slices by placing them on baking sheets without touching. Then I put them in flat packages to take up little freezer space. They do not stick together and I can take out as many as I need.

Vegetables

GREEN TOMATOES: Slice and dip in cornmeal; package and freeze. To serve, pan- or deep-fry without thawing. Excellent with pork.

CUCUMBERS: Peel, seed and put them through food chopper. Pack in refrigerator trays, freeze. Wrap each cube and place in freezer. *Do not thaw;* crush cubes at last minute to toss in salads for summertime flavor.

BAKED SWEET POTATOES: Select firm sweet potatoes of good quality, wash and dry. Place in your oven on baking sheets, filling both racks. Bake in hot oven (400°F.) until soft, 30 to 40 minutes. Cool and package in meal-sized quantities. I use heavy-duty foil. Freeze. When ready to fix for a meal, take the required number of potatoes from the freezer, thaw in foil wrapper, peel, season as you like and heat.

SWEET POTATOES: When we dig sweet potatoes, some are bruised or cut. I trim, cook and freeze them. It's quite

a saving and the salvaged sweets make many tasty dishes.

GREENS: (spinach, beet, chard, collard, kale, mustard, turnip): Use young, tender leaves. Remove tough stems. Wash in cold running water. Scald 2 minutes, except for collards and chard. Steam these 3 to 4 minutes. Immediately chill in iced water. Drain; package with water that clings to leaves. Freeze. When ready to use, thaw and cook until tender. Season greens with bacon drippings.

VEGETABLES IN BULK: After scalding corn, carrots, peas and snap beans I spread them on trays and freeze them. Then I pour the frozen vegetables into plastic freezer bags or other containers, seal and return them to the freezer. That way I can take out as many cupfuls as I need for a meal. Corn is good and handy fixed this way, but when you freeze it on trays, the freezer has a strong "corn odor." If the food in the freezer is well wrapped, it will not be affected, but I dislike to have food odors noticeable in my freezer. Use cut-up carrots and beans and corn cut from the cob.

BAKED BEANS: I bake 5 pounds of beans at a time, using two huge bean pots and baking them all night at 300° F. By morning, they are deep brown and luscious. When cooled, I put them in the freezer.

BLANCHING SHORT CUT: To speed the blanching of vegetables for freezing, I use my electric deep-fat fryer. The temperature control keeps the water at the proper temperature.

DICED BEETS: In the fall before frost, I always put away a few containers of beets ready to heat quickly. I cook the beets until barely tender so they will not be spongy. Then I peel and dice or cube them, cool quickly and package. To serve the beets, I thaw them in a double boiler or heavy pan with butter, salt and pepper added. Sometimes I freeze them in a vinegar sauce instead of plain.

THANKSGIVING DINNER: A couple of weeks or so in advance, I freeze cooked squash in a casserole, cranberry/orange relish, and apple, pumpkin or mince pies. They are ready to combine with turkey for dinner.

PEPPER RELISH: The recipe I used to make pepper relish last fall directed that you cover the chopped peppers and onions with boiling water, let mixture stand 5 minutes, drain and discard liquid. When I was ready to add the boiling water, the vegetables were covered with their own juices. So I

drained them off before adding the water. I froze the drained juices in an ice cube tray, bagged the cubes and put them in the freezer. We found they seasoned soups and meat gravies delightfully throughout the winter.

CELERY: When cleaning celery for table use, save the leaves and little scraps. Put them in a plastic freezer bag, twist to exclude as much air as possible, seal and freeze. You will always have a touch of celery to season poultry stuffing, soups, stews and Chinese dishes. A great convenience!

SWEET PEPPERS: I freeze red and green peppers separately, to add to winter cabbage slaw and other salads and to cooked dishes. I either cut them in slender strips or chop them fine and package and seal in small plastic containers. I store the little bags in a box or a larger plastic bag so I can quickly find them.

FRESH HERBS: Freeze fresh herbs in small labeled foil or plastic packages. To use, cut fine with sharp knife while crisply frozen, or cut with kitchen shears. Best way to keep parsley on hand for spur-of-the-moment use.

PARSLEY: When there is plenty of parsley in the garden, I grind it in the food chopper (fine blade), saving the juice that is extracted. I freeze the juice in a refrigerator tray, adding a little water to it. When frozen, I wrap each cube in foil and store in the freezer. Handy flavor for adding to soup, white sauce and gravies in winter.

CUTTING CORN FROM COB: When you are cutting corn from the cob to freeze, stand the tip of ear in the center hole of a tube cake pan. The deep pan catches the corn and it's easy to hold the ear steady while cutting kernels. Speeds up the work!

BROCCOLI: I freeze broccoli in measured recipe amounts for making soufflés. I store all the little packages in large plastic or stockinet bags.

ASPARAGUS TRIM: Directions for washing asparagus before freezing usually suggest cutting off the scales with a sharp-pointed knife. I find this isn't always necessary. When I cut and bring asparagus into the kitchen, I remove the scales from several stalks to find out if they hide sand or dirt. If they don't, I omit this tedious step. Sand under the scales depends largely on weather—rains or winds.

Sauces

THICKENING FOR SAUCES: I mix *measured amounts* of butter and flour for making sauces, package, label and freeze them for quick use. I use more of the mix made with equal parts flour and butter than others (2 tblsp. each to use with 1 c. liquid). To use, I melt the frozen mixture and add liquid (milk for white sauce, tomato juice for red sauce) and seasonings and stir as the mixture cooks and thickens.

SAUCES: Add a paste, made of ¼ of the flour or cornstarch in recipe and a little water, after sauce has been made, cooled and chilled. I find this helps prevent separation of fat. The uncooked paste cooks while the food mixed with the sauce heats.

Hostess Tricks

ROSEBUDS IN ICE: I freeze tiny, perfect rosebuds in water poured into refrigerator trays. Then I put the decorative cubes in a plastic bag and store them in the freezer. Women make quite a fuss when they see them floating in the party punch or in glasses of lemonade.

PLATES: Chill salad and dessert plates in freezer when weather is warm before serving food on them.

COLORED ICE CUBES: I tint water with food colors and freeze it in refrigerator trays. Then I store the cubes in plastic bags in the freezer. The children like colored ice cubes in their lemonade or other fruit drinks.

CANDLES: Buy them ahead to use on the table for anniversary celebrations and other special occasions. Store them in the freezer. They keep their shape, burn with a bright flame and are not so likely to drip on the table cover.

COFFEE AND TEA: Freeze leftover coffee or tea in ice cube trays. Place cubes in plastic bags. Use them for quick servings. Or use them in iced tea or coffee to keep it undiluted.

FRESH GINGER: I wash, dry, wrap, label and store fresh ginger roots in the freezer. All I need do when a Chinese-style recipe calls for ginger is to grate the frozen root. Many supermarkets sell fresh ginger.

PIE SHORTCAKES: Roll pastry ⅛" thick and cut in circles with 3" cutter. Place on an ungreased baking sheet. Prick rounds with fork. Bake in a very hot oven (450°F.) 8 to 10 minutes. Cool. Package layers of pastry in rigid freezer containers, cover and seal. Freeze. When you need a dessert in a hurry, stack 3 pastry rounds on a plate with pie filling between and on top. You can use canned or frozen berries, heated and thickened with cornstarch with a little butter and sugar added. Or use canned pie filling. If you have mounds of whipped cream in your freezer, put one on top of each shortcake. They're easier-than-pie and just as delicious and appealing.

Cream and Butter

SURPLUS CREAM: We are a "one-cow" family. When I have extra cream, I freeze it in an ice cube tray, than remove cubes and store them in the freezer in a plastic freezer bag. They are wonderful to season garden vegetables, like peas, and for use in casseroles. Freeze only pasteurized cream with at least a 30 to 35% fat content. Use within 4 months.

DILL BUTTER: I cream ½ c. butter until fluffy, add 1 tsp. dill weed (from seasoning counters in supermarkets). Then I package it in foil and freeze. I like to baste broiling fish with the butter and add it to the white sauce for creamed and scalloped fish. It adds a gourmet touch.

BUTTER: I don't have much cream for churning so I rarely have more than enough to make a pound of butter. I like to keep at least 1 pound of country butter in the freezer. I salt the cream before I churn and avoid the white "salt streaks" that sometimes show up in homemade butter. Churn only pasteurized cream.

Time and Money Savers

SCRAPS OF FOIL: Save foil scraps and wrap them around the sharp bones of meats and poultry when you are wrapping them for the freezer. The foil makes a cushion that protects the freezer paper, plastic bag or other wrap.

TO REMOVE FREEZER TAPE: You can pull it off easily if you place the frozen casserole dish in a warm oven for a few minutes.

NYLON MESH BAGS: Keep small packages together in the freezer by putting them in a large nylon mesh bag—the kind often used to hold fragile fabrics when laundering them in the automatic washer. You can find them in a jiffy.

SPECIAL DISHES: If you fix special dishes for children, oldsters or invalids, prepare them in quantity and freeze menu-size portions in freezer. It saves work and dishwashing.

TV SURPRISE DINNERS: Empty trays for TV dinners, washed and dried, make ideal containers for dinner or supper leftovers—meat, chicken, vegetables, etc. I fill a tray, cover tightly with foil and freeze. After I have accumulated enough trays for everyone in my family, we have a "Surprise Dinner." I could label them, but our family prefers and enjoys the element of surprise as everyone eats what he "draws." Sometimes we swap dinners.

BROWN SUGAR: Pour into freezer containers or glass jars; seal and store in freezer. The easiest way to avoid lumps and annoyance on baking day.

MARSHMALLOWS: Keep them packaged in the freezer. They do not dry out and when you cut them to add to salads and desserts, you or your kitchen shears don't get stuck up.

Farm Favorites

ICE-CREAM SANDWICHES: My children like pretty pink-dappled peppermint ice cream frozen between layers of crushed cocoa graham crackers. On special occasions, I pass chocolate sauce to pour over this dessert.

HOMEMADE NOODLES: "I have plenty of eggs so I make noodles. My family and friends are enthusiastic about them. They freeze successfully and I find it convenient to keep a supply in the freezer," writes an Ohio country cook. Here is the way she fixes them:

Beat 3 egg yolks and 1 whole egg until very light. Beat in 3 tblsp. cold water and 1 tsp. salt. Then stir and work in with the hands 2 c. flour to make a stiff dough.

Divide dough into 3 parts. Roll each one out on lightly floured, cloth-covered board as thinly as possible—paper thin. Place each piece of dough between towels until it is partially dry like a chamois skin. Roll up like a jelly roll and cut with a sharp knife to make strips the width you like— ⅛" for fine noodles and ½" for broad ones. Shake out the strips and let them dry before packaging, sealing and freezing. Makes 6 cups.

FRIED CORNMEAL MUSH: I make mush, pour it into a pan, cool quickly and wrap in aluminum foil or plastic wrap. When ready to use, I slice it unthawed and brown the slices in a greased heavy skillet. The mush keeps satisfactorily in freezer for about 6 months. Ours never lasts that long!

Fruits
THREE STEPS TO GLAMOROUS GARNISHES

1. Pick the prettiest, most nearly perfect berries. Wash carefully and drain. Leave the hulls on strawberries. Handle lightly to prevent crushing. Place them in rows, ½″ apart, on baking sheets.

2. Set baking sheets in freezer. When berries are frozen firmly, package in freezer containers.

3. Put back in freezer. At serving time, remove only what you need.

APPLES, WHOLE: I'm so busy in summer that I often freeze whole apples for cooking. We like the tart taste of the early fruit later on in pies, sauce and other desserts. This is how I do it —I wash firm apples without blemishes, place in plastic freezer bags and put them in freezer. To fix fruit for cooking, I run cold water over each frozen apple until it thaws enough so I can peel, core and slice it like fresh fruit. You have to work fast because apples that thaw before peeling darken quickly.

CRANBERRIES: Instead of freezing cranberries in the transparent bags in which you buy them, look them over, wash and drain thoroughly. Then pack them in plastic freezer bags (original bags, washed, may be used if airtight) or containers and freeze. It is easier to clean the berries before they are frozen. And they are ready to use.

BREAKFAST PEACHES: "Ripe peaches, sliced and frozen in orange juice,

make a cheerful breakfast eye-opener —tastes like pure gold," says a Minnesota homemaker. She puts up a big supply of this fresh-tasting fruit combination. To fast-fix the mixture for freezing, she uses frozen orange juice concentrate. Here is her recipe.

PEACHES IN ORANGE JUICE

A refreshing way to start a winter day—serve this fruit for breakfast

1	(6 oz.) can frozen orange juice concentrate
3	cans water
¼	c. sugar
¼	tsp. powdered ascorbic acid
10	medium peaches, peeled and pitted (about 2¾ lbs.)

· Mix orange juice concentrate as directed on can with 3 cans water. Add sugar and ascorbic acid or other color protector, following directions on package. Stir to dissolve sugar.

· Fill freezer containers one third full of the orange juice mixture. Slice prepared, ripe peaches directly into containers. Leave head space. Add enough orange juice to cover. Place crumpled pieces of freezer paper under the lids to hold the peaches submerged in the orange juice. Pack, label, date and freeze. Makes 7 half pints.

To serve, partially thaw in original container. Serve while fruit still contains a few ice crystals.

GRAPES AND MELON IN LEMONADE: Another excellent farm cook freezes summer's small, green seedless grapes and muskmelon or cantaloupe balls in orange- and lemon-flavored syrups. She adds them to fruit salads and fruit cocktails. Sometimes she tops the green-and-yellow mixture with small scoops of lemon sherbet.

Select firm, ripe seedless green grapes; leave them whole. Remove stems or leave in small clusters.

Choose ripe, meaty muskmelons or cantaloupes that are not stringy. Cut melon in halves, remove seeds and cut flesh in balls with ball cutter or ½ teaspoon measuring spoon, or dice it.

Place a mixture of grapes and melon balls, the desired proportions, in freezer containers. Mix 1 (6 oz.) can frozen lemonade concentrate with 3 cans water as directed on can. Mix thoroughly. Pour over grapes and melon to cover. Leave head space. You need ¾ c. syrup for each pint of grapes and melon balls. To serve, partially thaw in original container. Serve while fruit and melon contain a few ice crystals.

Note: Use Orange or Sugar Syrup for lemonade. Easy way to vary flavor:

ORANGE SYRUP: Mix 1 c. reconstituted frozen orange juice with ¼ c. sugar. Stir to dissolve sugar.

SUGAR SYRUP: Dissolve 2 c. sugar in 1 qt. water.

FRESH GRAPES IN WINTER: An Iowa farm woman treats her family and friends to seedless green grapes during the winter. She washes the grapes and packs them in small clusters or with stems removed, in freezer containers. She makes lemonade with 1 (6 oz.) can frozen lemonade concentrate using 1 can less water than called for on lemonade can. This she pours over the grapes, covers and seals containers, puts them in the freezer. She partially thaws the grapes when serving them in their lemonade syrup for an evening snack with crisp crackers and cheese. Often she tosses drained grapes with sliced frozen peaches for an attractive, light dessert. If she thinks this meal ending is not hearty enough, she passes coconut, nut or chocolate cookies, too.

RIPE BANANAS: To salvage ripe fruit, I put it through my food mill and add lemon juice or powdered ascorbic acid to prevent darkening, and freeze. Then when I want to make a banana nut bread or a banana cake, the fruit is ready to add to batter.

LEMONS: I make lots of lemonade in haying time for the men in the field. I cut off some of the white from the discarded peels, grind the yellow part fine, package and freeze it. The rest of the year it's handy for flavoring salad dressing, cakes, cookies and other baked foods.

LEMON JUICE: One reader says, "I buy lemons in large quantities, especially when they are bargains. I extract the juice and freeze it in ice cube trays. The cubes, stored in plastic freezer bags in the freezer, enable me always to have lemon juice on hand."

Another farm homemaker mixes 1 c. sugar with 1 c. lemon juice and freezes it in tight containers. And a third one freezes measured amounts of lemon juice in foil "cups."

APPLE/RHUBARB SAUCE: Equal parts of apples and rhubarb cooked together make a delightful sauce. Of course, these two foods are not in season at the same time, but with frozen rhubarb in the freezer, we enjoy this sauce from autumn on through winter.

RHUBARB SAUCE: I like to cook fresh rhubarb, sweeten it to taste and freeze it in plastic or glass containers with tight lids. It's ready to use when you take it out. Some women cut the fresh rhubarb stalks and freeze them, but they have to cook the rhubarb before serving it. That takes time.

SUGARING STRAWBERRIES: Most directions for freezing strawberries suggest that you add sugar and let the mixture stand until the juices start to flow. Then you stir gently to mix, using care not to crush the berries. I have a better way—it's easier and quicker. I add the sugar to the berries and mix at once, using a rubber spatula to fold the berries over and over. There's almost no crushing if you use a light hand.

GELATIN FRUIT SALADS: I find whipped gelatin freezes well, as do chiffon pies with beaten egg whites folded into the filling. But I had trouble with unwhipped gelatin salads "weeping" until I cut back the liquid from 2 c. to 1½ c. They "weep" less, often not at all.

FRUIT COCKTAIL: Freeze a can of unopened fruit cocktail or apricots. Open at both ends to serve. Push out frozen fruit and slice. Top with mayonnaise or fruit salad dressing and serve on lettuce—you have a jiffy salad. Or top with whipped cream and maraschino cherries.

Breads

MUFFINS AND BISCUITS: When there are two or three leftover muffins or biscuits, I store them in the freezer in a plastic bag. When I need a quick topping for a casserole dish, I crumble the frozen muffins or biscuits on top the food, dot it with butter and often sprinkle it with cheese.

ASSORTED BREADS: I buy several different kinds of bread at a time and repackage and freeze slices of different kinds in loaves to fit my family's size.

We have a choice of breads at our meals. Everyone approves.

TOASTED PARMESAN ROLLS: Split hard rolls in halves, spread with butter, sprinkle with grated Parmesan cheese and freeze. Wrap in foil or package in plastic freezer bags. To serve, place roll halves, cheese side up, on broiler pan and broil to melt cheese and heat rolls.

BISCUITS: Cut rolled biscuit dough

with empty juice can. Fit the rounds of biscuit dough in the washed and dried juice can; seal ends with foil and freezer tape. Freeze. To use, remove foil, push the biscuits out from one end and bake immediately.

FROZEN MUFFINS: I bake muffins, cool them, put them back in the pans; wrap with foil and freeze. To serve, I heat them, unwrapped, in the pans in a hot oven (400°F.) about 25 minutes.

HOT BUTTERED HARD ROLLS: These rolls, resembling little loaves of bread, I slice in ½″ slices (but not through the lower crust). I butter the slices liberally, wrap each roll in foil and freeze the small packages. When company comes, I heat the rolls, wrapped, in a slow oven (325°F.) 30 to 40 minutes or until heated through. Everyone breaks off the hot slices of his roll—easier to eat. When I'm in a hurry, I serve the rolls in the packages and let everyone unwrap his own. They are bound to be hot when left in the foil.

BREAD FOR DRESSING: I start dressing for chicken or other poultry and meats by cutting leftover slices of dry bread in small pieces. Package and freeze it—ready to toast and season for dressing. A timesaving trick!

HOMEMADE BREAD: The bread I baked and froze seemed to break just below the upper crust. My County Extension Home Economist showed me how to avoid the trouble and here are the rules I now follow for success: Bake the bread before it gets too light. Press it gently with your finger tips; if the dent remains, it is time to put the bread in the oven. Bake it in loaf pans with vertical sides. This keeps the dough from overstretching and breaking away from the crust. And do not bake too much dough in a pan. If you do, it forms ears on the sides and again the side walls stretch too much; the loaf is unattractive.

Cakes

ANGEL FOOD CAKE: When the angel food cake is cool, I slice it in individual servings, place them on a tray and freeze. They do not touch during freezing, so you can wrap each one separately in good packaging material and store them in a plastic bag. Any desired number of servings can be taken out on a few minutes' notice. The cake thaws very quickly.

CAKE TO CARRY: Freeze the frosted cake before you tote it to a potluck supper. It is firm and carries well and will be thawed by the time you are ready to serve it.

CHRISTMAS FRUITCAKE: Last year I was chairman of the food committee for our church's big holiday tea. I bought round fruitcakes with holes in the center at the bakery and froze them. Then I sliced each cake into fourths—I cut each wedge in halves to make eighths. I placed each wedge on a board, cut side down, and with a sharp knife, cut thin crosswise slices that resembled triangles—or Christmas trees. At the wide end of each, I placed a thin 1″ stick of candy for the tree trunk. At the narrow top, I pressed in a piece of sticky, green gumdrop. The little Christmas trees, arranged on trays, were beautiful—they made a hit.

CAKE CUTOUTS: I freeze unfrosted cake before I attempt to cut it in fancy shapes to frost for parties and birthday cakes. You can make clean, neat cuts and eliminate crumbs.

FROZEN FRUITCAKES: I always freeze fruitcakes. They taste better than cakes stored the old way at room temperature. My pet slick trick is to slice fruitcakes while they are frozen, using a sharp knife. That's the best way to handle cakes that crumble. You avoid the crumbs and waste.

CAKE LAYERS: I like to keep at least one unfrosted cake layer in my freezer. When I need a dessert in a hurry, it will thaw in about 30 minutes. I cut it in wedges like pie and top with lemon instant pudding or a mixture of frozen strawberries and miniature marshmallows—2 c. berries to 1 c. marshmallows. Often I thaw

the berries in a slow oven to gain time.

MARSHMALLOW CAKE FROSTING: Add 10 to 12 marshmallows to your favorite 7-minute cake frosting. They add new flavor and the frosting stays firm when frozen.

CAKE CRUMBS: Freeze leftover cake crumbs. Add a touch of cinnamon and a little brown sugar for a crunchy topping on open-face fruit pies or quick coffee cakes.

BAKED FOODS: After baking and cooling cake, pies, brownies, gingerbread and similar foods, I cut them in serving pieces. Or leave them uncut, spread out on baking sheets, and freeze overnight. Then I store them in moisture-vaporproof packages without wrapping them individually. In this way, I manage to keep a variety of baked goods on hand for almost instant use.

CAKE FROSTINGS: Frostings made with butter or cream cheese and confectioners sugar freeze satisfactorily. I also have success freezing fudge- and penuche-types of frosting, but those made with egg whites become frothy and spongy.

For Your Cat

CATNIP: If you have a cat, gather, wash and dry catnip leaves. Pack them in layers in plastic containers with waxed paper between. Your cat will be happy all winter.

Postscript—More Slick Tricks

Letters from country women to FARM JOURNAL often end with postscripts that describe kitchen discoveries they've made. Many of these good ideas deal with freezing. Here are two examples of favorite short cuts.

CHEESE WAFERS: Women in our neighborhood often serve salad for the main dish at party luncheons. I find that crisp, freshly baked Cheese Wafers are popular salad go-withs. I make the dough, shape it in small rolls about 1" in diameter, wrap and freeze. Usually I do this a week or two before the luncheon.

The dough is a snap to fix. I grate 4 oz. sharp process cheese into a bowl and sift in 1½ c. flour, ¾ tsp. salt and a dash of ground red pepper. Next, I cream ½ c. butter until fluffy and combine it with the flour-cheese mixture, blending thoroughly. The mixture looks crumbly and dry, but I quickly knead it into a smooth ball,

refrigerate 1 hour, shape the rolls, wrap and freeze.

To bake, I thaw the rolls about an hour in the refrigerator. Then I slice them about ¼" thick, line them up on a baking sheet and bake in a hot oven (400°F.) about 10 minutes. They're wonderful hot or cold. My recipe makes about 6 dozen wafers.

BAKED APPLES: I do not cut through the bottom of the apples when coring them. The fruit juices blended with sugar and butter remain in the fruit. To cut down on shrinkage, I remove about ½" peel from top of apples. I bake the fruit in an open pan, adding little or no water, about 30 minutes, using a hot oven (400°F.). I cool the apples quickly, package them in meal-size portions and freeze. To serve, I reheat them in a slow oven (325°F.) only until warm. Use apples that bake well. I like Winesaps.

CHAPTER 2

FRUITS AND VEGETABLES

Selection of Right Varieties for Freezing · How to Prepare and Freeze · Buying Fruits in Big Containers · Freezer Recipes for Cranberry Applesauce, Peach Purée Delicious, Golden Glow Melon Freeze · French Fried Potatoes · How to Cook Frozen Vegetables, Orange-Glazed Carrots, Broccoil Soufflé, Stuffed Baked Potatoes, Oven-Fried Potato Slices · Heat-and-Eat Potato Treats · Ham/Vegetable Casserole, Baked Stuffed Zucchini

Country women mentally start freezing vegetables in winter with seed catalogs in their hands. And when trees blossom pink and white, that's when they ponder how much fruit to freeze. For they don't have long to wait. When the rosy-red rhubarb stalks and tender asparagus spears push their heads above the earth, harvesting and freezing time begins.

Freezing is the quickest, easiest—and coolest—way to put up fruits and vegetables. And it keeps more of their fresh taste and bright color than other methods of preservation—especially for farm people, because they can pick fruits and vegetables at the exact flavor peak, and in the morning before the sun has a chance to heat them. Hurried into the freezer, time stands still until the frozen produce is used.

Desirable as freezing is, garden and orchard products must pass an entrance examination for admittance to many freezers. Space is at a premium. Every woman must decide what to can and what to freeze—to consider that some foods, like strawberries, are best frozen and others, like tomatoes and pears, are best canned. Another question: Is it economical to freeze root vegetables if you have a cool cellar for storing them?

Busy cooks fast-fix frozen fruits and vegetables for meals because they are partly prepared—peaches are sliced, peas are shelled, for instance.

"Compare your meals with your grandmother's," one country cook suggests. "Look at recipes in old cookbooks. Then you'll know why freezers bring blessings to homemakers, along with astonishingly good meals to farm tables." Follow our directions for top-quality frozen products.

Fresh Fruits, Year Round
THEY'RE ALWAYS IN SEASON

One of the wonders of freezing is that strawberry time never needs to end. Peaches with a fresh-picked flavor and the juiciness of summer are at home in midwinter meals. And the country cook with a freezer can combine fruits that ripen at different times of the year for excellent dishes.

If there is any rule a cook experienced in freezing fruits can give a beginner, it is: *Freeze the best.* And that means ripe, full-flavored fruits and berries. And do hold their beauty by using a color protector or ascorbic acid powder if they are fruits that air darkens. Handle them gently to avoid crushing and use imagination with them in meals. Look in our Index for recipes to use your frozen fruits.

Freezing Fruits and Berries

Choose Ripe Fruits: They should be riper for freezing than canning—"eating ripe." Tree- and vine-ripened fruits have superior flavor and more vitamins than fruits picked green, then ripened. Discard immature fruits.

Select Right Varieties: Every region has fruits that retain the maximum amount of color, texture and flavor when frozen. Varieties vary with the place where they grow. Ask your County Extension Home Economist or write your State Agricultural Experiment Station to find out which are best for you.

Prepare Quickly: Sort, wash in ice water or cold water and fix fruit as for table use. Work fast.

Package Properly: Use one of these three ways to pack fruits for freezing (see recipes for specific amounts).

1. Sugar Syrup Pack. Dissolve the sugar in water. *Do not heat.* Add the sugar to the water and let it stand, stirring occasionally, until sugar dissolves. You can make it a day or two ahead and store it in the refrigerator. *Always add it cold.* If you add 1 part light corn syrup to 2 parts sugar syrup, you often get frozen fruit with

better texture, flavor and color. Fruits packed in sugar syrup retain the most vitamins.

2. Sugar Pack. Sprinkle the sugar on fruit. Stir carefully with a rubber spatula until the sugary juices coat every piece of fruit. Many homemakers especially like to use this method for fruits to freeze for pies. This method also is excellent for sliced strawberries.

3. Unsweetened Pack. Either pack the fruit dry or pack it in water with powdered ascorbic acid or other color protector added. Use 1 tsp. powdered ascorbic acid to 1 qt. water. Berries packed without syrup or sugar collapse and lose flavor more quickly when thawed, however. Use partly thawed. Blueberries and cranberries, whole, are fine in dry pack.

Keep Colors Bright: Some fruits, like peaches, apricots, sweet cherries and figs, darken unless you add a color protector. In syrup pack, add the protector or powdered ascorbic acid *just before you combine the fruit and syrup.* You can buy packaged products that protect color in supermarkets. These contain ascorbic acid and another fruit acid, such as citric. Follow label directions when using them. Or use powdered ascorbic acid available in many drugstores. Add the ascorbic acid mixture or ascorbic acid powder to the syrup; mix thoroughly, but use care not to beat air into the syrup. Add the color protector or ascorbic acid mixture to the syrup when you are ready to pack the fruit. You lose some of these products' effectiveness if you let the syrup stand after you add them. In the sugar pack, add it to the sugar and if it is used in the unsweetened pack, to water. Be sure to mix the color protector thoroughly with sugar or water.

Pack the Right Way: For the sugar syrup pack, fill containers one third full of cold syrup, add the fruit and cover with cold syrup. To keep fruit that darkens readily submerged, place a generous piece of crumpled waxed paper under the lid. For the sugar pack, place the fruit in a bowl, sprinkle the sugar on and mix gently with a rubber spatula. Ripe berries are so delicate and soft that it is a good idea to add sugar to a small quantity at a time, about 1½ qts. Or place berries in a large shallow pan, sprinkle on sugar and mix gently until each is coated with sugar and juice.

Leave Head Space: In wide-topped rigid freezer containers, leave ½" head space for pints and 1" for quarts. When packing liquid (fruit packed in juice, syrup or water; crushed or purée): In wide-mouth jars with no shoulders allow ½" for pints and 1" for quarts; in wide-mouth jars with shoulders, 1" for pints, 1½" for quarts; in regular-mouth jars with shoulders, 1½" for pints and quarts.

When packing fruit juices, soups and sauces: In wide-mouth jars with no shoulders, 1" for pints and 1½" for quarts; in wide-mouth jars with shoulders, 1½" for pints and quarts; in regular-mouth jars with shoulders, 1½" for pints, 2" for quarts.

When packing fruit or vegetables without liquid (dry pack), or fruit in sugar pack: In wide-mouth jars with no shoulders, ½" for pints and quarts; in wide-mouth jars with shoulders, ¾" for pints, 1" for quarts; in regular-mouth jars with shoulders, 1" for pints and quarts.

Hurry to Freezer: Cover, seal if necessary and label every container with the name of the fruit and the date of packaging. Spread packages in freezer *at once* and freeze at 0°F. or lower.

Be sure fruit is completely frozen before stacking to save space.

Storage Time: 9 to 12 months.

How to Thaw: Let frozen fruits thaw in their original, *sealed containers* at room temperature. Quality and nutritive values are retained by fairly rapid thawing. If packages are watertight, you can submerge them in cool water. Serve fruit cold, preferably while it contains a few glistening ice crystals. Or cook like fresh fruit.

Directions for Freezing Fruits
(in alphabetical order)

APPLE SLICES: Wash firm-fleshed apples suitable for making pies or sauce. Remove bruises and decayed spots, peel, quarter and core. Cut each quarter into three slices. To prevent discoloration while fixing the apples, slice them into a salt water solution, ½ c. salt to 1 gal. water. When all the fruit is sliced, drain, rinse in cold water and drain. To freeze apple slices in sugar syrup, use 3 c. sugar to 1 qt. water and add ½ tsp. ascorbic acid powder to syrup before adding it to fruit. If you freeze apples for pies, omit syrup. For each quart of apple slices, blend 1 tsp. ascorbic acid powder with ½ to 1 c. sugar according to desired taste. Coat fruit evenly with the mixture. Pack, label, date and freeze.

(Commercially prepared ascorbic acid powder is available in supermarkets.)

APPLESAUCE: Canned applesauce may have better flavor than the frozen sauce. To freeze the sauce, cook apples in the usual way, then put them through a food mill if you wish. Sweeten to taste. Cool, package, label, date and freeze.

APRICOTS: Use directions for freezing peaches (see Index), selecting fully ripe fruit of uniform color. Unless you peel apricots before freezing them, the canned fruit is better for dessert use. (The skin tends to toughen in freezing.) Frozen unpeeled apricots are satisfactory for making pies, however. Cut the washed fruit in halves, discard pits and steam 4 minutes. Crush and pack with sugar, 1 lb. sugar to 4 lbs. fruit, or about ½ c. sugar to 1 qt. fruit. You will not need to add a color protector if you steam the fruit. If you do not steam the apricots, mix in ¾ to 1 tsp. powdered ascorbic acid for every 10 c. sugar. Mix powdered acid and sugar.

AVOCADOS: Select avocados that are soft-ripe with rinds free of dark blemishes. Peel, cut in halves, remove pits and mash pulp. For a superior product, add ⅛ tsp. powdered ascorbic acid to every quart of purée. Unsweetened avocados are best for salads, sandwiches and dips. Package, label, date and freeze.

BERRIES: Boysenberries, Dewberries, Loganberries and Youngberries: Follow directions for blackberries.

BLACKBERRIES: Wash firm, glossy, ripe berries of rich flavor in ice or very cold water. Lift from water into colander; hold in hands to drain. This avoids crushing berries. For dessert, use uncooked. Pack berries in sugar syrup made with 3 c. sugar to 1 qt. water. Pack without sugar for pies and jams. Or add ¾ c. sugar to 1 qt. berries. Label, date and freeze.

BLUEBERRIES: Wash stemmed, ripe berries in ice or very cold water, lift from water into colander and drain. For dessert use (uncooked) and superior quality, pack in sugar syrup made with 3 c. sugar to 1 qt. water. For pies and other cooked dishes, pack whole berries without sweetening. Or crush or sieve berries and mix with sugar, 1 to 1⅛ c., depending on sweetness of berries, to 1 qt. crushed blueberries; pack. Label, date and freeze.

CANTALOUPE: See Melons.

CHERRIES, SWEET: Use fully ripened, dark-red cherries. Chill them in ice or very cold water to prevent bleeding when pitted. Lift from water, stem and pit. Pack in sugar syrup made with 2 c. sugar to 1 qt. water. Add ½ tsp. powdered ascorbic acid. For the most delicious frozen cherries, add 1 tsp. citric acid or 4 tsp. lemon juice to the syrup in addition to the ascorbic acid. (Frozen sweet cherries are tasty in salads.) Package, label, date and freeze.

CHERRIES, TART: Wash, stem and pit bright-red cherries. For pies and other cooked dishes, pack cherries with sugar, ¾ c. to 1 qt. cherries. Mix until sugar dissolves. To improve color retention, add 1 tsp. powdered ascorbic acid to every cup of sugar. Or crush cherries coarsely and increase sugar—mix in 1 to 1½ c. sugar for every quart of fruit until sugar dissolves. Package, label, date and freeze.

CITRUS FRUITS: Fresh oranges and grapefruit are available the year round in most regions, but you may wish to include them, for the flavor they contribute, to mixed fruits for freezing (see Mixed Fruits). If you have a surplus of grapefruit and oranges, you may wish to freeze them. Select tree-ripened, firm fruit that is heavy for its size. Do not use fruit with soft spots. Wash and peel with a knife. Take out fruit sections, removing all membrane and seeds. Slice oranges if you prefer. If grapefruit has many seeds, cut it in halves across and scoop out half-sections with a knife or spoon. Pack the fruit sections or sliced oranges in containers with a sugar syrup made with 3 c. sugar to 1 qt. water, adding ½ tsp. powdered ascorbic acid. Use excess juices of fruit for part of the water in making the syrup. Label, date and freeze.

COCONUT: Shred fresh coconut meat or put it through a food chopper, or cut in pieces. Pack into containers and cover with milk from coconut. Package, label, date and freeze. Partially thaw and use like fresh coconut, grated or packaged, dehydrated shredded or flaked.

CRANBERRIES: Select firm, glossy berries that are plump. Stem, sort and wash in ice or very cold water; drain. Pack without sugar. Or make cranberry sauce; add 2 c. water to 1 qt. berries and cook until skins pop. Put through food mill if you wish. Add sugar to taste—about 2 c. for 1 qt. purée. Package, label, date and freeze.

CURRANTS: Stem large-fruited varieties of currants, wash in ice or very cold water, lift from water and drain. Mix each quart of fruit with sugar to taste, about ¾ c. Stir until most of the sugar dissolves. If you crush the currants slightly, the syrup will penetrate the berries. Or pack currants without adding sugar. Label, date and freeze.

DATES: Select ripe dates with good flavor and tender texture. Wash, slit and remove pits. Leave whole or put through a food mill to make a purée. Package, label, date and freeze.

ELDERBERRIES: Follow directions for blueberries.

FIGS: Use tree-ripened, soft-ripe fruit, making certain centers of figs are not soured. Sort, wash and cut off stems. Peel if desired. Slice or leave whole. Pack in sugar syrup made with 2½ c. sugar and 1 qt. water with ¾ tsp. powdered ascorbic acid added. Or omit ascorbic acid and add ½ c. lemon juice to every quart of syrup. You can pack figs without adding syrup, either dry or by covering with cold water with ¾ tsp. powdered ascorbic acid added to each quart of water. If you prefer to freeze crushed figs, mix 1 qt. fruit with ⅔ c. sugar with ¼ tsp. powdered ascorbic acid added. Package, label, date and freeze.

FRUIT JUICES: See Chapter 10.

GOOSEBERRIES: Remove stems and blossom ends. Wash, lift from water and drain. Pack without sugar or syrup; label, date and freeze.

GRAPES, BUNCH: Sort, stem and wash seedless green grapes (Thompson) or Tokay grapes. Pack Thompson seedless grapes whole or halved; cut Tokays in halves or quarters and discard seeds. Pack in sugar syrup made with 3 c. sugar to 1 qt. water. Label, date and freeze.

GRAPES, MUSCADINE: Sort, stem, wash and pack in sugar syrup made with 2 to 4 c. sugar for 1 qt. water. These grapes include the native American variety, the Scuppernong. Label, date and freeze.

HUCKLEBERRIES: Follow directions for blueberries, selecting berries with tender skins.

MELONS: Choose firm, ripe, fine-textured melons. Immature melons are inferior in quality when frozen. Wash, cut in halves, discard seeds and rind. Cut melon flesh into ½ to ¾″ cubes or balls and pack in sugar syrup made with 2 c. sugar to 1 qt. water. Whole seedless grapes may be added. Package, label, date and freeze.

Serve melon when partially thawed. Use same directions for Cantaloupes, Crenshaw, Honeydew, Muskmelons and Persian melons.

MIXED FRUITS: Select ripe fruits that contrast pleasantly in taste, color and texture. Wash, sort and prepare them as for table use. Cut fruits into attractive sizes and shapes for use in salads and cocktails.

Fruits that are good mixers are apricots, cherries, grapefruit, oranges, pineapples and Thompson seedless grapes. Fruits that are *not* especially good mixers are strawberries, raspberries, cantaloupe and apples.

A good way to fix grapefruit and oranges for freezing with other fruits is to arrange the sections, free of membrane, in layers with sugar to sweeten. Cover and set in the refrigerator until the fruit is just about covered with juices. Combine with the desired fruits and freeze in a syrup made with 2 to 3 c. sugar (depending on natural sweetness of fruits) to 1 qt. water with ½ tsp. powdered ascorbic acid added. Package, label, date and freeze.

Thaw fruit combinations in original, sealed containers. For molded salads, completely thaw; for cocktails and mixed salads, partially thaw so fruits retain a few ice crystals.

NECTARINES: Follow directions for peaches, using fully ripe, well-colored, firm fruit. Overripe nectarines may have an unpleasant flavor when frozen.

NUTS: Fresh, unprocessed nuts will keep in the freezer 9 to 12 months. If they are salted, the storage time is cut in half. Hold fresh nuts in damp place overnight to prevent brittleness of kernels in cracking. Pack in glass jars or metal containers, label and freeze.

PEACHES: Select fruit slightly riper than for canning. It should not have green spots. If you buy shipped-in peaches for freezing, let them ripen in a temperature of 65 to 70°F. for best results. Sort, wash and peel fruit. A good way to peel peaches (and apricots) for freezing is to dip 3 or 4 of them at a time in boiling water for 15 to 20 seconds or until the skins loosen. Chill quickly in ice or very cold water and peel and cut in halves or slices, working fast.

Slice the peaches directly into the freezer container filled one third full of cold syrup. Make the syrup with 3 c. sugar to 1 qt. water with ½ tsp. powdered ascorbic acid added just before syrup is used. Completely cover fruit with the cool syrup. For best color and flavor, keep the fruit submerged in the syrup by placing a generous piece of crumpled waxed paper under the lid. Cover, label, date and freeze.

If you cannot package the cut peaches immediately, you can hold them a short time without darkening by submerging them in 1 gal. water containing 1¼ tsp. powdered ascorbic acid. (This is a good way to hold sliced peaches for table use too.) For a water pack, if you cannot use sugar, substitute cold water for the syrup, adding 1 tsp. powdered ascorbic acid to each quart water. (See also Peach Purée Delicious, this chapter.)

PEARS: Better results are obtained by canning pears than by freezing them.

PERSIMMONS, NATIVE AND CULTIVATED: Select soft-ripe fruit. Sort and wash. Press the native variety through a food mill or sieve, add ⅛ tsp. powdered ascorbic acid to 1 qt. purée and pack without sugar. Select orange-colored, soft-ripe cultivated persimmons and peel. Prepare like native persimmons, but add 1 c. sugar to 1 qt. purée if you wish. Package, label, date and freeze.

PINEAPPLE: Peel and core firm, ripe pineapple with fragrant aroma, indicating ripeness. Slice, dice or cut in wedges or sticks. Pack in sugar syrup made with 3 c. sugar to 1 qt. water. If pineapple juices are available, use them for all or part of the water in making the syrup. For the sugar pack, mix 1 c. sugar with 8 or 9 c. cut-up pineapple. Package, label, date and freeze.

Frozen pineapple must be cooked before you add it to a gelatin mold. Otherwise an enzyme in the fruit will prevent the jellying.

PLUMS: They are better canned for dessert than frozen. If you want to freeze plums, choose fruit of deep color, remove pits and cut in halves or quarters or leave whole. Pack in syrup made with 3 c. sugar to 1 qt. water. Cover, label, date and freeze.

If no sugar is added, it (packed dry) makes good jam and pies.

PRUNES, FRESH: Wash, cut in halves and pit. Pack into containers and cover with sugar syrup made with 3 c. sugar to 1 qt. water. Cover, label, date and freeze.

Or freeze whole prunes without adding syrup or sugar.

RASPBERRIES: Wash firm, fully ripe red or black raspberries in ice or very cold water, but do not let them soak. Lift berries from water; drain small amounts through fingers, shaking hands. Pack them in sugar syrup or sugar. For sugar syrup, use 3 c. sugar to 1 qt. water; for sugar pack, use 1 lb. sugar to 4 to 5 lbs. berries—1 c. sugar to 7 to 8 c. berries. The exact amount of sugar needed depends on the sweetness of the berries. Package, label, date and freeze.

Freeze red and black raspberries for jam without adding syrup or sugar. For a purée, add ¾ to 1 c. sugar for 1 qt. crushed or sieved berries. Mix until sugar dissolves.

RHUBARB: Select crisp, tender red stalks early in spring. Remove leaves, woody ends and blemishes. Wash, cut in 1″ lengths and cover with sugar syrup, 3½ c. sugar to 1 qt. water. For a few months of storage, you can use a sugar pack successfully. Package, label, date and freeze.

Add 1 c. sugar to 4 c. rhubarb and you will not need to add sugar when making pie. Some homemakers like to freeze rhubarb cut in pieces without sugar.

STRAWBERRIES: Select ripe berries of bright color, rich flavor and pleasing aroma. Wash in cold water, lift into colander, drain, hull and slice each berry lengthwise in thirds. Pack in either syrup or sugar. Many people prefer the sugar pack. Use 1 lb. sugar to 4 to 5 lbs. berries, depending on how sweet they are, or 1 c. sugar to 7 to 8 c. hulled strawberries. Use a rubber spatula to mix berries and sugar. Small whole berries are best packed in sugar syrup made with 3 to 4 c. sugar to 1 qt. water, but their flavor is not so good as the sliced. Package, label, date and freeze.

Berries, chopped with a stainless steel chopper may be packed in the syrup or sugar, as preferred. Unsweetened strawberries are inferior in flavor when frozen.

Buying Frozen Fruits in Big Containers

Some farm women, who live in non-fruit-growing regions, find it economical to buy large packs of frozen fruits, like cherries, peaches and strawberries from locker plants or wholesale grocers that supply restaurants and other institutions. It is best to repack these fruits in smaller, handy containers.

Let the fruits stand at room temperature until they thaw just enough so you can separate the individual frozen pieces of fruit without breaking them. Pack in smaller containers and return to the freezer at once.

FROZEN CINNAMON APPLES

Keep the red beauties in your freezer —wonderful served with roast pork

1   c. sugar
1   c. water
½   c. red cinnamon candies
      (red hots)
8   to 12 medium apples

· Combine sugar, water and candies in saucepan. Cook over medium heat until candies are dissolved, stirring frequently. Simmer 5 minutes.

• Peel apples, cut in halves and remove cores. Cook them, a few at a time, in the syrup until they are just tender. Do not overcook and do not crowd apples in syrup.
• Cool, package, label, date and freeze. Makes 16 to 20 servings for relish, 8 to 12 servings when used for salad.
Recommended storage time: 9 months.
• To use, partially thaw apples and place one on each serving plate or place them on a relish tray. Or fill centers with cream cheese mixed with chopped nuts, top with spoonfuls of salad dressing and serve on lettuce for a colorful salad.

CRANBERRY APPLESAUCE

Keep a few jars in freezer for a change from plain applesauce

6   apples, cored and sliced
1   c. fresh cranberries
½   c. water
⅔   c. sugar
½   tsp. ground cinnamon
1   tblsp. lemon juice

• Combine apples, cranberries and water in saucepan; bring to a boil; cover. Cook slowly until apples are tender, about 15 minutes.
• Add remaining ingredients; cook until sugar dissolves. Refrigerate overnight. Serves 8.
• To freeze, ladle into foil-lined casserole and place in freezer. Remove foil-wrapped block, overwrap, label, date and return to freezer.
Recommended storage time: 6 months.
• To serve, remove outer wrap and

place in casserole; cover and heat in hot oven (400°F.) 35 minutes.

FROZEN CRANBERRY CHUTNEY

Make up this American fruit special and keep it in your refrigerator

4   c. cranberries
2   small oranges, seeded
1   lemon, seeded
2   apples, cored
1   c. raisins
1   c. brown sugar, firmly packed
½   tsp. ground ginger
2   tblsp. candied ginger
2   tblsp. grated onion
6   tblsp. chopped sweet green pepper

• Grind cranberries, oranges, lemon, apples and raisins. Add remaining ingredients; mix well.
• Pack in freezer containers. Seal and freeze. Makes about 3 pints.

Note: Chutney will keep up to 1 month stored in refrigerator.

PEACH PURÉE DELICIOUS

If you have overripe, soft peaches, you can salvage them in a delightful purée. It makes a delicious topping for ice cream and other desserts. The following directions were developed by the Colorado Experiment Station.

Divide peaches into two lots according to degree of bruising. Use ripest, softest fruit. Dip peaches in boiling water for 30 seconds, cool in running water and remove skins. Place in bowl of salted water (about 2½ tblsp. to a gallon) while you trim and pit peaches.

Mash drained fruit with a mesh-type potato masher. Four to five average-size peaches make 3 c. purée—to this quantity add ¼ tsp. powdered ascorbic acid to prevent discoloration. Add 1 pkg. powdered pectin; stir to dissolve; let stand 15 minutes, stirring. Add 3 c. sugar and stir to dissolve completely.

Remove peel, pits and bruised spots from less bruised fruit in same way. But instead of mashing, cut each peach in 12 slices and then run the knife around the center of the fruit to cut slices in halves.

Fill pint-size glass or other freezer containers with equal parts peach purée and slices mixed together lightly. Cover, label, date and freeze.

Melon-Patch Treat

When melons are abundant and your family finally tires of eating them plain, fix them in different ways. You'll never taste a more refreshing dessert than a cantaloupe purée, frozen. It's a perfect light ending for a meal that's otherwise heavy, a delightful topping for fruit salads. And if you use ripe melon with pink-orange or yellow-orange flesh, the dessert is a bright, colorful beauty.

GOLDEN GLOW MELON FREEZE

Lovely to look at, luscious to eat— serve it when you want to splurge

1   cantaloupe (3 c. cantaloupe purée)
¾   c. sugar
1   tblsp. lemon juice
⅛   tsp. salt
1   envelope unflavored gelatin
¼   c. cool water

· Use ripe, sound cantaloupe; cut in half. Remove seeds and peel. Slice and press through a food mill or sieve to make purée.

· Mix cantaloupe purée, sugar, lemon juice and salt. Soften gelatin in cool water 5 minutes; then dissolve by heating over boiling water. Add cantaloupe mixture slowly to gelatin, stirring while adding to mix thoroughly.

· *For electric ice cream freezer*, pour into freezer container, surround with 6 to 8 parts ice to 1 part rock salt. Keep freezer turning about 20 minutes until mixture becomes firm and clings to dasher. Remove dasher. Serve immediately. Makes about 1 quart.

· *For refrigerator trays*, pour mixture into trays and freeze until firm. Remove trays and stir rapidly to incorporate air and make it smoother. Return trays to freezer a few hours to harden. Serve immediately or pack in freezer containers, label, date and place in freezer.

Recommended storage time: 3 weeks.

SUNRISE PINK DESSERT

This pink beauty gives the springtime taste to winter meals

2   (3 oz.) pkgs. strawberry flavor
      gelatin
2   c. boiling water
2   (10 oz.) pkgs. frozen
      strawberries (2 ½ c.)
1   medium banana, mashed
2   tblsp. lemon juice
2   c. dairy sour cream

• Dissolve gelatin in boiling water; add frozen berries; stir until thawed.
• Add banana and lemon juice.
• Stir mixture into sour cream. Pour into 2-qt. mold. Chill until set.
• To serve, unmold; garnish with slightly thawed berries. Makes 8 servings.

Note: You can substitute 1 c. heavy cream, whipped, for the sour cream.

VARIATION

STRAWBERRY SALAD: Add ½ c. mayonnaise and use only 1½ c. sour cream. Pretty on greens.

GINGER PEACHES

• Melt ½ c. butter or regular margarine in skillet. Add ⅓ c. slivered crystallized ginger or ½ tsp. ground ginger, 2 tblsp. grated lemon peel and 1 tsp. lemon juice, then 1 qt. frozen peaches, thawed, or 1 qt. canned peach halves and juice. The lemon-ginger taste is special. Heat through. Best served warm over ice cream. Makes 6 servings.

Flavor-Fresh Vegetables
THEY COOK IN ALMOST NO TIME

Farm women use vegetables from their gardens all winter long—via their freezers. They know the lift fresh vegetables give to meals, and they're a snap to fix. Best of all, they taste so good.

Most farm cooks have their own seasoning touches for cooked vegetables—a snip of parsley, mint or other herb, a squirt of lemon juice or a few toasted nuts, chopped.

But the first step is to freeze the vegetables right. Then they will be worth talented treatment. Do hustle them from the garden to the freezer. *And follow directions for scalding them—don't omit this hot water bath.* Even if you hear about homemakers having success freezing vegetables without scalding, don't try it. Too many failures result when you skip this important step. Play safe.

Freezing Vegetables

Hurry from Garden to Freezer: It is the best way to keep top quality. If the weather is hot, gather vegetables early in the morning before they have absorbed much heat from the sun. When you must keep them a short time before preparing for freezing, spread in a cool, ventilated place or pack loosely and put in the refrigerator. Cooling unshelled peas and asparagus immediately after picking protects flavors and vitamins. Place these vegetables in ice or very cold water until cold, drain and refrigerate. Or pack them in crushed ice. Do not hold shelled or cut vegetables before freezing or they may sour. Other causes of souring are inadequate scalding, or stacking packages in the freezer before they are thoroughly frozen. First, spread packages out in freezer; stack later if space is scarce.

Plant Varieties for Freezing: Many varieties of all vegetables freeze successfully, but some are not good freezers. Ask your County Extension Home Economist or write to your State Agricultural Experiment Station to find out which ones in your area freeze well.

Scald Vegetables: Scalding is extremely important. It prevents loss of flavor, toughening, retains vitamins, increases potential storage time in freezer and results in products of superior quality. Use rapidly boiling water. Properly scalded, vegetables may be stored in the freezer from 9 to 12 months. Green vegetables will have a brighter color when scalded, and the heat will shrink vegetables slightly so they handle more easily and conserve freezer space. Scalding also removes objectionable odors and bitter flavors from some vegetables. Here are up-to-date detailed directions:

SCALD VEGETABLES THIS WAY:

1. Place water in a large aluminum, stainless steel or enamelware kettle with cover. Use at least 1 gal. water to 1 pt. vegetable, except for the leafy greens. For them, use 2 gals. water. Bring the water to a full rolling boil.

2. Put the prepared vegetable in a wire basket (a covered one is excellent) or loosely in a cheesecloth bag and *submerge in boiling water.* Start counting time immediately. The time is so important in scalding that we recommend use of a timer. Keep the heat high, kettle covered and the water boiling. A practical test for sufficient scalding is to cut a few pieces of the product to see if it has been heated to the center. Beans with green and yellow pods will bend without breaking if scalded long enough. But avoid overscalding; it results in soft textures, destroys vitamins and nutrients and produces inferior flavors. Use the same water several times if you wish, but add more from time to time to keep it at the proper level throughout the scalding process.

3. *Increase scalding time if you live in high elevations.* At 2000 to 4000 feet, add ½ minute; 4000 to 6000

feet, add 1 minute; over 6000 feet, add 2½ minutes to the time given.

Chill Quickly: Plunge basket or cloth bag of scalded vegetable into cold running water or ice water immediately (1 lb. ice per 1 lb. vegetable). Rapid chilling checks the cooking, saves nutrients and helps make for top quality. A practical test for sufficient chilling is to bite into a few pieces. If they feel cold to the tongue, drain the vegetable in a colander or wire basket and pack. It takes about as long to chill as to scald vegetables.

Use Steam Scalding for Broccoli: Some people believe they get a better product if they scald broccoli with steam rather than in hot water. However, steaming is not recommended for most vegetables and fruits because it is difficult to scald thoroughly with the equipment available in most home kitchens. Pumpkin, winter squash and sweet potatoes sometimes are scalded in steam, but most homemakers prefer to bake them before freezing.

To scald with steam, place from 1 to 3″ water in the bottom of a large kettle. Bring to a full rolling boil. Place a single layer of the prepared vegetable in a wire basket or in a cheesecloth bag. Suspend over the rapidly boiling water, preferably on a rack. Keep the cover on the kettle during the steaming and start counting the time when the lid is placed on the kettle. Steaming takes longer than scalding in water.

Leave Head Space: Allow ½″ for pints and quarts in rigid freezer containers. Leave ½″ for dry pack and 1″ for liquid pack (as with syrup) in standard glass canning jars and pack firmly, but not tightly. Vegetables that pack loosely, like broccoli and asparagus, need no head space.

Directions for Freezing Vegetables
(in alphabetical order)

ARTICHOKES, GLOBE: Select small artichokes; pull leaves from them and cut top from buds. Trim stem to within 1″ of base. Wash thoroughly.

Scald artichokes in boiling solution of 1 tblsp. citric acid crystals (or 1 tblsp. lemon juice) and 1 qt. water for 8 to 10 minutes, counting time when solution returns to boiling again. Cool 15 minutes under cold running water or in ice water. Drain and package.

Artichoke hearts may be frozen separately. Scald them in the boiling solution 2 to 3 minutes. Cool like whole artichokes. Package, label, date and freeze.

ASPARAGUS: Select young, bright-colored, brittle stalks that snap when broken and have compact tips. Harvest early in the morning if weather is warm. Discard woody, blemished stalks. Wash in cold running or ice water. Remove bracts (scales). Sort into medium and large stalks. Pack in lengths to fit package or cut in 2″

lengths, discarding woody ends. For top quality, process as soon as possible after harvesting. Asparagus becomes tough or woody and loses vitamins after picking. The tips are rich in vitamin C and full of flavor.

Scald medium stalks 3 minutes, large stalks (½ to ¾″ in diameter) 4 minutes. Chill in cold running or ice water. Drain, package, label, date and freeze.

BEANS, GREEN: Home economists in our Countryside Test Kitchens experimented with various ways to freeze green beans, and their results prove the following two methods are best. It is especially important to choose varieties recommended for freezing in your area—check with the Horticulture Department of your state agricultural college. Pick young, tender beans that snap when broken and that have small, tender seeds. Wash in cold running water and process them right after picking. (If you can't process them immediately, keep beans in ice cold water until processing time.) Snip off tips and sort for size. Cut or break beans in 1½″ pieces, or leave them whole, if you wish.

Standard 3-Minute Blanch: Have ready a kettle with at least 1 gal. rapidly boiling water. Place 1 pt. beans in wire basket and immerse in boiling water. Cover and count time for 3 minutes. Remove basket from boiling water and immerse it in ice water to chill beans. Test coolness by biting into the vegetable. When it is cool to the tongue, it is ready to pack. Drain beans right away and package them. Label, date and freeze immediately.

Cooked, Frozen in Seasoned Bouillon: Combine 2 qts. water, 8 beef bouillon cubes, 1 tsp. onion powder and 1 tsp. salt in 8-qt. kettle; heat to boiling. Add 4 qts. cut green beans; cover and bring to a boil again. Boil 12 minutes. Remove cover and place kettle in ice water bath. Cool quickly, stirring occasionally. Fill containers with beans and liquid; *be sure liquid covers beans.* Seal and freeze. Makes 8 pints. To serve, dip freezer container in hot water to loosen beans. Slip block of beans and liquid into heavy saucepan. Cover; heat slowly until defrosted and liquid begins to boil (about 20 minutes).

BEANS, ITALIAN: Select any good garden variety. Wash in cold water and cut or break in 1 to 1½″ pieces. Scald in water 3½ minutes. Chill in cold running or ice water. Drain, package, label, date and freeze.

BEANS, LIMA: Harvest well-filled pods containing green, tender young beans. Do not freeze white beans; they are overmature. Wash and remove beans from pods, using scissors to snip tough pods. Do not wash after shelling. Discard blemished beans. Process them at once because shelled beans lose flavor quickly if allowed to stand.

Scald small and medium bean 3 minutes, larger beans 4 minutes. Chill in cold running or ice water. Drain, package, label, date, freeze.

BEANS, SOY: Harvest well-developed pods containing green beans. Wash in cold running water.

Scald in pods 5 minutes. Chill in cold running or ice water; shell, discarding blemished beans; package, label, date and freeze. You need not scald them after shelling.

BEANS, YELLOW: Follow directions for green beans.

BEETS: Select smooth, tender beets of small to medium size. Discard blemished beets, remove green tops and wash thoroughly.

Scald by cooking in water until tender. Chill in cold running or ice water, slip off the skins, slice or dice larger beets; package, label, date and freeze.

BROCCOLI: Use tender, firm stalks with compact heads. Discard off-color heads and those that have started to blossom. Remove tough leaves and woody stalks. Cut through stalks lengthwise. When cut, heads should be about 1″ in diameter. (The cutting makes uniform scalding possible and gives attractive servings when cooked.) Soak stalks, heads down, for ½ hour in salt water (¼ c. salt to 1 qt. cold water). This drives out the small insects. Rinse in cold water.

Scald 4 minutes or steam 5 minutes. (For steaming see directions that precede.) Steaming usually is preferred. Chill in cold running or ice water; drain. Place heads and stalks alternately in the container to make compact package. Label, date and freeze.

BRUSSELS SPROUTS: Select firm, compact heads of good color. Wash, trim and discard discolored heads. Soak in salt water (¼ c. salt to 1 qt. water) ½ hour to drive out small insects. Rinse in cold water and drain.

Scald medium heads 4 minutes; larger heads, 5 minutes. Chill in cold running or ice water; drain, package, label, date and freeze.

CARROTS: Harvest smooth, tender carrots before roots are woody. Plan plantings so you can harvest them in cool weather. The small, immature roots often harvested in hot weather contain less carotene and they rarely are of good quality when frozen. Remove tops, wash and scrape. Dice or slice ¼″ thick.

Scald 3½ minutes. Chill in cold running or ice water; drain, package, label, date and freeze.

CAULIFLOWER: Pick well-formed, compact white heads with fresh leaves. Trim, discard leaves and wash. Slit heads into pieces about 1″ in diameter. Soak about ½ hour in salt water (¼ c. salt to 1 qt. water) to drive out small insects. Rinse in cold water and drain. Work fast to prevent discoloration. Scald 4 minutes. Chill in cold running or ice water; drain, package, label, date and freeze.

CELERY: If freezer space is limited, it is questionable whether it is wise to freeze celery. But the green varieties may be frozen for use in cooked dishes. Trim, discarding tough and blemished stalks. Wash and cut in 1″ pieces or finely dice.

Scald 4 minutes. Chill in cold running or ice water; drain, package, label, date and freeze.

CORN, SWEET: Harvest early in morning if weather is warm. Freeze corn when at its "eating best." It remains at this stage of optimum maturity a short time, usually only about 48 hours. A practical test for maturity: press the thumbnail into a kernel. If the milk spurts out freely, the corn is at or near the stage of desired maturity. Immature corn kernels will be watery; when overmature, doughy.

Process as quickly as possible after harvesting. A delay of more than a few hours often results in loss of quality unless ears are refrigerated.

Husk ears, remove the silk and trim ends. Scald, using a large kettle that holds 12 to 15 qts. boiling water. Keep kettle covered during scalding. For whole kernel corn, scald the ears 4½ minutes. Cool in cold running water or ice water, drain and cut kernels from cobs at about ¾ depth of kernels. Package, label, date and freeze.

For corn on the cob, scald small ears (up to 1½″ in diameter) 8 minutes, and large ears (diameter more than 1½″) 11 minutes. (Measure diameter of corn at large end, after trimming.) Chill quickly in cold running or ice water; drain and freeze on a tray or baking sheet. Then wrap in moistureproof packaging material and seal, label, date and freeze.

EGGPLANT: Harvest eggplant before it is too mature and when the seeds are tender. For top quality, select firm, heavy eggplant of uniform dark color. Peel and slice in ¼ to ⅓″ slices, or dice. Drop pieces into cold water containing ¼ c. salt to 1 gal. water to prevent color loss.

Scald eggplant in boiling salted water (¼ c. to 1 gal. water) 4½ minutes. Chill in cold running or ice water. Drain and package in layers separated by sheets of freezer paper. Label, date and freeze.

Many homemakers prefer to freeze cooked eggplant.

GREENS: (spinach, beet, chard, collard, kale, mustard, turnip): Pick young, tender leaves early in morning if weather is warm. Remove large, tough stems and discard blemished leaves. Wash in cold running water.

Scald 2 minutes, except collards and stem portions of Swiss chard. Steam these 3 to 4 minutes. Very tender young spinach is best scalded 1½ minutes. Chill in cold running or ice water; drain and package with the water that clings to leaves. Label, date and freeze.

A good way to chill greens after scalding is to swish them in ice water or to spread them on ice, turning often.

HERBS, GARDEN: Wrap a few sprigs of leaves in foil or seal in plastic bags and place in a glass jar or carton. Freeze.

Do not scald leaves—just wash them thoroughly and drain.

KOHLRABI: Pick when young and tender. Cut off tops, wash, peel and cut in ½″ cubes.

Scald 2½ minutes. Chill in cold running or ice water; package, label, date and freeze.

MIXED VEGETABLES: Prepare each vegetable and scald separately according to directions. Freeze the vegetables separately if desired, thaw just enough to separate the pieces, combine as desired; package, label, date and refreeze.

MUSHROOMS: Process young, firm mushrooms as soon as possible after picking. They bruise and deteriorate rapidly. Wash and remove base of stem. Freeze small mushrooms whole. Cut large ones in four or more pieces. To prevent browning, add 1 tsp. citric acid, 3 tsp. lemon juice or ½ tsp. powdered ascorbic acid to every quart of water used in scalding.

Scald medium or small whole mushrooms 4 minutes; cut pieces, 3 minutes. Chill, drain and package. If the mushrooms are very mild in flavor, steam them instead of scalding. Before steaming, put them in water containing 1½ tsp. citric acid or 1 tsp. lemon juice to 1 pt. water for 5 minutes. Steam whole mushrooms not larger than 1″ across for 5 minutes, small or quartered, 3½ minutes and sliced, 3 minutes. (See general directions for steaming earlier in this chapter.) Chill at once in cold running or ice water; drain, package, label, date and freeze.

Or cut washed mushrooms in slices ¼″ thick and sauté in butter for 2 minutes. Cool quickly and pack. Pour excess butter over packed mushrooms. Package in meal-size amounts. Label, date and freeze.

OKRA: Select young, tender pods 2 to 4″ long. Remove stems and wash. Scald under water, 3 to 4 minutes. The large-podded varieties grown in the West need to be scalded 5 minutes. Chill in cold running or ice water; drain, package, label, date and freeze.

ONIONS: Onions keep well in a cool, dry place. Usually, they are not home frozen, but you can freeze chopped onions successfully. They will hold from 3 to 6 months, but after that they tend to lose flavor. Select mature sweet Spanish or any good garden onion. Peel, wash and cut in quarters. Chop and scald in water 1½ minutes. Chill in cold running or ice water. Drain, package, label, date and freeze.

PARSNIPS: Select smooth, firm roots of top quality that are not woody. In northern areas, parsnips may be harvested in spring or late fall. Remove tops, wash and peel. Slice, dice or cut in lengthwise strips.

Scald 3 minutes. Chill in cold running or ice water; drain, package, label, date and freeze.

PEAS, CHINESE OR EDIBLE POD: Select any good variety with bright green, flat tender pods. Wash well and remove stems, blossom ends and strings; leave whole. Scald in water 2½ to 3 minutes. Chill in cold running or ice water. Drain, package, label, date and freeze.

PEAS, ENGLISH OR GREEN: Pick bright green, crisp pods containing tender peas that are sweet, but not overmature. Peas are at their best for a short time, about 24 hours. If peas are hard to shell, scald pods in boiling water for 1 minute. Scald and shell a few at a time; you need not wash them after shelling. Discard small, undeveloped peas. Or before scalding, you may separate overmature peas from tender ones by floating the peas in cold salt water—½ c. salt to 1 gal. water with 55°F. temperature. After 10 seconds, remove the floaters, which are the tender peas; the overmature will sink. *Avoid delay between shelling and freezing to prevent toughening of skins.* Some homemakers like to mix 2 to 3 tsp. sugar in 3 to 3¼ c. peas (1 lb.) after scalding and chilling.

Scald shelled peas 1½ to 2 minutes. Chill in cold running or ice water; drain, package, label, date and freeze.

PEAS, FIELD (like Black-eyed): Follow directions for green peas, except scald them 2 minutes.

PEPPERS, GREEN AND PIMIENTOS: Pick crisp, well-developed peppers of good color, green or red. Wash, cut out stem; remove seeds from green peppers. Cut in halves, dice or slice. Pimiento peppers may be peeled by roasting them in a hot oven (400°F.) 3 to 4 minutes or until peel is charred. Cool peeled pimientos and pack dry. Label, date and freeze.

Scald green pepper halves 3 minutes; sliced and diced, 2 minutes. Chill in cold running or ice water; package, label, date and freeze.

Peppers lose crispness in freezing but are satisfactory for cooked dishes. They are one vegetable that may be packed and frozen without scalding.

PEPPERS, HOT: Wash; package without scalding, label, date and freeze.

POTATOES, FRENCH FRIES: Peel and cut potatoes in thin strips, about ⅜" wide and ⅜" thick. Fry in hot fat (370°F. on deep-fat frying thermometer) until potatoes are a *light* brown. Drain on paper towels spread in a baking pan. Cool and package. Label, date and freeze immediately. To serve, spread potatoes on a baking sheet and place in medium oven (350°F.) 8 to 10 minutes or until

brown. Or spread in broiler pan and broil 8 to 10 minutes. Salt to taste.

POTATOES, SWEET: Pick firm, smooth roots of bright color. Wash and bake in moderate oven (350°F.) until soft. Cool, peel and slice into ½" slices. To keep the bright color, dip slices in solution made by dissolving ¼ c. lemon juice in 1 pt. cold water. For candied sweet potatoes, drain slices and roll in granulated or brown sugar. The color is less bright when they are rolled in brown sugar.

Or freeze sweet potatoes in purée form. Steam or bake them, cool, remove pulp from skins and mash or put through food mill. Add 2 tblsp. lemon juice for every 10 c. purée to help preserve color. You can add 1 c. sugar if you wish. You can freeze this sweetened purée mixed with milk, eggs and spices (except cloves) for pie filling. Package, label, date and freeze.

POTATOES, WHITE OR IRISH: Select any good potato. Wash, peel, cut out deep eyes and any green spots (sun or light burn). Cut in ¼ to ½" cubes. Scald 5 minutes. Chill in cold running or ice water. Drain; package, label, date and freeze.

PUMPKIN: Select good pie pumpkins. Pick at maximum maturity, indicated by good color and a stem that breaks easily from vine. Wash, cut or break into uniform pieces, remove seeds and bake in moderate oven (350°F.) or steam until tender. Cool, scoop pulp from skins and mash or put through food mill. Package, label, date and freeze.

Or make pie filling by your favorite recipe and freeze.

RUTABAGAS: Freeze tender, young rutabagas. Wash, remove tops, peel and slice, or dice in ¼" cubes.

Scald 3 minutes, chill in cold running or ice water; drain, package, label, date and freeze.

SPINACH: See Greens.

SQUASH, SUMMER (Crookneck, Zucchini and Straightneck): Pick when small, 5 to 7" long, and while rind is tender and seeds are small. Wash, but do not peel. Cut in pieces not more than 1½" thick.

Scald 3 minutes for ¼" slices, 6 minutes for 1½" slices. Chill in cold running or ice water; drain, package, label, date and freeze.

SQUASH, WINTER: Pick fully ripe or mature squash, with shells hard enough so that you cannot push your thumbnail through them. "Dry" types are recommended. Wash and cut or break into fairly uniform pieces and remove seeds. Bake in moderate oven (350°F.) or steam until tender. Cool, scoop out pulp and mash or put through food mill. Package, label, date and freeze.

You can fix your favorite pie filling with sugar, milk, eggs and spices (except cloves) and freeze.

Some homemakers like to mix one or two varieties or to blend squash and pumpkin purées.

TOMATOES: Whole tomatoes may be wrapped and frozen. Use them for cooking within 2 months. For best results, stew the tomatoes before freezing, but do not add bread or crackers until you heat the frozen tomatoes for serving. Stew the tomatoes and cool them by placing saucepan in larger pan containing ice water. Package, label, date and freeze.

You can freeze uncooked tomato pulp and store it for a few months without great flavor loss.

TOMATOES, HUSK (Ground Cherries): Husk, scald 2 minutes, chill and pack in sugar syrup. Use 3 c. sugar to 1 qt. water. Package, label, date and freeze.

TURNIPS: Harvest young tender turnips. Remove tops, wash, peel, slice, or dice in ½" cubes. Scald 2½ minutes; chill in cold running or ice water; drain, package, label, date and freeze.

VEGETABLE PURÉES: Scald the prepared vegetables as directed, cool, drain and put through food chopper. Package, label, date and freeze.

How to Cook Frozen Vegetables

Cook all vegetables, except corn on the cob, without thawing. (Or thaw vegetables frozen in a solid block just enough so that you can separate the pieces with a fork.) Drop vegetables, except purées, into boiling water over high heat. You will hasten the cooking if you will break the vegetable block apart with a fork as the hot water thaws it. When the water, cooled by the frozen food, boils again, reduce the heat, cover and simmer until the vegetable is just tender. The time depends on the vegetable, the variety, maturity, the size of the pieces, the length of the scalding period in preparation and the degree of thawing before cooking. Most vegetables will cook in from 4 to 15 minutes. Time is slightly longer at high altitudes.

Use as little water as possible in cooking frozen vegetables. Usually from ¼ to ½ c. is adequate for 1 pint. Add salt and other desired seasonings to the water. Plan the cooking time so that the vegetable may be served piping hot when cooked to avoid a loss of food nutrients, attractiveness and flavor.

Partially or completely thaw frozen corn on the cob before cooking. Cook it like other frozen vegetables only a very short time, 3 to 6 minutes, because the kernels were practically cooked when scalded. It is especially important to serve at once or corn on the cob will be soggy. Cook second servings separately instead of keeping them warm in hot water.

Usually enough water clings to the leaves of home-frozen greens for cooking, but this is not always true of those commercially frozen. Always follow package directions for cooking commercially frozen vegetables from retail markets. Read package labels.

Heat or cook puréed or mashed vegetables in top of a double boiler without water. If vegetable seems dry, add a little melted butter or milk. Season to taste. Use imagination.

ORANGE-GLAZED CARROTS

Quick to get in freezer, no work to freeze. Glistening glaze seasons

1 ½	lbs. carrots, cut in strips
2	tsp. flour
¼	c. brown sugar, firmly packed
½	tsp. salt
1	tblsp. vinegar
1	tblsp. lemon juice
½	c. orange juice
1	tblsp. grated orange peel
2	tblsp. butter

· Blanch carrots in boiling water 5 minutes. Drain.

· Blend together flour, sugar and salt. Add vinegar, juices and orange peel. Bring to a boil. Add butter; cook 5 minutes.

· Pour over carrots in 1-qt. foil-lined pan; freeze. Remove from pan; wrap, label, date and store in freezer. Makes 6 servings.

Recommended storage time: 6 weeks.

· To serve, turn carrots upside down in same pan; bake, covered, in a moderate oven (350°F.) about 1 hour, until tender. Uncover last 20 minutes.

BROCCOLI SOUFFLÉ

A dish that rises to the occasion—a guest luncheon special

3	tblsp. butter or regular margarine
3	tblsp. flour
1	c. milk
¼	tsp. salt
⅛	tsp. pepper
½	lb. (about 2½ c.) grated process cheese
1	(10 oz.) pkg. frozen chopped broccoli, partially thawed
½	c. finely chopped onion
3	eggs, separated

• Melt butter in saucepan, stir in flour to make smooth paste; add milk, salt and pepper; cook 5 minutes.

• Add cheese; stir until melted. Fold in broccoli and onion.

• Fold in well beaten egg yolks. Lightly fold in egg whites, beaten until stiff but not dry (you'll still see some white pieces). Pour into foil-lined 2-qt. baking dish with straight sides.

• Cover, label, date and freeze. When frozen, remove from dish; store in plastic freezer bag; return to freezer. Recommended storage time: 6 to 8 weeks.

• To serve, remove foil; place in same dish and set in shallow pan filled with ½" hot water. Cover with foil and bake in moderate oven (350°F.) about 45 minutes, then uncover and bake about 1 hour, until puffy and browned. Makes 6 to 8 servings.

Note: Takes less baking time if you freeze this in individual baking cups;

makes about 8 cups. To bake, set cups in shallow pan filled with ½" hot water; bake in moderate oven (350°F.) about 45 to 50 minutes, uncovered.

To bake without freezing, bake in unlined dish set in pan of hot water in moderate oven (350°F.) for 1 hour.

STUFFED BAKED POTATOES

• Prepare and stuff as usual but do not brown.

• Cool quickly; place in flat containers and wrap, label, date and freeze. Or freeze on trays; store in plastic freezer bags.

Recommended storage time: 1 month.

• To serve, bake unthawed in moderate oven (350°F.) 30 minutes; brown last few minutes at 400°F.

OVEN-FRIED POTATO SLICES

• Slice 5 medium, peeled potatoes ¼" thick; scald 2 minutes; drain.

• Pour ⅓ c. salad oil in each of two large shallow pans. Add half of potatoes to each; turn to coat slices with oil. Arrange one layer deep.

• Bake in very hot oven (450°F.) until light brown, 20 to 25 minutes, turn once. Drain. Makes 6 servings.

• Cool quickly; freeze on baking sheets. Store in plastic freezer bags; label, date and freeze.

Recommended storage time: 1 month.

• To serve, spread frozen slices on baking sheets. Heat in hot oven (400°F.) 5 to 10 minutes, drain. Add salt and pepper to taste.

Heat-and-Eat Frozen Potato Treats

With so many meat-and-potato men in the United States, it's not surprising that home economists in our Countryside Kitchens received many letters asking for recipes for potato dishes that freeze successfully. Our Heat-and-Eat Potato Treats are their delicious answer to the questions. The trick is to cook and freeze the potatoes in ready-to-use shapes so you can take them from the freezer and place in the oven at once to reheat. It is important not to let the food thaw before heating. Thawing makes potatoes mushy.

Here are recipes for the potato dishes. You can store them in the freezer up to 2 months.

FROZEN HASHED BROWN POTATOES

Cook two skilletfuls of these golden, crisp-crusted potatoes for 8 or 9

To Freeze: Boil baking-type potatoes in their jackets until just tender but still firm (10 to 15 minutes). Drain, cool and peel. Grate potatoes on a coarse grater.
· Line a 10″ skillet with aluminum foil, bringing foil up to cover sides. Mix 1½ tsp. salt with 4 c. grated potatoes. Pack in foil-lined skillet, pressing down firmly. Remove from skillet with foil. Seal, label and freeze. Repeat to stock your freezer.

To Cook: Heat ½ c. shortening over medium heat (350°F. in electric skillet) in same skillet in which potatoes

were shaped for freezing. Remove foil and add the disk of frozen potatoes (shortening will spatter, so quickly cover the skillet). Cook 5 minutes over medium heat. Uncover and continue cooking 10 to 12 minutes, or until potatoes are browned on the bottom. Cut into 4 wedges; turn each piece separately with spatula or pancake turner. Continue cooking 5 minutes, or until attractively browned. Makes 4 generous servings.

BASIC MASHED POTATOES

Freeze these plain or make into one of our five interesting variations

4   lbs. boiling potatoes
1   c. milk (amount varies with moisture in potatoes)
¼   c. butter
1 ½   tsp. salt

· Peel potatoes. Boil until soft; drain. Press potatoes through a ricer or mash.
· Heat milk, butter and salt together. Gradually whip in until the potatoes are smooth and fluffy.
· Form into shapes that are ready to use with no thawing. Freeze by directions in variations that follow.

VARIATIONS

POTATO PUFFS: Add ½ c. grated Cheddar cheese or 2 egg yolks to Basic Mashed Potatoes. Chill. Form into balls; roll in mixture of ¾ c. corn flake crumbs and 3 tblsp. toasted sesame seeds. Freeze on tray until firm. Package, label and return to freezer. Makes 48 small or 24 medium balls.

To Serve: Place frozen puffs on baking sheet. Brush lightly with melted butter. Bake in hot oven (400°F.) 20 minutes for small puffs and 30 minutes for medium puffs. To serve without freezing, omit brushing with butter and bake puffs only until they brown, 5 to 10 minutes.

SNOWCAPS: Add 2 egg yolks to Basic Mashed Potatoes. Spoon hot potatoes in mounds on baking sheet. Cool; freeze until firm. Remove from baking sheet; place in plastic bags. Seal, label and return to freezer. Use to top meat and vegetable casseroles. Makes 24 snowcaps.

PIMIENTO NESTS: Add ½ c. chopped, drained pimiento to Basic Mashed Potatoes. Line a 1½-qt. casserole with aluminum foil. Spoon half the potato mixture into casserole. Shape into a nest, building up the sides to top of casserole. Remove from casserole with foil to hold shape of the nest. Reline casserole with foil and shape remaining potato mixture. Cool; freeze nests until firm. Remove from freezer; package, seal and label. Return to freezer. Serve with chicken filling (see recipe for Chicken in Potato Nest).

CHEESE NESTS: Add ½ c. grated Cheddar cheese to hot Basic Mashed Potatoes; omit the pimiento and proceed as for Pimiento Nests. Serve with onion filling (see recipe for Cheese/Onion Pie).

POTATO NESTS: Omit the pimiento and shape like Pimiento Nests.

CHICKEN IN POTATO NEST

For company use two Pimiento Nests and double the other ingredients

1   frozen Pimiento Nest
4   tblsp. melted butter or regular margarine
2   tblsp. flour
1   c. chicken broth
Salt
Pepper
1   (4 oz.) can sliced mushrooms, drained
½   c. diced celery
1   c. diced cooked chicken

· Remove wrapper from frozen Pimiento Nest. Place in casserole in which it was shaped originally. Drizzle with 2 tblsp. melted butter. Cover and bake in hot oven (400°F.) 30 minutes. Uncover, bake 30 minutes.

· In the meantime, combine remaining 2 tblsp. butter and flour in heavy saucepan. Slowly add broth; stir constantly until sauce is smooth and thick. Season with salt and pepper. Add remaining ingredients; heat. Spoon hot mixture into baked Pimiento Nest. Makes 6 servings.

CHEESE/ONION PIE

Potatoes make the crust for this pie— serve with fish, ham or fried chicken

1   frozen Cheese Nest
2   tblsp. melted butter
1   beef bouillon cube
½   c. boiling water
2   c. chopped onions
¼   c. butter or regular margarine
3   tblsp. flour
1   c. milk
Salt
Pepper

· Remove wrapper from frozen Cheese Nest. Place in casserole in which it was shaped originally. Drizzle with 2 tblsp. melted butter. Cover and bake in hot oven (400°F.) 30 minutes. Uncover, bake 30 minutes.

· In the meantime, dissolve bouillon cube in boiling water. Add onions, cover and simmer until tender; drain.

· Melt ¼ c. butter in heavy saucepan. Add flour to make a smooth paste. Add milk slowly; stir constantly until white sauce is smooth and thick.

· Season with salt and pepper. Add drained onions. Spoon onion mixture into baked Cheese Nest for serving. Makes 6 servings.

HAM/VEGETABLE CASSEROLE

Frozen vegetables win praise when teamed with ham and baked this way

2	c. frozen corn or 1 (10 oz.) pkg.
2	c. frozen peas and carrots or 1 (10 oz.) pkg.
2	c. frozen succotash or 1 (10 oz.) pkg.
1	tsp. salt
¼	tsp. pepper
3	tblsp. chopped onion
1	can condensed cream of mushroom soup

Ham slices, individual servings, cut ¼" thick

· Place frozen vegetables in greased 3-qt. casserole. Sprinkle with salt, pepper and onion. Spread soup over the top.

· Cover with foil and bake in a hot oven (400°F.) 40 minutes. Stir vegetables, spreading them evenly over the bottom of the casserole.

· Cover with ham. Return to oven and bake, uncovered, 10 minutes. Turn meat and continue baking 10 minutes. Makes 8 servings.

VARIATION

BACON/VEGETABLE CASSEROLE: Substitute 10 to 15 slices frozen Canadian-style bacon or fresh side meat (lean) for the ham.

BAKED STUFFED ZUCCHINI

Perfect example of why families of Italian descent like this squash

8	small to medium zucchini
2	medium onions
1	clove garlic
12	sprigs parsley
3	tblsp. olive oil
1	c. Swiss chard or spinach, cooked and drained
1	tsp. orégano leaves
1 ½	tsp. salt
⅛	tsp. pepper
½	c. grated Parmesan cheese
3	eggs, beaten
⅔	c. dry bread crumbs

· Cook zucchini in boiling water 5 minutes. Drain and cool. Cut in halves lengthwise; scoop out center pulp, leaving ¼" shell all around.

· Chop onions, garlic and parsley in blender or food chopper. Sauté in olive oil.

· Put zucchini pulp and chard through food chopper or in blender; drain off excess liquid. Add to onion mixture and sauté a few minutes. Add seasonings and cheese; mix well. Add eggs and blend; then add crumbs.

· Sprinkle zucchini shells lightly with salt. Fill with pulp mixture. Sprinkle

lightly with more bread crumbs. Makes 6 to 8 servings.
• To freeze, place on a tray. When frozen, pack, label, date and freeze. Recommended storage time: 6 to 8 weeks.

• To serve, take from freezer and place in covered baking pan. Bake in moderate oven (350°F.) 45 minutes. Uncover and bake 10 minutes longer.

Vegetable Seasoning Ideas

Imaginative country cooks collect and use seasoning ideas to give cooked frozen vegetables unusual and intriguing flavors. Here are favorites from farm kitchens. You start with the hot, cooked vegetable.

ASPARAGUS: Instead of buttering it, pour on heated Italian salad dressing.

BROCCOLI: Dress with butter or cream sauce seasoned with a suggestion of curry powder. Or add chopped pimiento-stuffed olives to the sauce.

CAULIFLOWER OR GREEN BEANS: Butter the hot vegetable and scatter crisp, brown bread cubes on top. To fix the bread, cut either rye or white bread slices into tiny squares. Melt a small amount of butter in a skillet and add the bread. Cook, stirring to brown evenly. Season with salt and pepper.

CORN: Butter as usual but sprinkle with chili powder, garlic salt or both.

GREEN BEANS: Sauté ¼ c. cut-up almonds or cashew nuts and 2 tblsp. finely chopped onion in 2 to 3 tblsp. butter. Toss with 1 (10 oz.) pkg. green beans, cooked. Or toss the hot beans,

buttered, with thin strips of cooked ham just before serving. Boiled ham is especially good.

LIMA BEANS: Add canned tomatoes and a touch of orégano. Heat piping hot. This dish waits patiently if dinner is delayed. Or add 2 tblsp. finely chopped pimiento, 1 tblsp. butter and ½ c. dairy sour cream to 2 c. cooked lima beans. Heat and season with salt and pepper.

PEAS: Stir finely chopped chives into the cream sauce before combining with the peas. Or add 2 to 3 tsp. mint jelly to buttered peas.

SPINACH: To hot, drained, chopped and buttered spinach, add a little light cream pointed up with a dash of prepared horse-radish. For company, garnish with hard-cooked egg slices. Or sprinkle buttered spinach with lemon juice and grated onion.

SUCCOTASH: Add chopped pimiento to buttered vegetable mixture.

SWEET POTATOES OR SQUASH: Fold a little grated orange peel into the mashed vegetable. Or season sweet potatoes with butter and maple syrup.

CHAPTER 3

MEAT, POULTRY, FISH AND GAME

Directions for Freezing Beef, Veal, Lamb, Ground Beef, Pork Sausage, Ham, Bacon, Game Animals, Lard · Recipes for Barbecued Ribs, Barbecued Brisket and Swedish Flank Steaks · Directions for Freezing Chickens, Turkeys and Other Poultry · Game Birds · Freezing Cooked Poultry · Freezing Fish and Shellfish

Fresh meat the year round—farmers consider this the prime advantage of frozen meats. "Time was," a Texas rancher says, "when beef and pork were pretty scarce in summer. We had so much chicken and salt pork that I used to get hungry for winter."

When farm homemakers talk of frozen meats, they say how glad they are to skip the pickling, salting, grinding and smoking processes and to get variety in their meals. City women go to meat counters to get fresh meats. Most country women don't leave home for this—they step to their freezers and make their selections from meats, poultry, fish and game.

Locker plants and other commercial establishments slaughter, chill and quick-freeze much of the beef, veal, pork and lamb farm people take home to their freezers. When the supply runs low, turnover gives space in the freezer at times for other frozen foods, some from the supermarket.

Frozen chickens, ready to cook, the meaty pieces separated from the bony, insure good company dinners with less work . . . no flurry of catching chickens, dressing and chilling them at the last minute. Farmers freeze fish after a big catch, venison when they shoot a deer.

If you render lard at home, be sure to notice in this chapter how to handle it so it will stay fresh and sweet in or out of the freezer.

Meats and chicken take up more room in the freezer than all other foods put together, but most farmers put it first. One of them explains it this way: "No complaints when you can slice tender, juicy beef roasts in summer or come hungry from the field to fork-tender pork chops and brown gravy for dinner one day, lamb chops the next noon."

Mainstay Platter Treats
THEY MAKE THE MEAL

Meat, poultry, fish, and game when it's available . . . , are the mainstay of country meals—and of farm freezers. Many other foods have to surrender space to them in the home's zero-storage plant. They are important, for these perishable protein foods are money.

While most of the meats, poultry and fish are frozen fresh, country cooks like to have a few cooked or partially cooked meat combination dishes made to reheat when there's almost no time to spend in the kitchen. (See the chapter on Main Dishes.)

Meats are valuable nutritionally, too. It behooves homemakers to make sure they're handled and stored the correct way. Don't skimp on the packaging—that's poor economy. Wrap them right. And do pay attention to the directions that follow.

Freezing Meats

Meats and animal products usually fill at least half the space in home freezers. Farm women hold that no better way than freezing has been discovered to preserve for several months the natural, fresh qualities.

While beef, veal, pork and lamb often are produced on the farm and the meats go into home freezers, most farmers find it advisable to have animals slaughtered, chilled and frozen in locker plants or other commercial establishments. There they can be handled in a sanitary way and inspected by local authorities. And the animals can be slaughtered and frozen throughout the year as needed.

The home freezer is not designed to freeze several hundred pounds of meat at a time. If you want to freeze more than 5% of the freezer's capacity at one time, it is best to have the freezing done at a locker plant and to bring the frozen meats home for storage.

The quality of frozen meat depends on (1) the original selection of good quality meat, (2) the way it is handled when prepared for the freezer, (3) use of the right wrapping materials and (4) always keeping the freezer temperature at zero or below.

Recommended storage time: Unground beef, 9 months; ground beef, 4 months; lamb, 9 months; pork, 4 months; veal, 6 months; sausage, unsalted, 2 to 3 months.

Animal Selection: Select healthy, quality animals with adequate finish (fattening). Though freezing for several weeks has a tenderizing effect on meats, remember that *a tough steak will never become a tender one in the freezer.* Don't expect the impossible.

Slaughtering: Use sanitary methods.

Chilling:

1. *Beef.* Hang the meat and chill it quickly to minimize the development of off-flavors and odors. Chill the carcass at 32 to 34°F. After chilling, age the hind quarters in temperatures of 36 to 38°F. from 10 to 12 days, forequarters 6 to 8 days. Do not age beef as long as for use unfrozen. Age young beef of standard and utility grades or lower quality 5 to 6 days.

2. *Pork.* Hang the carcass whole to chill with body cavity open and the leaf fat pulled loose but left attached to the hams. Chill 24 hours at 34°F. Failure to chill pork quickly may result in souring at the ham bone, which causes spoilage during the curing. Cut and package pork as soon as it is chilled to the bone, always within 3 days after slaughtering. Meat from hogs fed fish or fish meal develops rancidity more quickly when frozen.

3. *Veal and lamb.* Hang carcasses whole during chilling. Allow 10 to 16 hours for them to reach an internal temperature of 38°F. Veal, like pork, should be cut, wrapped and frozen as soon as it chills to the bone. Lamb and mutton may be aged like beef, but for less time—6 to 7 days.

Cutting: Make cuts the right size for a family meal. Remove excess fat and bone. Fat becomes rancid quicker than lean meat; the bones waste freezer space and make wrapping

more difficult. Meat tastes just as good without them and boning will save from 5 to 35% in storage space. Do not make packages larger than necessary. They are awkward to handle and take longer to freeze and thaw than smaller ones.

Wrapping Materials: Poor wraps often cause unpleasant flavors in frozen meats. Use moisture-vaporproof materials to prevent freezer burn or the light gray spots that sometimes form on meats. Be sure the wraps also efficiently exclude oxygen to slow down the development of rancidity. Use a pliable material that will make a tight wrap and crowd out air pockets. The wrapping needs to be odorless, strong when wet, greaseproof and it should not adhere to the meat. Among the best materials for packaging meats are aluminum foil, plastic wrap and combination films like cellophane and polyester. A single layer of the wrapping material is adequate if well sealed. Usually a packaging material 18″ wide is satisfactory, although 24″ width is needed for large cuts.

Wrapping: The best method is one that excludes the most air, and usually the "freezer wrap" is considered best. It also takes less wrapping material than the "butcher wrap."

Freezer Wrap: Place the meat in the center of the sheet of paper. Bring the two longest sides together over the meat and fold these edges over about 1″ making a lock seam. Fold again as many times as necessary to bring the paper flat and tight against the meat. To avoid waste, wrapping material need be only long enough to make two folds. Turn the package over and fold the end corners toward each other. Then fold the ends over, stretching tight, and fasten with locker tape or cord. Aluminum foil needs no tape or cord. Do not draw the foil too tightly in making the lock seam. Allow a little surplus to mold tightly around the meat, pressing the foil against the meat while the two ends are open. Close the foil ends by pressing them, starting next to the meat. Then fold ends over and make a lock seam with both of them, pressing the seam tightly against the meat to exclude air.

To Stack Meats: Several chops, steaks and ground meat patties often are packaged together for a meal. Place two thicknesses of freezer paper between pieces of meat. This allows quick and easy separation when used. If the paper is waxed only on one side, put the shiny side next to the meat.

Ground Meats: Pack in rolls or blocks. Season if desired, but do not add salt to meat you'll keep longer than 2 to 3 weeks. Place double pieces of freezer paper, shiny side next to the meat, between small blocks and rolls for easy and quick separation and use.
Recommended storage time: 4 months.

Pork Sausage: Use of the proper packaging materials and spices helps keep sausage in good condition when frozen. You can buy sausage seasonings containing antioxidants at many retail food markets, feed stores and some locker plants. Smoked sausage, everything being equal, keeps longer than fresh sausage. Bologna does not freeze successfully—its texture changes.
Recommended storage time for sausage: With antioxidant added, 3 to 4 months. Unsalted sausage, *properly wrapped,* may keep that long without the antioxidant, but often it loses quality before then.

Ham and Bacon: Freezer life of these cured meats depends on their freshness, the cure and the smoking. Salt has an undesirable effect on frozen meats. Usually hams and bacon, unsliced, keep from 2 to 3 months when frozen. Whole or half hams and bacon sides hold up better than the slices when frozen and they may be sliced as needed with a power saw. Or you can freeze the fresh hams and pork sides and cure and smoke them as needed. Ham and bacon purchased in retail markets, when frozen, may keep a very short time, depending on its freshness.

Game Animals: Handle them much like beef, only age them a shorter time—5 to 6 days—especially if they are lean. Or if they are not in top condition when they reach home, cut, package and freeze them without aging. Bleed, dress and cool the carcass at once after killing. Sprinkle the inside body cavity with pepper to keep flies away. Trim off and discard portions damaged by gun shot. Hang to cool in a breezy place; it often is desirable to spread the ribs apart with a stick to speed up the cooling. Since the hide helps to prevent contamination of the meat, usually it is best to leave it on. Wrap carcass loosely on the trip home to protect from dust.

Recommended storage time: 9 months.

To Thaw Meat: Leave it in the original wrapper. Partially thaw small cuts at room temperature or completely thaw in the refrigerator. It takes from 2 to 2½ hours to thaw a pound of meat at room temperature, 5 to 8 hours in the refrigerator. Thaw large cuts in the refrigerator (or in front of an electric fan to speed it up).

To Cook Frozen Meats: Meats are equally flavorful and juicy whether cooked before or after thawing. Often it is convenient to start cooking thin cuts, like some steaks, chops and cutlets, while they are frozen or partially frozen. The cooking of roasts and steaks more than 1½" thick will be more uniform and quicker if they are thawed or partially thawed first. Sometimes unthawed meat becomes too dark and overcooked on the outside and is undercooked inside.

Thaw ground meats if you want to shape them in patties or loaves. Thaw or partially thaw sliced meats, like liver and cutlets, which you dip in flour before frying or broiling.

Cook thawed meats like fresh. To cook without thawing, allow extra time—10 to 15 minutes per pound for roasts and 13 to 23 minutes to total cooking time for thick steaks.

How to Render Lard

Trim the fat from the pork carcass and render it into lard as quickly as possible after slaughtering. Cook the leaf fat, backfat and fat trimmings. Caul and ruffle fats from internal organs yield lard of darker color; if you use them, cook them separately.

Remove fat, wash and chill promptly. *Cut fat into small pieces or grind it* to hasten the rendering. Place in a large, heavy kettle and *cook slowly,* starting with a small quantity to make stirring easier. When the fat begins to melt, add more pieces, but do not fill kettle or it might boil over. Stir frequently and cook slowly to avoid sticking and scorching.

As cooking begins, the temperature will stay at 212°F. As the water evaporates from the fat, the temperature will rise slowly. Do not let it go higher than 255°F.

During the cooking the brown cracklings will start to float. When the lard is almost rendered, they sink to the bottom of the kettle. *Be careful not to let them stick and scorch.* You can stop the cooking while the cracklings still float, but complete rendering removes more water and results in lard that keeps better. If moisture is eliminated by proper rendering, water souring should not develop during storage.

Let the lard cool slightly and settle before emptying the kettle. Dip the lard carefully into 5- or 10-lb. containers. Put the cracklings through a press. Then strain all the lard through three thicknesses of cheesecloth.

Store immediately in a cool place, at near freezing or freezing temperature. Chilling it quickly produces a fine-grain lard.

Keep lard in metal containers or greaseproof freezer cartons, sealed with a tight cover, and store in a dark cool place or in freezer or locker. Air and light often cause chemical changes that result in rancidity. If lard becomes rancid, you cannot improve it.

Note: You can greatly increase the storage life of lard by adding an antioxidant (available at most locker plants). Another way to prolong the fresh flavor is to stir 1 (3 lb.) can of hydrogenated vegetable shortening into every 50 lbs. of lard while it is cooling.

Favorite Beef Recipes

BARBECUED RIBS

You're lucky if you have this in the freezer when company comes

1 large onion, chopped
2 tblsp. salad oil
½ c. molasses
1 c. ketchup
½ c. water
¼ c. Worcestershire sauce
¼ c. prepared mustard
1 tblsp. salt
3 lbs. short ribs

· Sauté onion in oil; combine remaining ingredients, except ribs, and add to onion. Cook 10 minutes.
· Divide ribs for serving; brush pieces with sauce; put in shallow baking pan.
· Bake in moderate oven (350°F.) 1½ to 2 hours, or until tender. Brush on sauce every half hour and turn.
· Cool, wrap, label, date and freeze. Recommended storage time: 2 to 3 months.
· To serve, thaw and heat in moderate oven (350°F.) about 30 minutes. Makes 4 servings.

BARBECUED BRISKET

Leftovers will make good sandwiches

3 to 4 lbs. beef brisket
1 c. ketchup
1 c. water
¼ c. vinegar
1 tblsp. sugar
1 tblsp. prepared horse-radish
1 tblsp. prepared mustard
1 tsp. salt
¼ tsp. pepper
2 onions, finely chopped
2 tblsp. chopped celery

· Place brisket in casserole.
· Mix remaining ingredients; pour over meat. Refrigerate overnight.
· Bake in moderate oven (350°F.) 1 hour per pound, or until tender.
· Cool. Place meat and sauce in freezer container; seal, label, date and freeze.
Recommended storage time: 2 to 3 months.
· To serve, thaw meat and heat, uncovered, in moderate oven (350°F.) 40 to 50 minutes, or until heated throughout. Makes 4 to 5 servings.

SWEDISH FLANK STEAKS

Thrifty dish with rich, brown gravy

½ lb. veal, ground twice
½ lb. lean pork, ground twice
1   egg, beaten
2   tblsp. chopped parsley
½ small onion, grated
1   tblsp. light cream
2   tblsp. bread crumbs
1   tsp. salt
½ tsp. freshly ground pepper
½ tsp. Worcestershire sauce
2   lbs. flank steak, cut in pieces
      3 to 4″ wide and 5″ long
½ lb. salt pork, cut into strips
      ⅓″ wide, 4″ long

· Mix all ingredients except steak and salt pork. Spread each steak with stuffing; cross with one strip of salt pork. Roll the long way with ends of pork extending beyond roll.

· Tie with string; wrap, label, date and freeze.

Recommended storage time: about 6 to 8 weeks (depends on freshness of salt pork).

· To serve, defrost flank steaks and coat with mixture of ½ c. flour, 2 tsp. salt and ¼ tsp. pepper; place in skillet and brown in 2 to 4 tblsp. salad oil; transfer to baking pan.

Sauté 1 c. sliced mushrooms in skillet, adding more oil if needed. Add 1 (12½ oz.) can chicken broth.

Mix 3 tblsp. flour and ½ c. milk; blend into broth; cook until thickened.

Pour over steaks; cover and cook in moderate oven (350°F.) 1 to 1½ hours, or until very tender. Makes 6 servings.

Note: You can use the large flank steak to make one big roll.

Exciting Venison Treats

Country cooks excel in cooking game. Here are examples of what they do with venison from their freezers. When we tested these recipes in our Countryside Kitchens, the men on our taste panel said they had never tasted better venison. Each is superior—try them all.

VENISON MEATBALLS IN SAUCE

Heavenly served over biscuits

2   c. grated raw potatoes
1½ lbs. ground venison
⅔   c. chopped onion
1½ tsp. salt
⅛   tsp. pepper
¼   c. milk
1   egg
¼   c. butter
3   c. water
2   to 3 tblsp. flour
2   c. dairy sour cream
1   tsp. dill seeds
1   (10 oz.) pkg. frozen peas,
        cooked

· Combine potatoes, venison, onion, salt, pepper, milk and egg; shape into 1½″ balls. Brown slowly in butter in large skillet. Add ½ c. water, cover and simmer until done, about 20 minutes. Remove meatballs.

· Stir in flour, then remaining water, simmer to thicken. Reduce heat; stir in cream and dill; add meatballs and peas. Heat but do not boil. Makes 8 servings.

When berries are ripe, freeze coral-red Fresh Strawberry Sherbet (recipe, page 80) for dessert and salad dress-ups. Or pack with ice cream, parfait-style, in molds for parties and special dinners.

Country hostesses like to serve Cake Rolls, rich with cream fillings. You'll find the rolls and variations delightful make-ahead-and-freeze desserts (recipes, page 108). Fine for parties or serving a crowd.

Two-step Brown-and-Serve Roast Chicken (recipe, page 137), is a hostess special. You bake chicken 30 minutes, cool and freeze. To serve, run frozen chicken in oven to complete cooking.

Keep a Lemon Meringue Pie Supreme in your freezer to serve on short notice when you want a glamorous dessert with nippy filling and tall meringue (recipe, page 123). The whole pie freezes successfully.

VENISON TERIYAKI

Developed by Oregon State University

2   lbs. venison sirloin or round
        (1½" thick)
1   can condensed beef
        consommé
⅓   c. soy sauce
¼   c. chopped onion
1   clove garlic
2   tblsp. lemon juice
2   tblsp. brown sugar
1   tsp. seasoned salt

• Slice meat diagonally across grain about ¼" thick.
• Mix other ingredients for marinade; pour over meat; refrigerate overnight.
• Drain meat; broil 3 to 4" from heat about 5 minutes first side, baste with marinade; broil 3 minutes other side, basting (do not overcook). Heat marinade to pass with meat. Makes 6 servings.

VENISON/NOODLE SKILLET

Flavor improves with reheating

1   lb. ground venison
3   tblsp. shortening
½   c. diced onion
½   c. diced green pepper
1   c. diced celery
1   (1 lb.) can red kidney beans
2   c. broad noodles, uncooked
1   qt. tomatoes
1   (4 oz.) can button
        mushrooms
2   tsp. seasoned salt
1   tsp. chili powder
1   tsp. salt
⅛   tsp. pepper

• In large skillet brown meat in shortening; sauté onion, green pepper and celery until transparent.
• Add remaining ingredients; mix well. Cover tightly; bring to a boil. Reduce heat; simmer 20 minutes. Makes 8 servings.

VENISON STEAK CASSEROLE

Old-fashioned stew goodness

2   lbs. venison round steak
        (1" thick)
6   tblsp. flour
1   tsp. salt
½   tsp. pepper
⅛   tsp. orégano leaves
1   clove garlic, crushed
3   tblsp. shortening
6   medium potatoes, sliced
2   medium onions, sliced
2   carrots, sliced or in strips
1   green pepper, cut in
        squares
3   c. beef bouillon

• Cut steak into serving pieces.
• Combine ¼ c. flour, ½ tsp. salt, ¼ tsp. pepper, orégano and garlic; pound into meat. Brown in shortening; place in one layer on bottom of 3-qt. oval baking dish.
• Layer half of potatoes, onions, carrots and green pepper on top; sprinkle with half remaining salt, pepper and flour. Repeat. Pour bouillon over top.
• Bake, covered, in moderate oven (350°F.) 1 hour; uncovered ½ hour. Makes 6 servings.

VENISON LIVER KABOBS

Traditional hunters' camp food

• Cut ½″ thick slices of venison liver in 1½″ squares. Sprinkle with salt and pepper. String on skewer alternating with bacon, pineapple chunks and 1½″ squares of green pepper.
• Broil 3 to 5″ from heat about 5 minutes per side; do not overcook. Brush often with mixture of ½ c. melted butter and ¼ tsp. garlic salt.

VENISON BACKSTRAP BARBECUE

This cut of meat lies along both sides of the backbone; it is equivalent to the rib eye in beef and may extend, if you wish, into loin. A camp favorite

• Strip out backstrap in one piece (remove bones if animal is large).
  Put on long skewer or lay on rack over broiler pan; wrap strips of bacon loosely around meat, fasten with toothpicks.
• Broil about 5 minutes per side for backstrap 2″ thick. Brush often with your favorite barbecue sauce (reduce sugar one fourth), or mixture of ½ c. melted butter and ¼ tsp. garlic salt or 2 tblsp. lemon juice.

BUTTERFLY VENISON STEAKS: Cut raw backstrap into 2″ slices; slice each piece in half sideways, cutting almost through; open flat to butterfly. Broil 3 to 4″ from heat about 5 minutes per side, brushing often with barbecue sauce.

VENISON HERB ROAST

Crust keeps moisture inside roast

3	to 4 lbs. venison rump, loin or rib roast
1	tblsp. salad oil
½	tsp. salt
¼	tsp. pepper
¼	c. flour
2	tsp. marjoram leaves
1	tsp. thyme leaves
2	tsp. rosemary leaves
1	clove garlic, crushed
1	c. apple juice
1	c. water

• Dry meat well; cut several slits in meat about ½″ deep. Rub roast with oil, sprinkle with salt and pepper.
• Combine flour, marjoram, thyme, rosemary and garlic; pat mixture on roast and stuff into slits. Insert meat thermometer.
• Pour apple juice and water into shallow pan. Set roast in liquid (no rack); bake, uncovered, in slow oven (325°F.) about 1 hour until flour mixture adheres to meat. Baste frequently with liquid in roaster. Finish baking about 1 hour (or 25 to 30 minutes per pound total time), basting often. Meat thermometer should read 160°F. for medium, 170°F. for well done. Makes about 6 servings.

VENISON MINCEMEAT

Team with pastry to make that famous Christmas pie of the Old West

4	lbs. venison "trim" meat with bones
Water	
¾	lb. beef suet

3   lbs. apples, peeled and
        quartered
2   lbs. seedless raisins
1   (15 oz.) box seeded raisins
1   (12 oz.) box currants
1   tblsp. salt
1   tblsp. ground cinnamon
1   tblsp. ground ginger
1   tblsp. ground cloves
1   tblsp. ground nutmeg
1   tsp. ground allspice
1   tsp. ground mace (optional)
2   qts. apple cider, grape or
        other fruit juice
1   lb. brown sugar

· Trim fat from venison. Cover with water; simmer until meat is tender. Refrigerate venison in cooking liquid overnight. Remove all fat from top of liquid. Separate meat from bones and put meat through food chopper using coarse blade. (There should be enough ground venison to make at least 2 qts. ground meat.)
· Grind suet and apples.
· Combine all ingredients in large kettle. Simmer 2 hours to plump fruit and blend flavors. Stir often to prevent sticking.
· Cool, pack in pint containers. Label, date and freeze. Makes about 11 pints.
Recommended storage time: 3 months.

Note: You can also can this mincemeat. After simmering, pack and process like State-of-the-Union Mincemeat (see Index for recipe).

Chicken—a Country Special

In all popularity polls of good country eating, chicken wins honors. With chicken, turkey and other poultry dressed and in the freezer, the cook has a head start on festive meals. No wonder farm feasts continue to put the spotlight on these platter treats.

Don't miss the Sunday-best chicken recipes in other chapters in this cookbook. Save time by looking for them in the Index under "Chicken." You will be pleased with the favorite dishes from country kitchens.

Freezing Chickens and Turkeys

Select the Best: Freeze healthy, well-finished birds that have grown rapidly. Young birds have tender flesh, but older ones, like mature hens, often have more flavor. Among the good freezers are broiler-fryer chickens at 8 to 12 weeks of age, roasters at 3 to 5 months, mature hens (stewing chickens), fryer-roaster turkeys at 12 to 15 weeks and young tom and hen turkeys at 5 to 7 months.

Starve before Killing: If practical, starve chickens and turkeys overnight or at least 6 to 8 hours before killing. When you draw them, there will be less danger of rupturing the digestive tract, contaminating the birds and producing off-flavors. Do not feed birds fish or fish oil for several weeks before killing.

Suspend to Kill: Hang birds by legs from a rope or shackle to avoid bruises. Since the head hangs down, the bleeding will be better. Stretch the head in a line with the neck and make a clean cut across the throat just back of the jaw. Use a sharp knife.

Scald to Easily Remove Feathers: When bleeding ceases, scald the birds by swishing them from 40 to 60 seconds in hot water, 140°F. Scalding removes the outer skin layer and the birds will dry out quickly if allowed to stand. *Keep them wet.* If you plan to cool the birds by air or think you will have delays in getting them into the freezer, scald them in cooler water, 125 to 130°F. (You will find the pin feathers more difficult to pull out if you use the cooler water.) Pull out the wing and tail feathers first. After feathers are removed, singe off the hairs, cut off head and feet and wash birds thoroughly.

Draw Birds Promptly: Freeze only drawn birds. Draw them at once after plucking feathers, to check development of off-flavors. Cut out the oil sac, which is on top of the tail. Then, cut a circle around vent below the tail, freeing it for removal with the internal organs. Make a crosswise slit large enough for drawing between this circle and the rear of the breastbone. If you want to freeze the bird whole, leave a band of skin between the two cuts.

Remove internal organs and vent. Slit skin lengthwise at the base of the neck. Then slit the skin down and remove the crop and windpipe. Cut the neck off short and save it. Leave neck skin on bird. Wash bird, inside and out, in cold running water. Trim off excess abdominal fat.

Trim and cut blood vessels from the heart. Cut away the gall sac from liver, being careful not to break. Cut through one side of the gizzard to the inner lining. Remove and discard inner lining and contents. Wash giblets.

Chill Thoroughly: Lower the temperature of the washed birds as quickly as possible to around 36°F. by packing them in crushed ice. Use plenty of ice, about 1 lb. to 1 lb. chicken or turkey. Or pack the birds in a slush of ice and water. It is especially important to chill the inside of the bird quickly for spoilage is likely to start there. Some farm homemakers omit the cooling in ice and place the birds in a refrigerator with a temperature of 40°F. to chill overnight. Thorough chilling helps insure tenderness.

Age Whole Birds: Turkeys and large chickens will be more tender after freezing if you age them by icing them for 12 to 24 hours. After the first 3 or 4 hours of chilling, frequent draining is necessary to prevent birds from absorbing too much water and the flavors from leaching out. Add more ice as it melts.

Before packaging birds, drain them thoroughly for 10 to 15 minutes. Fold the neck skin under bird. Truss the wings and legs close to the body with butcher's twine.

Cut-up Chicken and Turkey: Birds for frying, or cooking in water will take up less space in the freezer if cut up before packaging. After the pieces are washed, dry them thoroughly. Paper toweling is excellent for this.

To Freeze: Sort the pieces, the meaty ones like the legs, breast and wings from the bony ones like the neck, back and wing tips. If you are processing several birds, package the different cuts separately. Place the meaty pieces close together in layers with 2 sheets of freezer paper between or lay each piece in a fold of freezer paper. Pack close together in moisture-vaporproof plastic freezer bags or cartons. Seal, label, date and freeze. Place broiler halves together with 2 pieces of freezer paper between. Use paper waxed on both sides. Wrap with foil, or place in moisture-vaporproof plastic freezer bags. Press out as much air as possible before tying with a twist-seal. Package bony pieces for making broth. Recommended storage time: 9 months.

Package giblets separately from whole carcass to speed freezing, and use them within 2 to 3 months.

Some homemakers freeze chicken in water; research indicates the flavor of the chicken is inferior to that packaged in plastic freezer bags and aluminum foil.

To Partially or Completely Thaw Chicken Pieces (until pliable): Leave them in original wrap at room temperature, 2 to 3 hours. Or leave them in the refrigerator; complete thawing will take place in about 9 hours. Stewing chicken need not be thawed.

To Cook: Cook as you would freshly dressed poultry. Cook stewing hens without thawing if you desire.

Whole Chickens and Turkeys: Do not stuff birds before freezing. It takes time to heat the frozen dressing in frozen birds and food-spoiling and food-poisoning bacteria may develop. (This caution does not apply to commercially frozen chicken and turkey which are handled by methods unavailable in home kitchens.)

To Freeze: Place the trussed bird in a moisture-vaporproof plastic freezer bag, press out all the air and fasten with a twist-seal. Or submerge the bag containing the chicken or turkey, except the open end, in water. When the air is out, twist to seal. Or mold heavy-duty foil tightly around the bird to exclude the air. Overwrap with freezer wrap. Freeze immediately at 0°F. or below. Recommended storage time: 9 months.

To Thaw: If the chicken or turkey is in a watertight package, you can thaw it in cold running water. Place it in a steady stream of water. It takes from 1 to 2 hours to thaw chickens weighing less than 4 lbs.; 2 to 2½ hours for chickens 4 lbs. or over; 4 to 6 hours for 4- to 11-lb. turkeys; 6 to 7 hours for 12- to 24-lb. turkeys.

Since running cold water is not plentiful in some homes, the USDA recommends thawing watertight packages of poultry in cold water. It is important to change the water several times.

Many women like to thaw poultry at room temperature (70 to 80°F.). When doing this, provide additional protection. It will help prevent the growth of enough bacteria on a bird to cause food poisoning. Research at the U. S. Department of Agriculture Western Research Laboratory in Albany, California, shows that the use of a protective overwrap, such as a paper bag, can be a safe method of thawing at room temperature because it reduces the hazards of bacterial growth. The paper bag keeps the surface temperature low without greatly increasing the thawing time. The thawing time for 4-lb. and over birds in a paper bag should not exceed 15 hours, 12- to 24-lb. birds no more than 20 hours. (No food should be thawed at room temperature longer than 6 hours without protective covering.)

It takes longer to thaw poultry in the refrigerator, but it requires little or no watching. You need to allow 12 to 16 hours for chickens under 4 lbs.; 24 to 36 hours for chickens 4 lbs. and over; 24 to 36 hours for turkeys weighing 4 to 11 pounds; 48 to 72 hours for 12- to 24-lb. turkeys.

Thaw frozen poultry in its original wrap. Cook or refrigerate it promptly when thawed and while the bird is very cold.

To Cook: Roast thawed birds like freshly dressed.

Freezing Domestic Ducks and Geese

Handle like chickens and turkeys, but scald in warmer water, 160°F., for 1 to 1½ minutes, with ½ c. vinegar added to every 10 gals. of hot water. Many farm cooks find use of a commercial wax helpful in removing down and pin feathers. Pack and freeze like chickens and turkeys. Recommended storage time: Ducks and geese, 9 months.

To Thaw: It takes from 2 to 2½ hours to thaw 3- to 5-lb. ducks in cold running water, 1 to 1½ days in the refrigerator. Geese weighing 4 to 14 lbs. thaw in 3 to 5 hours in cold running water, 1 to 2 days in refrigerator.

Freezing Game Birds

Handle them much the same way as poultry. Do not scald wild ducks—pluck them dry. Scald pheasants in warm water, 155 to 160°F. Remove body heat as quickly as possible after killing. Avoid heaping birds together, for this retains heat. Allow space between birds, rather than piling them in a car trunk, for air circulation and quicker cooling. Deterioration is rapid when birds are stacked. Often it is best to have birds frozen at a locker plant near the hunting grounds before returning home if it's a long trip. Observe state game laws for "tagging" and length of time in storage.

Freezing Cooked Poultry

It is handy to have cooked poultry in the freezer ready to use. Stewing is an excellent method to prepare birds for freezing. When stewing chicken, save the broth. Pour it into glass jars or other rigid, moisture-vaporproof containers and freeze.

To save freezer space, remove bones from stewed chicken. Chicken covered with broth or gravy keeps longer when frozen than if no moisture is added.

Leftover roasted chicken and turkey, sliced or cut up, freeze successfully if packaged in moistureproof packages.

Recommended storage time: Slices or pieces of cooked poultry covered with broth or gravy, 6 months; without broth or gravy, 1 month. Fried chicken, 4 months.

Note: Do not be disturbed if there is a darkening around the bones of frozen, young birds. This is caused by a seepage of the hemoglobin from the bone marrow. It does not affect the taste of poultry and is harmless.

If you want to freeze a large number of chickens, turkeys or other poultry at a time, it may be best to have them frozen at a commercial freezing plant. This eliminates the danger of overloading the home freezer and getting a slow, uneven freeze. It also avoids the possibility of increasing the freezer temperature enough to affect the quality of the other frozen foods in the freezer.

Freeze Fish and Shellfish Right

Freeze fish as soon as possible after catching; it spoils quickly. Kill immediately if practical. If fish flop around in the bottom of a boat, they bruise themselves. Let the blood drain from the flesh, remove viscera and gills and pack in ice. Prepare all fish for freezing as for table use; wash in cold water and drain. Properly wrapped fish will not affect the flavor of other food in the freezer. Aluminum foil and plastic wrap are excellent wrappings for fish.

Small Fish: Freeze them whole. One of the best ways is to freeze them in a block of ice. Place the fish in a clean, watertight container, like a 2-lb. coffee can or loaf pan. Cover with water and freeze. If you use a loaf pan, remove the block of frozen fish; package it in freezer wrap. There is no need to remove the frozen fish from a coffee can. Just adjust the lid. Hurry back to freezer before thawing starts. When ready to use, thaw in cold running water.

Large Fish: They will handle easier if cut into steaks or filets ready for the pan. Place two layers of freezer paper between steaks, filets or pieces of fish and wrap in meal-size packages for convenient use.

Ice Glazing: Whole fish, prepared for table use, may be glazed with ice for freezer storage. Place the fish on a tray and freeze. Remove from freezer, dip fish in near freezing water, and return to freezer. Repeat several times or until a coating of ice about ⅛" thick covers the fish. Wrap in aluminum foil or other materials that exclude the most oxygen (as for meats).

Freeze fish in the coldest part of the freezer, near the bottom of chest type and directly on the refrigerated shelves of upright types.

Recommended storage time: 3 to 4 months.

Fish Roe: Wash thoroughly, place in moisture-vaporproof containers, label, date and freeze.

To Thaw and Cook Fish: Partially or completely thaw fish in its original wrapper. You can thaw fish in the refrigerator, there will be less drip. It will take about 20 hours to thaw a 4½-lb. (about) whole fish, 8 hours for 1-lb. fish steaks or filets and 8 hours for a 1-lb. container or package of shellfish. If fish is in a watertight package, the best and quickest way to thaw it is to place it in cold running water. It takes 1¼ hours for a 4½-lb. whole fish, ½ hour for 1-lb. fish steaks or filets and ½ hour for a 1-lb. package of shellfish. Cook like fresh fish while still chilled, but allow additional cooking time and use a lower cooking temperature if the fish is only partially thawed.

Shellfish: It is desirable to freeze them near the source of supply because they deteriorate quickly.

Clams: Keep cold. Shuck at once and save liquid. Wash in salt water (⅓ c. salt to 1 gal. water). Drain. Wash thoroughly, eviscerate and wash again. Pack them in freezer containers and cover with their natural liquor or brine (⅓ c. salt to 1 gal. water). Place waxed paper or cellophane under the lid to keep the pieces submerged in the liquid. This prevents darkening.

Recommended storage time: 3 to 4 months.

Crabs: Keep cold. Clean at once and wash in cold water. Eviscerate and wash again. Cook in salted water (½ tsp. salt to 1 qt. water) 15 to 20 minutes. Cool quickly, shell and pack meat in freezer containers and freeze. Frozen crabmeat is apt to be tougher.

Recommended storage time: 3 to 4 months.

Lobsters: You can freeze them alive, but the meat is difficult to remove from the shell. Or plunge them in boiling salt water for 1 to 2 minutes, just long enough to cook the meat next to the shell. Cool quickly, package and freeze. Or cook the lobsters 20 minutes in salted water as if they were to be used at once, or cook them 10 minutes. Cool quickly, wrap and freeze.

Recommended storage time: 2 months.

Oysters: Handle like clams. If they have been held on ice for a week, they are not of high enough quality and flavor to freeze.

Recommended storage time: 3 to 4 months.

Scallops: Handle like clams, only do not save liquid when shucking them. Recommended storage time: 3 to 4 months.

Shrimp: Freeze cooked or uncooked shrimp. The cooked shrimp is easier to use, but uncooked has the best flavor. Wash. Pack in ice as soon as possible after catching. They darken if allowed to stand any length of time.

To Raw Pack: Wash uncooked shrimp thoroughly, remove heads and sand veins; wash in brine (1 tsp. salt to 1 qt. water); drain. Place in freezer containers or pile together in blocks and pour ice water over them and freeze to obtain a protective glaze. Tightly wrap glazed shrimp in foil or other moisture-vaporproof packaging material. Label, date and freeze. Recommended storage time: 3 to 4 months.

To Freeze Cooked Shrimp: Place washed shrimp in boiling salt water (⅔ c. salt to 1 gal. water) and cook. Drain, cool quickly and, if you desire, remove veins and shells. Rinse in cold water, drain and package with head space in moisture-vaporproof containers. Label, date and freeze.

People who live inland may wish to cook frozen shrimp and refreeze it. Recommended storage time: Cooked peeled shrimp, 2 to 3 months; cooked unpeeled shrimp, 4 to 6 months; Shrimp Creole and Shrimp Cocktail, about 6 weeks.

CHAPTER 4

DAIRY FOODS AND EGGS

Homemade Butter · Freezing Milk for Cooking · Storing Ice Cream · Recipes for Coconut/Honey, Quick Vanilla, Vanilla Custard Ice Creams · Peach Melba Parfait · Grape Sherbet, Fresh Strawberry Sherbet · Right Kinds of Cheese to Freeze · Cheese Cake, Sour Cream/Raspberry Topping, Hot Cheese Dip · How to Freeze Eggs, Measuring, Using Frozen Eggs · Frozen Egg Dessert · Angel Meringues

Think of the best country meals you've enjoyed. You will find that liberal use of milk, cream, butter and eggs helped make them memorable. Farm women's reliance on these foods started when every place had cows and poultry. Now dairy and poultry are specialized businesses and many farmers keep no cows or chickens. Even so, their wives often continue their habit of using a free hand in cooking with dairy foods and eggs.

When surplus cream, butter and eggs pile up—whether they're produced on the farm or purchased at a bargain—country women store some in their freezers. Often they also freeze small amounts of milk and buttermilk to use in cooking. Many country children still have a chance to eat ice cream from dashers. Home-cranked ice creams get space in freezers for special occasions—sometimes for Christmas gifts. (Do make Mariella's Ice Cream and the tropical Coconut/Honey Ice Cream from recipes in this chapter.) Wrap the ice cream and sherbets you buy to store according to directions in this chapter to keep their best flavors and textures.

Relatively few country kitchens have churns, but read how some farm women whip up a pound of butter in their electric mixers—often in 5 minutes. This way they always have the perfect seasoning for garden-fresh new potatoes, succulent peas and sweet corn.

Fresh eggs, when plentiful, go into freezers in recipe-measured amounts, ready to use. This chapter shows how good country cooks keep an abundance of dairy foods and eggs on hand even if they live on "cowless, chickenless" farms. They depend on the freezer.

Plenty of Cream, Milk and Eggs
COUNTRY COOKS KNOW HOW TO USE THEM

Country cooks use dairy products and eggs freely. It's an old farm custom too much appreciated to change. When they have a supply on hand in their freezers, they know good-to-taste and good-for-you foods will reach their tables.

Homemade Country Butter

Good country cooks know that foods made or seasoned with butter have superior flavor. One-cow families may not have much heavy cream to churn. But if you have a quart of it and an electric mixer, you can make a pound of butter in 5 minutes. On farms with several cows, there is often enough cream to make extra butter for freezing. Properly made and packaged, it will keep 6 months at 0°F.

Either sweet or sour cream may be used. (One way to sour the cream quickly is to stir ¼ c. cultured buttermilk into it.) Each one results in different flavors and each has its champions. Experts on freezing advise that you *pasteurize home-produced cream because butter made with it is less likely to become rancid or develop off-flavors in storage.*

Many farm homemakers write the Food Department of FARM JOURNAL that they do have success with freezing butter made from unpasteurized cream. Usually such butter, according to research, will not keep in top condition longer than 2 or 3 months.

To PASTEURIZE CREAM: Heat it in a regular home pasteurizer or in a double boiler, stirring frequently, to 160 to 165°F. Chill quickly to 50°F.

MIXER-MADE BUTTER

Churn the butter if you have a churn or pour 1 qt. heavy cream (35% butterfat) into the large bowl of your mixer. Cover the bowl with foil, inserting the beaters through a hole made in the center of the foil. This eliminates spattering and clean-up work.

Beat cream at high speed until flecks of butter begin to form. Then turn to low speed and beat until the butter "comes"—or until buttermilk separates from butter.

Pour off the buttermilk.

Add cold water equal in quantity to the buttermilk. Use water 2 or 3°F. cooler than the buttermilk. Agitate at lowest speed. Pour off water and repeat, using slightly cooler water each time, until water drained off is clear. This is important. *Butter that is not washed thoroughly will not retain its prime quality long when frozen.*

Work out water by pressing butter against the sides of bowl with a wooden spoon if you do not have a butter paddle.

Salt the butter slightly, ½ tsp. to 1 lb. butter, if cream is pasteurized. (You can add more salt—2 tsp.— but the butter will not keep as well.) *Do not salt butter made from unpasteurized cream.*

Press butter into glass jars or plastic containers with tight-fitting lids, or mold it and cover it with a moistureproof wrap. Freeze at once. One quart cream makes about 1 pound butter, although it depends on how heavy the cream is.

Recommended storage time: Up to 9 months.

A good Colorado cook saves time by freezing butter measured in the recipe amounts she most often uses (½ and 1 c.). And a North Dakota homemaker freezes the buttermilk she cannot use immediately. She bakes with it later.

BUYING BUTTER FOR FREEZING

Be sure the butter you buy to freeze is fresh. Sometimes butter offered for sale in retail markets has been in storage several months. You may be able to get freshly churned butter from a creamery. Rewrap it in good, moistureproof packaging material. Oxidation is a common cause of frozen butter changing in flavor. You can prevent this by using a good wrap and sealing it tightly with freezer tape. Fresh creamery butter may be stored in freezer for 9 months.

Milk for Cooking

You can freeze milk in moistureproof, sealed containers. The flavor is not so good as fresh milk, but you can use it in cooking. If you buy milk, you can store the whole pasteurized, homogenized milk in its paper containers. You can freeze nonhomogenized milk, but there is a tendency for the fat to separate or "oil off" when thawed. But many homemakers use it for cooking.

Recommended storage time: 3 weeks.

Frozen Cream Has Many Uses

Heavy cream, or that with 30 to 35% butterfat content, freezes satisfactorily. Use pasteurized cream. You will find it convenient to use if packaged in small containers—enough cream to use at one time. Completely fill containers. To discourage fat separation, thaw it in the refrigerator.

You will find that frozen cream is smoother when 1 to 1½ tblsp. sugar is added to every cupful, but cooks say this limits the ways it can be used. Frozen cream, sweetened or with considerable fat separation, will not whip. You can use it in cooking and making ice cream. Recommended storage time: 4 months.

WHIPPED CREAM: Mounds of whipped cream, sweetened with confectioners sugar, freeze successfully. Good cooks like to keep them on hand to serve on desserts. Drop the whipped cream on a chilled baking sheet and freeze. Package in tightly covered containers or in plastic bags, twisted to exclude air. To use them, place unthawed on top of the dessert. They thaw rapidly and will defrost adequately by the time the dessert reaches the table. Recommended storage time: 1 month.

Keep Ice Cream on Hand
YOU'LL NEVER HAVE A DESSERT PROBLEM

If you buy ice cream to keep in the freezer, you can store it for 3 weeks in the original container without drying out. If you want to keep it 6 weeks, overwrap it with good packaging material. And when you serve ice cream from the carton, either lay a piece of plastic wrap, cut to fit, on top of the remainder, or fill the empty space with crumpled cellophane to exclude the air. Large ice crystals may form if ice cream experiences high storage temperatures.

HOMEMADE ICE CREAM: Among the favorites for freezing are ice creams with a cooked custard base and those that contain gelatin or evaporated milk. Remove it from the freezer can, pack in rigid containers with tops as wide as the bottoms for easy removal, leaving ½" head space. Top with a piece of plastic wrap, cut to fit, and cover tightly. Store it in the bottom or the coldest part of the freezer. Soften it before serving by placing it in the refrigerator for 20 to 30 minutes, the time depending on size of the container. You will find ice cream mellowed this way tastes better than when hard frozen. Recommended storage time: Up to 6 weeks.

Many ice cream desserts are favorite freezer foods for hostesses. Among them are cream puffs, cake rolls, pastry or crumb pie crusts, eclairs and cake layers split and put together with ice cream. Serve these desserts directly from the freezer. Recommended storage time: Up to 1 month.

How to Freeze and Ripen Ice Cream

1. Pour the cool ice cream mixture into the freezer can. Fill can two thirds to three fourths full to leave room for expansion. Fit can into freezer; follow manufacturer's directions if using an electric freezer.

2. Adjust the dasher and cover. Pack crushed ice and rock salt around

the can, using 6 to 8 parts ice to 1 part rock salt. (Freezing is faster if you increase the amount of salt—4 parts ice to 1 part rock salt—but sometimes you do not get quite as smooth a product.) Turn the dasher slowly until the ice melts enough to form a brine. Add more ice and salt, mixed in the proper proportions, to maintain the ice level. Turn the handle fast and steadily until it turns hard. Then remove the ice until its level is below the lid of the can; take the lid off. Remove the dasher.

3. To ripen the ice cream, plug the opening in the lid. Cover the can with several thicknesses of waxed paper or foil to make a tight fit for the lid. Put the lid on the can.

4. Pack more of the ice and salt mixture, using 4 parts ice to 1 part rock salt, around the can, filling the freezer. Cover the freezer with a blanket, canvas or other heavy cloth, or with newspapers. Let ice cream ripen at least 4 hours, sherbet 1 hour. Or put the can in the home freezer.

Note: If you buy ice by the pound, you can use 20 lbs. ice to about 1 lb. rock salt for a 1-gal. freezer.

COCONUT/HONEY ICE CREAM

For a lush, tropical flavor blend, make this with orange blossom honey

1 ½	c. honey
4	eggs, slightly beaten
3	c. heavy cream
2	tsp. vanilla
½	tsp. lemon extract
½	tsp. salt
3	c. milk
1	(3 ½ oz.) can flaked coconut

2	(8 ½ oz.) cans crushed pineapple

· Add honey to eggs; mix well. Add cream, flavorings, salt and milk; stir until well blended. Chill.

· Pour into freezer can; put dasher and cover in place. Pack chopped ice and rock salt around can, 6 parts ice to 1 part salt. (See "How to Freeze and Ripen Ice Cream" in this chapter.) Turn dasher.

· When partly frozen, add coconut and pineapple; continue freezing until crank turns hard. Remove dasher. Let ice cream ripen, using 4 parts ice to 1 part salt. Or spoon into freezer containers; seal, label, date and store in freezer. Makes 1 gallon.

MARIELLA'S ICE CREAM

A Kansas dairyman's wife freezes this ice cream for Christmas giving

1	qt. milk, scalded
4	eggs, beaten
2 ½	c. sugar
2 ½	to 3 c. heavy cream
1	qt. cold milk
2	tblsp. vanilla
¼	tsp. salt
3	drops lemon extract

· Stir hot milk slowly into eggs and sugar; cook slowly over direct heat until thick, stirring; cool.

· Add remaining ingredients to cooled egg mixture; stir until smooth. Pour into freezer can; put dasher and cover in place. Pack chopped ice and rock salt around can, using 6 parts ice to 1 part salt; turn dasher until crank turns hard. (See "How to Freeze and Ripen Ice Cream" in this chapter.) To store, spoon lightly into air-

tight freezer containers (do not
pack). Seal, label and date. Freeze.
Makes about 1 gallon.
Recommended storage time: Up to
1 month.

VARIATIONS

CHOCOLATE: Stir 1 (5½ oz.) can chocolate syrup into vanilla mixture.

STRAWBERRY: Mix 3 (10 oz.) pkgs.
frozen strawberries, thawed, and ½
c. sugar; stir into vanilla mixture;
add red food color for pink ice cream.

Note: You can make 4 batches con-
secutively. By time the custard for
the fourth one is cooked, the first is
cool enough to put in freezer can.
When that gallon is frozen, the second
batch is ready for freezing. This assembly line method makes economical use of ice. A 50-lb. bag of
cracked ice is enough to freeze 4
gallons. You save time by using the
same bowls and pans for each batch.
A good selection is to make 2 gallons
vanilla, 1 chocolate and 1 strawberry.

QUICK VANILLA ICE CREAM

*You're lucky if you have a chance to
clean dasher—stores well in freezer*

1	tblsp. unflavored gelatin
½	c. cold water
7	c. light cream
1½	c. sugar
1	c. evaporated milk
1	tblsp. vanilla

• Soften gelatin in cold water.
• Scald 2 c. cream; add gelatin and
stir to dissolve. Add sugar; stir to
dissolve. Combine remaining cream,
evaporated milk and vanilla; add
slowly to gelatin mixture, stirring.

• Pour into 1-gal. freezer container.
Pack with 6 parts ice to 1 part rock
salt; freeze. (See "How to Freeze and
Ripen Ice Cream" in this chapter.)
Makes about 3 quarts.
• Pack in rigid containers with tight
lids. Label and date. Store in freezer.
Recommended storage time: 3 to 6
weeks.

VANILLA CUSTARD ICE CREAM

*A good keeper if you hide the freezer's
key where no one can find it*

2	c. sugar
⅛	tsp. salt
¼	c. cornstarch
1	qt. milk
4	eggs, separated
2	tsp. vanilla
1	(13 oz.) can evaporated milk
2	c. light cream
½	c. milk (about)

• Thoroughly mix sugar, salt and
cornstarch; stir into 1 qt. milk, heated
to just boiling point. Remove from
heat.
• Beat yolks; gradually add 1 c. of
the hot milk mixture, beating constantly. Stir egg yolk mixture into
remaining hot milk and bring to a
boil. Remove from heat; add vanilla,
evaporated milk and cream to hot
custard. Cool.
• Fold in egg whites, beaten to stiff
but not dry peaks. Pour into 1-gal.
freezer container. Add remaining milk
to fill can three fourths full.
• Pack with 6 parts ice to 1 part
rock salt; freeze. (See "How to Freeze
and Ripen Ice Cream" in this chapter.) Makes 1 gallon.
• Package in rigid containers with

tight lids. Label and date. Store in coldest part of freezer.
Recommended storage time: 3 to 6 weeks.

Note: Substitute 2 (13 oz.) cans evaporated milk for cream, if you wish.

PEACH MELBA PARFAIT

Midsummer's dessert dream—fresh peaches, raspberries and ice cream

1   (3 oz.) pkg. raspberry
    flavor gelatin
2   c. hot water
1   (10 oz.) pkg. frozen
    raspberries (1 ¼ c.)
1   (3 oz.) pkg. peach flavor
    gelatin
½   c. cold water
1   pt. vanilla ice cream
1 ½ c. diced fresh peaches

· Dissolve raspberry gelatin in 1 c. hot water in bowl. Add unthawed raspberries. Stir occasionally to separate berries. Let thaw (it will begin to set).
· Pour 1 c. hot water over peach gelatin in another bowl; stir to dissolve. Add ½ c. cold water. Add ice cream in 8 chunks; stir to dissolve. Refrigerate until thick enough to mound up.
· Spoon slightly thickened raspberry mixture into 8 dessert dishes.
· When ice cream mixture has thickened, fold in peaches and spoon over raspberry mixture. Chill at least 30 minutes. Makes 8 servings.

COUNTRY GRAPE SHERBET

Sour cream adds distinctive flavor

1   c. dairy sour cream
1   c. milk
1 ½ c. sugar
1   egg, well beaten
1   c. grape juice (Concord)
¼   c. lemon juice

· Combine ingredients and beat until sugar dissolves.
· Pour into 2 refrigerator trays or loaf pans; freeze until nearly firm.
· Turn mixture into chilled bowl and beat until fluffy and smooth. Work fast and do not let mixture melt.
· Return to trays and freeze until firm. Makes 6 servings.
· To freeze, wrap blocks of sherbet, seal, label and date.
Recommended storage time: Up to 1 month.

FRESH STRAWBERRY SHERBET

Pretty, coral-red dessert to make when the strawberries are ripe

4   qts. fresh strawberries,
    sliced
4   c. sugar
2 ⅔ c. milk
⅔   c. orange juice
⅛   tsp. ground cinnamon

· Mix strawberries and sugar; let stand until juicy (about 1½ hours). Mash, or purée in blender. Strain out seeds (optional, but we prefer seedless sherbet).
· Add milk, orange juice and cinnamon. Mix well. Freeze in crank-type freezer. (See "How to Freeze

and Ripen Ice Cream" in this chapter.) Or pour mixture into refrigerator trays or loaf pans; freeze about 3 hours; stir 2 or 3 times. Makes about 1 gallon. Pack in airtight containers; label, date and freeze. Recommended storage time: 1 month.

VARIATIONS

STRAWBERRY PARFAIT RING: Spoon strawberry sherbet and soft vanilla ice cream in alternating layers in chilled ring mold. Freeze. When frozen, unmold on serving plate; return to freezer. To serve, fill center with fresh berries for color-bright garnish.

STRAWBERRY/LEMON PARFAIT: Spoon strawberry and lemon sherbets alternately into parfait glasses or tumblers. Return to freezer until time to serve. Garnish with fresh berries.

CHOCOLATE/STRAWBERRY RING: Spoon strawberry sherbet into ring mold. Freeze. When frozen, unmold on plate; return to freezer. To serve, fill with scoops of chocolate ice cream.

Choose the Right Cheese to Store

Much research has been done on freezing cheese. These studies show that certain kinds freeze well, while others become crumbly and mealy. Pasteurized process cheese keeps well in freezer for 1 to 2 months. And regardless of the kind of cheese, small portions freeze best. Package the cheese in ½ lb. or smaller lots in pieces from ½ to 1" thick. Larger portions freeze too slowly at 0°F. Among the types that freeze with good results are Cheddar, Brick, Port du Salut, Swiss, Provolone, Mozzarella, Liederkranz, Camembert, Parmesan and Romano. Some Limburger, Gouda, Club and Colby cheeses freeze successfully, but others do not. Cream cheese becomes crumbly when frozen but dips and sandwiches made with it as an ingredient freeze well. Cottage cheese does not freeze successfully.

To Package: Wrap the cheese in airtight packages. Heavy-duty aluminum foil and plastic wrap are excellent. Camembert cheese, which comes in small, foil-wrapped packages need not be rewrapped. Freeze process cheese in original polyethylene package, but overwrap with foil.

If you have grated cheese or scraps of cheese, freeze them in plastic bags, twisting to exclude the air, or in other airtight packages. They're handy for seasoning and topping casseroles. Recommended storage time: 6 months.

CHEESE CAKE

When guests taste, the women will ask, "May I have your recipe?"

1 ½	c. zwieback crumbs
¼	c. butter or regular margarine
2	(8 oz.) pkgs. cream cheese
1	c. sugar
4	eggs, separated

1 ½   tsp. grated lemon peel
4   tsp. lemon juice
½   tsp. vanilla
½   c. sifted flour
½   tsp. salt
1   c. milk
Sour Cream/Raspberry Topping

· Blend together crumbs and butter. Press into bottom and 1″ up the sides of a 9″ spring-form pan. Bake in a slow oven (325°F.) 5 minutes. Cool.
· Mix together cheese, sugar and egg yolks. Beat until light. Blend in lemon peel, juice and vanilla.
· Mix in flour and salt, sifted together. Blend in milk. Fold in stiffly beaten egg whites.
· Pour into crumb-lined pan. Bake in a slow oven (325°F.) 1 hour. Turn off heat and allow cake to cool in oven 1 hour. Remove from oven; cool. Makes 12 servings.
· Freeze, then wrap, label and date. Return to freezer.
Recommended storage time: Up to 1 month.
· To use, thaw in refrigerator. Just before serving, add Sour Cream/Raspberry Topping.

SOUR CREAM/RASPBERRY TOPPING: Spread 1 c. dairy sour cream on top of cheese cake. Ring 1 c. fresh raspberries (or drained, partly frozen) around edge of cake.

Note: If you don't have a spring-form

pan use a round (9″) layer cake pan. For extra height, fit a 22″ length of 12″ foil across bottom of pan; fold long ends back to build up sides at least an inch. To complete extra height around rim, cut a 6″ length of foil in two; fit pieces, fill gaps and fold above rim. When cake is baked, lift it out by grasping edges of long foil sheet.

HOT CHEESE DIP

Crackers and nippy cheese party-style

2   (5 oz.) jars sharp cheese spread
1   (8 oz.) can minced clams (not drained)
1   tblsp. chopped green onion
2   tblsp. chopped green pepper
2   tsp. Worcestershire sauce
⅛   tsp. paprika

· Thoroughly mix together all ingredients. Put in freezer container or ovenproof dish. Makes about 2 cups.
· Wrap, label, date and freeze.
Recommended storage time: 2 to 4 weeks.
· To use, thaw enough to remove from container or leave in ovenproof container. Heat in a slow oven (325°F.) about 45 minutes. Serve in chafing dish or casserole over candle warmer with crackers or cubes of French bread on toothpicks.

Store Eggs in Freezer

Grandmother put eggs down in waterglass in springtime when they were abundant. She was thrifty and knew that eggs, kept for weeks when they were scarce, came in handy on baking day. Today's country cooks often freeze top-quality eggs when they have a big supply. It's convenient to have them—they stretch the budget.

You can freeze eggs whole, or whites and yolks separately. The important point is to use *fresh, clean, chilled eggs.* Select only sound-shelled eggs. If convenient, chill them almost to the freezing point before breaking. Here are the steps to follow:

1. Wash fresh eggs in water warm to the hands (120°F.) with detergent added to help loosen dirt. Dry quickly.

2. Break eggs, one at a time, into a cup before adding to the bowl. Do not freeze eggs that have an odor or blood spots.

3. Stir whole eggs with a fork or electric mixer on low speed to mix whites and yolks, but do not beat; avoid adding air. To 1 c. eggs (about 12 eggs) add 1 tblsp. sugar or light corn syrup or ½ tsp. salt, depending on how you want to use them. This prevents gumminess when thawed. To use them, thaw in the refrigerator, or under cold running water, or at room temperature. Stir them before using. Do not let them wait longer than 24 hours in the refrigerator before using and do not refreeze. Thawed frozen eggs sour rapidly.

4. Freeze and package egg whites in recipe amounts—for an angel food cake or meringue shells. Be careful not to include even a particle of the yolk. If you do, remove it carefully with the tip of the spoon. Even a small drop will prevent the whites from beating well.

5. Break egg yolks by stirring with a fork, but do not beat them. Into 1 c. yolks, mix 2 tblsp. light corn syrup or 1 tsp. salt, depending on how you want to use them.

6. Package small amounts or *measured-recipe amounts,* leaving ½" head space, in moistureproof containers. Leave ½" head space in half-pint and pint containers, ¾" in narrow-top jars; seal tightly. Label every package so you will know the quantity and whether eggs contain salt or sweetening (sugar or corn syrup). You will use the sweetened eggs for desserts like custards, cakes and other dishes containing sugar; those with salt for omelets, scrambling and other dishes made without sweetening. Recommended storage time: 6 to 8 months.

MEASUREMENTS FOR FROZEN EGGS

1 to 1½ tblsp. frozen yolks equal 1 egg yolk

2 tblsp. whites equal 1 egg white

3 tblsp. yolks and whites equal 1 whole egg

1 c. equals 5 whole eggs, 12 yolks, or 8 whites

FROZEN EGG DESSERT

Good way to use extra eggs (*developed at University of Connecticut*)

¾ c. butter or regular margarine
1½ c. confectioners sugar
4 large eggs
¾ c. chopped pecans
¾ tsp. vanilla
3¾ c. vanilla wafer crumbs

· Cream butter and sugar; add eggs, one at a time, beating well after each addition. Mix in nuts and vanilla. Add 2¾ c. wafer crumbs; mix.

· Spread remaining crumbs over bot-

tom of buttered 8″ square pan. Spread creamed mixture evenly over crumbs. Makes 16 (2″) squares.
· Wrap, seal, label, date and freeze. Recommended storage time: About 1 month.
· Serve without thawing, topped with whipped cream.

VARIATIONS

CHOCOLATE EGG DESSERT: Substitute 2 (1 oz.) squares unsweetened chocolate, melted, for the vanilla.

LEMON EGG DESSERT: Substitute ¼ c. lemon juice and 2 tsp. grated lemon peel for the vanilla.

ANGEL MERINGUE SHELLS

Tint egg whites in delicate pastels with food colors for festive parties

4	egg whites
¼	tsp. salt
½	tsp. cream of tartar
1	c. sugar

· Beat egg whites to a foam; add salt and cream of tartar; beat slightly.
· Add sugar by tablespoons, beating well after each addition. Beat until glossy and stiff peaks form.
· For each shell drop ⅓ c. meringue on heavy brown paper on baking sheet. Use back of spoon to hollow out center and build up sides.
· Bake in preheated, very slow oven (250°F.) 1 hour; immediately turn off heat. Leave meringues in closed oven overnight. Next morning shells will be completely dry, but not browned. Makes about 12.
· To freeze, wrap each shell in plastic wrap and seal with freezer tape. Overwrap with heavy-duty foil. Label and date. To thaw, remove foil wrapping and let shells stand at room temperature in plastic wrap about 6 hours. Recommended storage time: Up to 1 month.

CHAPTER 5

HOMEMADE BREADS

Freezing and Serving Breads · Recipes for White, Crusty French, Honey Whole Wheat, Orange Yeast and Breads · Raisin Bran · Yeast Breads Made from Frozen Dough, Savory Buns, Petite Brioche, Cottage Cheese Rolls and Coffee Breads · Fruit and Nut Quick Breads · Popovers · French Toast

Many mothers believe children are short-changed if they never stand wide-eyed in the kitchen when rounded, crusty loaves of gold-brown bread come from the oven. How pleasant to sniff the yeasty aroma—and to remember it. Food fragrances, research shows, are among the most cherished memories people have of their childhood homes.

Home freezers deserve much credit for keeping bread baking a flourishing art in country kitchens. True, lots of the good daily bread comes from bakery counters, but when a farm woman finds time, loaves, rolls and coffee cakes move from oven to cooling rack and into the freezer. Reheated, these fresh-again breads, sliced and spread with butter and jelly or jam, make coffee hours and mealtimes something special. Be sure to try Freezer White Bread, Apricot Braid and Orange Blossom Buns made with frozen dough.

You will find recipes for unusual, superior breads in this chapter. And all of them freeze successfully. Some are prize winners—Honey Whole Wheat Bread, which contains potatoes, for instance. It won blue ribbons for a California FARM JOURNAL reader at county and state fairs.

Don't miss the frozen popovers that become light as balloons and crisp-crusted when baked; the muffin-like Petite Brioche. Note the distinctive, quick fruit and nut breads for dainty party sandwiches. We suggest that you serve Cranberry/Orange Bread at your next club luncheon, with chicken salad. The garnet chunks of berries give it a fascinating tart-sweet flavor.

Watch your family and friends help themselves again and again to your homemade breads. Keep a supply in your freezer!

Homemade Breads
TASTE LIKE THOSE MOTHER USED TO BAKE

Farm women of all ages and in all parts of the country like to bake bread. And they do bake it! We know because every time we feature a bread-making story in FARM JOURNAL, we really rejoice in the enthusiastic response from our readers.

Many a loaf spends time in the farm freezer, awaiting its chance to glorify a meal. Warmed and sliced thin, with golden butter melting into it, homemade bread pleases everyone. Here are "breads for spreads," and the jellies, jams and marmalades for which there are recipes in this cookbook. Slice some of the loaves for sandwiches that get rave notices.

Freezing Yeast Breads

We believe the best way to freeze most yeast breads, rolls and coffee cakes is to bake them first. We do recommend Freezer White Bread, Apricot Braid and Orange Blossom Buns (see Index) for which the dough freezes before baking by methods developed in our Countryside Test Kitchens. To get light loaves every time from frozen dough may be a problem. Sometimes a part of the yeast is inactivated and in addition to poor volume, the loaves may have a dry, tough crust.

BAKERY BREAD: If it comes to the kitchen in a good wrap, you can put it directly in the freezer. It will stay in *good condition about 4 months*. In case you want to store it longer, overwrap the loaves and rolls with moistureproof packaging material or place them in plastic freezer bags.

HOMEMADE BREADS: Use your favorite bread, roll and coffee cake recipes or use the wonderful ones that follow in this chapter. Let the shaped dough for loaf bread rise until doubled. Then bake in a hot oven (400°F.) 45 to 50 minutes. It will be less crumbly after frozen than bread baked an hour in a moderate oven (375°F.). Bake all breads to a light golden brown to prevent upper crust from separating from inside of loaf. (Specialty breads and rolls, rich in sugar and eggs, often need to be baked at temperatures lower than 400°F. Use temperatures specified when using recipes in this chapter.) Remove from pans, cool quickly to room tempera-

ture, wrap in foil or plastic wrap or place in plastic freezer bags, seal, label, date and freeze.
Recommended storage time: 9 months to 1 year.

Bake rolls and buns when dough doubles, in a hot oven (400°F.) 15 to 20 minutes. Cool and wrap like bread loaves or place in a rigid container, overwrap, label, date and freeze. Many women like to wrap, freeze and warm rolls in foil.
Recommended storage time: 9 months.

Bake coffee cakes when dough is light, in a moderate oven (375°F.) 20 to 30 minutes, or until a light golden brown. Cool and wrap like bread loaves. Frost before serving.
Recommended storage time: 9 months.

To use, thaw the bread in its wrapper at room temperature if you wish to serve it cold. A 1-lb. loaf will thaw in about 3 hours. You need not thaw bread slices for toast. Thaw rolls in their wrapper to serve cold. To heat them, place unwrapped rolls in a covered container or wrap in aluminum foil. Heat in a moderate oven (350°F.) about 20 to 25 minutes, or until hot. Do not heat them longer than necessary or they will dry out. Put unthawed coffee cakes in a moderate oven (350°F.) and heat, uncovered, about 20 to 25 minutes. Frost if desired.

To Freeze Bread Dough: We do not recommend freezing doughs for yeast breads except those made by the freezer method. See the recipes in this chapter for Freezer White Bread, Apricot Braid and Orange Blossom Buns, examples of breads that may be successfully frozen before baking.

Doughnuts: Fry doughnuts of yeast-leavened dough, drain on layers of paper toweling; cool, wrap in meal-size amounts or individually in foil.
Recommended storage time: 2 months.

To use, let thaw in wrap and heat in a slow oven (300°F.) about 15 minutes. Or unwrap, brush lightly with butter, place on a baking sheet and heat quickly in a hot oven (400°F.).
Recommended storage time: Up to 2 months.

HOMEMADE WHITE BREAD

Winter's best snack—bread warm from oven, spread with butter and jelly

3	pkgs. active dry yeast
½	c. warm water (110 to 115°F.)
½	c. sugar
4	tsp. salt
⅓	c. melted shortening
5	c. water
16	to 18 c. flour

· Sprinkle yeast on warm water; stir to dissolve.
· Combine sugar, salt, shortening and water in 5-qt. bowl. Stir in 8 c. flour. Add yeast and enough of remaining flour (8 to 10 c.) to make stiff dough that cleans the bowl when you stir.
· Knead on lightly floured surface until smooth and satiny (5 to 8 minutes). Place in greased bowl; turn to

bring greased side up. Cover; let rise in warm place (80 to 85°F.) until doubled, about 1½ hours. Punch down. Turn out on floured board.

· Divide in half. Set aside one half to rise again. Divide other portion in half; shape each half into smooth ball; let rest 10 minutes. Shape into two loaves; place in greased 9×5×3″ loaf pans. Grease top lightly; cover and let rise until doubled, about 1 hour. Bake in hot oven (400°F.) 40 to 50 minutes. Immediately turn out of pans on rack. Cool thoroughly.

· When portion of dough set for second rising is doubled, punch down and repeat process. Makes 4 loaves.

· Wrap loaves individually as soon as they cool. Label, date and freeze. Recommended storage time: 9 months to a year.

· To serve, let thaw in wrapper at room temperature (on rack to allow air circulation) and heat in foil wrapper in moderate oven (375°F.) 20 minutes. Foil may be opened for last 5 minutes to crisp the crust.

VARIATIONS

WHOLE WHEAT BREAD: Substitute whole wheat flour for half the white.

RAISIN COFFEE BREAD: Make 3 loaves and knead ½ c. raisins into fourth loaf just before shaping. Place in greased 8″ square pan to rise. Before baking, brush top with melted butter and sprinkle with mixture of cinnamon and sugar.

POTATO BREAD: Reduce amount of water to 3 c. Add 2 c. instant mashed potatoes to water mixture before adding flour and yeast.

MILK BREAD: Substitute 5 c. scalded milk for 5 c. water. Add sugar, salt and shortening. Cool to lukewarm before adding yeast to batter.

CRUSTY FRENCH BREAD

Keep a golden loaf in the freezer to make garlic bread for the barbecue

2	c. warm water (110 to 115°F.)
1	pkg. active dry yeast
1	tblsp. sugar
2	tsp. salt
5½	c. flour (about)
1	egg white, beaten

· Pour water into a large bowl. Sprinkle on yeast and stir until dissolved. Add sugar, salt and 3 c. flour. Stir to mix; then beat until smooth and shiny. Stir in about 2½ c. more flour.

· Sprinkle a little flour on bread board or pastry cloth. Turn dough out on board and knead until satiny and smooth, 5 to 7 minutes. Shape in a smooth ball.

· Rub bowl lightly with shortening. Press top of dough into bowl, then turn dough over. Cover with waxed paper, then with a clean cloth. Let rise until doubled, about 1 hour.

· Punch down, divide in half and shape each portion in a ball. Place balls on lightly floured board, cover and let stand 5 minutes.

· Rub a little shortening on the palms of hands. Start shaping the loaves by rolling ball of dough at center and gently working the hands toward ends of loaf. Do this several times to get well-shaped, long, slender loaves.

· Place the two loaves about 4″ apart on lightly greased baking sheet. With a sharp knife or razor blade,

cut diagonal gashes about ¾″ deep, 1½″ apart into top of each loaf. Cover and let rise until a little more than doubled, about 1 hour. Bake in hot oven (425°F.) 30 to 35 minutes.
· Remove from oven. Brush with egg white. Return to oven for 2 minutes. Remove; cool on racks. Makes 2 loaves.
· Wrap loaves individually as soon as they cool. Label, date and freeze. Recommended storage time: 9 months to a year.
· To serve, let thaw in wrapper at room temperature (on rack to allow air circulation) 3½ hours or heat in foil in moderate oven (375°F.) 20 minutes.

CRUSTY ROLLS: Bake 1 loaf of French Bread and use other half of dough to make rolls. Cut the dough into pieces the size of an egg. Shape each piece into a smooth ball by folding the edges under. Place them 3″ apart on a lightly greased baking sheet. With scissors, cut a cross ½″ deep in top of each roll. Cover and let rise until doubled. Bake in a hot oven (425°F.) 15 to 20 minutes. Remove from oven, brush rolls with egg white and return to oven for 2 minutes. Remove from baking sheet. Serve hot or cold. Makes 12.
· To freeze, package rolls in foil or place in a freezer box and overwrap. Label, date and freeze. Recommended storage time: 9 months to a year.
· To serve, thaw package at room temperature (on rack to allow air circulation) about 1 hour. To serve hot, place foil-wrapped frozen rolls in hot oven (400°F.) 20 minutes. If wrapper on rolls cannot be heated, place in paper bag and heat in moderate oven (350°F.) until hot, about 15 to 20 minutes.

CHEESE BRAIDS

Unusual seasoning: black pepper.
Slice thin, serve with crisp salads

2   c. warm water (110 to 115°F.)
2   pkgs. active dry yeast
¾   c. instant dry milk
¼   c. sugar
2   tsp. salt
7   to 8 c. flour
¼   c. soft lard or butter
3   eggs, beaten
2   tsp. coarsely ground black pepper
2   c. coarsely shredded dry Cheddar cheese (½ lb.)
Melted fat
1   egg yolk
2   tblsp. cold water

· Measure ½ c. warm water into large bowl. Add yeast and stir to dissolve. Add remaining warm water, dry milk, sugar, salt and 3 c. flour. Stir until smooth.
· Add lard, eggs, pepper and enough remaining flour to make dough that cleans the bowl when stirred.
· Turn out on floured board; knead until smooth and satiny, about 5 minutes. Flatten with hands into rectangle. Sprinkle with ½ c. cheese; roll up like jelly roll, flatten again. Repeat process until all cheese is worked in. Knead lightly to be sure cheese is evenly distributed. Place in greased bowl; turn dough so top is greased. Cover with damp cloth and let rise in warm place (80 to 85°F.) until doubled, about 1½ hours.

· Punch down. Divide in six equal parts. Cover; let rest 5 minutes. Roll each part into strips as long as baking sheet with tapered ends. Lay 3 strips on each of two greased baking sheets. Starting in middle, braid loosely to each end; turn ends under and press down lightly to baking sheet. Brush with melted fat. Cover; let rise until light, about 40 minutes (do not let size double). Brush tops with mixture of egg yolk and cold water.

· Bake in moderate oven (350°F.) 20 minutes; reduce heat to 325°F. and bake about 25 minutes more. Brush again with egg yolk glaze about 5 minutes before end of baking time. Makes 2 loaves.

· Wrap or package loaves individually as soon as they cool. Seal, label, date and freeze.

Recommended storage time: 9 months to a year.

· To serve, let thaw in wrapper at room temperature (on rack to allow air circulation) or heat in foil wrapper in moderate oven (375°F.) 20 minutes. Foil may be opened for last 5 minutes to crisp the crust.

HONEY WHOLE WHEAT BREAD

A bread for spreads—try it with butter, jelly, jam, apple butter

5	c. warm water (110 to 115°F.)
2	pkgs. active dry yeast
6	tblsp. lard or other shortening
¼	c. honey
4	c. whole wheat flour
½	c. instant potatoes (not reconstituted)
½	c. instant dry milk
1	tblsp. salt
6½ to 8	c. all-purpose flour
	Melted fat

· Combine ½ c. water and yeast in bowl. Stir to dissolve yeast.

· Melt lard in 6-qt. saucepan; remove from heat. Add honey and remaining water.

· Mix whole wheat flour, instant potatoes, dry milk and salt. Add to saucepan. Beat until smooth.

· Add yeast mixture and beat until smooth. Then with a wooden spoon mix in enough all-purpose flour to make a dough that cleans the pan. Knead on lightly floured board until smooth and satiny, and small blisters appear, 8 to 10 minutes.

· Place in greased bowl; turn dough so top is greased. Cover; let rise in warm place (80 to 85°F.) until doubled, 1 to 1½ hours. Punch down dough; divide in thirds; cover and let rest 5 minutes. Shape into 3 loaves. Place in greased 9×5×3″ loaf pans; brush with melted fat. Cover; let rise until doubled, about 1 hour.

· Bake in hot oven (400°F.) about 50 minutes. Remove from pans; cool on rack. Makes 3 loaves.

· Wrap or package loaves individually as soon as they cool. Label, date and freeze.

Recommended storage time: 9 months to a year.

· To serve, let thaw in wrapper at room temperature (on rack to allow air circulation) or heat in foil wrapper in moderate oven (375°F.) 20 minutes. Foil may be opened for last 5 minutes to crisp the crust.

Note: You may use 1 c. unseasoned mashed potatoes in place of the instant potatoes. Combine with the honey-water mixture.

ORANGE BREAD

*Watch—it browns quickly. Team with
date-nut filling for party sandwiches*

½	c. warm water (110 to 115°F.)
2	pkgs. active dry yeast
1½	c. warm orange juice (110 to 115°F.)
5	to 6 c. flour
½	c. sugar
2	tsp. salt
¼	c. soft lard or butter
¼	c. grated orange peel
Melted butter	

· Measure warm water into large
bowl. Add yeast and stir to dissolve.
Add orange juice and 2 c. flour; beat
thoroughly. Add sugar, salt, lard,
orange peel and about 4 c. flour, to
make dough that cleans bowl when
you stir.
· Turn out on lightly floured board
and knead until satiny and elastic, 5
to 8 minutes. Place in greased bowl,
turning dough so top is greased.
Cover with damp cloth; let rise in
warm place (80 to 85°F.) until doubled, about 1½ hours.
· Punch down dough; divide in half.
Cover; let rest 5 minutes. Shape into
loaves and place in greased 8½ × 4½
× 2¾" ovenproof glass loaf pans.
Brush tops with butter; cover and let
rise until doubled, about 1 hour.
· Bake in moderate oven (350°F.)
about 45 minutes. (Increase oven temperature to 375° if you use metal
pans.) Cool on racks. Makes 2 loaves.
· Wrap or package loaves individually as soon as they cool. Label, date
and freeze.
Recommended storage time: 9
months to a year.

· To serve, let thaw in wrapper at
room temperature (on rack to allow
air circulation) or heat in foil wrapper in moderate oven (375°F.) 20
minutes. Foil may be opened for last
5 minutes to crisp the crust.

ORANGE-CINNAMON SWIRL: Roll half
of dough into rectangle ¼" thick, 6"
wide, 20" long. Brush with 1 tblsp.
melted butter. Mix 3 tblsp. sugar and
1½ tsp. ground cinnamon. Sprinkle
evenly over dough, reserving 1 tblsp.
for top of loaf. Roll like jelly roll.
Seal ends. Place in greased 8½ × 4½
× 2¾" ovenproof glass loaf pan.
Brush top with melted butter; sprinkle with remaining sugar mixture. Let
rise until a little more than doubled,
about 1¼ hours. Bake in moderate
oven (350°F.) about 45 minutes. (Increase oven temperature to 375° if
you use metal pans.)

RAISIN BRAN BREAD

*Light tender bread. Dough rises more
slowly than white bread*

1¾	c. milk, scalded
1	c. all-bran cereal
2	tblsp. shortening
2	tblsp. light molasses
1	tblsp. light brown sugar
1½	tsp. salt
1	pkg. active dry yeast
¼	c. warm water (110 to 115°F.)
1½	c. raisins
¼	c. water
5⅓	c. flour (about)

· Stir into milk the cereal, shortening, molasses, sugar and salt; cool.
· Sprinkle yeast on warm water; stir
to dissolve.

· Steam raisins in ¼ c. water over medium heat; drain.

· Add 2 c. flour to bran mixture; beat vigorously by hand or with mixer. Stir in yeast. Add raisins and enough remaining flour until dough forms around spoon.

· Turn out on well-floured surface; cover, let rest 5 minutes. Knead dough lightly until springy, about 5 minutes. Dough may be sticky.

· Place in greased bowl; turn to bring greased surface to top. Cover; let rise until doubled, about 1½ hours. Punch down, let rise until doubled.

· Turn out on floured surface; cut in half; cover, let rest 5 minutes. Shape into 2 loaves. Place in well-greased 9×5×3″ loaf pans. Let rise in warm place (80 to 85°F.) until doubled.

· Bake in hot oven (400°F.) 10 minutes; then in moderate oven (375°F.) about 30 minutes. Cool 5 minutes; remove to racks. Brush with butter. Makes 2 loaves.

· Wrap or package loaves individually as soon as they cool. Label, date and freeze.

Recommended storage time: 9 months to a year.

· To serve, let thaw in wrapper at room temperature (on rack to allow air circulation) or heat in foil wrapper in moderate oven (375°F.) 20 minutes. Foil may be opened for last 5 minutes to crisp the crust.

Yeast Breads by the Freezer Method

Many questions from women came to Countryside Kitchens through the years about a dough to freeze that would produce excellent bread every time. The following three recipes are the answers of our food editors. They are the result of many tests. Do follow the directions when making these treats. They were developed especially for the frozen dough method.

FREEZER WHITE BREAD

Nice evenly shaped loaves, good results every time—a large recipe

12½ to 13½ c. flour
½   c. sugar
2   tblsp. salt
⅔   c. instant nonfat dry milk solids
4   pkgs. active dry yeast
¼   c. softened butter or regular margarine
4   c. very warm water (120 to 130°F.)

· In a large bowl thoroughly mix 4 c. flour, sugar, salt, dry milk solids and yeast. Add butter.

· Gradually add water and beat 2 minutes at medium speed of electric mixer, scraping bowl occasionally. Add 1½ c. flour. Beat at high speed 2 minutes, scraping bowl occasionally. Stir in enough additional flour to make a stiff dough. Turn out onto lightly floured board; knead until smooth and elastic, about 15 minutes. Cover with a towel; let rest 15 minutes.

· Divide dough into 4 equal parts. Form each piece into a smooth round ball. Flatten each ball into a mound 6″ in diameter. Place on greased baking sheets. Cover with plastic wrap. Freeze until firm. Transfer to plastic freezer bags and store in freezer. Recommended storage time: Up to 1 month.

· Remove dough from freezer, place on ungreased baking sheets. Cover; let stand at room temperature until fully thawed, about 4 hours. For round loaves, let thawed dough rise on ungreased baking sheets until doubled, about 1 hour. Or roll each ball into a 12×8″ rectangle. Shape into loaves. Place in greased 8½ × 4½ × 2½″ loaf pans. Let rise in warm place until doubled, about 1½ hours.

· Bake in moderate oven (350°F.) about 35 minutes, or until done. Remove from pans and cool on wire racks. Makes 4 loaves.

APRICOT BRAID

Keep this attractive, flavorful loaf on hand, ready to bake for guests

5½	to 6½ c. flour
¾	c. sugar
1	tsp. salt
3	pkgs. active dry yeast
½	c. softened butter or regular margarine
1	c. very warm water (120 to 130°F.)
3	eggs (at room temperature)

Apricot Filling
Crumb Topping

· In a large bowl thoroughly mix 1¼ c. flour, sugar, salt and yeast. Add butter.

· Gradually add water and beat 2 minutes at medium speed of electric mixer, scraping bowl occasionally. Add eggs and ¼ c. flour. Beat at high speed 2 minutes, scraping bowl occasionally. Stir in enough additional flour to make a soft dough. Turn out onto lightly floured board; knead until smooth and elastic, about 8 to 10 minutes.

· Divide dough into 3 equal pieces. Roll one piece into a 12×7″ rectangle. Transfer to greased baking sheet. Starting at a short side, spread one third of Apricot Filling down center third of rectangle. Cut 1″ wide strips along both sides of filling cutting from filling out to edges of dough. Fold strips at an angle across filling, alternating from side to side. Sprinkle with one third of Crumb Topping. Cover tightly with plastic wrap; place in freezer. Repeat with remaining pieces of dough, filling and topping. When firm, remove from baking sheets and wrap each loaf with plastic wrap, then with aluminum foil. Store in freezer.

Recommended storage time: Up to 1 month.

· Remove dough from freezer; unwrap and place on ungreased baking sheets. Let stand covered loosely with plastic wrap at room temperature until fully thawed, about 2 hours. Let thawed dough rise in warm place, free from draft, until more than doubled in bulk, about 1½ hours.

· Bake in moderate oven (375°F.) 20 to 25 minutes, or until done. Remove from baking sheets and cool on wire racks. Makes 3 coffee cakes.

APRICOT FILLING: Combine 2¼ c. dried apricots (11 oz. pkg.) and 1½ c. water in saucepan. Bring to a boil; cook until liquid is absorbed and apricots are tender, about 20 minutes. Sieve; stir in 1½ c. brown sugar, firmly packed. Cool.

CRUMB TOPPING: Combine ½ c. unsifted flour, 3 tblsp. sugar and ¾ tsp. ground cinnamon. Mix in 3 tblsp. softened butter or regular margarine until mixture is crumbly.

ORANGE BLOSSOM BUNS

Just form dough into balls and coat with Orange Sugar—easy

5½   to 6½ c. flour
¾   c. sugar
1   tsp. salt
3   pkgs. active dry yeast
½   c. softened butter or regular margarine
1   c. very warm water (120 to 130°F.)
3   eggs
Melted butter or regular margarine
Orange Sugar

· In a large bowl thoroughly mix 1¼ c. flour, sugar, salt and yeast. Add ½ c. softened butter.
· Gradually add water and beat 2 minutes at medium speed of electric mixer, scraping bowl occasionally. Add eggs and ¼ c. flour. Beat at high speed 2 minutes, scraping bowl occasionally. Stir in enough additional flour to make a soft dough. Turn out on lightly floured board; knead until smooth and elastic, 8 to 10 minutes.
· Divide dough into 3 equal parts. Divide one part into 8 equal pieces; form each piece into a smooth ball. Dip each ball into melted butter, then coat with one third of Orange Sugar.

Place in greased 8″ round cake pan. Cover pan tightly with plastic wrap, then with aluminum foil; place in freezer. Repeat with remaining pieces in dough and coating. Store in freezer. Recommended storage time: Up to 1 month.
· Remove dough from freezer. Let stand covered loosely with plastic wrap at room temperature until fully thawed, about 3 hours. Let thawed dough rise in a warm place, free from draft, until more than doubled in bulk, about 2 hours and 15 minutes.
· Bake in moderate oven (350°F.) 25 to 30 minutes, or until done. Remove from pans and cool on wire racks. Makes 2 dozen.

ORANGE SUGAR: Mix together 1 c. sugar and 2 tblsp. grated orange peel.

SAVORY BUNS

Fix hamburgers with seasoned buns— they'll ask where you found the buns

2   pkgs. active dry yeast
½   c. warm water (110 to 115°F.)
1½   c. milk
½   c. soft shortening
½   c. sugar
1   tsp. salt
½   tsp. celery salt
½   tsp. spaghetti sauce mix
2   eggs, beaten
7   to 7½ c. flour

· Dissolve yeast in warm water in large mixing bowl.
· Scald milk; add shortening, sugar, salt, celery salt and spaghetti sauce mix; cool until lukewarm. Add milk mixture, eggs and half the flour to the yeast. Beat with spoon until smooth.

• Add remaining flour gradually, mixing first with spoon and then by hand. Turn onto a lightly floured surface and knead until smooth and elastic, about 5 minutes.

• Place in greased bowl, turning to grease all sides. Cover with towel and let rise in warm place (80 to 85°F.) until doubled, about 1½ hours. Punch down, let rise 30 minutes.

• Divide dough into thirds. Roll each third into a square about ½" thick. Cut in 9 small squares. Tuck square corners under slightly to shape buns. Place on a greased baking sheet. Pat buns out so they are about ½" thick. Cover with a towel; let rise until doubled, about 30 minutes.

• Bake in hot oven (400°F.) 12 to 15 minutes. Cool on racks. Makes 27.

• Freeze buns as soon as cool. Place in plastic freezer bags or wrap in foil, label and date. Return to freezer. Recommended storage time: 9 months.

• To serve cold, thaw in package at room temperature 2 to 3 hours. To serve hot, place in covered container or aluminum foil wrap and heat in moderate oven (350°F.) until hot, about 20 to 25 minutes.

PETITE BRIOCHE

You'll like the hint of lemon

1   c. milk
½   c. butter or regular margarine
1   tsp. salt
½   c. sugar
2   pkgs. active dry yeast
¼   c. warm water (110 to 115°F.)
4   eggs, beaten
1   tsp. grated lemon peel
5   c. sifted flour (about)
Melted butter

• Scald milk; stir in butter, salt and sugar. Cool until lukewarm.

• Sprinkle yeast over warm water; stir to dissolve.

• Add eggs and lemon peel; mix well. Combine with cooled milk mixture. Add flour gradually to make a soft dough.

• Knead lightly until dough is smooth and satiny. Place in greased bowl; cover with cloth and let rise in warm place until doubled, about 2 hours. Punch down, turn out on lightly floured board. Knead lightly.

• Shape two thirds of dough into smooth balls about 2" in diameter. Shape other third into smaller balls, about 1" in diameter. Place large balls in greased muffin-pan cups; set one small ball firmly on top of each of larger ones. Brush surface with butter; let rise until doubled in bulk. Bake in hot oven (425°F.) about 10 minutes. Remove from pans at once. Cool on racks. Makes about 3 dozen.

• Wrap rolls, as soon as they are cool, in moistureproof material or place in plastic freezer bags or freezer containers. Label, date and freeze. Recommended storage time: 9 months.

• To serve cold, thaw in package at room temperature approximately 2 to 3 hours. To serve hot, place frozen rolls in covered container or aluminum foil wrap and heat in moderate oven (350°F.) 20 to 25 minutes.

COTTAGE CHEESE ROLLS

Delicate, sweet rolls with distinctive flavor—perfect coffee go-with

2 ¾   c. sifted flour
¼   c. sugar
1   tsp. salt
1   c. small curd creamed cottage cheese (room temperature, drained)
½   c. soft shortening (half butter)
2   pkgs. active dry yeast
¼   c. warm water (110 to 115°F.)
1   egg

Filling:

⅔   c. finely chopped pecans
⅔   c. brown sugar, firmly packed
3   tblsp. melted butter
½   tsp. vanilla

• Measure flour, sugar, salt and cheese into a large bowl. Cut in shortening, like making pastry.

• Add yeast to warm water; let stand a few minutes. Blend egg into yeast mixture. Thoroughly mix yeast into flour mixture. Dough will be sticky.

• Pat dough out on a lightly floured surface. Turn over a few times to coat with flour. Roll out to a 12″ square.

• Mix together filling ingredients. Spread evenly over dough. Roll up like jelly roll. Seal edges. Cut into 18 slices and place in 2 greased 8″ round layer cake pans. Let rise in a warm place (80 to 85°F.) until doubled, about 45 minutes.

• Bake in moderate oven (375°F.) until browned, 20 to 25 minutes. Cool on rack. Makes 18 rolls.

• Wrap rolls, as soon as they are cool, in moistureproof material or place in plastic freezer bags or freezer containers. Seal, label, date and freeze. Recommended storage time: Up to 9 months.

• To serve cold, thaw in package at room temperature about 2 to 3 hours. To serve hot, place in covered container or aluminum foil wrap and heat in moderate oven (350°F.) until hot, about 20 to 25 minutes. Sprinkle with confectioners sugar.

Wisconsin Coffee Specials

Travel around the world and you'll not find yeast-leavened coffee breads that excel those baked in many Wisconsin country kitchens. Here are two recipes from the Milwaukee area that explain why the cooks there are famous for their yeast breads.

Both Kolaches and Holiday Coffee Cake are perfect with coffee. They taste as good as they look.

Notice the home baker's trick—judging when the dough is light enough to bake by pressing a finger deep into it. If the dent remains, the bread is ready for the oven.

KOLACHES

Fruit topknots on this coffee bread tempt and reward

¾   c. milk
¼   c. sugar
1   tsp. salt

¼   c. soft shortening (part butter)
3 ½   to 4 c. flour
1   egg (room temperature)
2   pkgs. active dry yeast
¼   c. warm water (110 to
        115°F.)

Filling:
1   c. dried prunes
1   c. dried apricots
½   c. sugar
¼   tsp. ground cinnamon
1   tblsp. lemon juice

· Scald milk. Pour into large bowl with sugar, salt and shortening. Cool until lukewarm. Add 1 c. flour; blend in egg. Beat until smooth.
· Add yeast to warm water in small bowl. Let stand 3 to 5 minutes. Stir to dissolve. Add yeast to bowl containing milk-flour mixture. Beat until smooth. Stir in remaining flour, a little at a time. First use a spoon, then the hands. Squeeze dough through fingers to blend. The dough should be soft, but stiff enough to clean sides of bowl.
· Knead dough on lightly floured surface until smooth and elastic. Place in greased bowl; turn once to grease all sides. Cover and let rise in warm place (80 to 85°F.) until doubled, 1 to 1½ hours, or until dent made deep in dough with finger remains.
· Prepare filling. Cover prunes and apricots with water and simmer until tender, 20 to 30 minutes. Cool, drain and chop fruits fine. Combine with remaining ingredients.
· Punch down dough. Let rise 15 more minutes. Shape into 1½" balls. Place smooth side up about 3" apart on lightly greased baking sheet. Cover and let rise 10 minutes.
· Make a dent in each ball by press-

ing finger to the pan. Leave about ½" edge around outside of circle. Spoon filling into center. Brush sides of rolls with melted butter.
· Let rise 20 to 30 minutes. Dent remains when sides of dough are pressed gently with fingers.
· Bake in hot oven (400°F.) until golden brown, 10 to 15 minutes. Remove from baking sheet and cool on racks. Makes about 3 dozen.
· Place cool rolls on baking sheet and put in freezer. When frozen, wrap in foil, label, date and return to freezer. Recommended storage time: Up to 9 months.
· To serve, thaw in wrapper on rack at room temperature about 2 to 3 hours. Or heat frozen rolls, uncovered, in moderate oven (350°F.) 20 to 25 minutes and sprinkle with confectioners sugar.

HOLIDAY COFFEE CAKE

Good yuletide selection but a fine choice for all special occasions

1   c. buttermilk
⅓   c. sugar
1 ½   tsp. salt
2   pkgs. active dry yeast
¼   c. warm water (110 to 115°F.)
4 ¾   to 5 ¼ c. flour
2   eggs
¼   c. soft shortening

Filling:
½   c. strained honey
⅓   c. finely chopped nuts
¼   c. sugar
1   tblsp. grated orange peel
1   tblsp. orange juice
1   tsp. ground cinnamon

⅓ c. raisins
1 tblsp. butter or regular
   margarine

Frosting:
1 c. sifted confectioners sugar
Warm water or light cream

· Heat buttermilk to lukewarm, stirring constantly. (If overheated, it will separate.) Pour into large bowl; add sugar and salt.
· Dissolve yeast in water.
· Beat half the flour into buttermilk mixture; add yeast mixture and continue beating until well blended.
· Add eggs, shortening and more flour, a little at a time. Blend until dough starts to clean sides of bowl. This dough will be soft.
· Turn out on floured surface; knead until smooth and elastic. Round up dough and place in lightly greased bowl. Turn once to grease all sides.
· Cover and let rise in warm place 1 hour or until deep dent, made by pressing finger into dough, remains.
· Prepare filling by mixing together all ingredients except butter.
· Punch down dough. Turn out on floured surface and divide into 2 equal parts. Keep one half covered with cloth. Roll out other half to make a 10″ square. Brush with butter and sprinkle with half the filling. Roll up like jelly roll. Pinch edges into the roll. Turn pinched edge to bottom and seal by rolling back and forth.
· Cut dough into 1″ slices. Place layer of slices in greased 10″ tube cake pan so slices barely touch. For second layer, place slices alternately around the pan; the third layer as the first. Prepare remaining dough and add slices to pan as before.
· Cover and let rise in warm place about 30 minutes or until doubled. Bake in a moderate oven (350°F.) 45 to 60 minutes. Turn out of pan and cool on rack. (Frost after freezing.)
· Wrap with foil, label, date and freeze.
Recommended storage time: Up to 9 months.
· To serve, thaw in wrapper overnight if you want to serve it for breakfast. To serve warm, place thawed coffee cake in moderate oven (350°F.) 20 to 25 minutes.
· Combine sugar and enough warm water for spreading consistency. Spread on heated coffee cake.

Freezing Quick Breads

Be sure to use a double-acting baking powder to leaven the quick breads you freeze.

BISCUITS: You can roll out the dough and cut it. Package the rounds in layers, separated with locker paper. Some Southern cooks prefer to freeze biscuits before baking them, but they sometimes are tough and have a poorer texture and less volume.
Recommended storage time: 2 weeks.

To serve, bake without thawing on a baking sheet in a hot oven (400°F.) 20 to 25 minutes.

Or bake biscuits, cool, store in rigid containers, seal, label, date and freeze.
Recommended storage time: 3 months.

To serve, heat them in a slow oven

(300°F.) 10 to 15 minutes. Many women save leftover biscuits this way.

MUFFINS: Pour the batter into muffin-pan cups lined with paper baking cups. Stack with locker paper between layers. Overwrap with moisture-vaporproof paper. Seal, label, date and freeze.
Recommended storage time: 12 to 14 days.
To serve, thaw at room temperature for 1 hour. Bake as usual.
Or bake the muffins, cool quickly, package, label, date and freeze.
Recommended storage time: 2 to 3 months.
To serve, reheat in a slow oven (300°F.) about 20 minutes.

DOUGHNUTS: Same as for yeast leavened doughnuts.

COFFEE CAKES: Follow directions for fruit and nut breads.

FRUIT AND NUT BREADS: Use your favorite recipes or the ones in this chapter. Bake, cool, package, label, date and freeze.
Recommended storage time: 2 to 3 months.
To serve, thaw in wrapper at room temperature, 1½ to 2 hours.

Or place unthawed in wrapper (if foil wrapped) in slow oven (325° F.) 15 to 25 minutes.
Or pour batter into pans, wrap in moisture-vaporproof material and freeze.
Recommended storage time: Up to 2 months.
To serve, thaw batter at room temperature, but do not let stand longer than necessary. Bake the usual way.

WAFFLES: Bake, cool and freeze in rigid containers with locker paper between waffles. Seal, label and date.
Recommended storage time: 2 to 3 months.
To serve, do not thaw. Reheat in electric toaster, set to "light." Or heat 2 to 3 minutes in a hot oven (400°F.).

PANCAKES: See directions for waffles.
Or pour the waffle or pancake batter into tightly covered containers, seal, label, date and freeze.
Recommended storage time: 1 week.
To serve, thaw at room temperature. Many country cooks like to thaw the batter overnight in the refrigerator to bake for breakfast. Add a little milk if the batter is too thick.

FRENCH TOAST: (See recipe in this chapter.)

Fruited Nut Breads

Many a farm homemaker depends on frozen fruit and nut-filled loaves to make extra-good sandwiches in a hurry. Slice them thin and spread with butter—it's that quick. Or let the guests spread their own. For a

change, you can whip softened cream cheese until fluffy to use for the butter.
"I depend on quick fruit and nut breads on a Sunday summer evening," says one country cook, "when I find our home is as popular as a resort

hotel." She serves sandwiches with tea or coffee. And when she has several kinds of the cake-like breads in the freezer, she arranges dark and light sandwiches on the tray for pleasing color and flavor contrasts.

APRICOT/NUT BREAD

Bits of golden fruit show in sliced bread giving it appetite appeal

2 ¾	c. sifted flour
¾	c. sugar
3	tsp. baking powder
½	tsp. baking soda
½	tsp. salt
2	eggs
¼	c. melted shortening or salad oil
1	c. buttermilk
1 ½	c. dried apricots, cut in thin strips
1	c. chopped nuts

· Sift together dry ingredients, saving out 2 tblsp. flour to coat apricots and nuts.
· Beat eggs well, add melted shortening and buttermilk. Add this mixture to the dry ingredients. Stir only until dry ingredients are moistened. Coat apricots and nuts with the 2 tblsp. flour; fold into batter.
· Pour batter into greased 9×5×3″ loaf pan. Bake in moderate oven (350°F.) about 1 hour. Cool on rack. Makes 1 loaf.
· Wrap, label, date and freeze. Recommended storage time: 2 to 3 months.
· To serve, thaw in wrapper on rack at at room temperature 1½ to 2 hours.

BLACK WALNUT/DATE BREAD

Makes the best bread-and-butter sandwiches you ever tasted

¾	c. black walnuts, finely chopped
1	c. sliced dates
1 ½	tsp. baking soda
½	tsp. salt
¼	c. shortening
¾	c. boiling water
2	eggs
½	tsp. vanilla
1	c. sugar
1 ½	c. sifted flour

· Combine nuts, dates, soda and salt in mixing bowl. Add shortening and water. Let stand 15 minutes, blend.
· Beat eggs slightly, add vanilla. Sift in sugar and flour and stir until dry ingredients are moistened. (This is a very stiff mixture.) Add to date mixture, mixing until well blended.
· Grease 4 soup cans. Pour batter into cans, filling two thirds full. Cover with aluminum foil. Bake in moderate oven (350°F.) 25 minutes. Remove foil and bake 10 minutes longer or until center tests done. Cool 15 minutes on rack, remove from cans. Cool.
· To freeze, leave in cans, wrap, label, and date. Or wrap loaves in foil.
Recommended storage time: 2 to 3 months.
· To serve, thaw in wrapper on rack room temperature 1½ to 2 hours.

LEMON BREAD

Keep this loaf with glazed top on hand for teatime or party sandwiches

⅓	c. melted butter
1 ¼	c. sugar

2   eggs
¼   tsp. almond extract
1 ½   c. sifted flour
1   tsp. baking powder
1   tsp. salt
½   c. milk
1   tblsp. grated lemon peel
½   c. chopped nuts
3   tblsp. fresh lemon juice

• Blend butter and 1 c. sugar; beat in eggs one at a time. Add extract.
• Sift together dry ingredients; add to egg mixture alternately with milk. Blend just enough to mix. Fold in lemon peel and nuts. Turn into greased 8½ × 4½ × 2¾" glass loaf pan.
• Bake in slow oven (325°F.) 70 minutes, or until loaf tests done. (Increase oven to 350° if you use metal pan.)
• Mix lemon juice and ¼ c. sugar; immediately spoon over hot loaf in pan. Cool 10 minutes. Remove from pan; cool on rack. Do not cut for 24 hours. Makes 1 loaf.
• Wrap bread, label, date and freeze. Recommended storage time: 2 to 3 months.
• To serve, thaw in wrapper on rack at room temperature 1½ to 2 hours.

PRUNE/OATMEAL BREAD

Makes really good sandwiches

2   c. sifted flour
3   tsp. baking powder
1   tsp. salt
½   tsp. baking soda
¾   c. sugar
1   c. quick-cooking rolled oats
2   eggs
¼   c. salad oil
1   c. milk
1   c. chopped pitted prunes, uncooked

• Sift flour, baking powder, salt, soda and sugar into bowl. Stir in oats.
• Beat eggs, add salad oil and milk. Add to dry ingredients and stir just enough to moisten. Stir in prunes.
• Pour into greased 9×5×3" loaf pan. Bake in moderate oven (350°F.) about 1 hour. Cool on rack. Makes 1 loaf.
• Wrap bread, label, date and freeze. Recommended storage time: 2 to 3 months.
• To serve, thaw in wrapper on rack at room temperature 1½ to 2 hours.

CRANBERRY/ORANGE BREAD

Favorite Christmas bread in homes of Wisconsin cranberry growers—not cake-like, but rich enough

2   c. sifted flour
1   c. sugar
1 ½   tsp. baking powder
½   tsp. baking soda
1   tsp. salt
½   c. chopped nuts
2   c. fresh cranberries, cut in halves
1   orange, juice and grated peel
2   tblsp. melted shortening
1   egg, well beaten

• Sift together flour, sugar, baking powder, soda and salt. Add nuts and cranberries.
• Combine orange juice, grated peel and shortening in measuring cup and add enough water to fill cup three quarters full. Stir in egg. Pour into dry ingredients, stir just to mix.
• Spoon mixture into a greased 9× 5×3" loaf pan, spreading evenly, but making the corners and sides a little higher than the center.

· Bake in a moderate oven (350°F.) about 1 hour. Remove from pan, cool on rack. Makes 1 loaf.
· Wrap, label, date and freeze. Recommended storage time: 2 to 3 months.
· To serve, thaw in wrapper on rack at room temperature 1½ to 2 hours.

Note: If the cooled bread is wrapped tightly, it may be stored in the refrigerator for a few weeks. Do not slice bread until it is chilled.

HIGH-HAT POPOVERS

They turn golden and puff way up in the oven—a Maine hostess favorite

1	c. sifted flour
¾	tsp. salt
2	eggs, beaten
1	tblsp. melted shortening
1	c. milk

· Sift together flour and salt. Combine eggs, shortening and milk; add to flour. Beat smooth with rotary beater.
· To freeze, grease custard cups generously; fill half full of batter. Set cups on tray and put in freezer.
· To package, dip cups in warm water quickly so frozen batter can be slipped out. Place in plastic freezer bags, seal, label, date and return to freezer. Makes 7 popovers. Recommended storage time: 1 month.
· To bake, put frozen batter back in greased custard cups. Set cups on baking sheet. Place in a cold oven and heat to 400°F. Bake 1 hour.

FROZEN FRENCH TOAST

Don't waste dry bread slices. Make French toast and freeze it

4	eggs, beaten
2	tsp. sugar
½	tsp. salt
¼	tsp. ground nutmeg
¼	tsp. vanilla (optional)
1 ½	c. milk
8	slices day-old bread (very dry)

Butter or regular margarine

· Combine eggs, sugar, seasonings, vanilla and milk in large bowl; beat well. Dip each bread slice so it will absorb as much mixture as possible.
· Brown bread on both sides in butter in skillet over moderate heat. Cool.
· To freeze, lay slices on greased baking sheet; put in freezer. When frozen, stack slices with foil or freezer paper between; wrap, label, date and freeze. Makes 8 slices. Recommended storage time: 2 to 3 months.
· To serve, place frozen bread in toaster until heated through.

CINNAMON/SUGAR DOUGHNUTS

Our best-loved cake-style doughnuts

4	eggs, beaten
⅔	c. sugar
⅓	c. milk
⅓	c. melted shortening
3 ½	c. sifted flour
3	tsp. baking powder
¾	tsp. salt
1	tsp. ground cinnamon
¼	tsp. ground mace or nutmeg

Salad oil

• Beat eggs and sugar until light. Add milk and shortening. Sift dry ingredients together and add to egg-sugar mixture, mixing well. Cover bowl with plastic wrap, refrigerate about 1 hour.
• Remove half the chilled dough from refrigerator to a well-floured pastry cloth or board. Turn over to coat dough with flour. Roll ⅓" thick, cut with floured (3") doughnut cutter. Let rest, uncovered, 10 minutes.
• Heat salad oil 2" deep in electric skillet to 375°F. Drop 3 or 4 doughnuts at a time into hot oil. As doughnuts rise to surface of fat, turn and continue cooking until doughnuts are golden brown on both sides.
• Lift doughnuts from hot oil, letting each doughnut drain a few seconds. Drain on paper towels. Cool on racks.
• Repeat with remaining dough, re-rolling scraps. Makes 22 doughnuts.
• Place in freezer containers, seal, label, date and freeze. Recommended storage time: Up to 2 months.
• To serve, spread doughnuts in pan and heat, uncovered, in slow oven (300°F.) about 20 minutes. Shake them in paper bag with 1 c. sugar mixed with 1 tsp. ground cinnamon.

WHITE NUT BREAD

Checkerboard: Alternate light and dark nut bread sandwiches on tray

¾   c. sugar
2   tblsp. shortening
1   egg
1½ c. milk
3   c. sifted flour
3½ tsp. baking powder
1   tsp. salt

¾   c. chopped hickory nuts or walnuts

• Blend together sugar, shortening and egg. Stir in milk. Sift flour, baking powder and salt together; stir into first mixture. Add nuts.
• Pour into greased 9×5×3" loaf pan. Let stand 20 minutes.
• Bake in moderate oven (350°F.) 60 to 70 minutes or until toothpick inserted in center comes out clean.
• Cool on rack. Makes 1 loaf.
• Wrap, label, date and put in freezer. Recommended storage time: 2 to 3 months.
• To serve, thaw in wrapper at room temperature for 1½ to 2 hours.

BUTTERSCOTCH LOAF

Delicious with taste of brown sugar

2   c. sifted flour
1¼ tsp. baking powder
¾   tsp. baking soda
¼   tsp. salt
½   c. chopped walnuts
1   egg, slightly beaten
1   c. brown sugar, firmly packed
1   c. buttermilk
1   tblsp. melted shortening or salad oil

• Combine flour, baking powder, soda and salt; add walnuts and mix well.
• Combine egg, brown sugar, buttermilk and shortening. Pour into flour mixture and stir only enough to moisten ingredients. Do not beat.
• Turn into a greased 9×5×3" loaf pan and bake in a moderate oven (350°F.) 45 to 50 minutes. Cool. Makes 1 loaf.

· Wrap cooled bread, label, date and freeze.

Recommended storage time: 2 to 3 months.

· To serve, thaw in wrapper at room temperature 1½ to 2 hours.

Note: To avoid crumbling, slice this and other nut breads while partially frozen. Some make-ahead cooks slice the frozen loaf, fit the slices back together, wrap and refreeze it. Then it is ready to serve when thawed.

CHAPTER 6

CAKES, COOKIES AND PIES

Directions for Freezing Baked Goods · Butterscotch Nut Torte, Frozen Cake Roll, Oregon Apple Dapple, Coconut Cupcakes · Recipes for Cakes · Bar, Drop, Rolled and Refrigerator Cookies · Fruit and Berry, Ice Cream, Lemon Meringue, Chiffon Pies, Pies Made with Frozen Fruits and Berries

When people want to give special praise to cakes, cookies and pies, they say they have a "country-kitchen" taste and look—a tribute to farm women. And country cooks depend on freezing these baked foods to relieve the humdrum of meals on busy days, to make entertaining easier.

Of all baked foods, pies and cookies go into farm freezers in the largest quantities. The reasons are simple—they're great farm favorites and timesavers. You can stretch minutes by baking two pies instead of one and doubling the cookie recipe, baking a big batch. When days are crowded, farm homemakers freeze cookie dough to bake when needed. Then they can serve cookies still faintly warm and fragrant from the oven. And if they have several kinds of dough frozen, they can pass an impressive choice of cookies to drop-in guests.

The trend in pies is to freeze fillings to add, unthawed, to pastry at baking time. Fillings frozen in pie pans, then removed, wrapped and put in freezers, are economical of space. Some women prefer to store the fillings in freezer containers or plastic freezer bags, thawing them enough to stir before pouring into pastry-lined pans. If you want to awaken appetites dulled by spring fever, bake Apple/Cranberry Pie—a New Jersey special that in March still has autumn's fresh, tart-sweet taste and rich coloring. You'll have requests for second helpings.

Cakes often go into freezers unfrosted. Farm women find they are easy to wrap and that a frosting quickly spread on before serving gives the cake a freshly made appearance. Be sure to try our Cake Roll, Four Ways, a popular FARM JOURNAL fix-and-forget party dessert introduced to us by a Wisconsin homemaker.

Country Baked Goods
THEY'RE LIKE MONEY IN THE BANK

Farmers put home-baked pies, cakes and cookies high on their list of something wonderful to eat. Their wives know that a supply in the freezer is the badge of a good manager. With these desserts, they are ready for guests and extra people to feed no matter how busy the day. And even if the remainder of the meal is plain-Jane, a cake, tender and rich, a juicy fruit pie or an assortment of cookies makes it special.

The recipes in this chapter are choice. They come from our readers across the country and from our own Countryside Test Kitchens. You won't want to miss any of them. There's nothing like frozen homemade cakes, cookies and pies to give quick meals a carefully planned look and taste.

Freezing Cakes

Most cakes freeze successfully—especially angel food, sponge, butter, chiffon, fruit and pound cakes. One-bowl cakes stay moist because they contain high proportions of shortening and sugar. And many homemakers find that their fruit cakes actually improve in flavor during freezer storage.

Cakes, baked and then frozen, have better volume and are of superior quality to those made from frozen batter. Good country cooks usually cut down on the clove measurement because this spice's flavor tends to strengthen during freezing. They use pure vanilla, too, because the artificial flavor often gives the cake an undesirable taste. Recent research indicates that chocolate cakes made with part butter and vegetable shortening freeze best.

To Freeze Baked Cakes: Cool the cake quickly on racks. (You can speed up the cooling with an electric fan.) If you plan to serve it within a couple of days, you need not be as particular about the wrap. For longer storage, you will want to wrap the cake in moisture-vaporproof packaging material. Because few cakes are solid when frozen, freeze the wrapped cake and then place it in a freezer carton or metal container to prevent crushing. Return to freezer. Many women like to bake, freeze and store cakes in covered cake pans.

Frosted Cakes: If you want to frost a cake before freezing it, an uncooked confectioners sugar frosting is the best choice. You can use a candy-type frosting like fudge or penuche, but it may become brittle and crack after a month of storage. Some good cooks like to use boiled frosting on the special-occasion cakes they freeze. It is difficult to wrap such cakes so the frosting will not stick to the wrapping. One way to reduce the annoyance is to insert toothpicks around edge of cake to hold wrapping so it just misses contact with the frosting.

Always freeze frosted cakes before wrapping. You will find them much easier to handle. You can store confectioners sugar frosting in a rigid freezer container with a tight-fitting lid. When you want to use the frosting, thaw it in the covered container at room temperature. If too thick to spread, stir in a little milk.

Unfrosted Cake: An unfrosted cake thaws more quickly than a frosted one and you can use it in more ways.

Cupcakes: Bake as usual, cool, pack in freezer containers and seal or wrap individually in foil and freeze. Individually wrapped cupcakes may be tied "daisy chain" style in stockinet. Recommended storage time:

Unfrosted cakes, 4 to 6 months

Frosted cakes, 2 to 3 months

Cupcakes, 2 months

To use, *thaw cakes in their wrappers* at room temperature.

Frosted cakes (large), about 2 hours

Unfrosted cake layers, about 1 hour

Cupcakes, 30 minutes

You can reduce defrosting time about one third by thawing wrapped cake in front of an electric fan. Thawing wrapped cake on a rack permits air circulation and speeds up the defrosting.

Note: Some farm women like to thaw unfrosted cake by putting it in a sealed container or aluminum foil wrap and heating it in a very slow oven (250 to 300°F.) for 20 to 25 minutes. They say the heat redistributes the moisture and gives the cake a fresh taste. The trick is not to heat the cake too long and dry it out. An excellent way to thaw frosted cake is to put it, loosely covered, in refrigerator for 3 to 4 hours.

BUTTERSCOTCH NUT TORTE

Keep rich, nutty layers in freezer to frost quickly. Wonderful with coffee

6   eggs, separated
1½ c. sugar
1   tsp. baking powder
2   tsp. vanilla
1   tsp. almond extract
2   c. graham cracker crumbs
1   c. chopped nuts
Whipped Cream Frosting
Butterscotch Sauce

• Beat egg yolks well, slowly adding sugar, then baking powder and flavorings. Mix well.

• Beat egg whites until they hold stiff peaks; fold into yolk mixture. Fold in crumbs and nuts. Pour into two 9″ round layer cake pans, greased and lined with waxed paper.

• Bake in slow oven (325°F.) 30 to 35 minutes. Cool 10 minutes, then remove from pans; frost with Whipped Cream Frosting when completely cooled if you wish to use at once. Pour Butterscotch Sauce over top, letting it drizzle down sides of torte. Or freeze unfrosted. Makes 12 servings.

• To freeze, wrap layers individually, label and date.

Recommended storage time: Unfrosted torte, 6 months.

• To serve, thaw in wrapper at room temperature about 1 hour. Frost.

WHIPPED CREAM FROSTING: Whip 2 c. heavy cream, slowly adding 3 tblsp. confectioners sugar. Spread frosting between layers and over top of torte.

BUTTERSCOTCH SAUCE

¼ c. water
¼ c. melted butter
1 c. brown sugar, firmly
    packed
1 tblsp. flour
1 egg, well beaten
¼ c. orange juice
½ tsp. vanilla

· Add water to melted butter; blend in brown sugar and flour.
· Add egg, orange juice and vanilla and mix well.
· Bring to boil and cook until mixture thickens. Cool thoroughly. Pour over torte so it drizzles down sides.

ROCKY MOUNTAIN CAKE

Black walnuts in the frosting make the "rocks" which give cake its name

2   c. sifted flour
1 ½ c. sugar
1   tblsp. baking powder
1   tsp. salt
1   tsp. ground cinnamon
½   tsp. ground nutmeg
½   tsp. ground allspice
¼   tsp. ground cloves
7   eggs, separated
2   tblsp. caraway seeds
½   c. salad oil
¾   c. ice water
½   tsp. cream of tartar
Rocky Mountain Frosting

· Sift flour, sugar, baking powder, salt and spices together several times.
· Combine egg yolks, caraway seeds, oil and water in large bowl. Add dry ingredients. Beat about 30 seconds at low speed on mixer or 75 strokes by hand. (Add a few drops of lemon extract for different flavor.)
· Add cream of tartar to egg whites. Beat until stiff peaks form.
· Gradually pour egg yolk mixture over beaten whites; gently fold in.
· Pour into ungreased 10″ tube pan. Bake in slow oven (325°F.) 55 minutes, then in moderate oven (350°F.) 10 to 15 minutes.
· Invert pan to cool cake. When completely cool, spread Rocky Mountain Frosting over top and sides of cake.

ROCKY MOUNTAIN FROSTING: In saucepan, blend ½ c. butter with 2½ tblsp. flour and ¼ tsp. salt. Cook 1 minute; do not brown. Add ½ c. milk; cook until thick. While hot, add ½ c. brown sugar, firmly packed; beat well. Add 2 c. confectioners sugar, sifted; beat until thick and creamy. Add 1 tsp. vanilla and 1 c. chopped black walnuts (or other nuts). Spread over top and sides of cooled cake.
· Freeze, wrap, label, date and return to freezer.
Recommended storage time: 2 to 3 months.
· To serve, thaw in wrapper at room temperature about 2 hours.

Note: You can make a double batch of frosting and freeze for that extra cake. If you do not freeze cake, increase amount of cloves to ½ tsp.

FROZEN CAKE ROLL, FOUR WAYS

Basic recipe for cake roll. Look at pictures of cakes in this book

4   eggs, separated
¾   c. sugar

1   tsp. vanilla
¾   c. sifted cake flour
¾   tsp. baking powder
¼   tsp. salt

· Beat egg yolks until light and lemon-colored. Slowly add sugar, beating to cream. Add vanilla; beat.
· Sift together flour and baking powder; gradually add to egg yolk mixture. Beat only until smooth.
· Whip egg whites with salt until stiff, but not dry. Fold into batter.
· Spread batter evenly in greased 15½ × 10½ × 1" jelly roll pan lined with heavily greased brown paper.
· Bake in moderate oven (375°F.) 15 minutes, or until top springs back when lightly touched. Loosen cake edges at once; invert onto clean towel sprinkled with confectioners sugar. Cut off hard edges. Roll up, leaving towel in; cool. Unroll; fill with Strawberry Filling (recipe follows); reroll.
· Wrap, label, date and freeze seam side down.
Recommended storage time; Unfilled rolls, 6 months; filled, up to 1 month.
· To serve, take from freezer, spread top with Strawberry Sauce, slice. Makes 1 roll, or 10 (1") slices. Repeat recipe for Pineapple and Butterscotch Rolls.

CHOCOLATE CAKE ROLL: Follow recipe, sifting ¼ c. cocoa with flour.

CAKE ROLL FILLINGS, SAUCES

BASIC FILLING: Whip 1 c. heavy cream until it begins to thicken. Gradually add 3 tblsp. sugar and ¼ tsp. vanilla (use almond extract instead of vanilla for Pineapple Roll); beat stiff.

STRAWBERRY ROLL: Fold 1 (10 oz.) pkg. frozen strawberry slices, drained, into whipped cream. Spread on cake; roll. Bring to boil ¼ c. strawberry jam and ¼ c. light corn syrup; brush on roll. Serve with Strawberry Sauce.

STRAWBERRY SAUCE: Mix 1 c. strawberry jam and 1 c. light corn syrup; bring to boil. Cool. Makes 1 pint.

PINEAPPLE ROLL: Fold 1 (9 oz.) can crushed pineapple, drained, into whipped cream. Spread over cake; roll. For glaze, bring to boil ¼ c. apricot jam and ¼ c. light corn syrup; brush on top of roll. Serve with Pineapple Sauce.

PINEAPPLE SAUCE: Mix 1 (9 oz.) can crushed pineapple, drained, with 1 c. light corn syrup. Bring to boil and cook until thickened. Makes 1 pint.

BUTTERSCOTCH ROLL: Fold 1 (3 oz.) can chopped pecans into whipped cream. Spread over cake; roll. For glaze, heat ¼ c. light corn syrup and 1 tblsp. melted butter or regular margarine. Brush on top of roll. Sprinkle with ¼ c. chopped pecans. Serve with Butterscotch Sauce.

BUTTERSCOTCH SAUCE: Combine ⅔ c. light corn syrup, 1¼ c. brown sugar, firmly packed, ¼ c. butter and ¼ tsp. salt; boil to heavy syrup; cool. Add 1 (6 oz.) can evaporated milk. Makes about 1 pint.

CHOCOLATE ROLL: Spread whipped cream over cake; roll. Sift ¼ c. confectioners sugar over roll. Serve with Chocolate Sauce.

CHOCOLATE SAUCE: Put 4 squares unsweetened chocolate, ½ c. butter and 2¼ c. evaporated milk in top of double boiler; heat until butter and chocolate melt. Slowly add 3 c. sugar; heat until sugar dissolves. Cool; refrigerate. (Sauce will thicken. If too thick, thin with corn syrup.) Makes 1 quart.

Note: Cake rolls may be filled with different kinds of ice cream, softened just enough to spread, and returned to the freezer. Serve with a sundae sauce.

BOILED RAISIN CAKE

Preferred above all fruit cakes by a Nevada ranch family. Do try it

1 ½	c. sugar
¼	c. cocoa
2 ½	c. water
⅔	c. butter
2	c. raisins
2	tsp. ground cinnamon
½	tsp. ground cloves
½	tsp. ground nutmeg
¼	tsp. ground allspice
½	tsp. salt
3 ½	c. sifted flour
2	tsp. baking powder
1	tsp. baking soda
1	c. chopped walnuts

• Mix sugar and cocoa. Add water, butter, raisins, spices and salt. Boil 4 minutes. Cool to room temperature.
• Sift together flour, baking powder and soda. Add to raisin mixture and mix until well blended. Stir in walnuts. Pour into greased 13×9×2″ pan. Bake in moderate oven (350°F.) 35 minutes or until done. Remove from oven and cool on rack.
• Wrap, label, date and freeze.
Recommended storage time: 6 months.

• To serve, thaw in wrapper at room temperature about 1 to 2 hours.

PINK AND WHITE WONDER CAKE
They'll wonder what makes the bon-bon-pink in filling so pretty and good

1	loaf (9×5×3″) angel food cake
1	qt. vanilla ice cream
2	tblsp. frozen pink lemonade concentrate
1	c. heavy cream, whipped

• Slice cake lengthwise in thirds.
• Stir ice cream to soften or beat with electric beater. With spoon zig-zag partly thawed lemonade concentrate through ice cream.
• Spread ice cream evenly between cake layers; place in freezer.
• Frost cake with whipped cream.
• Wrap, label, date and return to freezer.
Recommended storage time: 1 month.
• To serve, let cake stand at room temperature about 10 minutes.

OREGON APPLE DAPPLE

Two words describe the way this torte tastes—extra-delicious

¼	c. butter or regular margarine
1	c. sugar
1	egg
1	c. sifted flour
1	tsp. baking soda
¼	tsp. salt
1	tsp. ground cinnamon
¼	tsp. ground nutmeg
1	tsp. vanilla
2	c. grated tart apples
½	c. chopped walnuts

• Cream together butter and sugar. Beat in egg.

• Sift together flour, soda, salt and spices. Stir into creamed mixture. Stir in vanilla, apples and nuts.

• Bake in a greased 8″ square pan in moderate oven (350°F.) about 45 minutes. Serve warm with sauce or ice cream. Makes 6 to 8 servings.

• Or freeze. When torte is cool, wrap, label, date and freeze.
Recommended storage time: 2 to 3 months.

• To serve, place unthawed in slow oven (300°F.) 1 to 2 hours. Excellent served with Elin's Sauce, which will keep in the refrigerator 2 to 3 months.

ELIN'S SAUCE: Heat ½ c. butter or regular margarine, ½ c. light cream and 1 c. sugar to boiling point and simmer, stirring occasionally, 20 minutes.

COCONUT CUPCAKES

Coconut serves for frosting, but you may add frosting if you desire

½	c. soft shortening
2	c. sifted cake flour
1	c. sugar
2½	tsp. baking powder
¾	tsp. salt
1	egg, slightly beaten
¾	c. milk
1	tsp. vanilla
Flaked coconut	

• Stir shortening in bowl to soften. Sift in dry ingredients. Add the egg and half the milk. Beat 2 minutes on low speed of mixer. Add rest of milk and vanilla. Beat 1 minute.

• Place paper liners in medium muffin-pan cups. Fill half full with batter. Top each with 1 tsp. coconut.

• Bake in a moderate oven (375°F.) 20 to 25 minutes. Remove from oven, cool on racks. Makes 20 cupcakes.

• Wrap, label and date, or freeze without wrapping, place in plastic freezer bags and return to freezer.
Recommended storage time: 2 months.

• To serve, thaw in wrapping at room temperature, about 1 hour.

CARROT/PECAN CAKE

A spiced, nut cake that keeps well—if you hide it in freezer

1¼	c. salad oil
2	c. sugar
2	c. sifted flour
2	tsp. baking powder
1	tsp. baking soda
1	tsp. salt
2	tsp. ground cinnamon
4	eggs
3	c. grated raw carrots
1	c. finely chopped pecans
Orange Glaze	

• Combine oil and sugar; mix well.

• Sift together remaining dry ingredients. Sift half of dry ingredients into sugar mixture; blend. Sift in remaining half alternately with eggs, one at a time, mixing well after each.

• Add carrots and mix well; then mix in pecans. Pour into lightly oiled 10″ tube pan. Bake in slow oven (325°F.) about 1 hour and 10 minutes. Cool in pan upright. Remove from pan.

• Freeze, wrap, label, date and return to freezer.
Recommended storage time: 2 to 3 months.

• To serve, thaw in wrapper at room temperature 2 hours.

• Split frozen cake into 3 horizontal

layers. Spread Orange Glaze between layers and on top and sides.

ORANGE GLAZE

1	c. sugar
1/4	c. cornstarch
1	c. orange juice
1	tsp. lemon juice

2	tblsp. butter
2	tblsp. grated orange peel
1/2	tsp. salt

• Combine sugar and cornstarch in saucepan. Add juices slowly and stir until smooth. Add remaining ingredients. Cook over low heat until thick and glossy. Cool and spread on cake.

Wonderful Lard Cakes

No collection of FARM JOURNAL's cake recipes is complete without including lard cakes made by the meringue method invented in our Countryside Kitchens. They are treasures in hundreds of recipe files across country. Cakes they produce continue to bring happiness and compliments. And they are never better than when teamed with the frostings and glazes designed especially to glamorize them. Do try these cakes.

ORANGE LARD CAKE

Dress up this cake by sprinkling coconut on freshly spread frosting

2	eggs, separated
1/2	c. sugar
1/3	c. lard
2 1/4	c. sifted cake flour
1	c. sugar
2 1/2	tsp. baking powder
1	tsp. salt
1/4	tsp. baking soda
3/4	c. milk
1/3	c. orange juice, fresh or reconstituted frozen
1/4	tsp. almond extract
	Orange Butter Cream Frosting

• Beat egg whites until frothy. Gradually beat in 1/2 c. sugar. Continue beating until very stiff and glossy.
• In another bowl stir lard to soften. Add sifted dry ingredients and milk. Beat 1 minute, medium speed on mixer. Scrape bottom and sides of bowl constantly.
• Add orange juice, egg yolks and almond extract. Beat 1 minute longer, scraping bowl constantly.
• Fold in egg white mixture.
• Pour into 2 greased and floured 9" round cake pans. Bake in moderate oven (350°F.) 25 to 30 minutes.
• Cool layers in pans on racks 10 minutes; then remove from pans. Frost with Orange Butter Cream Frosting. Or freeze unfrosted cake and frost shortly before serving.
• Freeze; wrap, label, date and return to freezer.
Recommended storage time: 2 to 3 months for frosted cake, 4 to 6 months for unfrosted cake.
• To serve, thaw in wrapper at room temperature about 2 hours.

ORANGE BUTTER CREAM FROSTING: Cream 1/2 c. butter. Gradually add 3 c. sifted confectioners sugar alternately with ⅓ c. orange juice concentrate, thawed, creaming well after each addition until light and fluffy.

YELLOW LARD CAKE

A 2-egg cake with an old-time country taste made in a new way

2	eggs, separated
½	c. sugar
⅓	c. lard
2¼	c. sifted cake flour
1	c. sugar
3	tsp. baking powder
1	tsp. salt
1	c. plus 2 tblsp. milk
1½	tsp. vanilla

Peanut Butter Frosting

· Beat egg whites until frothy. Gradually beat in ½ c. sugar. Continue beating until very stiff and glossy.

· In another bowl stir lard to soften. Add sifted dry ingredients, ¾ c. milk and vanilla. Beat 1 minute, medium speed on mixer. Scrape sides and bottom of bowl constantly.

· Add remaining milk and egg yolks. Beat 1 minute, scraping bowl constantly. Fold in egg whites.

· Pour into 2 greased and floured 9″ round layer cake pans. Bake in moderate oven (350°F.) 25 to 30 minutes. Cool layers on racks 10 minutes; then remove from pans.

· Brush crumbs from cake while warm for ease in frosting. Frost with Peanut Butter Frosting. Or freeze unfrosted, add frosting before serving.

· Freeze; wrap, label, date and return to freezer.

Recommended storage time: 2 to 3 months for frosted cake, 4 to 6 months for unfrosted cake.

· To serve, thaw in wrapper at room temperature about 2 hours.

PEANUT BUTTER FROSTING: Whip ¾ c. crunchy peanut butter with mixer (or wooden spoon). Add ¾ c. cold Basic Sugar Syrup (see recipe in this chapter) gradually, beating.

FUDGE PUDDING CAKE

Made with lard, it's chocolate all the way—moist fudgy cake

⅓	c. lard
3	squares unsweetened chocolate
¾	c. sugar
2	tblsp. cornstarch
1	c. milk
2	c. sifted flour
1	c. sugar
1¼	tsp. baking soda
½	tsp. salt
¾	c. milk
2	eggs

Glossy Fudge Frosting

· Melt lard in 2- or 3-qt. saucepan over low heat. Add chocolate and stir until melted. Remove from heat.

· Mix ¾ c. sugar and cornstarch thoroughly. Stir into chocolate mixture. Add 1 c. milk; stir and cook over low heat until smooth and thick. Remove from heat and cool to room temperature. (Set pan in cold water to speed cooling.)

· Sift remaining dry ingredients together 3 times. Add ½ to chocolate mixture, blend and beat ½ minute (75 strokes). Add ¾ c. milk and blend. Add remaining dry ingredients, blend; beat 1 minute (150 strokes).

· Add eggs, blend and beat ½ minute (75 strokes).

• Bake in paper-lined 13×9×2″ pan in moderate oven (350°F.) about 35 minutes. Cool.
• Frost with Glossy Fudge Frosting.
• Freeze; wrap, label, date and return to freezer.
Recommended storage time: 2 to 3 months.
• To serve, thaw in wrapper at room temperature, about 2 hours.

GLOSSY FUDGE FROSTING

2   tblsp. butter or regular margarine
1   (6 oz.) pkg. semisweet chocolate pieces
⅓   c. Basic Sugar Syrup

• Melt butter over hot (not boiling) water. Remove from heat before the water boils.
• Add chocolate pieces to butter over hot water and stir until melted, blended and thick.
• Add Basic Sugar Syrup gradually, stirring after each addition until blended. Mixture will become glossy and smooth.
• Remove from hot water and cool until of spreading consistency. Spread thinly over cake. Apply quickly by pouring a small amount at a time on top of cake; as it runs down on sides, spread with spatula. Frost top of cake last. Makes frosting for two 8″ layers, or one 13×9×2″ cake.

BASIC SUGAR SYRUP

2   c. sugar
1   c. water

• Boil sugar and water together 1 minute. Pour into jar. Cool, cover and refrigerate. Makes about 2 cups.

Note: Frostings made with Basic Sugar Syrup in higher altitudes (above 3500 feet) take longer and more beating to become thick enough to stay on the cake.

Freezing Cookies

You will kindle delight in your children's eyes if they come home from school to baked cookies from the freezer, or to freshly baked cookies from frozen dough. Take your pick of the two methods, or use both of them at different times, depending on which is more convenient at the moment. Both methods give satisfactory results. Most country cooks prefer to freeze the dough because it takes up less space in the freezer than cookies.

Unbaked Cookies: Here are directions for freezing dough for four types of cookies.

Refrigerator-type:
1. Shape the dough in a roll with a diameter of the desired size. Wrap in plastic wrap or foil; freeze.

To use, thaw just enough to slice with sharp knife, place slices on a lightly greased baking sheet; bake.
2. Or chill the roll of dough in the

refrigerator several hours. Slice and store slices in layers, pieces of plastic wrap or aluminum foil between, in freezer containers. Seal, label, date and freeze. You will reduce the chances of crushing the dough if you hold number of layers to a minimum.

To use, bake slices without thawing.

3. Or pack the dough into empty juice cans, opened at both ends. Seal with foil and freezer tape; label, date and freeze.

To use, remove end wrappings; push out the dough. Slice and bake.

Bar-type:

1. Spread the dough evenly in greased pans; cover with plastic wrap or foil. Seal, label, date and freeze.

To use, bake dough in pan, frozen.

2. Or store dough in wide-topped jar or other freezer container; cover with tight-fitting lid. Seal, label, date and freeze.

To use, thaw dough just enough that you can spread it in a greased pan. Bake as usual.

Drop-type:

1. Store dough in airtight containers and cover or wrap in plastic wrap or foil. Seal, label, date and freeze.

To use, thaw dough at room temperature, just enough that you can drop it from a spoon onto a lightly greased baking sheet. Bake as usual.

2. Or drop dough from spoon onto lightly greased baking sheet and freeze. Remove from freezer, pack unbaked cookies in freezer containers. Cover, seal, label, date and freeze.

To use, bake unthawed cookies.

Rolled-type:

Roll dough, cut and store cutouts in rigid freezer containers with plastic wrap or aluminum foil between layers. Seal, label, date and freeze.

To use, bake unthawed cookies.

Baked Cookies: Cool the cookies quickly when you take them from the oven. Arrange baked cookies in a sturdy box lined with plastic wrap or aluminum foil, separating cookie layers with more plastic wrap or foil. Fold over plastic wrap to cover top of cookies and seal with freezer tape, or press foil over cookies to seal. Close box, label, date and freeze.

To use, let cookies thaw at room temperature in their wrappings. This takes about 10 minutes.

Recommended storage time: Baked and unbaked cookies, 9 to 12 months.

OATMEAL CHIPPERS

All members of the family will like this cookie with chocolate nuggets

½	c. butter or regular margarine
½	c. shortening
1	c. sugar
1	c. brown sugar, firmly packed
2	eggs
1	tsp. vanilla
2	c. sifted flour
1	tsp. baking soda
1	tsp. salt
1	tsp. ground cinnamon
1	tsp. ground nutmeg
2	c. quick-cooking rolled oats
1	(6 oz.) pkg. semisweet chocolate pieces (1 c.)
1	c. chopped walnuts

• Cream together butter and shortening. Add sugars gradually, beating until light and fluffy. Beat in eggs and vanilla. Blend in sifted dry ingredients, mixing thoroughly. Stir in oats, chocolate and nuts.

• Drop by rounded teaspoonfuls 2" apart onto greased baking sheet. Bake in moderate oven (375°F.) 9 to 12 minutes. Makes 8 dozen.

• Cool cookies quickly on racks; package, label, date and freeze.

Recommended storage time: 9 to 12 months.

• To serve, let thaw in containers or wrap a few minutes.

add in thirds to creamed mixture; mix until smooth. Add fruit mixture; blend well. Let stand 1½ hours in refrigerator, or overnight.

• When ready to bake, spread dough in greased 15½ × 10½ × 1" jelly roll pan. Bake in hot oven (400°F.) 15 to 20 minutes, until lightly browned. Cool in pan. When cool, cut in bars about 3 × 1". Makes about 4 dozen.

• Package, label, date and freeze.

Recommended storage time: 9 to 12 months.

• To serve, thaw cookies in containers or wrap a few minutes.

FRUIT BARS

Excellent cookies to mail for gifts—they're good keepers

2	c. seedless raisins
1 ½	c. chopped mixed candied fruit
1	c. chopped walnuts
½	c. orange or pineapple juice
2	tsp. vanilla
1	c. butter or regular margarine
1	c. sugar
1	c. brown sugar, firmly packed
2	eggs, beaten
4 ½	c. sifted flour
2	tsp. ground cinnamon
2	tsp. baking powder
1	tsp. baking soda

• Rinse raisins in hot water, drain; dry on towel.

• Combine raisins, candied fruit, nuts, juice and vanilla; let stand.

• Cream together butter, sugars and eggs. Sift together dry ingredients and

SIX-IN-ONE COOKIES

You make 18 dozen cookies of six flavors from one batch of dough

2	c. butter
1	c. sugar
1	c. light brown sugar, firmly packed
2	eggs, beaten
1	tsp. vanilla
4	c. flour
1	tsp. baking soda
½	tsp. salt

Dough: Cream butter; gradually add sugars. Cream until light and fluffy.

• Add eggs and vanilla; mix well.

• Sift together flour, soda and salt; gradually add to creamed mixture, beating well after each addition.

Flavors: Divide dough in 6 parts. Add ½ c. shredded coconut to one; ½ c. finely chopped pecans to second; ½ tsp. nutmeg and 1 tsp. cinnamon to third; 1 square unsweetened chocolate, melted, to fourth; ¼ c. finely chopped candied cherries to fifth;

leave last portion plain. Chill 30 minutes or longer.
· Shape dough into 6 rolls about 1¾" in diameter.
· Wrap, seal, label, date and freeze. Recommended storage time for dough: 9 to 12 months.
· When ready to use, slice frozen dough ⅛" thick. Bake slices on lightly greased baking sheet in moderate oven (375°F.) 10 to 12 minutes. Cool on racks. Makes 18 dozen.

GINGER COOKIES FOR A CROWD

A big recipe to make when you wish to put cookies in the freezer

5½	c. sifted flour
1	tblsp. baking soda
2	tsp. baking powder
1	tsp. salt
¾	tsp. ground ginger
1	tsp. ground cinnamon
1	c. shortening
1	c. sugar
1	egg, beaten
½	tsp. vanilla
1	c. dark molasses
½	c. strong coffee

· Sift together flour, soda, baking powder, salt, ginger and cinnamon.
· Cream shortening; add sugar gradually; beat until light; add egg and vanilla. Add molasses and coffee, then dry ingredients; mix well; chill.
· Roll out on lightly floured board ¼" thick; cut with round 2" cutter.
· Place about 2" apart on greased baking sheet. Bake in hot oven (400°F.) 8 to 10 minutes. Spread on racks to cool. Makes 12 dozen.

· Package, label, date and freeze. Recommended storage time: 9 to 12 months.
· To serve, thaw cookies in containers or wrap a few minutes.

PEPPER NUTS (WITH LARD)

Nibblers like this new version of pfeffernuesse—a German cookie

½	c. lard
1½	c. sugar
1½	c. light corn syrup
¼	tsp. vanilla
6	c. sifted flour
4½	tsp. baking powder
¼	tsp. salt
¼	tsp. ground cardamom
¼	tsp. ground cinnamon
¼	tsp. ground nutmeg
¼	tsp. ground cloves
¼	tsp. ground allspice
¼	tsp. pepper
½	c. milk

· Cream lard; beat in sugar gradually. Blend in corn syrup and vanilla.
· Add dry ingredients, sifted together, alternately with milk. Roll in strips the width of a pencil on a floured surface. Cut in ½" pieces.
· Place on greased baking sheet and bake in moderate oven (375°F.) about 15 minutes, until browned. Makes 4½ quarts.
· Package, label, date and freeze. Recommended storage time: 6 months if lard contains antioxidant; without, 3 to 4 months.
· To serve, thaw in container or wrap a few minutes. Serve in bowls like nuts or popcorn.

Freezing Pies

Country pie bakers, the best in the world, divide into three groups: those who freeze baked pies, those who freeze pies and bake them later and the up-to-the-minute girls who fix the fillings and freeze them to combine with pastry at baking time. All agree that the freezer saves time and work because it is almost as easy to make two or three pies or fillings as one.

Many kinds of pies freeze successfully, like those with fruit, vegetable (pumpkin, sweet potato and squash) and mincemeat fillings. Chiffon pies with whipped cream or egg whites folded into the gelatin mixture freeze well and do not "weep" when served. On the other hand, custard pie rarely retains its top quality when frozen.

Pie Shells: You can freeze both pastry and crumb crusts, baked or unbaked. Almost every farm cook has her favorite way of packaging unbaked pastry and here is one system some pie bakers like. Roll pastry the size and shape you will need when baking pie. Cut a piece of cardboard the same size and cover it with plastic wrap taped in place or with foil. Lay a layer of pastry flat on the cardboard, top with two layers of plastic wrap or foil, then with another layer of pastry. Repeat until you have several layers. Put this stack in a plastic freezer bag, twist to exclude air and fasten with a twist seal.

To use, remove one piece of pastry from the plastic freezer bag, with a sheet of plastic wrap or foil beneath and on top to prevent moisture from condensing on pastry during thawing.

Thaw at room temperature 10 to 15 minutes, use like freshly made pastry.

Baked and Unbaked Pies: You can freeze pies before or after baking. Both kinds are satisfactory, although frozen unbaked pies often have a soggy undercrust. We recommend freezing baked pies.

Pie and Tart Shells: Bake pie and tart shells and rounds of pastry in a very hot oven (475°F.) 8 to 10 minutes. Cool; package in rigid containers to prevent crushing and overwrap with moisture-vaporproof packaging material. Or freeze without baking, wrap like baked ones.

Recommended storage time: Baked, 4 to 6 months. Unbaked, 2 months.

To serve, heat baked tart and pie shells and pastry rounds in a slow oven (325°F.) 5 to 8 minutes. Put unbaked pie and tart shells and rounds of pastry in a very hot oven (475°F.) 8 to 10 minutes.

If you bake pies in shiny, lightweight aluminum pans, set them on a baking sheet for baking. *Bake and reheat pies on the lower shelf of the oven.* And if you use frozen fruit for the filling, thaw it and drain. Also drain canned fruits. Use only a small part of the juice and thicken it either with tapioca or cornstarch, or a combination of tapioca and cornstarch. You can use flour for thickening, but the filling will not be so clear or bright in color.

Unbaked Pies: When using fresh peaches or raw apples, you need to treat them to prevent darkening. Add 1 tblsp. lemon juice or ¼ tsp. powdered ascorbic acid, mixed with 1 tblsp. water to the peaches for a pie. (Handle apricots like peaches.) Dip the apple slices in a solution of ½ tsp. powdered ascorbic acid and 1 c. water (enough for apples to make 5 pies). Or steam apple slices 2 or 3 minutes and cool quickly. Coat sweet cherries and berries with sugar and flour before adding to pie pan. Freeze the pie and then wrap with plastic wrap and seal with freezer tape. Or wrap in aluminum foil and seal with double fold. Place in plastic freezer bag; seal, label, date and freeze. Recommended storage time: 2 to 3 months.

To serve, unwrap pie and bake on the lower shelf of very hot oven (450°F.) 10 to 15 minutes; complete baking at 375°F. If pie rim browns too quickly, cover with strips of foil.

Baked Pies: Remove the two-crust pies from the oven while crust is light brown. They will brown more when you reheat them. Cool and freeze without wrapping, but be sure the pie is level while freezing. Package like unbaked pies and return to freezer. Recommended storage time: 4 to 6 months.

To serve, partially thaw baked pie in its original wrap at room temperature, about 30 minutes. Unwrap and place on lower shelf of moderate oven (350°F.) 30 minutes, until warm.

Chiffon Pies: Freeze and overwrap like unbaked and baked pies.

Recommended storage time: up to a month. (Some cooks freeze chiffon pies 2 to 3 months, but the longer storage often results in rubbery filling.)

To serve, thaw at room temperature about 45 minutes or in refrigerator 2 to 3 hours. Do not heat.

Pie Fillings: An increasing number of farm homemakers freeze pie fillings rather than pies. They take up less space in the freezer. Freeze fruit pie fillings in foil-lined pans, remove filling from pans, overwrap and return to freezer. Place the unwrapped, unthawed filling in pastry-lined pan, add top crust and bake in a hot oven (425°F.) from 10 to 20 minutes longer than for pie with unfrozen filling. Or thaw filling until you can almost stir it before adding to pastry. Recommended storage time: 2 to 3 months.

Among the favorite mixes containing eggs for freezing are those for pumpkin, squash and sweet potato pies. The usual method is to combine the vegetable, milk, sugar and eggs. Some cooks omit the spices, especially cloves, which increase in strength during storage, and add them at baking time. Recommended storage time: 5 weeks.

To serve, partially thaw the filling in its container. Add spices if needed. Pour filling into pastry-lined pans and bake pies in the regular way, in a hot oven (400°F.) 45 to 55 minutes, adding 10 to 15 minutes because filling is cold. Test for doneness by inserting a knife 1″ from side of filling to see if it comes out clean.

STRAWBERRY CHIFFON PIE

Pie is lovely in color and flavor

Baked 9" pie shell
¼   c. sugar
1   envelope unflavored gelatin
1   (10 oz.) pkg. frozen
       strawberry halves, thawed
3   egg whites
¼   tsp. cream of tartar
Dash of salt
⅓   c. sugar
½   c. heavy cream, chilled

· Stir together in saucepan ¼ c. sugar and gelatin; add strawberries and cook over medium heat, stirring constantly, just until mixture reaches a boil. Remove from heat at once. Set pan in bowl of ice water to chill. Stir occasionally while chilling. Chill until mixture mounds slightly when dropped from a spoon.

· Beat egg whites with cream of tartar, salt and ⅓ c. sugar until mixture is stiff and glossy (do not underbeat). Fold into strawberry mixture.

· Beat cream until stiff; fold into strawberry mixture. Pile into pie shell. Freeze; then overwrap and return to freezer.

Recommended storage time: Up to 1 month.

· To serve, thaw in refrigerator 2 to 3 hours, or at room temperature about 45 minutes. To use without freezing,

PEACH PIE FILLING

Stack several of these in your freezer when peaches are ripe

4   qts. sliced peeled peaches
       (9 lbs.)
1   tsp. powdered ascorbic acid

1   gal. water
3½   c. sugar
½   c. plus 2 tblsp.
       quick-cooking tapioca
¼   c. lemon juice
1   tsp. salt

· Place peaches in large container. Dissolve ascorbic acid in water and pour over peaches. Drain.

· Combine peaches, sugar, tapioca, lemon juice and salt.

· Line four 8" pie pans with heavy-duty aluminum foil, letting it extend 5" beyond rim. Divide filling evenly between pans. Makes fillings for four 9" pies.

To freeze, fold foil loosely over fillings; freeze. Remove from freezer, turn filling from pans and wrap snugly with foil. Return to freezer.
Recommended storage time: 6 months.

To bake, remove foil from frozen pie filling and place it, unthawed, in a pastry-lined 9" pie pan. Dot with butter and if you like, sprinkle on ¼ tsp. ground nutmeg or cinnamon. Adjust top crust; flute edges and cut vents. Bake in hot oven (425°F.) 1 hour and 10 minutes or until syrup boils with heavy bubbles that do not burst.

APPLE/CRANBERRY PIE FILLING

Taste-testers voted pies made with frozen filling extra-good and pretty

3   c. sliced peeled apples
2   c. cranberries
1¾   c. sugar
¼   c. flour
1   tsp. ground cinnamon
1½   tsp. melted butter

refrigerate until set, about 3 hours.

• Combine all ingredients. Arrange in a 9" pie pan lined with heavy-duty aluminum foil, letting foil extend 5" beyond rim. Freeze like Peach Pie Filling.

Recommended storage time: 3 months.

• To bake, remove foil and place in pastry-lined 9" pie pan without thawing. Top with pastry strip lattice.

• Bake in a hot oven (425°F.) 1 hour and 10 minutes.

CONCORD GRAPE COBBLER

What a midwinter treat! It's bound to get a royal table reception

10	c. stemmed and washed grapes
2	c. sugar
2 ½	tblsp. quick-cooking tapioca
¼	tsp. salt
⅛	tsp. ground cinnamon
2	tblsp. lemon juice
1	tblsp. butter
Biscuit Topping	

• Slip skins from grapes; set aside. Heat pulp to boiling; rub through coarse sieve or food mill to remove seeds. Discard seeds.

• Combine sugar, tapioca, salt and cinnamon. Add lemon juice and grape pulp. Cook until thickened, stirring.

• Remove from heat; add skins; mix.

• Pour into 8" square foil-lined baking pan; cool and freeze.

• Remove block of filling from pan; overwrap and return to freezer.

Recommended storage time: 2 to 3 months.

• To serve, return unthawed filling to pan. Dot with butter. Bake in hot oven (400°F.) about 35 to 40 minutes until bubbling, stir occasionally.

• Remove from oven, cover with Biscuit Topping; return to oven and bake about 20 minutes. Serve warm. Makes 9 servings.

Note: This filling will make two 8 or 9" pies. Pour into foil-lined pie pans; cool and freeze. Remove from pans; overwrap and return to freezer.

Recommended storage time: up to 3 months.

• To serve, place unthawed filling in pastry-lined pan; dot with butter; top with lattice crust. Bake in very hot oven (475°F.) 15 minutes; reduce oven to 375°F. and cover pastry rim with foil; bake 40 to 50 minutes.

BISCUIT TOPPING

1 ½	c. sifted flour
2 ¼	tsp. baking powder
1	tblsp. sugar
¼	tsp. salt
¼	c. butter or regular margarine
¼	c. milk
1	egg, slightly beaten

• Sift together dry ingredients.

• Cut in butter. Make well in center; add milk and egg all at once; stir with fork until mixture is a soft dough. Turn out on lightly floured pastry cloth and knead dough 10 times. Roll dough into 9×7" rectangle; cut in seven 9" strips. Place 4 strips on hot filling one way, lattice other 3 strips opposite way. Start with center strip. Bake as directed.

ROSY CRAB APPLE PIE

Red, red apples make the prettiest pie

Pastry for 2-crust pie
1	c. sugar
1	tblsp. flour
¼	tsp. salt
6	c. finely chopped unpeeled crab apples
1	tsp. vanilla
1½	tblsp. lemon juice
⅓	c. water
1½	tblsp. butter

• Combine sugar, flour and salt; toss together with apples.
• Pour apple mixture into pastry-lined 9" pie pan. Sprinkle with mixture of vanilla, lemon juice and water. Dot with butter. Cover with top pastry; flute edges and cut vents.
• Bake in very hot oven (450°F.) 10 minutes, reduce heat to 375°F. and bake about 45 minutes. Cool.
• Put cooled baked pie in freezer. When frozen, wrap, label, date and return to freezer.

Recommended storage time: 4 to 6 months.
• To serve, partially thaw pie in its wrapping at room temperature, about 30 minutes. Unwrap, place on lower shelf of a moderate oven (350°F.) for 30 minutes, or until warm.

In our Countryside Kitchens we also liked the unbaked pie. Freeze it, then wrap like the baked pie and return to freezer.

Recommended storage time: 2 to 3 months.
• To serve, bake unthawed on lower shelf of preheated very hot oven (450°F.) about 15 minutes; reduce heat to 375°F. and bake about 45 minutes or until done.

Note: Before mixing filling, steam apple bits 1 to 2 minutes and cool quickly to preserve color.

PINK PARTY PIE

FARM JOURNAL'S *famous ice cream pie*

1	recipe Pink Pastry
1	qt. strawberry ice cream
1	(10 oz.) pkg. frozen strawberries, thawed and drained
2	egg whites
¼	tsp. cream of tartar
¼	c. sugar

Few drops red food color

• Line a 9" pie pan with Pink Pastry and bake as directed (see recipe which follows).
• Pile softened ice cream into pie shell and spread; freeze overnight.
• You can wrap, label, date and store in freezer.

Recommended storage time: 2 to 3 weeks.
• To serve, heat oven to extremely hot (500°F.) Arrange strawberries on ice cream.
• Make meringue with egg whites, cream of tartar and sugar. Tint a delicate pink. Spread over pie, covering edges so ice cream will not melt.
• *Set pie on wooden bread board* in oven and bake about 5 minutes, or until lightly browned. Serve at once.

VARIATION

PINK AND WHITE PARTY PIE: Put 2 c. fresh strawberries in baked pie shell, top with 1 pt. vanilla ice cream, 1 c. berries and meringue. Brown.

PINK PASTRY

Good standard pastry recipe—you can of course omit the food color

1	c. sifted flour
½	tsp. salt
⅓	c. lard
3	to 4 drops red food color
2	tblsp. water

• Mix sifted flour and salt; cut in lard with pastry blender. Add food color to water. Sprinkle on the water and mix with a fork until all the flour is moistened. Gather the dough together and press firmly into a ball. Line pie pan with pastry; flute edges and prick pastry. Bake in hot oven (425°F.) 8 to 10 minutes. Cool. Makes enough pastry for 1 (8 or 9") pie shell.

Note: You can substitute ⅓ c. plus 1 tblsp. hydrogenated fat for the lard.

LEMON MERINGUE PIE SUPREME

Meringue billows top nippy, butter-cup-yellow filling—a luscious pie

	Baked 9" pie shell
7	tblsp. cornstarch
1½	c. sugar
¼	tsp. salt
1½	c. hot water
3	egg yolks, beaten
2	tblsp. butter or regular margarine
1	tsp. grated lemon peel
½	c. fresh lemon juice
3	egg whites (room temperature)
¼	tsp. cream of tartar
6	tblsp. sugar

• Mix cornstarch, 1½ c. sugar and salt in saucepan; gradually stir in hot water. Cook over direct heat, stirring until thick and clear, about 10 minutes.
• Remove from heat. Stir ½ c. hot mixture into yolks; stir this back into hot mixture. Cook over low heat, stirring constantly, 2 to 3 minutes. Remove from heat; stir in butter. Add lemon peel and juice, stirring until smooth. Cool. Pour into pie shell.
• Beat egg whites with cream of tartar until frothy; gradually beat in 6 tblsp. sugar, a little at a time. Beat until meringue stands in firm, glossy peaks. Spread meringue on filling, making sure it touches inner edge of crust all around pie.
• Bake in moderate oven (350°F.) 15 minutes, until lightly browned; cool.
• Place in freezer. When frozen, wrap in plastic wrap or aluminum foil and place in plastic freezer bag or box. Seal, label, date and return to freezer. Recommended storage time: Up to 1 month.
• To serve, remove from freezer 2 to 3 hours before serving.

FLORIDA ORANGE/LIME PIE

Just the pie to end a heavy meal—it's tart-sweet, light and airy

2	baked 9" pie shells
1	envelope unflavored gelatin
⅔	c. orange juice
8	egg yolks
⅔	c. sugar
2	tblsp. grated orange peel
½	c. lime juice (or lemon)
8	egg whites
½	tsp. salt
1	c. sugar

• Stir gelatin into orange juice.

· Combine egg yolks, ⅔ c. sugar, orange peel and lime juice in top of double boiler. Stir until smooth. Cook over boiling water, stirring constantly, until thickened.

· Add orange-gelatin mixture; stir well. Remove from heat.

· Beat egg whites with salt added until stiff. Gradually beat in 1 c. sugar. Fold in hot orange mixture. Pour into pie shells. Chill until set. Makes 2.

· Freeze. When frozen, wrap, label and date. Return to freezer. Recommended storage time: Up to 1 month.

· To serve, unwrap and thaw in refrigerator 1 hour. Spread top with whipped cream.

CHOCOLATE/WALNUT PIE

Rich dessert with snowy coconut halo to serve at your next club luncheon

Baked 9″ pie shell
30   marshmallows
1   c. milk
1   tsp. vanilla
⅛   tsp. salt
1   c. heavy cream, whipped
½   c. chopped walnuts
½   c. grated sweet cooking
      chocolate
¼   c. shredded or flaked coconut
2   tblsp. grated sweet
      chocolate

· Put marshmallows and milk in top of double boiler. Cook over boiling water until marshmallows are melted, stirring occasionally. Cool.

· Fold in vanilla, salt, whipped cream, walnuts and ½ c. grated sweet chocolate. Pour into pie shell. Sprinkle with coconut and 2 tblsp. chocolate.

· Place in freezer; when frozen, wrap, label, date and return to freezer. Recommended storage time: Up to 1 month.

· To serve, thaw in refrigerator.

Wonderful Pies Made with Frozen Fruits

If you want to rate as the county's best pie baker, use frozen fruits for fillings when the fresh are out of season. Thicken with a mixture of quick-cooking tapioca and cornstarch for a just-right filling—clear, smooth juices, neither too thick nor too runny.

Combine two fruits for new taste adventures. You will have an unforgettable pie.

We developed some recipes for pies made with frozen fruits in our Countryside Kitchens. When you bake them, be sure to notice the proportions of sugar to fruit. The thickenings are adjusted to them.

Which pie will you bake first, Double Cherry, Peach/Strawberry or Golden Peach? After you taste one or all of them, you may decide to freeze fruits sweetened especially for these pie fillings. Or you may prefer to buy them at your supermarket.

COUNTRY BLUEBERRY PIE

Tastes as if you rushed berries from the blue thickets into the pie

Pastry for 2-crust pie
3   c. frozen blueberries
Blueberry juice

Water
¾   c. sugar
2   tblsp. quick-cooking tapioca
1 ½ tblsp. cornstarch
1   tsp. lemon juice

• Thaw berries until most of free ice has disappeared. Drain off juice, measure and add water to make ½ c. liquid; stir into mixture of sugar, tapioca and cornstarch in saucepan. Heat rapidly until thickening is complete. Boiling is not necessary. Cool.

• Add berries and lemon juice to cooled, thickened juice. Pour filling into pastry-lined 9″ pie pan. Adjust top crust; flute edges and cut vents.

• Bake in hot oven (425°F.) 30 minutes, or until nicely browned. For a brown undercrust, bake on lowest oven shelf. When pie is cool, put in freezer; when frozen, package, label, date and return to freezer. Recommended storage time: 4 to 6 months.

Note: Blueberries in this recipe are frozen without sugar.

PERFECT CHERRY PIE

Once they taste this pie, you'll freeze cherries just to make it

Pastry for 2-crust pie
3   c. pitted tart frozen cherries
1   c. tart cherry juice
3   tblsp. sugar
2   tblsp. quick-cooking tapioca
1 ⅔ tblsp. cornstarch (5 tsp.)
⅛   tsp. almond extract

• Thaw cherries until most of the free ice has disappeared. Drain off the juice; measure and stir it into mixture of sugar, tapioca and cornstarch in

saucepan. Heat rapidly until thickening is complete. Boiling is not necessary. Set aside to cool.

• Add cherries and extract to cooled, thickened juice. Pour filling into pastry-lined 9″ pie pan. Adjust top crust; flute edges and cut vents.

• Bake in hot oven (425°F.) 30 to 35 minutes, or until nicely browned. For a brown undercrust, bake on lowest oven shelf. When pie is cool, put in freezer. When frozen, package, label, date and return to freezer. Recommended storage time: 4 to 6 months.

Note: Proportions of sugar, tapioca and cornstarch are based on 5 parts cherries frozen with 1 part sugar.

DOUBLE CHERRY PIE

Two kinds of cherries between the same crust make a doubly good pie

Pastry for 2-crust pie
2   c. pitted tart frozen cherries
1   c. pitted dark sweet frozen cherries
⅔   c. tart cherry juice
⅓   c. sweet cherry juice
¼   c. sugar
2 ⅓ tblsp. quick-cooking tapioca
1 ½ tblsp. cornstarch
1   tsp. lemon juice

• Thaw cherries until most of the free ice has disappeared. Drain off juices, measure and stir into mixture of sugar, tapioca and cornstarch in saucepan. Heat rapidly until thickening is complete. Boiling is not necessary. Set aside to cool.

• Add cherries and lemon juice to cooled, thickened juice. Pour filling

into pastry-lined 9" pie pan. Adjust top crust; flute edges and cut vents.
· Bake in hot oven (425°F.) 30 to 35 minutes, or until nicely browned. For a brown undercrust, bake on lowest oven shelf. When pie is cool, put in freezer. When frozen, package, label, date and return to freezer. Recommended storage time: 4 to 6 months.

Note: Proportions of sugar, tapioca and cornstarch are based on 5 parts cherries frozen with 1 part sugar.

GOLDEN PEACH PIE

Winter pie—juicy and luscious with summer's fresh peach taste

Pastry for 2-crust pie
3	c. frozen sliced peaches
1	c. peach juice
1 ½	tblsp. brown sugar
1 ½	tblsp. sugar
2 ⅓	tblsp. quick-cooking tapioca
1 ½	tblsp. cornstarch
⅛	tsp. ground cinnamon
1	tsp. lemon juice

· Thaw peaches until most of free ice has disappeared. Drain off the juice, measure and stir it into mixture of sugars, tapioca, cornstarch and cinnamon in saucepan. Heat rapidly until thickening is complete. Boiling is not necessary. Set aside to cool.
· Add peaches and lemon juice to cooled, thickened juice. Pour filling into pastry-lined 9" pie pan. Adjust top crust; flute edges and cut vents.
· Bake in hot oven (425°F.) 30 minutes, or until nicely browned. For a brown undercrust, bake on lowest oven shelf. When pie is cool, put in

freezer. When frozen, package, label, date and return to freezer. Recommended storage time: 4 to 6 months.

Note: Proportions of sugar, tapioca and cornstarch are based on 5 parts peaches frozen with 1 part sugar.

PEACH/STRAWBERRY PIE

Tune your ears for compliments when forks cut into this lovely pie

Pastry for 2-crust pie
1 ½	c. frozen sliced peaches
1 ½	c. frozen strawberries
½	c. peach juice
½	c. strawberry juice
3	tblsp. sugar
2 ½	tblsp. quick-cooking tapioca
1 ½	tblsp. cornstarch
1	tsp. lemon juice

· Thaw fruit until most of free ice has disappeared. Drain off the juices and measure, then stir into mixture of sugar, tapioca and cornstarch in saucepan. Heat rapidly until thickening is complete. Boiling is not necessary. Set aside to cool.
· Add fruit and lemon juice to cooled, thickened juice. Pour filling into pastry-lined 9" pie pan. Adjust top crust; flute edges and cut vents.
· Bake in hot oven (425°F.) 30 to 35 minutes or until nicely browned. For a brown undercrust, bake on lowest oven shelf. When pie is cool, put in freezer. When frozen, package, label, date and return to freezer. Recommended storage time: 4 to 6 months.

Note: Proportions of sugar, tapioca and cornstarch are based on 5 parts peaches frozen with 1 part sugar; 4 parts strawberries frozen with 1 part sugar.

VARIATION

PEACH/BLUEBERRY PIE: Substitute blueberries for strawberries. If blueberries were frozen unsweetened, use ⅓ c. sugar; add water to the combined fruit juices to make 1 c. liquid.

WONDERFUL STRAWBERRY PIE

The best two-crust strawberry pie you'll ever make or taste

Pastry for 2-crust pie
2 ⅔	c. frozen strawberries
1 ⅓	c. strawberry juice
3	tblsp. sugar
2 ½	tblsp. quick-cooking tapioca
1 ½	tblsp. cornstarch
1	tsp. lemon juice

• Thaw berries until most of free ice has disappeared. Drain off the juice; measure and stir it into mixture of sugar, tapioca and cornstarch in saucepan. Heat rapidly until thickening is complete. Boiling is not necessary. Set aside to cool.

• Add berries and lemon juice to cooled, thickened juice. Pour filling into pastry-lined 9″ pie pan. Adjust top crust; flute edges and cut vents.

• Bake in hot oven (425°F.) 30 minutes, or until nicely browned. For a brown undercrust, bake on lowest oven shelf. When pie is cool, put in freezer. When frozen, package, label, date and return to freezer.

Recommended storage time: 4 to 6 months.

Note: Proportions of sugar, tapioca and cornstarch are based on 4 parts strawberries frozen with 1 part sugar.

CHAPTER 7

MAIN DISHES

Directions for Cooking, Cooling, Freezing and Serving · Recipes for Hamburger Mix, Busy-Day Meat Mix, Meat Loaves, Swiss Steak, Pot Roast, Beef Stroganoff, Stuffed Peppers · Macaroni and Cheese · Chicken Dishes, Stuffed Crepes and Hot Tamales · Liver Paste, Ham Combinations, Chop Suey, Sausage Casseroles · Seafood Scallop, Shrimp Creole · Barbecued Lima Beans · Baked Beans · Busy-Day Chicken Dinner Menu, Chicken Mounds · Menu for Meat Loaf Dinner · Menu for Fish Dinner, Mustard-Glazed Tuna Cups

Listen to a group of farm women discuss frozen main dishes and you'll notice great changes in country cooking. You'll know why meals on the busiest days are now so wonderfully good. Homemakers fix them weeks ahead on less crowded days. These dishes are so hearty that they are almost a meal by themselves.

Most country cooks like best to freeze slow-cooking food combinations—those that must bubble lazily over low heat. They couldn't possibly fix them when they have almost no cooking time. Stewed chicken is one; baked beans another. And Meat Ball Chowder is our classic—you'll find the recipe in this chapter. Several farm women keep a supply of it in their freezers so they will have the right food to tote to community suppers even if they can spend little time in the kitchen. Such dishes give the impression the cook wasn't in a hurry—a tribute to her good management.

Of course, you have to reheat frozen main dishes, but most of them take care of themselves. A Western ranch mother, whose teen-age daughter takes music lessons and participates in many after-school activities, calls her specialties shove-in-the-oven dishes. She puts one in the oven to heat for dinner before she drives to town to bring her daughter home. An excellent dinner is on the table within 10 minutes after they step into the kitchen. Magic? No, just intelligent, planned use of the freezer.

Take golden, puffed Broccoli Soufflé (recipe, page 53) proudly to the table—everyone will rave over this spectacular vegetable dish, revel in its fine flavor. Oven-ready for your freezer.

Men like the taste of Sunday Swiss Steaks (recipe, page 132); their wives like to have the frozen steaks heating in a slow oven while they're at church. Ranchero Pot Roast (recipe, page 133) also freezes well.

These two bread winners—Crusty French Bread and Orange Cinnamon Swirl (recipes, pages 88, 91)—freeze well. You reheat them to fill the kitchen with come-hither aroma and to melt butter as it's spread.

Serve your guests Rocky Mountain Cake (recipe, page 108), a grand finale for gala meals. Its beauty tempts; its blended black walnut, caraway, spice flavor delights. An excellent chiffon cake.

Hearty Main Dishes
FREEZE THEM AND YOU'RE MEALS AHEAD

Farm women agree that nothing helps more in getting meals easily, when they must rush, than main dishes to transfer from freezer to range. Carefully chosen recipes, like those that follow, result in food with a fresh-cooked taste.

Many homemakers on less busy days like to make two main dishes at a time—one to serve that day, the other, cooked a little less, to freeze for use later. They say it takes little more time to fix two than one.

Steps to Freezing Main Dishes

Select Ingredients of Good Quality: Especially is this important with the shortening you use. Make certain it is fresh and of high quality, for it has much to do with how successfully dishes freeze. Lard sometimes changes in flavor after frozen 4 months.

Do Not Overcook: Add vegetables, like those for stews and soups, near the end of the cooking period. They should not be tender because you will cook them more when reheating to serve. The meat should be tender, but firm. If you completely cook macaroni, spaghetti, noodles and rice, they will be soft and mushy when served. Parboiled rice is excellent for freezing. Cook it only until the hard center disappears, about 20 minutes. Overcooking not only destroys the texture of foods, but it also gives them a warmed-over taste.

Cool Cooked Foods Quickly: This will stop the cooking. Loss of flavor is rapid when foods are held at high temperatures, and spoilage bacteria develop quickly. To hasten cooling, set the saucepan of cooked food in

a large pan of cold water (ice water is best). Stir it occasionally with a rubber spatula, using care not to break up or mash the food. When you store a main dish in a Pyroceram or metal container, you can cook and freeze it in the same utensil. A timesaver!

Pack Food Solidly: A solid pack helps keep out the air. If you pour sauces or gravies over meat, they fill the air spaces and crowd out the air. The meat will taste better.

Thaw in Refrigerator: You can *partially thaw* main dishes at room temperature. If you want to *thaw them completely, place in refrigerator.* There is danger of spoilage if you leave them at room temperature too long, especially in warm weather. You can reheat many of the main dishes in this chapter without thawing.

Reheat Correctly: You can quickly reheat and thaw the food in a saucepan containing a small amount of melted butter. Or you can set it over low heat, watching and stirring it frequently. Put a covered casserole in a moderate oven (350°F.) or a hot oven (400°F.); it usually heats in about 1 to 1½ hours. Or defrost it in refrigerator overnight before reheating or at room temperature until partly thawed. Reheat foods that scorch easily, like stews and creamed dishes, in a double boiler about 30 to 45 minutes, breaking up the chunks of frozen food carefully. *Time for thawing and reheating is approximate.*

Rotate Frozen Dishes: Keep frozen dishes going to the table and new ones coming into the freezer. Almost all combination dishes lose flavor after 3 to 4 months. It is a good idea to use them within 6 to 8 weeks.

How to Adapt Favorite Recipes

Almost all families have special dishes they like. Often slight changes make them satisfactory for freezing. Here are some facts to keep in mind:

Flavor Changes: Cloves, garlic, black pepper, green peppers, pimiento and celery increase in flavor during freezing. Use them more sparingly. You may wish to add more onion because its flavor often decreases. Salt and chili powder sometimes decrease in strength.

Casserole Toppings: Add bread crumbs and grated cheese at reheating time rather than before freezing.

Rice and Macaroni: Some combination dishes that contain rice, macaroni, spaghetti and noodles may appear dry when taken from the freezer. *Add a little milk or water, about ⅓ c., when reheating them.*

Chopped Cooked Meats: Freeze them in sauces or gravies to prevent their drying out.

Turkey Fat: It becomes rancid more quickly than chicken fat. Use chicken broth, when available, for making turkey dishes to freeze.

Fat in Sauces and Gravies: It often separates in freezing. Whipping while heating often will recombine it. In making gravy or sauce, use a minimum amount of fat and remove sauce from heat when it starts to thicken. The uncooked flour or cornstarch will finish cooking when reheated.

Beans: Small white beans (navy) are good freezers. Some varieties get mushy.

HAMBURGER MIX

This basic recipe came from Arizona—a busy cook's special

2	c. chopped onions
3	cloves garlic
2	c. chopped celery
¼	c. fat
4	lbs. ground beef
4	tsp. salt
½	tsp. pepper
3	tblsp. Worcestershire sauce
2	(14 oz.) bottles ketchup

• Put onions, garlic and celery in large skillet and cook in fat until soft. (Run toothpick through garlic to aid in removal.) Add ground beef; cook until pink color disappears. Remove garlic and discard.

• Add remaining ingredients; simmer 20 minutes. Cool quickly. Skim off excess fat. Makes 6 pints.

• Pack in moisture-vaporproof containers; seal, label, date and freeze. Recommended storage time: 3 to 6 months.

• To use, partially thaw in container in refrigerator overnight or if container is airtight, under running cold water. Thaw until mixture will slip out of container. Use Hamburger Mix in recipes that follow.

HAMBURGER-FILLED BUNS

Freezer to table with little work

3   c. Hamburger Mix
8   hot buttered buns

• Heat partially thawed Hamburger Mix. Serve between hot buns, buttered. Makes 8 sandwiches.

VARIATION

STUFFED ROLLS: Spoon 2½ c. thawed Hamburger Mix generously between wiener buns, split. Wrap in foil or place in tightly covered pan and heat in moderate oven (350°F.) 30 minutes. Makes 8 sandwiches.

HAMBURGER/NOODLE CASSEROLE

Good "dress-up" for leftover corn, carrots, green and lima beans, peas

1½   c. noodles, uncooked
2   c. Hamburger Mix, partly thawed
1   c. canned or cooked vegetables
½   c. grated cheese
1   tsp. chopped parsley

• Cook noodles in boiling salted water until tender; drain.

• Heat Hamburger Mix in skillet. Stir in noodles and vegetables. Sprinkle cheese and parsley over the top.

• Heat, covered, over low heat until cheese melts. Makes 4 to 6 servings.

BUSY-DAY MEAT MIX

The best way to salvage roast beef, lamb or veal—it has many uses

4   c. ground cooked meat
½   lb. bulk pork sausage
2   c. bread cubes
2   eggs, slightly beaten
1   (4 oz.) can chopped mushrooms
¼   c. chopped parsley
1   tsp. salt
¼   tsp. pepper
2   tsp. Worcestershire sauce
1   can condensed cream of mushroom soup

• Mix all ingredients. Makes 3 pints.

• Pack into freezer containers, seal, label, date and freeze. Recommended storage time: 2 to 3 months.

• To use, partially thaw and use to stuff cabbage leaves, green peppers or squash, or as a filling for biscuit rolls or pastry turnovers, which may be prepared and frozen. Or you can make individual meat loaves.

INDIVIDUAL MEAT LOAVES: Shape Busy-Day Meat Mix in ½ c. measure. Makes 12 individual loaves.
· Freeze on baking sheet; wrap individually in foil or plastic wrap, label, date and return to freezer.
· To serve, remove wrapping, place frozen in baking pan. Bake in moderate oven (375°F.) 45 minutes.

COLORADO MEAT LOAVES

Individual frozen meat loaves cook quicker than a single big loaf

2   eggs
1   c. milk
2   c. soft bread crumbs
2   tsp. salt
1   tsp. dry mustard
1   tsp. celery salt
¼   tsp. pepper
6   tblsp. grated onion
2   lbs. ground beef

· Beat eggs slightly in large bowl; blend in milk. Add remaining ingredients. Mix thoroughly.
· Shape mixture into 12 small loaves. Makes 6 to 8 servings.
· Place on baking sheet; freeze. When frozen, remove from freezer, package in foil or plastic wrap, label and date. Return to freezer.
Recommended storage time: 2 to 3 months.
· To serve, place frozen loaves, uncovered, in baking pan. Bake in moderate oven (375°F.) 45 minutes.

MEAT LOAF

Good gravy comes with this tasty loaf

2   eggs, slightly beaten
½   c. ketchup

¾   c. warm water
1   (1½ oz.) pkg. onion soup mix
1½   c. soft bread crumbs
2   lbs. ground beef

· Mix eggs, ketchup, water, onion soup mix and crumbs; blend into beef. Shape into loaf. Makes 8 servings.
· Wrap, label, date and freeze. Recommended storage time: 2 to 3 months.
· To serve, bake frozen loaf, uncovered, in shallow pan in very hot oven (450°F.) 45 minutes; reduce heat to moderate (350°F.) and bake about 15 minutes longer. Transfer loaf to platter; keep warm.
· Make gravy from drippings. Pour over loaf and serve.

SUNDAY SWISS STEAKS

Saucy meat that cooks by itself

½   c. flour
2   tsp. salt
¼   tsp. pepper
6   slices eye of round, 1½" thick
½   c. thinly sliced onion rings
¼   c. shortening
1   (8 oz.) can tomato sauce
1   c. pizza sauce

· Combine flour, salt and pepper; pound into meat.
· Brown onions lightly in hot fat in large skillet; remove onions and brown meat. Place onions on top of meat.
· Add tomato and pizza sauces. Cover; simmer 1½ to 2 hours until tender. Serve sauce with meat. Makes 6 servings.
· Package cooked steaks individually,

with sauce, in small foil pie pans;
wrap with foil. Seal, label, date and
freeze.

Recommended storage time: 3 to 6
months.

• To serve, heat in skillet.

RANCHERO POT ROAST

*An untended dish—the rich, spicy
aroma and flavor mount as it simmers*

2	tsp. salt
¼	tsp. freshly ground pepper
¼	tsp. paprika
1	clove garlic, finely chopped
3	lbs. bottom round roast
2	tblsp. shortening
1	c. beef broth
½	c. chopped onions
½	c. chili sauce

• Rub salt, pepper, paprika and garlic
into meat. Cover; refrigerate overnight.

• Next day, brown meat slowly in
hot fat to a deep brown.

• Place meat on rack in deep pan.
Add broth and onions; cover and simmer 1½ hours (add more broth if
necessary). Add chili sauce and cook
30 minutes. Makes 6 servings.

• Cool quickly. Pack into containers,
seal, label, date and freeze.

Recommended storage time: 3 to 4
months.

• To serve, partially thaw and simmer
until heated and tender, about 1 hour.

BEEF STROGANOFF

*Hostess special to fix and freeze a few
days before you entertain*

| 1½ | lbs. sirloin steak, cut in |
| | 1 × ¼ " strips |

3½	tblsp. flour
¼	c. butter or regular margarine
1	c. chopped onion
1	can condensed beef bouillon
1	tblsp. Worcestershire sauce
1	tsp. salt
½	tsp. dry mustard
2	tblsp. tomato paste
1	c. dairy sour cream
1	(6 oz.) can chopped mushrooms, drained

• Dredge meat in 1½ tblsp. flour.
Brown quickly in melted butter in
heavy skillet, turning meat to brown
on all sides. Add onion and cook
until barely tender, 3 to 4 minutes.

• Remove meat and onion from skillet. Blend remaining flour (2 tblsp.)
into drippings in skillet. Add bouillon
and Worcestershire sauce and cook,
stirring constantly, until thickened.
Stir in salt, mustard and tomato paste.
Blend in sour cream. Add meat and
mushrooms. Cool. Makes 6 cups.

• Pour into freezer containers, seal,
label, date and freeze.

Recommended storage time: 3 to 6
months.

• To serve, partially thaw. Heat in
double boiler. Serve over parslied rice,
wild rice or noodles.

MEAT BALL CHOWDER

*Don't let the number of ingredients
scare you—the chowder is simple to
fix and there's plenty for two meals*

| 2 | lbs. ground lean beef |
| 2 | tsp. seasoned salt |

⅛   tsp. pepper
2   eggs, slightly beaten
¼   c. finely chopped parsley
⅓   c. fine cracker crumbs
2   tblsp. milk
3   tblsp. flour
1   tblsp. salad oil
4   to 6 onions, cut in eighths
6   c. water
6   c. tomato juice
6   beef bouillon cubes
3   c. sliced carrots (about 6)
3   to 4 c. sliced celery
2   to 3 c. diced potatoes
¼   c. long grain rice
1   tblsp. sugar
2   tsp. salt
2   bay leaves
½   to 1 tsp. marjoram leaves
       (optional)
1   (12 oz.) can Mexicorn

· Combine meat, seasoned salt, pepper, eggs, parsley, cracker crumbs and milk. Mix thoroughly. Form into balls about the size of a walnut (makes about 40). Dip in flour.

· Heat oil in 8- to 10-qt. kettle. Lightly brown meat balls on all sides (or drop unbrowned into boiling vegetables).

· Add remaining ingredients (except add corn last 10 minutes of cooking). Bring to boil; cover. Reduce heat and cook at slow boil 30 minutes, or until vegetables are tender. If dinner must wait, turn off heat at this point. Takes only minutes to reheat. Makes 6 to 7 quarts.

· To freeze, cook until the vegetables are crisp-tender. Cool quickly. Ladle into freezer containers, cover, seal, label and date.

Recommended storage time: 2 to 3 months.

· To serve, partially thaw until chowder softens. Heat until piping hot, about 45 minutes.

PLANTATION STUFFED PEPPERS

Choose plump, crisp peppers to fill with this flavorful meat mix

1   lb. ground beef
1   c. chopped onion
1   clove garlic, chopped
2   tsp. chili powder
1   tsp. salt
½   tsp. pepper
2   cans condensed tomato
       soup
½   lb. sharp process cheese,
       shredded or sliced
1½   c. cooked parboiled rice
8   medium green peppers

· Cook ground beef, onion and garlic in skillet until meat is browned. Add seasonings and tomato soup; simmer, covered, 10 minutes. Add cheese. Cook slowly, stirring occasionally until cheese melts. Stir in rice. Cool.

· Cut peppers in halves lengthwise. Remove membranes and seeds. Cook in boiling salted water to cover until barely tender, about 3 minutes. Drain and cool.

· Place peppers on baking sheet. Stuff with rice mixture. Serves 8.

· To freeze, place in freezer until peppers are frozen. Remove, wrap frozen peppers in foil or plastic wrap. Label, date and return to freezer. Recommended storage time: 2 to 3 months.

• To serve, remove wrapping, place partially thawed peppers in shallow pan. Cover with foil. Bake in hot oven (400°F.) 30 to 45 minutes.

MACARONI AND CHEESE

You couldn't pick a more popular dish to freeze for busy-day meals

1 ½	c. macaroni, uncooked
2	tsp. salt
2	tblsp. butter or regular margarine
2	tblsp. flour
¼	tsp. pepper
3	c. milk
2	c. grated sharp Cheddar cheese
½	tblsp. grated onion
1	tsp. Worcestershire sauce
½	c. buttered bread crumbs

• Cook macaroni with 1½ tsp. salt in 3 qts. rapidly boiling water; cook about 2 minutes less than for complete doneness. Drain and rinse.

• Make a white sauce of butter, flour, ½ tsp. salt, pepper and milk. Stir cheese into sauce until melted. Add macaroni, onion and Worcestershire sauce. Cool quickly. Place in greased shallow baking dish. Serves 6 to 8.

• Wrap, label, date and freeze.

Recommended storage time: 6 to 8 weeks.

• To serve, thaw 18 hours in refrigerator, or 4 hours at room temperature. Bake, covered with foil, in moderate oven (350°F.) 25 minutes. Remove foil, add crumbs; bake 15 minutes.

FRICASSEE CHICKEN WITH PARSLEY NOODLES

A good start on Sunday dinner— chicken and homemade noodles

1	(3 ½ to 4 lb.) stewing chicken, cut up
6	c. water
1	branch celery
1	carrot, cut in chunks
1	onion, sliced
1 ½	tsp. salt
⅛	tsp. marjoram leaves
⅛	tsp. thyme leaves
1	bay leaf

Noodles:

1	tblsp. water
½	tsp. salt
1	egg, beaten
1	c. sifted flour
¼	c. finely chopped parsley

• Simmer chicken in water with vegetables and seasonings until chicken is tender. Strain broth to remove vegetables and herbs. Cool chicken. Reserve broth.

• In the meantime, prepare noodles. Add water and salt to egg. Stir in flour to make a stiff dough, adding parsley with last portion. Knead dough slightly with hands until it doesn't stick. Cut into thirds. Roll one third at a time until very thin on a lightly floured board. Let stand 20 minutes to dry slightly. With long knife cut into ⅛" strips.

• Bring chicken broth to boiling. Add noodles slowly so broth does not stop boiling, and cook 20 minutes, or until tender. Cool. Makes 6 servings.

• Put cooled chicken pieces in freezer containers. Cover with broth, then with cooled noodles and broth. Seal,

label, date and freeze. Recommended storage time: 3 to 6 months.
• To serve, thaw and heat slowly in heavy pan over low heat, until chicken is heated and sauce is bubbly. Add more water, if needed.

CHICKEN/CORN SUPPER

You can't beat the chicken-corn combination in this old-time special

1   c. butter or regular margarine
¾   c. flour
2   qts. hot chicken broth
2   tsp. salt
½   tsp. pepper
2   tblsp. finely chopped onion
1 ¾   qts. chopped cooked chicken (2 stewing hens)
1 ½   qts. cooked or canned whole kernel corn, or 3 (1 lb.) cans, drained
1 ½   c. grated process cheese
¾   c. chopped pimientos
Buttered bread or cracker crumbs

• Melt butter; blend in flour. Add hot broth and cook over medium heat until bubbling and thickened, stirring. Stir in salt, pepper and onion.
• Combine with remaining ingredients, except crumbs, in a very large bowl. Cool quickly. Makes 4½ quarts.
• Pack in freezer containers, label, date and freeze.
Recommended storage time: 3 to 6 months.
• To serve, thaw food enough to remove from container. Place in a greased casserole and bake, covered, in a hot oven (400°F.) 30 minutes or until food is thawed enough to press

into the shape of the baking dish. Sprinkle with buttered crumbs.
• Continue baking, uncovered, until bubbly hot and crumbs are browned. Total baking time, about 1 hour for pints, 1 hour 45 minutes for quarts.

CHICKEN IN BARBECUE SAUCE

Flavor of lemon peel is a nice accent; it made a hit with our taste-testers

1   egg, beaten
1   c. water
2   stewing hens, cut up
2   c. flour (about)
½   c. fat
2   lemons, thinly sliced
2   onions, thinly sliced
Barbecue Sauce

• Beat together egg and water. Dip chicken in egg, then shake in flour in plastic bag. Brown all sides in hot fat; cool on rack; do not stack.
• Place chicken, skin side up, in large roasting pan; do not stack. Top each piece with half slices lemon and onion. Pour cooled Barbecue Sauce over chicken. Makes 6 to 8 servings.
• Cover, seal, label, date and freeze. Recommended storage time: 3 to 6 months.
• To serve, partially thaw chicken in pan at room temperature or in refrigerator overnight. Bake, covered, in moderate oven (350°F.) about 3 hours (2½ hours for fryers), basting occasionally. Remove cover during last half hour.

BARBECUE SAUCE: Combine following ingredients: 4 (6 oz.) cans tomato paste, 8 (6 oz.) cans water, 1 c.

ketchup, ⅓ c. Worcestershire sauce, ⅛ tsp. Tabasco sauce, 2 tblsp. brown sugar, 1½ tblsp. liquid smoke, 1 tblsp. vinegar, ¼ tsp. chili powder, ⅛ tsp. pepper, 1 tblsp. salt, 1 minced clove garlic, 2 branches celery, finely chopped, and 1 crushed bay leaf. Simmer 10 minutes; cool.

ALABAMA CHICKEN SPAGHETTI

For families with children who prefer Italian-type dishes on the bland side

1   (4 to 5 lb.) stewing chicken
3   branches celery
2   tblsp. salt
4   c. boiling water
6   c. chopped onions
1   c. chopped celery
1   clove garlic, minced
2   (1 lb.) cans tomatoes (1 qt.)
1   c. ketchup
1   (6 oz.) can chopped
      mushrooms (stems and
      pieces)
3   tblsp. Worcestershire sauce
2   tsp. salt
½   tsp. pepper
1   (1 lb.) pkg. spaghetti,
      uncooked

• Place dressed chicken, cut up if desired, in large kettle with celery branches and 2 tblsp. salt. Add boiling water; simmer until tender, about 3 hours. Remove chicken. Cool. Cut chicken from bones and dice.
• Skim ½ c. fat from cooled chicken broth. Place in large kettle. Cook onions, chopped celery and garlic in fat until onions are soft (not browned). Add chicken, broth, tomatoes, ketchup, mushrooms and juice, Worcestershire sauce, salt and pepper. Bring to a boil. Add spaghetti and cook until spaghetti is about half-cooked. (Do not cook spaghetti completely or it will be mushy when reheated.) Cool quickly. Makes 4½ quarts.
• Package in moistureproof containers, seal, label, date and freeze.
Recommended storage time: 3 to 6 months.
• To serve, let thaw in package in refrigerator 8 hours or until mixture can be removed from container. Turn into casserole or baking pan, cover and bake in a hot oven (400°F.) until thoroughly heated, about 45 minutes for 1 pint; 1 hour for a quart. If mixture appears dry, add ⅓ c. chicken broth or water before reheating.

BROWN-AND-SERVE ROAST CHICKEN

You'll want to try this new, high temperature way of roasting chicken

2   (2½ to 3 lb.) whole
      broiler-fryers
3   tsp. salt
¼   tsp. pepper
6   tblsp. melted butter

• Wash outside of chickens in cold water; wipe out inside with damp cloth; dry thoroughly. Rub cavities with 1 tsp. salt. Fasten neck skin to back with skewers. Tie legs together.
• Coat chickens with mixture of 2 tsp. salt and pepper. Brush with butter. Roast breast side down in a very hot oven (450°F.) 30 minutes. Makes 8 servings.
• Cool quickly. Wrap, label, date and freeze. Freeze drippings separately.
Recommended storage time: 1 month.

· To serve, place frozen chicken on rack in shallow pan, breast side up. Roast in a hot oven (400°F.) about 1 hour or until drumstick-thigh joint moves easily. Baste while cooking with drippings or Lemon Sauce.

LEMON SAUCE: Crush 1 clove garlic into 2 tsp. salt. Add 2 tblsp. finely chopped onion, 2 tblsp. finely chopped parsley, ½ c. lemon juice and ¼ c. salad oil or drippings. Use to baste chickens while roasting.

CONNECTICUT BAKED CHICKEN

Easy-to-fix chicken with gourmet flavor and many uses—do try it

2   (2½ to 3 lb.) broiler-fryers, cut in serving pieces
1   c. diced celery
2   to 3 sprigs parsley
2   tsp. salt
¼   tsp. pepper
1   tsp. basil leaves
½   c. tomato juice

· Place chicken in Dutch oven or large casserole. Top with remaining ingredients.
· Cover and bake in a moderate oven (350°F.) until chicken is tender but still firm, about 1½ hours. Cool.
· Pack chicken as compactly as possible in freezer containers. Cover with chicken broth. (If more broth is needed, dissolve 1 chicken bouillon cube in 1 c. hot water.) Makes about 2 quarts. Or to save freezer space, cut meat off the bone in as large pieces as possible and pack as directed.
· Seal, label, date and freeze.
Recommended storage time: 3 to 6 months.

· To serve, partially thaw and place chicken with bones, covered, in a moderate oven (350°F.) until heated thoroughly. If chicken seems dry, add a little broth while heating. Or use cut-up chicken in casseroles, salads, curry, creamed dishes and chop suey.

CHICKEN PIE SUPREME

FARM JOURNAL'S *famous chicken pie*

Pastry for 2-crust pie
1   (5 lb.) whole stewing chicken
1½   qts. water
2   tsp. salt
1   small onion
1   carrot
1   branch celery
½   c. sifted flour
½   tsp. onion salt
½   tsp. celery salt
Dash of pepper
3½   c. chicken broth
2   or 3 drops yellow food color (optional)

· Place chicken in large kettle and add water, 1 tsp. salt, onion, carrot and celery. Simmer, covered, until tender, 3 to 3½ hours.
· Remove chicken and strip meat from bones in large pieces. Refrigerate chicken and broth when cool.
· Combine flour, onion salt, celery salt, pepper and 1 tsp. salt with ½ c. chicken broth. Mix until smooth.
· Put 3 c. chicken broth in skillet; heat and add flour mixture, beating with a wire whip to prevent lumping.
· Cook over medium heat, stirring constantly until mixture is smooth and thickened. Add food color.
· Add chicken and blend well. Cool.
· Line 9″ deep-dish pie pan with

pastry. Fill with cooled chicken mixture. Adjust top crust; cut vents and seal edges. Makes 6 to 8 servings.
• Freeze pie. When frozen, wrap, label, date and return to freezer.
Recommended storage time: 3 to 6 months.
• Cool remaining broth and freeze in glass jars or freezer containers.
• To serve, bake frozen pie in hot oven (400°F.) 45 minutes to 1 hour. Chicken filling should be hot, the crust a golden brown. Make gravy with frozen broth to serve with pie.

COUNTRY COMPANY CHICKEN

Do try this treat from kitchens in Kentucky's bluegrass country

1	c. parboiled rice
1	tsp. salt
2	c. boiling chicken broth
1	can condensed cream of celery soup
1	c. milk
2	c. cooked chicken
1	c. chopped celery
2	tblsp. grated onion or 2 tsp. onion flakes
1	c. slivered, toasted almonds
1	tsp. salt
½	tsp. Worcestershire sauce

• Add rice and salt to broth. Stir until mixture begins to boil. Cover, reduce heat and simmer 15 minutes. (Rice will complete cooking when reheated.)
• Blend together soup and milk. Stir in rice, chicken, celery, onion, ½ c. almonds and seasonings. Cool quickly.
• Line a 2-qt. casserole with aluminum foil. Pour mixture into casserole, sprinkle remaining ½ c. almonds on top. Makes 6 to 8 servings.

• Freeze. Remove from dish, wrap, label, date and store in freezer.
Recommended storage time: 3 to 6 months.
• To serve, grease original casserole. Remove foil from frozen block of chicken mixture and place in casserole. Let partially thaw. Bake, covered, in hot oven (400°F.) 30 to 45 minutes. Remove cover and continue baking until thoroughly heated, about 30 minutes.

RANCH-STYLE CHICKEN

A good Nevada cook gives this baked chicken a savory Italian accent

6	tblsp. shortening or salad oil
½	c. flour
3	tsp. salt
¼	tsp. pepper
2	(2 to 3 lb.) broiler-fryers, cut in serving pieces
1	onion
8	sprigs parsley
1	clove garlic
2	tblsp. olive oil
1	(8 oz.) can tomato sauce
1	(1 lb.) can tomatoes
½	c. pitted, sliced ripe olives and juice
1	(3½ to 4 oz.) can sliced mushrooms
1	tsp. salt
¼	tsp. Italian herb seasoning
⅛	tsp. pepper

• Line two 13×9×2″ baking dishes with aluminum foil. Melt 3 tblsp. shortening in each dish.
• Combine flour, salt and pepper in paper bag. Shake chicken pieces to coat with flour. Lightly moisten chicken pieces in melted fat. Arrange

in one layer, skin side up in baking dishes. Bake in very hot oven (450°F.) 30 minutes.

· Chop onion, parsley and garlic. Sauté in olive oil. Add tomato sauce, tomatoes, olives, mushrooms and juice, and seasonings. Pour sauce evenly over the 2 dishes of chicken. Cool. Makes 4 to 6 servings.

· Cover and place in freezer. When frozen, lift foil from baking dish. Wrap in foil or plastic wrap; label, date and return to freezer. Recommended storage time: 3 to 6 months.

· To serve, remove foil, place in baking dish. Bake, uncovered, in moderate oven (350°F.) 1 hour and 15 minutes.

ARIZONA CHICKEN-STUFFED CREPES

Pancakes that go to company supper or dinner tables and make a hit

1 ⅓	c. milk
2	tblsp. butter
2	eggs, beaten
½	c. sifted flour
1	tsp. baking powder
½	tsp. salt
1	pt. dairy sour cream
2	whole chicken breasts, cooked and cut in strips

1 ¼	c. cooked ham, cut in strips
¼	c. canned sweet chili peppers, cut in strips
½	c. grated Gruyère cheese

· Heat 1 c. milk and butter in saucepan until butter is melted; cool.

· Beat in eggs, then flour, baking powder and salt, sifted together; beat until smooth and well blended.

· To bake, lightly grease 4 or 5" skillet; heat and pour in 3 tblsp. batter for each crepe; tilt skillet to cover evenly. Cook about 1 minute to brown, flip and brown other side.

· Spread one side of all crepes with sour cream (takes about 1 c.); place several strips of chicken, ham and chili peppers on crepes, roll and place in 11×7×1½" baking dish. Makes 10.

· Wrap, label, date and freeze. Recommended storage time: 1 month.

· To serve, let thaw in refrigerator. Mix ⅓ c. milk with 1 c. sour cream, pour over crepes. Top with cheese. Bake, uncovered, in moderate oven (350°F.) 20 minutes, to melt cheese.

Note: If you do not freeze stuffed crepes, let dish stand in refrigerator 24 hours, then bake and serve.

Hot Tamales—Supper Money-Makers

Adaptations of Mexican hot tamales, a main dish packed in corn shucks, are gaining wide acceptance. They are especially popular in Mississippi and Louisiana and on west to the Pacific Ocean. You can open the little husk packages and eat their contents with a fork—or informally with your fingers.

Home cooks say they're work to fix, but that there's a redeeming feature. You can make, cook, cool, package and freeze them. Then you quickly reheat them at serving time.

A group of Arkansas farm women are extremely successful in raising money for their church by giving chicken tamale suppers. They like to put them on at Halloween time, although they sometimes have them in winter. With the tamales the group make, they serve homemade dill and sweet pickles, ketchup, crisp cabbage slaw or a green salad, coffee and a choice of pies they bake. They set individual servings on a table so everyone can take his pick.

If the corn shucks you have are green, you can dry them. Spread them in sunshine for 3 to 5 days or until they turn yellow. Store them in a clean, dry place until you are ready to use them. If you do not have corn shucks, use 8×6″ pieces of foil.

CHICKEN TAMALES

Golden corn shucks make jackets for this chicken-cornmeal main dish

1	(4 to 5 lb.) stewing chicken, cut up
2	tsp. salt
1	large onion, chopped
1	clove garlic, minced
2	tblsp. salad oil
½	tsp. paprika
1	tblsp. salt
½	tsp. ground red pepper
2	tblsp. chili powder
1	tsp. ground cumin
3	c. white cornmeal
1½	tsp. salt
10	c. chicken broth
Corn shucks	

• Place chicken in large kettle; cover with water; add 2 tsp. salt. Simmer until tender, and meat falls from bones, 2½ to 3 hours. Remove chicken; save broth (you'll need at least 10 c.). Take meat off bones; put through coarse blade of food chopper.

• Cook liver, heart and gizzard separately; grind. Mix with chicken.

• Sauté onion and garlic in oil until clear. Mix with chicken and seasonings.

• Mix cornmeal and 1½ tsp. salt with 3 c. lukewarm broth. Bring rest of broth to boil; slowly pour cornmeal mixture into boiling broth, stirring constantly. Cook until very thick. Cool in shallow pans.

• Trim shucks to 7×6″ rectangles; rinse with cold water. Place in shallow pan; cover with boiling water for 10 minutes until shucks are pliable. Drain on paper towels; brush with salad oil.

• Spread 2½ tblsp. mush in 4″ square on each shuck, from bottom edge to about 2″ from top edge. Spoon on 2 tblsp. chicken.

• Fold over bottom of shuck; overlap top 2″. Secure each end with string cut from shuck.

• Place tamales on rack in a large kettle or roasting pan that has about 2″ water in the bottom. Arrange tamales loose enough that steam can circulate around them freely. Make certain tamales will not touch the water. Set covered kettle over medium heat (water should boil gently). Steam tamales about 1 hour. To test for doneness, remove a tamale and open. If the cornmeal does not stick to the shuck, it is ready to eat or cool for freezing. Makes about 4 dozen.

VARIATION

PORK TAMALES: Cover 3 to 4 lbs. pork loin with water seasoned with 2 tblsp.

chili powder and 1½ tsp. salt. Simmer 30 minutes. Put through coarse blade of food chopper; set aside. Sauté ¼ c. chopped onion in 2 tblsp. butter or regular margarine until clear. Add 2 (6 oz.) cans each of tomato paste and water, 2 crushed cloves garlic and 1 tsp. curry powder (optional). Add pork and simmer 10 minutes. Spoon 2 tblsp. mixture on the corn shucks spread with cornmeal mush, as directed for Chicken Tamales.

· To freeze, arrange tamales in neat stacks on foil or plastic wrap. Wrap tightly; label, date and freeze.

Recommended storage time: 6 to 8 weeks.

· To serve, reheat by steaming as in making the tamales. Steam 20 minutes.

Note: In Mexico the cooked chicken, pork and other meats are cut in fine pieces instead of being put through a food chopper.

MICHIGAN TAMALE BAKE

Dinner is well on the way when you put this freezer special in oven

Topping:

1   c. yellow cornmeal
1   tsp. salt
1   c. cold water
3   c. boiling water

Filling:

1½   lbs. ground beef
1   c. chopped onion
2¼   tsp. salt
4   tsp. chili powder
2   c. canned tomatoes
1   c. sliced pitted ripe olives
1   c. grated process cheese

· Combine cornmeal, salt and cold water. Stir slowly into boiling water. Cook until mixture thickens, stirring frequently. Cover and continue cooking over low heat 10 minutes.

· Brown beef and onion in large skillet. Pour off excess fat. Add salt, chili powder and tomatoes. Simmer, covered, 20 minutes. Add olives; cool.

· Spread into a 13×9×2″ pan. Top with cornmeal mush. Serves 9.

· Cool, cover with foil, seal, label, date and freeze.

Recommended storage time: 3 to 6 months.

· To serve, bake, uncovered, without thawing, in moderate oven (350°F.) 1 hour or until hot. Sprinkle with cheese and bake 15 minutes longer.

MEXICAN BEEF HASH

Your family will like this hash—it's hearty and full of flavor

1   c. chopped onion
1   c. chopped green pepper
1   lb. ground beef
3   to 4 tsp. chili powder
2   tsp. salt
¼   tsp. pepper
1   c. long grain rice
2   (1 lb.) cans tomatoes (4 c.)

· Sauté onion and green pepper with ground beef until beef is browned.

· Add remaining ingredients, except tomatoes, and mix well.

· Line two 1½-qt. casseroles with aluminum foil. Divide mixture evenly between the 2 casseroles. Pour 1 can tomatoes over each casserole and mix lightly to blend. Cover and bake in moderate oven (350°F.) 20 minutes. Remove from oven, leave covered,

and cool to room temperature. Each casserole makes 4 to 6 servings.
• Place casseroles in freezer. When hash is frozen, lift foil from casserole. Wrap in foil or plastic wrap; label, date and return to freezer.
Recommended storage time: 3 to 6 months.
• To serve, take package from freezer, remove wrappings and place in casserole. Cover and bake in moderate oven (350°F.) 1 hour.

PENNSYLVANIA LIVER PASTE

Good-for-you pork liver is very tasty fixed this Danish way

1	lb. frozen pork liver
6	slices bacon
1	medium onion
¼	c. flour
1	c. milk
2	eggs
1	tsp. salt
½	tsp. pepper

• Put liver, bacon and onion through food chopper two or three times, using finest blade. Liver is easier to handle if partially frozen. Blend in remaining ingredients.
• Spread mixture in greased 9×5×3″ loaf pan. Bake in slow oven (325°F.) about 1 hour and 35 minutes or until done. Makes 1 loaf.
• Cool, turn out of pan; wrap, label, date and freeze.
Recommended storage time: 6 to 8 weeks.
• To serve, thaw in refrigerator. Makes delicious sandwiches. You also can serve warm like meat loaf.

CREOLE JAMBALAYA ORLEANS

Taste this and you'll know why Louisiana is famed for superior food

1	tblsp. butter or regular margarine
1	tblsp. flour
1	c. cubed cooked ham
¼	c. chopped green pepper
2	c. cooked tomatoes
1¼	c. tomato juice
1	lb. shrimp, cleaned
1	onion, sliced
1	clove garlic, minced
2	tsp. salt
¼	tsp. pepper
1	sprig parsley, chopped, or 1 tsp. parsley flakes
⅛	tsp. thyme leaves
1	bay leaf
1	c. parboiled rice

• Melt butter in heavy skillet over medium heat. Stir in flour, ham and green pepper. Cook and stir 5 minutes.
• Add remaining ingredients, except rice. Bring to a boil. Stir in rice and simmer, covered, until rice is almost tender, about 25 minutes. (Rice will complete cooking when reheated.) Remove bay leaf. Makes 2 quarts.
• Cool quickly. Place in freezer containers, seal, label, date and freeze.
Recommended storage time: 3 to 6 months.
• To serve, partially thaw. Place in a 2-qt. casserole. Pour over ⅓ c. water. Bake, covered, in a hot oven (400°F.) 1 hour.

HOLIDAY HAM RING

Spicy ham loaf for special meals.
Serve buttered corn or peas in center

3	lbs. ground smoked ham
1	lb. ground pork
2	eggs
1 ¾	c. graham cracker crumbs
1 ½	c. milk
½	tsp. ground allspice
Sauce	

· Combine ingredients, except Sauce; mix well. In 15½ × 10½ × 1″ jelly roll pan, shape into ring (or loaf) about 10″ across. Makes 12 to 14 servings.
· Place pan in freezer. When meat is frozen, remove from pan, package, label, date and return to freezer.
Recommended storage time: 6 to 8 weeks.
· To serve, partially thaw meat mixture, pour half of Sauce over loaf.
· Bake in moderate oven (350°F.) 45 minutes; pour over remaining Sauce; bake 45 minutes longer, basting several times with sauce.

SAUCE: Combine 1 can condensed tomato soup, ½ c. vinegar, ½ c. brown sugar, firmly packed, and 1½ tsp. prepared mustard.

Note: Some cooks like to bake the loaf, cool quickly, wrap, seal, label and freeze. They defrost the loaf in the refrigerator, slice and serve cold.

CASSEROLE OF HAM AND ASPARAGUS

Special for your on-the-go days. It's color-bright and flavorful

1	c. hot milk
¼	lb. process cheese, grated
½	c. dry bread crumbs
¼	c. ham fat or butter
¼	c. chopped pimiento
1	tblsp. finely chopped onion
1 ½	tblsp. chopped parsley
3	eggs, well beaten
1 ½	(10 oz.) pkgs. frozen cut asparagus spears
3	c. diced, cooked ham
¾	c. buttered bread crumbs

· Combine hot milk and cheese.
· Blend ½ c. crumbs, fat, pimiento, onion and parsley; add to milk mixture. Blend in eggs. Cool.
· Cook asparagus briefly, boiling only 2 minutes; drain; cool. Combine ham, asparagus and egg mixture. Pour into buttered 1½-qt. shallow casserole. Makes 6 to 8 servings.
· Wrap, label, date and freeze.
Recommended storage time: 6 to 8 weeks.
· To serve, thaw and top with buttered crumbs. Bake in moderate oven (350°F.) 40 to 50 minutes.

SKILLET CHOP SUEY

Let company come—with this in the freezer it's easy to get a good meal

2	c. finely diced fresh pork
3	tblsp. salad oil
3	c. chopped celery
2	c. chopped onion
2	tblsp. soy sauce
2	chicken bouillon cubes
1	c. boiling water
3	tblsp. cornstarch
1	tblsp. molasses
½	c. water
1	(1 lb.) can bean sprouts
1	(4 oz.) can mushroom pieces

• Brown pork in hot oil; add celery, onion and 1 tblsp. soy sauce; cook 10 minutes.

• Dissolve bouillon cubes in boiling water. Add to pork along with cornstarch mixed with remaining 1 tblsp. soy sauce, molasses and ½ c. water. Stir in bean sprouts and mushrooms with their liquids. Cook, stirring until thickened. Makes 8 servings. To serve at once, cook 5 minutes longer.

• To freeze, cool quickly, place in freezer containers, seal, label, date and freeze.

Recommended storage time: 2 to 3 months.

• To serve, partially thaw at room temperature; quickly heat in skillet.

TWIN SAUSAGE CASSEROLES

The unusual seasoning and blend of meats give you tasty variety

1	(6 oz.) can sliced or chopped mushrooms
6	chicken bouillon cubes
1	lb. bulk pork sausage
1	lb. ground beef
2	c. chopped celery
1	c. chopped green pepper
½	c. grated Parmesan cheese
1	tsp. salt
½	tsp. marjoram leaves
⅛	tsp. pepper
2	c. long grain rice

• Drain mushrooms and add enough water to liquid to make 5 c. Add bouillon cubes and heat to dissolve.

• Brown meat and drain off fat and liquid. Combine meat with remaining ingredients except bouillon.

• Line two 2-qt. casseroles with aluminum foil. Divide mixture evenly between the 2 casseroles. Pour half of hot bouillon over each casserole. Stir lightly to blend. Cover and bake in moderate oven (350°F.) 15 minutes. Remove from oven, leave covered, and cool to room temperature. Each casserole makes 4 to 6 servings.

• Freeze. When frozen, lift foil from casserole. Wrap each in foil; label, date and return to freezer.

Recommended storage time: 1 month.

• To serve, take package from freezer, remove wrappings and place in casserole. Cover and bake in moderate oven (350°F.) 1½ hours.

SEAFOOD SCALLOP

It's a lucky fish day when you have this dotted-pink-with-shrimp scallop

1	lb. frozen or fresh shrimp, cooked and cleaned, or 2 (4½ oz.) cans, drained
2	(6½ oz.) cans crabmeat
2	(7 oz.) cans tuna
1	(4 oz.) can mushrooms
¼	c. butter or regular margarine
¼	c. flour
1	tsp. salt
¼	tsp. pepper
Milk	
⅓	c. minced green pepper
½	tsp. curry powder
¾	c. buttered bread crumbs

• Cut shrimp into bite-size pieces. Drain crabmeat and tuna; drain mushrooms, reserving liquid.

• Melt butter in saucepan. Stir in flour, salt and pepper (omit salt if us-

ing canned shrimp). Add enough milk to mushroom liquid to make 2 c. Stir into butter-flour mixture with green pepper and curry powder. Cook, stirring constantly, until thickened. Cool quickly. Combine with seafood and mushrooms. Makes 8 servings.
· Place in freezer container. Seal, label, date and freeze.
Recommended storage time: 6 weeks.
· To serve, thaw in refrigerator. Put in 2-qt. casserole or individual baking dishes. Top with crumbs. Bake in moderate oven (350°F.) 35 to 45 minutes, 15 to 20 minutes for individual dishes.

SHRIMP CREOLE

All-American favorite seafood main dish—it freezes successfully

½　c. chopped onion
½　c. chopped celery
½　c. chopped green pepper
2　cloves garlic, minced
3　tblsp. salad oil
1　(1 lb.) can tomatoes
1　(6 oz.) can tomato paste
1 ½　tsp. salt
½　tsp. pepper
1　tsp. Worcestershire sauce
⅛　tsp. Tabasco sauce
1　tsp. cornstarch
2　tsp. water
1 ½　lbs. cleaned raw shrimp

· Cook onion, celery, green pepper and garlic in oil until tender. Add tomatoes, tomato paste and seasonings. Bring to boil, simmer 30 minutes.
· Blend cornstarch and water; stir into sauce. Add shrimp, cover and simmer 15 minutes. Makes 6 cups.
· Cool quickly, pack in freezer container, seal, label, date and freeze.

Recommended storage time: Up to 6 weeks.
· To serve, partially thaw. Heat in skillet. Serve over hot cooked rice.

BARBECUED LIMA BEANS

They'll praise this economical dish at picnics and community suppers

1　lb. dried lima beans
4　c. water
1 ½　c. chopped onions
1　c. brown sugar, firmly packed
1　c. ketchup
⅔　c. dark corn syrup
1　tblsp. salt
1　tblsp. liquid smoke
9　drops Tabasco sauce
Bacon slices for topping (optional)

· Soak washed beans in water overnight. Do not drain. Add onions, bring to a boil and simmer until beans are almost tender, about 30 minutes.
· Mix remaining ingredients, except bacon. Stir into beans. Makes 9 cups.
· Cool quickly and pack into containers, or place in casserole and wrap; seal, label, date and freeze.
Recommended storage time: 6 months.
· To serve, thaw at room temperature until you can remove beans from container. Place in baking pan (or leave in casserole) and put in hot oven (400°F.). Bake, covered, until beans can be pressed into shape of pan or casserole.
· Place bacon strips on top if desired and bake uncovered until beans are bubbly hot and bacon browns, about 1 hour for 1 qt. beans.

INDIANA BAKED BEANS

Full-meal, brown-beauty beans, hot corn bread and coleslaw

2¼	qts. dried navy or pea beans (4 lbs.)
4	qts. water
1	c. brown sugar, firmly packed
2	tblsp. salt
3½	tsp. prepared mustard
2	c. ketchup
1	c. molasses
1½	c. chopped onion
¾	lb. salt pork, sliced

• Soak beans in large kettle overnight. Or bring them to a boil and boil 2 minutes. Remove from heat and let them stand, covered, 1 hour.

• Simmer beans in same water until almost tender, about 1 hour.

• Combine sugar, salt, mustard, ketchup, molasses and onion. Add to beans; bring to a boil.

• Pour beans into casseroles or bean pots or leave them in the kettle. Mix some of the salt pork slices into the beans; lay remaining pork on top.

• Bake covered in a slow oven (300°F.) 5 hours. Add boiling water during cooking if necessary to keep beans from becoming dry.

• Pack in freezer containers, seal, label, date and freeze.

Recommended storage time: About 4 to 6 months. (Storage time depends on how fresh the salt pork was when added to the beans.)

• To serve, partially thaw at room temperature about 2 hours; then heat in a saucepan with a little water added or in the top of a double boiler. Or bake beans in a moderate oven (350°F.) until heated, about 45 minutes for a pint, 1 hour for a quart.

Note: Some country cooks like to remove salt pork before freezing because it tends to become rancid. To use part of beans before freezing, cook 1 hour longer than for freezing; uncover the last 30 minutes.

Meals to Fix-and-Freeze
MEAT-AND-POTATO MEALS FROM FREEZER

Many clever country cooks fix and freeze meals for busy days. One of FARM JOURNAL's readers, an Ohio farm woman, shares three of her best-liked menus. She especially likes to cook for her freezer in March. She says: "Spring and summer are busy times. When I get off the tractor, milking demands my attention, along with the hens—and supper! I have to get something hearty and tasty in a hurry, so I plan ahead and have frozen dinners on hand for jiffy use."

(*Dishes from freezer. See Index for recipes.)

BUSY-DAY CHICKEN DINNER

*Chicken Mounds
*Orange-Glazed Carrots
*Oven-Fried Potato Slices
Mixed Green Salad
*Ginger Peaches on
*Ice Cream

MEAT LOAF DINNER

*Sweet-Sour Meat Loaf
Green Beans
*French Fried Potatoes
Cabbage/Carrot Slaw
*Frozen Egg Dessert

CHICKEN MOUNDS

*Good use for leftover chicken. Top
with ketchup or mushroom sauce*

3	eggs, beaten
1	c. milk
½	c. chicken broth, heated
1	tblsp. finely chopped onion
¾	tsp. salt
½	tsp. paprika
1	tblsp. chopped pimiento
2½	c. diced, cooked chicken
1¼	c. soft bread cubes

• Combine eggs, milk, broth, onion, salt, paprika and pimiento. Add chicken and bread; mix well.
• Pour into buttered custard cups. Set in pan partly filled with hot water; bake in moderate oven (350°F.) 40 minutes. Makes 6 servings.
• Cool quickly. Remove from cups. Wrap individually, label, date and freeze in plastic freezer bags.
Recommended storage time: 3 to 6 months.
• To serve, put back in cups; set in pan of hot water; bake unthawed and covered in moderate oven (350°F.) 1 hour (uncover last 20 minutes).

SWEET-SOUR MEAT LOAF

Sauce makes meat loaf extra-good

2	lbs. ground beef
½	lb. ground pork
2	tsp. salt
½	tsp. pepper
½	c. chopped onion
2	tsp. Worcestershire sauce
1	c. soft bread crumbs
2	eggs
Sauce	
2	tblsp. shortening

• Combine all ingredients except Sauce and shortening. Mix well. Add ⅔ c. Sauce; mix and shape into 8 loaves.
• Brown loaves in shortening; drain; place in shallow pan. Pour rest of Sauce over loaves. Bake in moderate oven (350°F.) about 50 minutes, basting often.
• Cool quickly; wrap in individual foil packages with sauce in each; label, date and freeze.
Recommended storage time: 2 to 3 months.
• To serve, bake unthawed, in foil, in moderate oven (350°F.) about 1 hour, uncover to brown. Serve with Sauce.

Sauce: Mix 5 tblsp. brown sugar, 2 tblsp. light corn syrup, 5 tblsp. cider vinegar, 2 tsp. soy sauce, 1 tsp. salt and 2 c. water.

FISH DINNER

*Mustard-Glazed Tuna Cups
Buttered Beets
*Stuffed Baked Potatoes
Lime Gelatin Salad
*Strawberries on
*Angel Food Cake

MUSTARD-GLAZED TUNA CUPS

Mustard Sauce adds just-right tartness

2   (7 oz.) cans tuna, drained
2   eggs, slightly beaten
½   c. milk
¼   c. ketchup
1   tblsp. melted butter
1   c. rolled oats
½   tsp. salt
¼   tsp. pepper
3   tblsp. chopped parsley or
     celery
¼   c. finely chopped onion
Mustard Sauce

· Mix all ingredients except sauce. Pour into buttered muffin-pan cups or custard cups; top with Mustard Sauce.
· Bake in moderate oven (350°F.) 25 minutes. Makes 6 servings.
· Cool quickly; remove from cups. Wrap individually; label, date, and freeze in plastic bags.
Recommended storage time: 4 to 6 weeks.
· To serve, put back in cups; bake unthawed and covered in moderate oven (350°F.) 55 minutes (uncover last 30 minutes).

Mustard Sauce: Melt 1½ tblsp. butter; stir in 1 tblsp. flour. Slowly add ½ c. chicken broth; bring to boil; cook to thicken. Add 1 tsp. prepared mustard, ½ tsp. prepared horse-radish, ¼ tsp. salt and ⅛ tsp. pepper. Cook 1 minute.

CHAPTER 8

SOUPS, SALADS AND SANDWICHES

Freezing Soups · Recipes for Beef/Vegetable and Country Bean Soups · Everyday and Fancy Sandwiches · Recipes for Frenched Ham and Ready-to-Go Bologna Sandwiches and Other Sandwiches · Frozen Chicken, Tuna and Fruit Salads

Supper may be the family's stepchild meal in some homes—not in country kitchens. There it is hearty and inviting even if it's often the easiest meal to get. And if you have a freezer, it isn't secondhand food from noontime dinner.

Getting a good country supper often starts when you put a kettle of substantial soup on the range to thaw and then bubble lazily while it heats. You take sandwiches from the freezer to thaw for serving cold or for heating, depending on the weather, and add a frozen salad that doubles for dessert. There's your menu. You may want to bring cookies from the freezer and open a jar of homemade pickles for bonus touches. And you'll pour glasses of milk or a hot beverage.

Not all the sandwiches and salads in this chapter are exclusively for family meals. You'll enjoy splurging with some of them when entertaining your club at luncheon. Chicken/Pineapple Salad, the favorite of a home economist in New Mexico, is a wonderful choice. So is Chicken/Blueberry Salad, made by a treasured New Jersey recipe. Serve either of these salads on crackling-crisp lettuce with hot rolls, muffins or corn sticks and the beverage of your choice. An easy luncheon to get and a compliment winner. Food looks as good as it tastes!

You'll find both everyday and Sunday-best sandwiches in this chapter. Let them inspire you to invent others. And keep a jar of Frozen Tuna Salad on hand for the salad plate or sandwich spreading.

Don't let supper be a dull meal. Give soups, salads and sandwiches a chance. Try some of the recipes in this chapter, put what you make in the freezer. Then when you wonder what to have for the evening meal, look in your freezer—or, better still, at the list of frozen foods it contains. You do keep a list, don't you?

Hearty Country-Style Soups
THEY'RE THRIFTY, SATISFYING AND TASTY

Even if the homemaker arrives home late from town, she often serves soup for dinner or supper. And it's the lazy-cooking, flavorful kind— from the freezer. Farm-style soups are hearty eating and husband-pleas-ing. And they pamper the pocket-book. Try the two recipes in this chapter. They'll make you want to freeze other soups your family likes. Just heed the rules for freezing.

Freezing Soups

Many of the best soups require long, slow cooking. Fortunately, country cooks find it takes little more time to make enough for two or three meals than for one. Soups pack solidly in freezer containers, excluding much of the air. And many of them freeze satisfactorily.

Their popularity in farm homes is due partly to the time they save homemakers. Once they are in the freezer, all you need do to get them ready for the table is to heat them slowly in a heavy kettle until piping hot. They thaw while they heat.

With space in freezers limited, it is best to concentrate the soups from one third to one half. Use less water in making them and add more when you reheat and thaw them.

Among the soups that freeze well are those made with dried beans, split peas, oysters, lobster, chicken and meats with vegetables. Most vegeta-bles, like carrots, celery and soybeans, are good in frozen soups unless overcooked. Do not cook them until tender; they will finish cooking in the reheating. Add them according to the time they require in cooking—carrots before potatoes, for instance. Potatoes tend to become soft when frozen, but they may be used in soups that are kept frozen a short time. In soups, as in other dishes when frozen, onions lose flavor, green pepper and garlic flavors intensify.

Cool the soup quickly to check the cooking and avoid the development of bacteria that may cause spoilage. Set the kettle of soup in a big pan containing very cold or ice water.

Vegetable purées are excellent in soups. Scald and chill the corn, carrots, peas or other vegetables the same as for freezing without chopping. Then put them through the food chopper, package, label and freeze.

The following recipes are examples of soups that freeze successfully. The time of storage varies with the soup, but is usually under 3 months.

BEEF/VEGETABLE SOUP

Soup's on—your family will rejoice if it's a beef-vegetable combination

1	meaty soup bone (2 to 3 lbs.)
3	c. water
1	tblsp. salt
2 ½	c. tomato juice
1	c. diced carrots
1	c. diced celery
1	c. diced potatoes
1	medium onion, diced (1 c.)

· Place soup bone, water and salt in kettle. Simmer, covered, 2 hours. Add remaining ingredients and simmer until vegetables are almost tender, about 30 minutes.

· Cool quickly by placing kettle in pan of very cold or ice water. Cut meat in cubes; discard bone. Add meat to soup. Ladle into freezer containers. Place in refrigerator until fat congeals on top. Makes 5 pints.

· To freeze, remove fat from containers; seal, label, date and freeze.

Recommended storage time: 2 to 3 months.

· To serve, partially thaw so you can remove soup from container. To every pint of soup, add 1 cup water. Heat until piping hot.

COUNTRY BEAN SOUP

Thick soup saves freezer space—add the water when reheating it

2	lbs. dried navy beans
2 ½	qts. water
1	meaty ham bone
2	c. chopped onions
1	tblsp. salt
½	tsp. pepper
1	bay leaf

· Wash and pick over beans. Add water to cover and soak overnight. Or boil beans in water 2 minutes and soak 1 hour.

· Add remaining ingredients. Cover and simmer until beans are tender, 3 to 3½ hours.

· Remove ham bone and bay leaf. Mash beans slightly with a potato masher. Cut meat off bone and add to soup. Makes 4 quarts.

· Pack in containers, seal, label, date and freeze.

Recommended storage time: 3 to 4 months.

· To serve, thaw slightly at room temperature. Add 2 c. water for each quart of soup mixture. Heat.

Sandwiches—Plain and Fancy

Keep substantial sandwiches in the freezer to round out meals and to serve the member of the family home late. Have a few foil-wrapped to heat in the oven for busy-day meals.

Make dainty, open-face sandwiches for the party. You can thaw them in a few minutes—serve them with pride. Let our recipe suggestions inspire you to invent others. Team your imagination with your free time and make satisfying sandwiches.

EVERYDAY SANDWICHES

If there are lunch boxes to pack, you will save considerable time by freezing sandwiches in advance. Make the sandwiches by the assembly line method—a supply for two weeks at a time. It takes much longer to fix them daily. Lay the bread slices out on the kitchen counter and spread from edge to edge with softened butter or regular margarine to completely cover. Add the fillings to half the slices; then cover with the remaining half.

Wrap as they will be used, individually or in pairs. Or wrap individually in waxed paper and then wrap in pairs in aluminum foil or plastic wrap. Label, date and freeze at once. If there is danger of the sandwiches being crushed in the freezer, you can put them in a box when frozen.

Most women become freehand cooks when they make sandwich fillings. They use imagination and the ingredients they have. But with sandwiches for freezing, certain foods should be avoided. Among them are mayonnaise and salad dressing (don't spread them on the bread instead of butter; like jelly and jams, they soak into the bread). Hard-cooked egg whites often develop off-flavors and become tough. Lettuce, tomatoes, carrots and other raw vegetables lose crispness and color. Natural cheese, sliced, may become crumbly, which may or may not be objectionable to you in sandwiches. You may prefer to

grate the cheese or use process cheese, which does not crumble.

Some of the best fillings for frozen sandwiches are sliced or ground cooked meats and poultry, peanut butter and other nut pastes, commercial cheese spreads like pimiento cheese, process cheese, cooked egg yolk, pickles and olives. Many farm cooks freeze sliced, cooked chicken and beef in broth for sandwiches.

You may prefer to make the fillings in large quantity and store them in small containers. They take up less freezer space and since many of the ingredients are ground, you save time by putting them through the food chopper in big amounts. This cuts down on the daily work, if lunch boxes are a feature of your life.

FROZEN PARTY SANDWICHES

Dainty, fancy-shaped sandwiches for teas, buffets and other special occasions may be frozen to save time on party day. The crusts will trim off easily if you use frozen bread slices. You can make open-face sandwiches or those with the filling between bread. Arrange them on baking sheets and freeze. Then pack them in layers, with two sheets of freezer paper between, in rectangular boxes. Overwrap the boxes with aluminum foil or plastic wrap; label, date and freeze. Do not pack different kinds of sandwiches in the same box—there may be a transfer of flavors.

To Thaw Sandwiches: Regular sandwiches, left in their wrappings, will thaw in 2 to 3 hours. So sandwiches packed in the lunch box in the morning will be ready to eat by noon.

Thaw the small container of sandwich filling in the refrigerator overnight. It will be ready to spread the next morning.

Thaw small, open-face sandwiches in their original wrapping at room temperature, 10 to 15 minutes. Do not refreeze sandwiches once you thaw them.

Recommended storage time: For sandwiches, about 3 weeks, and for fillings, packed separately, 3 months.

FILLINGS FOR FROZEN SANDWICHES

Add variety to sandwiches with different kinds of bread. When salad dressing is called for, use *only enough* to give filling spreading consistency.

REGULAR SANDWICHES

LIVERWURST with chopped, pimiento-stuffed olives or dill pickles mixed in to season.

PEANUT BUTTER with orange marmalade and honey added for spreading consistency.

BACON, cooked crisp and crumbled, in peanut butter.

CHEESE AND DATES, ground in equal parts, moistened for spreading consistency with orange juice. Point up flavor with a dash of grated orange peel. Add finely chopped nuts for variety.

BROWN BREAD, spread with butter and then with prepared mustard. Top with mashed baked beans, or omit mustard and add finely chopped mustard pickles to the beans.

GROUND COOKED CHICKEN and cream cheese, mixed and moistened with a little lemon juice.

DRIED BEEF, about 6 slices, chopped fine and mixed with 1 (3 oz.) pkg. cream cheese. Season with a bit of prepared horse-radish if desired.

SARDINES, canned in oil, drained, bones and skins removed, mashed with hard-cooked egg yolk. Add a dash of lemon juice.

HAM, cooked, chopped and mixed with cream cheese and finely chopped pimiento-stuffed olives or dill pickles.

ROAST BEEF, left over, chopped and mixed with a little chopped pickle and salad dressing.

CHICKEN, cooked, ground, with chopped pimiento added and just enough salad dressing for spreading.

SALMON OR TUNA, canned, drained and mashed with pickle relish and a little salad dressing.

HAM, cooked, chopped and mixed with pickle relish and a little salad dressing.

FANCY SANDWICHES

Use a variety of breads and cut buttered slices into fancy shapes with cookie cutters.

CREAM CHEESE, softened at room temperature and whipped until very light and fluffy. Use food color to tint cheese delicate pastel colors.

CHICKEN LIVER PÂTÉ, spread on bread and garnished with strips or cutouts of pimientos.

PEANUT BUTTER, mixed with chopped dates with orange marmalade added for spreading consistency.

CHEESE/TUNA, one cup grated Cheddar cheese mixed with ½ c. tuna, drained. Add finely chopped dill pickle and a little salad dressing.

CHEESE/OLIVE, 1 (3 oz.) pkg. cream cheese mixed with 8 ripe olives, pitted and finely chopped. Point up flavors with lemon juice.

DEVILED HAM, mixed with finely chopped nuts and spread on rye bread. Use canned ham. Add a little horseradish if desired.

BACON/CHEESE, crumbled, crisp-cooked bacon mixed into cream cheese with a little grated orange peel added.

FRENCHED HAM SANDWICH

Hearty—a snap to fix when you have French toast in your freezer

6	slices baked ham
6	slices mild cheese
12	slices frozen French toast
2	tblsp. butter or regular margarine

· Place 1 slice ham and 1 slice cheese between 2 slices toast; place in shallow baking pan with melted butter. Bake in hot oven (425°F.) 15 to 20 minutes. Turn once. Makes 6 sandwiches.

Note: See directions for freezing French toast in Chapter 5.

READY-TO-GO BOLOGNA SANDWICHES

Tuck them in the oven to heat while you get the rest of the supper

1	lb. bologna
¾	lb. sharp process cheese
3	(3″) dill pickles
1	slice onion or 2 tblsp. chopped green onion
½	c. salad dressing
1	tblsp. prepared mustard
Soft	butter or regular margarine
16	wiener buns

· Grind bologna, cheese and pickles in food chopper. If using onion slice, grind and add it to mixture. Or add chopped green onion. Stir in salad dressing and mustard.
· Butter inside of split buns evenly, spreading to the edge. Spread with bologna mixture. Put halves together to make 16 sandwiches.
· Wrap one layer deep in foil packages; label, date and freeze. (They reheat quicker than when stacked.) Recommended storage time: 2 to 3 weeks.
· To serve, if you wish to use some of the sandwiches without freezing, heat in a slow oven (275°F.) until filling is hot and cheese melted, about 30 minutes. Place unthawed frozen sandwiches, unwrapped, in a hot oven (400°F.) and heat 30 to 45 minutes.

Sunday Supper Salads

When company stops by at dusk Sunday afternoon, you often want to say: "Do stay for supper." You'll find the invitation comes easier when there's a good salad in the freezer.

This chapter contains several recipes you'll like—so take your pick. We know you're going to get compliments on the salads you try.

FROSTY SALADS

Country cooks find it convenient on busy days to take a salad from the freezer ready to serve. Especially does the hostess enjoy having a glamorous one on hand the day she entertains. It takes time to make a beautiful salad, but if the freezer holds one, about all the cook has to do to serve it is to thaw it partially and add last-minute garnishes and lettuce.

Fruit salads are favorites for freezing, but other kinds are gaining prestige with the discovery of satisfactory ways to handle them. If fresh fruits, like peaches, are used, combine them with citrus fruits, grapefruit and oranges, or add a little lemon juice or powdered ascorbic acid. Often fruit salads contain cream cheese or whipped cream.

Mayonnaise and home-cooked dressings tend to separate when frozen. If you do use them in fruit salads, it is a good idea to mix only a small amount of them with cream cheese or whipped cream. Commercial salad dressing gives good results in chicken, fish and meat salads. The trick is to use a little more commercial salad

dressing than usual in salads. In case such salads do separate a little after defrosting, you usually can recombine them by stirring.

Tuna, salmon, shrimp, crab, lobster, ham, pork and beef salads may be frozen. Many farm women like to keep cooked chicken and meat frozen for convenient salad making.

Gelatin salads freeze well if correctly handled. Research shows that it is important to use less liquid than usual—one fourth less. If the recipe calls for 2 cups water or other liquid, reduce it to 1½ cups unless the recipe is especially developed for a frozen salad, like those that follow. Tomato aspic, with the quantity of liquid adjusted, freezes beautifully. Celery, diced, retains some of its texture and color, but few vegetables are satisfactory in frozen salads.

Combinations of fresh fruits, frozen for mixed salads, never go begging. To serve them, partially thaw the fruits and mix in the salad dressing. Add nuts at the same time, if you wish—they sometimes discolor and acquire a bitter taste when frozen in salads. This is especially true if the salad is held more than a few days. Bananas usually are best added at serving time too. Raw apple slices tend to become flabby when frozen.

To Freeze: You can freeze the salad in a large block, wrap it in moisture-vaporproof packaging material and return it to the freezer. Or freeze it in a cylindrical carton if you want to push it out and cut it in round slices for serving. Some women like to slice frozen salads before packaging them, separating the servings with cellophane or plastic wrap. They add an overwrap of moisture-vaporproof paper and place in the freezer.

Or freeze salads in paper cups or individual molds. You can remove them from the cups or molds when they are frozen and wrap individually in foil or plastic wrap. Put them in a box or plastic freezer bag to keep them together in the freezer. If you prefer, freeze the salad in a refrigerator tray with dividers and treat the salad-cubes like individual salads. Recommended storage time: About 2 to 6 weeks.

To Serve: Never completely thaw frozen fruit salads before serving. Serve them as they come from the freezer or let mellow in refrigerator about 1 hour. You may thaw chicken and tuna salads overnight in refrigerator. Arrange on crisp salad greens and add any last-minute garnishes.

CHICKEN/BLUEBERRY SALAD

Something new and extra-good in chicken salad—a New Jersey favorite

1   envelope unflavored gelatin
¼   c. cold water
1   can condensed cream of
        celery soup
½   c. commercial salad dressing
¼   tsp. salt
2   c. finely cut cooked chicken
1   c. diced celery
1   c. fresh or frozen blueberries

· Soften gelatin in cold water. Heat soup over medium heat until boiling. Add to gelatin; stir to dissolve.

· Blend in salad dressing. Add remaining ingredients.
· Pour into a 1½-qt. mold. Chill until firm. Makes 8 servings.
· Wrap, label, date and freeze. Recommended storage time: Up to 1 month.
· To serve, thaw in refrigerator overnight. Serve on salad greens.

CHICKEN/PINEAPPLE SALAD

A choice recipe from New Mexico where hot corn sticks are a go-with

1 ½   c. cooked chicken, cut in
        ½" pieces
¾   c. drained crushed pineapple
1   c. chopped pecans
¼   tsp. salt
1   c. heavy cream, whipped
1   c. commercial salad dressing

· Toss together chicken, pineapple, pecans and salt. Blend together whipped cream and salad dressing. Fold into chicken mixture. Pour into a 1-qt. refrigerator tray. Makes 5 to 6 servings.
· Place tray in freezer. When frozen, unmold, wrap, label, date and return to freezer. Or slice and wrap each frozen portion individually in foil. Return to freezer. Recommended storage time: Up to 1 month.
· To serve, remove from freezer 15 minutes before serving. Serve on crisp greens. Top with salad dressing, if desired, and garnish each serving with a spoonful of cranberry jelly or sauce, drained, or seedless green grapes.

Note: Cut chicken in tiny pieces. Then you can cut neat slices.

FROZEN TUNA SALAD

Makes excellent sandwich filling

2   (7 oz.) cans tuna
Dash of pepper
2   tsp. prepared mustard
¼   c. pickle relish
½   c. commercial salad dressing
1   tblsp. lemon juice

· Mix together all the ingredients. Divide into 4 custard cups or molds. Makes 2½ cups (or enough filling for 10 sandwiches).
· Wrap, label, date and freeze. Recommended storage time: 6 weeks.
· To serve, partially thaw in refrigerator and unmold on salad greens.

REFRESHING FRUIT SALAD

Not so rich as most frozen fruit salads—doesn't "weep" when served

1   (1 lb.) can fruit cocktail
1   (8¼ oz.) can crushed
     pineapple
1   (1 lb.) can apricot halves
1   banana, diced
3   tblsp. lemon juice
½   tsp. grated lemon peel
1   (3 oz.) pkg. lemon flavor
     gelatin
1   c. heavy cream, whipped

· Drain fruit cocktail, pineapple and apricots, reserving juices. Cut apricot halves in fourths. Gently toss bananas with lemon juice and peel.
· Heat 1 c. reserved fruit juices to boiling. Dissolve gelatin in hot juice. Add ½ c. cool, reserved juice. Chill until mixture starts to thicken.
· Whip gelatin mixture with rotary or electric beater until thick and light.

Fold in fruits and whipped cream. Pour into two 9×5×3" loaf pans or 1-qt. molds. Makes 12 servings.
· Place in freezer; when frozen, remove. Wrap, label, date and return to freezer. Recommended storage time: About 2 weeks.
· To serve, let partially thaw in refrigerator several hours.

EVER-READY WALDORF SALAD

Serve topped with salad dressing and thin unpeeled apple wedges

1   (1 lb. 4 oz.) can crushed
     pineapple
3   eggs, slightly beaten
¾   c. sugar
⅓   c. lemon juice
¼   tsp. salt
¾   c. diced celery
3   medium unpeeled apples,
     diced
¾   c. chopped walnuts
1½   c. heavy cream, whipped

· Drain pineapple, reserving ¾ c. juice.
· Combine juice with eggs, sugar, lemon juice and salt. Cook over low heat until thick, stirring constantly. Cool.
· Add pineapple, celery, apples and nuts. Fold in whipped cream. Turn into two 9×5×3" loaf pans or a 9" square pan. Makes 12 servings.
· Place in freezer. When frozen, wrap, label, date and return to freezer. Recommended storage time: Up to 1 month.
· To serve, cut in serving-size portions and place on lettuce-lined plates. Garnish with spoonfuls of salad

dressing and insert slices of unpeeled red apples, skin side up, in fan shape.

Note: Apples soften but give salad a pleasing flavor; celery stays crisp.

THREE-WAY FROZEN SALAD

Choose from our trio of colors

2 (3 oz.) pkgs. cream cheese
1 c. heavy cream
⅓ c. mayonnaise
2 tblsp. lemon juice
1 c. miniature marshmallows
1 (10 oz.) pkg. frozen sliced strawberries, thawed and drained
1 (1 lb. 13 oz.) can crushed pineapple, drained

• Whip cheese; slowly add cream, beating until thick. Fold in remaining ingredients.
• Pour into muffin-pan cups lined with cupcake papers. Garnish with nuts, maraschino cherries or coconut. Makes about 18.
• Place in freezer. When frozen, remove from pans; put in plastic freezer bags; seal, and return to freezer. Recommended storage time: Up to 1 month.
• To serve, remove from freezer in the quantity desired; remove paper cups; place on crisp greens.

VARIATIONS

MINT/GRAPE: Substitute 1 c. white seedless grapes for berries; add green food color and ¼ tsp. peppermint extract.

GOLDEN PEACH: Substitute 1 (10 oz.) pkg. frozen peaches, drained, for berries; add yellow food color.

CREAMY FROZEN SALAD

Specialty of a Hoosier hostess—sour cream adds wonderful flavor

2 c. dairy sour cream
2 tblsp. lemon juice
¾ c. sugar
⅛ tsp. salt
1 (9 oz.) can crushed pineapple, drained
¼ c. sliced maraschino cherries
¼ c. chopped pecans
1 banana, sliced

• Blend cream, lemon juice, sugar and salt. Stir in other ingredients.
• Pour into 1-qt. mold, or cupcake papers. Makes 8 servings.
• Place in freezer. When frozen, remove from freezer; wrap, label, date and return to freezer. Recommended storage time: About 2 weeks.
• To serve, place on crisp greens.

Home Canning

Where and When to Start · Canning Equipment · Steps to Successful Canning · Raw and Hot Packs · Care after Processing · Opening for Use

Home canning is coming into its own. Not that it went out of style, but after World War II, freezers moved into kitchens by the thousands. And many homemakers, like little girls with new toys, froze just about every food their farms produced. By now they are more selective about what they freeze. Foods that are excellent when canned are not so frequently crowded into freezers where space is scarce.

Many incentives have restored popularity to home canning. Economy, for instance—canning is an inexpensive way of preserving food. And it saves many vegetables and fruits that otherwise would pile up and spoil at peak seasons. Improved methods are making canned products better. Certainly the greater convenience of farm kitchens has much to do with it, for canning is easier. Newer and remodeled homes have utility rooms where you can fix food for canning and keep the clutter out of kitchens. Many country cooks, like an Iowa homemaker and her three 4-H daughters, do the family canning in their cool basement—no interference with getting meals in the kitchen.

No letters from readers bring greater pleasure to our Food Staff than those that tell of prizes won at county and state fairs with FARM JOURNAL recipes for canned foods, and with their own original creations. We receive enough of these friendly notes to know smart country cooks consider canning an art—that they take pride in blue ribbons and money they win in competitive exhibits. Interest in gourmet canned foods is at an all-time high. Use this chapter's up-to-date methods to can praiseworthy fruits and vegetables. You'll be proud of the shining jars in your fruit closet.

Where and When to Start

A Wisconsin farm woman says she starts thinking about her summer canning the first spring evening she hears a cowbird on the pasture fence mock a phoebe in the woods. No doubt you have other signals—the run of smelts, bloom on the dogwood, shooting stars along the path to the garden, purple lilacs brightening bushes. Anything that announces spring is here and summer is not far behind!

So figure out your family's needs and take into consideration what you will can. This means you'll soon be getting the ground ready to plant your garden. And a Wisconsin friend says that's the best time to decide how much you want to can this season—much better than growing garden surpluses that may go to waste. The charts on the inside back cover of this book give you approximate yields of many foods when canned.

Your Canning Equipment and Supplies

Look over your canning equipment early in the season. Then buy the necessary jar lids and other supplies. Once you've done this, you are ready to tackle the job when the food—fruits, vegetables, meats, poultry and game—is available. Some homemakers "put up" foods in school canning centers. They, too, need to get their supply of jars and lids ready.

Jars and Lids: Look them over carefully. If they have cracks, chips or dents, don't use them—it's poor economy. Use new self-sealing lids or rubber rings. And don't test the rings by stretching. Tighten bails on glass-top jars if they are loose. Do it this way: Bend bail down in center; then bend on sides to snap it back in place.

Water Bath Canner: Use any kettle or metal container deep enough for water to cover jar tops by 2". There must be an additional 2" to allow space for boiling. Place a rack in the bottom of the kettle to hold the jars about 1" off the bottom of the container. Partitions in the rack are helpful; they keep jars from touching and from falling against the sides of the canner. The rack may be of wire or wood, but not of resinous wood. You can use your pressure canner if it is deep enough. Just set the cover in place, but do not fasten it, and leave the petcock open for steam to escape.

Steam Pressure Canner: If your canner has a dial gauge, either old or new, have it checked for accuracy before and at least once during the canning season. It is a good idea to have it checked more frequently during the canning season. If the gauge is not correct (10 lbs. pressure at 240°F.) the processing is not accurate. All the bacteria, including botulinus, may not be killed. Ask your County Extension Home Economist where to have it checked.

Clean the petcock and safety valve

by pulling a pipe cleaner or string through them.

Keep the kettle clean, but never put the cover in water. Wipe it off with a sudsy cloth and then with a clean cloth wrung from clear water. Dry thoroughly before putting away.

Pressure Saucepan: If saucepans are equipped with a gauge or weight for showing and controlling pressure at 10 pounds, they often are used to process small jars of food. Most authorities recommend adding 20 minutes to the pressure cooker time to make up for the quick climb in temperature at the beginning of the process and for the more rapid cooling to zero at the finish. In operating the pressure saucepan for canning, follow the directions of the manufacturer, but after processing *do not lower* pressure with cold water.

More Steps to Successful Canning

1. Wash standard canning jars and lids (except self-sealing lids) in sudsy warm water and rinse thoroughly. Or do it the easy way—in your electric dishwasher. Follow the manufacturer's directions for self-sealing lids. If none are given, dip them in clear, boiling water just before use. (Tongs are helpful.) Or scald by placing in pan and pouring boiling water over them. Wash and scald jars and invert on clean cloth, or leave in the scalding water; drain just before filling. It is not necessary to boil jars when food is processed.

2. Select fresh, firm fruits and young, tender vegetables. Can only freshly killed meats and poultry, chilled at once and kept chilled until canned.

3. Rush picked fruits and vegetables from orchard and garden into jars for processing as quickly as possible. If you must keep them a few hours, store them in a cool, dry and airy place. In case you must buy these foods for canning, try to get them from orchards and gardens nearby. This freshness will make a big difference in your success with canning —especially in the flavor.

4. Sort fruits and vegetables for ripeness or maturity and size so they will cook evenly. Wash them thoroughly, small lots at a time, under running water or through several changes of water even though you will peel them. Dirt contains bacteria that are difficult to kill. Lift the vegetables and fruits out of the water so the washed-off soil will not redeposit on them. Rinse out pans between changes of water, but don't let these foods soak or they may lose flavor and food value.

Wash poultry and game, if you like, but do not wash meats. Wipe them with a clean, damp cloth.

5. Select your pack. The two recommended ways of home canning most foods are the raw pack and the hot pack.

Raw Pack: This may be used for fruits, tomatoes, asparagus, green beans, carrots, cowpeas, black-eyed peas and summer squash. Pack the uncooked food firmly into clean jars, but do not crush it. Cover with boiling syrup, juice or water, leaving head space. Press tomatoes down so their juices cover them; do not add water to tomatoes. Work out air bubbles by putting a knife down the sides of the jar in several places or rotating jar. This helps keep the liquid over the top of the food and prevents top darkening. If more liquid is needed, add boiling water, but leave head space.

Meats may be canned by the raw-pack or hot-pack method. For the raw pack, cut pieces to fit into the jars. Pack loosely to within 1″ of jar top. Do not add liquid.

Hot Pack: Pack precooked foods into hot jars. The precooking eliminates shrinkage and the empty space that results in the jars. Be sure to precook foods the length of time given in the directions in the chapters that follow. Add hot syrup, cooking liquid or boiling water to within ½″ from top.

6. Cook meats one third to one half done.

7. Add 1 tsp. salt to each quart jar of vegetables and meats if you want to season them.

8. Wipe filled jar edges and rubber rings, if used, with a clean cloth to remove food spilled on them.

9. Adjust jar caps. When our directions state this you will do one of three things, depending on kind of lids you are using. If you use self-sealing lids, put the flat metal lid on the jar, composition next to the glass.

Screw the metal band on tight; lid has enough give to let air escape during processing. Do not tighten the band after processing. You will partially seal jars if you use one-piece metal caps and rubber rings—you screw the cap down tightly and then turn cap back ¼″. For glass-top jars, put the long wire over the top of lid so it fits in groove. Leave short wire up.

10. Water bath: This is commonly used for fruits and tomatoes. Have the water hot for the raw pack, but not boiling (it must be boiling hot for the hot pack). Lower jars carefully into water on rack, using care they do not touch. Cover canner. When the water comes to a full rolling boil, count your time. Keep water boiling vigorously throughout the processing. If you need to add more water, be sure it is boiling.

11. Pressure canner: Place jars on rack in pressure canner containing 1 to 2″ water. Leave room between jars for the steam to circulate freely. Exhaust all the air by letting steam escape for 10 minutes before closing the petcock.

Count time when gauge registers the specified pressure. To avoid drawing liquid from the jars, keep the pressure constant by adjusting the heat. Thermostatically controlled burners and units are helpful in processing food in pressure canners. When processing time is up, move pressure canner to a cooler place.

Do not open canner until the pressure gauge registers zero. Then open the petcock slowly until no more steam escapes.

Care After Processing

1. If food in jars is boiling vigorously, let the jars set in the canner for a few minutes. Remove and set jars upright on a board, rack or folded cloth, not on a cold surface. Leave room between for circulation of air, but keep out of drafts.

2. Complete your seals at once unless closures are self-sealing. These require no further tightening.

3. Test seals when jars are cold. Examine self-sealing metal lids; the center of the lid should look drawn in (concave). Or tap lid with a spoon. If sealed, it will have a clear, ringing sound. Remove metal bands. Tip jars with other closures. If they do not leak, they are sealed. If seals are imperfect, determine cause of sealing failure and recan at once, using new lids. (Empty jars, pack and process food as if it were fresh.) Or use the imperfectly sealed jar right away at meals, keeping it in refrigerator until time to heat.

4. Wipe jars clean and until they shine. Label with name of product and date. Store in a dry, cool place, away from danger of freezing.

Opening for Use

1. If you follow the directions in this cookbook, there is little or no chance of spoilage in your canned foods. But look for spoilage signs when you open a jar. If the cap bulges or the food has a peculiar odor or look, discard it. Even if there is no indication of spoilage, *do not taste*. Boil all nonacid vegetables, covered, at least 10 minutes, except corn and greens like spinach. Boil them, also meats and poultry, 20 minutes. For altitudes above 3000 feet, boil the food 15 minutes instead of 10; 30 minutes instead of 20. At very high altitudes, boil even longer.

Smell the food as it boils. Heating usually makes spoilage odors noticeable. It is possible for canned nonacid vegetables and meats and poultry to contain a food poisoning called botulism. It is caused by the toxin produced by botulism bacteria that grow in foods in the absence of air. This toxin is very poisonous. But it can be destroyed by boiling. That is why it is *important to follow the canning steps carefully, to make certain the pressure canner's gauge is accurate and to boil these foods before tasting them.*

2. Punch a hole in self-sealing lids and lift up. You should never reuse them anyway. If jars have rubbers, pull the rubber out with pliers to avoid necessity for prying open, which may dent or bend the lid and crack or chip the jar.

You will find detailed directions for canning fruits, vegetables, meats, poultry and game in the following chapters.

Make *altitude adjustments*. The time and pressures for processing foods in this book are for altitudes less than 1000 feet above sea level. The necessary adjustments are given in the following chapters.

CHAPTER 9

JAMS, JELLIES AND OTHER SPREADS

Recipes for Frozen Jellies, Equipment, Containers · Short-cook Jellies and Jams, Longer-cook Jellies and Jams · Jelly Sauces · Fruit Preserves · Special Occasion Conserves · Old-fashioned Fruit Butters · Cheerful Marmalades · Gourmet Spreads · Wild Fruit Specialties

The next two chapters deal with freezing and canning—making jams, jellies and other spreads and putting up fruit juices. While Grandmother canned spreads and juices, today's country cooks both can and freeze. They keep an array of jams, jellies, preserves, conserves and marmalades in their freezers and fruit closets to give meals color and appetite appeal. And on the spur of the moment!

You will find recipes in this chapter for the best frozen and canned sweet spreads that FARM JOURNAL'S readers make. You will notice that country cooks use different methods. Some farm women prefer the traditional, longer-cook way of making jelly, but more of them prefer the short-cook method or the newer, frozen jellies and jams. They have enthusiastic praise for the easier-to-fix frozen spreads that retain so much fresh fruit flavor and aroma.

With fewer city women making jams and jellies, fruit growers' wives often find it profitable to sell their specialties at roadside stands, by mail and in gourmet shops. Don't miss this chapter's Gourmet Corner, filled with potential sellers and winners in fair exhibits. And be sure to note the delicacies made from wild fruits, often to be had for the picking—bright red chokecherries, clusters of wild grapes on tangled vines, sweet strawberries ripening in the pasture.

These direct-from-the-farm-to-you recipes will add sparkle and flavor to your meals and boost your fame as a good cook. And they may inspire you to earn money in your own kitchen!

Luscious Fruity Sweets
MEAL PLANNERS RELY ON THESE ACCENTS

Gentle spring breezes brushing the purple iris are the signal that it's time for rhubarb jelly and strawberry jam. Many country cooks kick off the canning season by fixing these sweets.

You may prefer to can or freeze fruits and juices and make the jelly when the spirit moves you. Certainly there is something satisfying about ladling these sweets into glasses or jars when blizzards whip the trees. "The kitchen is so comfortable and cheery in stormy winter weather," a farm woman says. "I feel I've conquered nature on the warpath if I make jelly and jam then."

On the following pages you will find fruity treats to fix in season and the year round—and by various methods. So take your choice.

Jellies, Jams and Other Spreads

Even though new ways of making fruity sweets are popular, the yardstick for measuring their quality is the same as Grandmother's. The first requirement is that they carry the flavor and bright color of the fruit.

Jelly at its best is sparkling and clear. It quivers slightly when you turn it out in a dish, but it holds its shape. When you cut it with a spoon, it retains the angle of the cut. Topnotch jelly is tender and spreads easily.

Excellent jams are jelly-like in consistency and they are fairly smooth because fruits are crushed before cooking. Soft textures of berries make them ideal for making jams. According to Michigan fruit growers' wives who sell their homemade spreads, preferences for different kinds of fruity sweets depend much on the age of the customer. Younger people generally choose jams in which they can see the fruit, while the older generation selects jelly and fruit butters. Our readers sent us many more jam than jelly recipes. They say jams are easier to make.

How to Make Jellies and Jams

You can take your pick of three methods of making jellies and jams —the *uncooked, short-cook and longer-cook* ways. The taste and consistency of the products obtained varies according to the method followed. You will want to choose the one your family and friends like best.

Regardless of how you make these fruity spreads, four ingredients, in the right proportions, are important: *fruit, pectin, sugar and acid.*

You may obtain pectin directly from the fruit itself (underripe fruit contains more than fully ripe), or you may add commercial powdered or liquid fruit pectin, which also contains some acid.

Sugar helps to jell fruity mixtures and is a preservative, too. Use either cane or beet sugar—they have the same chemical composition.

Acids vary in quantity, but underripe fruits contain more than ripe, just as they contain more pectin. You may need to add more acid than is in the fruit. Most women use lemon juice for this, but you can buy crystalline citric acid at the drugstore and use it for lemon juice, ⅛ teaspoon for 1 tablespoon lemon juice.

Your chances of success will be greater if you *cook a small amount of fruit at a time*. Recipe sizes in this chapter are based on this rule.

All recipes have been tested. And most of them are highly prized favorites of superior farm cooks. Even so, you may sometimes have different results with a recipe. Variations are due to the amount of pectin and acid in fruits and berries, which fluctuates with the year, area, soil and variety.

Equipment to Simplify Jelly Making and Insure Success

First on the list of necessary equipment for jam and jelly making is a large kettle, holding 8 to 12 quarts, to permit the rapidly boiling fruit-sugar mixture to expand without boiling over. A utensil with a broad, flat bottom is best.

For jelly making you need a jelly bag of firm muslin or cotton flannel, or a fruit press. Or you may prefer to use, instead of the bag, cheesecloth layers spread in a colander. A stand for jelly bags is convenient.

In making short-cook and uncooked jellies and jams, a clock with a minute hand helps with correct timing. And a candy, jelly or deep-fat thermometer is a guide to the jellying point in the long-cook method.

Other kitchen tools you'll need: standard 1 quart and 1 cup measures, measuring spoons, paring and utility knives, food chopper, grater, masher, reamer, wire basket, ladle, long-handled spoon and bowls. Household scales come in handy.

CHOOSE CONTAINERS WITH CARE

Canning jars with lids that seal airtight are desirable, especially in warm climates. With them you eliminate the danger of the fruity mixture oozing out and causing spoilage. Straight-sided or shoulderless jars permit you to turn jelly out for serving. Do not use jars with cracks or chips. And follow the manufacturer's directions for using the lids. This is important.

You may prefer glasses for jellies; they must be sealed with paraffin and then covered. It is safer to seal cooked spreads in jars with lids because paraffin on them tends to loosen and break the seal. To get an airtight seal on any lid, fill one jar at a time with the boiling mixture and seal at once or process in boiling water bath.

In hot, humid climates it is especially desirable to process cooked jellies, jams, conserves, preserves, marmalades and fruit butters in boiling water bath to insure a good seal.

If you use paraffin, pour on only enough to make a layer ⅛" thick. Prick any bubbles that form; otherwise, in cooling, they may form holes. For a 6-ounce glass with a top diameter of approximately 2½", it takes about 1 tablespoon paraffin to make a good seal. One thin layer is better than two, or than a thick one, because one thin layer can expand or contract more readily and will give a better seal. Melt paraffin over water (in double boiler) and never let it heat enough to smoke or catch fire.

PREPARE CONTAINERS CAREFULLY

Get the jars or glasses ready before you start to make the jam, jelly or other spread. Your electric dishwasher is handy for this chore, if you have one. Or wash the jars and glasses in hot, soapy water and rinse with hot water. Keep them warm in a pan of hot water or in a slow oven so they will not break when the hot mixture is added to them. Invert them just before using to be sure they are dry inside before you fill them. Prepare the lids as manufacturer directs.

ALLOW HEAD SPACE WHEN FILLING

For longer-cook and short-cook spreads, fill jelly glasses to within ½" of top. Leave about ¼" head space in jars with self-seal lids. Allow about ½" head space with uncooked or frozen jellies, jams and spreads.

Three Ways to Make Jelly

No matter what method you use to make jelly, the first steps—preparing the fruit and extracting the juice—are the same. Wash sound, firm fruit. Discard blemished and spoiled spots and remove stem and blossom parts. Core, but do not peel hard fruits like apples. Cut fruit in small pieces or put it through the coarse blade of food chopper to insure extraction of the pectin. Crush soft fruits like berries to start flow of juices.

Add a minimum of water in the cooking process or you'll dilute the juice. Firm fruits, like apples, need about 1 cup water to 1 pound of fruit. Juicy plums require less, about ¼ cup to 1 pound fruit. Firm plums, like the Damson, require ½ to ¾ cup water to 1 pound fruit. Soft fruits and berries require no water unless they are not juicy—then you use the same amount as for plums.

To extract juice, bring the fruit (with water added if needed) to a boil and boil rapidly until tender, 10 to 20 minutes. Excessive boiling reduces jellying strength and destroys full fruit flavors. Pour the juice into a wet jelly bag of muslin or cotton flannel with the nap inside or into four thicknesses of cheesecloth spread in a colander, and *let it drip out* for the clearest jelly. Or gently twist the bag or cheesecloth to press out the juice. The juice then is ready for jelly making, although you may want to strain it again through layers of cheesecloth for exceptional clearness if you have forced it through the bag or press.

The next steps depend on the method you use. Since the uncooked or frozen jellies and jams are the newest ones, we'll explain them first.

Uncooked Jellies, Jams and Spreads

Uncooked, frozen jellies, jams and spreads have thousands of champions in country kitchens. Not only are they less work than longer-cook methods, but they keep more of the bright color and delightful aroma of fresh fruits. And because they are made of ripe fruits and are not cooked, they retain the maximum fresh fruity taste.

These frozen sweets are easy to fix; you do not make pectin and acid tests but merely add commercial pectin. The recipes call for more sugar and you obtain more jelly and jam from a given amount of fruit juice than when you follow the longer-cook method. You skip the greatest hazard in jelly making—determining the jellying point. Besides, you can make frozen jellies, jams and spreads the year round.

These newer-type jellies, jams and spreads were developed through research in laboratories and test kitchens. USDA's Research, on a commercial scale, by Western Research Laboratories, Albany, California, prompted our own FARM JOURNAL Test Kitchens to develop techniques for the homemaker to use in freezing jams. Other pioneers in research were Purdue, Colorado and Washington State universities.

Scientists first determined the correct proportions of sugar, fruit and pectin and studied the enzyme action in fruits. Then home economists simplified their methods of preparation for successful use in home kitchens. Here is the route to success:

Follow the directions in the recipes, measuring ingredients carefully. Use commercial pectin and do not attempt to substitute liquid and powdered pectins for each other unless the amount of each kind is specified. You will use more sugar than for cooked jellies and jams and will have to add acid, like lemon juice or ascorbic acid, for the less acid fruits.

Give the jams and jellies time to set before you store them in the freezer. It may take only a few minutes, but sometimes it takes two to three days. If they do not set within a few hours, put them in the refrigerator to finish setting.

If you notice a white moldlike formation in the frozen products when you take them from the freezer to serve, don't be alarmed. It occasionally forms during storage of several months, is harmless and will melt quickly at room temperature. And once you open a jam, jelly or spread, keep it in the refrigerator and use continuously. It will spoil if held at room temperature.

Store uncooked jellies and jams in the freezer at 0°F. or lower and they will keep six months or longer.

In the refrigerator they will keep two to three weeks, a month or longer in the refrigerator's freezer compartment. You can keep the uncooked spreads in the refrigerator several weeks and in the freezer a year. Favorite recipes follow.

Uncooked Jelly for Freezing

You can use frozen fruit juice concentrates, canned and bottled juices as well as juices extracted from fresh fruits—which, of course, have the freshest flavor. You can store these jellies successfully in the refrigerator for 3 to 4 weeks. They will keep their flavor 6 months or longer in the freezer at 0°F. or lower. Once you open them, continue using.

TART CHERRY JELLY

Sparkling, cherry-red—serve with hot rolls when ham is on platter

4 ¾	c. sugar
3	c. fresh cherry juice
1	pkg. powdered fruit pectin
½	c. water

• Add sugar to 1¼ c. cherry juice; stir thoroughly.
• Slowly add pectin to water. Heat almost to boiling point, stirring constantly. Pour hot pectin into remaining 1¾ c. cherry juice. Stir until pectin is dissolved. Let pectin mixture stand 15 minutes, but stir it occasionally.
• Add the juice-sugar mixture; stir until all the sugar is dissolved.
• Pour into containers; cover with tight lids.
• Let stand at room temperature until set, overnight or at least 6 hours.
• Freeze or refrigerate. Makes 5 to 6 half pints.

Note: Frozen cherries may be used. Grind whole frozen cherries and thaw. Pour into jelly bag and allow juice to drain. Squeeze bag to obtain the maximum quantity of juice. If juice is from commercially frozen cherries, reduce sugar to 4¼ c.

VARIATION

BERRY JELLIES: Follow recipe for Tart Cherry Jelly using juice from fresh berries instead of the cherry juice. Reduce the sugar from 4¾ c. to 4½ c. Use blackberries, black raspberries, boysenberries, loganberries or red raspberries.

CONCORD GRAPE JELLY

Glows like amethysts—good with chicken, veal and cold roast pork

1	pkg. powdered fruit pectin
2	c. lukewarm water
1	(6 oz.) can frozen grape juice concentrate
3 ¼	c. sugar

• Dissolve pectin in water in a 2-qt. bowl. Add pectin slowly, stirring constantly until completely dissolved. Let stand 45 minutes, stirring occasionally (stir, do not beat).
• Thaw grape juice concentrate by setting can in cold water. Pour it into a 1-qt. bowl. Add 1½ c. sugar to the

juice. Mix thoroughly (all sugar will not dissolve).

• Add remaining sugar to dissolved pectin. Stir until sugar dissolves.

• Add the juice mixture to the pectin mixture. Stir until sugar dissolves.

• Pour into containers. Cover with tight lids. Let stand at room temperature about 24 hours or until set. Freeze or refrigerate. Makes 5 to 6 half pints.

VARIATION

BOYSENBERRY JELLY: Make like Grape Jelly substituting 1 (6 oz.) can frozen boysenberry juice concentrate for the grape juice concentrate.

ORANGE/LEMON JELLY

Fine flavor accent with eggs and egg dishes—wonderful with roast duck

1	pkg. powdered fruit pectin
2	c. lukewarm water
1	(6 oz.) can frozen orange juice concentrate
¼	c. strained fresh lemon juice
4½	c. sugar

• Dissolve pectin in water in a 2-qt. bowl. Add the pectin slowly, stirring constantly until completely dissolved. Let stand 45 minutes, stirring occasionally (not beating).

• Thaw orange juice by placing can in cold water. Then pour juice into a 1-qt. bowl. Add the lemon juice and 2½ c. sugar. Mix thoroughly (all sugar will not dissolve).

• Add the remaining 2 c. sugar slowly to the dissolved pectin. Stir until sugar dissolves.

• Add juice mixture to pectin mixture. Stir constantly until sugar dissolves.

• Pour into containers. Cover with tight lids. Let stand at room temperature overnight or until set. Freeze or refrigerate. Makes 5 to 6 half pints.

Uncooked or Frozen Jams

If the jams seem a little stiff when you open them for serving, stir gently to soften. Or if they "weep" when cut, stir to blend them. They will mold or ferment if kept at room temperature more than a few days, so always store in refrigerator.

Jams from Frozen Fruits

STRAWBERRY JAM

Makes hot biscuits and vanilla ice cream taste equally special

2	(10 oz.) pkgs. frozen, sweetened strawberries
3	c. sugar
1	pkg. powdered fruit pectin
1	c. water

• Thaw frozen berries and grind or blend in blender to make a purée.

• Add sugar, mix thoroughly and let

stand 20 minutes; stir occasionally.
· Combine powdered pectin and water; boil rapidly 1 minute, stirring.
· Remove from heat. Add the fruit to the pectin; stir for 2 minutes.
· Pour into clean containers; cover with tight-fitting lids. Let stand at room temperature 24 hours. If jam does not set, refrigerate until it does.
· Freeze at 0°F. or lower, or refrigerate. Makes 4 to 5 half pints.

VARIATIONS

Omit powdered pectin and water and use ½ c. liquid fruit pectin. No heating is necessary.

CHERRY JAM: Put frozen tart cherries through food chopper. Add 2 tsp. lemon juice. Use cherries instead of strawberries.

PEACH JAM: Mash frozen peaches when thawed. Stir in 1 tsp. powdered ascorbic acid or 3 tblsp. lemon juice. Substitute for strawberries.

RED RASPBERRY JAM: Use 3 (10 oz.) pkgs. of frozen raspberries and 4 c. sugar. Prepare like Strawberry Jam.

Jams from Fresh Fruits

STRAWBERRY JAM

When spring gives you plump, juicy berries, use this recipe

2   c. finely mashed or sieved
       strawberries
4   c. sugar
1   pkg. powdered fruit pectin
1   c. water

· Combine fruit and sugar. Let stand 20 minutes, stirring occasionally.
· Boil powdered pectin and water rapidly for 1 minute, stirring constantly. Remove from heat. Add berries and stir about 2 minutes.
· Pour into containers and cover. Let stand at room temperature 1 hour. Refrigerate until set.
· Store in freezer. Once opened, refrigerate. Makes 5 to 6 half pints.

VARIATIONS

Omit powdered pectin and water. Use ½ c. liquid fruit pectin. No heating is necessary.

APRICOT JAM: Add 1 tsp. powdered ascorbic acid or 3 tblsp. lemon juice to finely mashed and measured fresh apricots. Substitute for strawberries.

BLACK RASPBERRY JAM: Substitute black raspberries for strawberries.

CHERRY JAM: Pit tart cherries and put through food chopper. Measure and substitute for strawberries.

PEACH JAM: Add 1 tsp. powdered ascorbic acid or 3 tblsp. lemon juice to mashed peaches. Substitute peaches for strawberries.

PLUM JAM: Pit *mild* plums and put through food chopper. Add 2 to 3 tsp. lemon juice, if desired. Measure and substitute for strawberries.

FRESH RED RASPBERRY JAM

Luscious when spread on warm-from-the-oven cakes and breads

3   c. finely mashed or sieved red raspberries
6   c. sugar
1   pkg. powdered fruit pectin
1   c. water

· Combine berries and sugar. Let stand at room temperature about 20 minutes, stirring occasionally.
· Boil pectin and water rapidly for 1 minute, stirring. Remove from heat.
· Add fruit and stir about 2 minutes.
· Pour into containers; cover. Let stand at room temperature 24 hours. If jam does not set, refrigerate until it does.
· Store in freezer. Makes about 8 to 9 half pints.

VARIATIONS

Omit powdered pectin and water. Use ½ c. liquid fruit pectin. No heating is necessary.

BLACKBERRY JAM: Substitute blackberries for red raspberries, but reduce sugar from 6 c. to 5½ c.

CONCORD GRAPE JAM: Heat stemmed grapes without adding water to break skins and soften grapes. Put through a food mill or colander to remove seeds. Measure pulp and substitute for raspberries.

TART PLUM JAM: Pit tart plums and put through food chopper or blend in blender. Measure and substitute pulp for raspberries.

Uncooked Spreads

Spreads are less sweet than jams and they hold more of the delicate fresh fruit taste and aroma. You add more pectin but since it controls the consistency, you can use a little less of it if you prefer thinner spreads, more if you like thicker spreads. Make up a test batch to determine if you wish to use more or less. Add light corn syrup to reduce formation of sugar crystals during storage.

The best way to make the fruit purée is to use a food mill, an electric mixer with a 1-qt. bowl, or a blender. Or you can mash the fruit very fine.

To make a luscious topping for ice cream, thin the spread when you open it with light corn syrup to the consistency you like.

You can store these spreads in the refrigerator several weeks—in the freezer at 0°F. or lower, a year.

BLUEBERRY SPREAD

Make with wild berries, sweetened by sunshine, or "tame" berries

¼   c. powdered fruit pectin
2   tblsp. sugar
1   c. sieved blueberries
¾   c. sugar
2   tblsp. light corn syrup
2   tblsp. lemon juice

• Combine pectin and the 2 tblsp. sugar; mix thoroughly. Add the finely sieved berries and mix at low speed for 7 minutes.

• Add remaining sugar, corn syrup and lemon juice. Mix 3 minutes longer.

• Pour into freezer containers and secure lids. Let stand at room temperature overnight or until jellied.

• Freeze. Makes 2 half pints.

CONCORD GRAPE SPREAD

Fresh-flavored—perfect teamed with pork roast, fried chicken or ham

¾   c. powdered fruit pectin
3   c. sugar
4   c. unsweetened grape juice
½   c. light corn syrup

• Mix pectin and ½ c. sugar. Add grape juice and mix at low speed for 7 minutes. Add the remaining sugar and the corn syrup. Mix 3 minutes longer.

• Pour into containers, secure lids. Let stand at room temperature for 24 hours.

• Store in freezer or refrigerator. Makes 6 half pints.

STRAWBERRY SPREAD

Brings the taste of May to Christmas —to all months on the calendar

1   c. powdered fruit pectin
3½   c. sugar
4   c. puréed or finely mashed strawberries, fresh or frozen without sugar
½   c. light corn syrup
2   to 3 tblsp. lemon juice

• Mix the pectin and ½ c. sugar. Add the puréed berries and mix at low speed for 7 minutes.

• Add remaining ingredients and mix 3 minutes longer.

• Pour into containers, fasten lids. Let stand at room temperature 24 hours.

• Store in freezer or refrigerator. Makes 6 half pints.

VARIATIONS

APRICOT SPREAD: Add 4 tsp. ascorbic acid powder to 4 c. puréed apricots; substitute for strawberries.

BERRY SPREADS: Substitute raspberries, loganberries, boysenberries or blackberries for the strawberries.

Note: Any fruit you can purée or chop very finely may be used to make these spreads. Peach, nectarine and pear spreads are delicious when fresh, but they are not good keepers.

Short-cook Jellies and Jams

Short-cook jellies and jams are simple to fix because you do not have to make acid and pectin tests or determine the jellying point. Use ripe fruit with fully developed flavor. The order of combining the ingredients varies with the kind of fruit pectin you use, liquid or powdered. Carefully follow the directions and recipes given by the pectin manufacturer or in the recipes in this cookbook.

The boiling time is brief—usually 1 minute—and you won't be successful if you change it! Use a timer.

Sparkling Jelly

One of FARM JOURNAL's readers makes especially beautiful and interesting jellies—she calls them Mystery Jellies. Her friends always praise them. She gathers most of the berries and fruits in the woods and on their Wisconsin farm.

All throughout the busy summer, she collects remnants of fruit juices, the leftovers from her regular jelly making. She pours them into containers and freezes them. When one container is full of mixed juices, she starts all over again. From them she makes jelly throughout the winter, "confident," she says, "that when I give a friend a glass of it for Christmas or at any other time, she will not have another one like it."

We asked her to freeze the different kinds of juices separately and experiment with measured proportions of them in making jellies. Each of her five boys—her husband and four sons —picked his favorite. Here is the quintet of recipes she sent us.

MYSTERY JELLIES

No. 1

2	c. frozen ripe gooseberry juice
1¾	c. frozen red raspberry juice
1¾	c. frozen red currant juice
1	pkg. powdered fruit pectin
6	c. sugar

No. 2

2	c. frozen red raspberry juice
2	c. frozen black raspberry juice
1½	c. frozen red currant juice
1	pkg. powdered fruit pectin
7	c. sugar

No. 3

1	c. frozen red currant juice
2¼	c. frozen tart cherry juice
1¾	c. frozen blueberry juice
1	pkg. powdered fruit pectin
7	c. sugar

No. 4

1½	c. frozen black raspberry juice
1	c. frozen plum juice
1	c. frozen ripe gooseberry juice
¾	c. frozen red currant juice
1	pkg. powdered fruit pectin
7	c. sugar

No. 5

3	c. frozen plum juice
2½	c. frozen ripe gooseberry juice
1	pkg. powdered fruit pectin
7	c. sugar

· Thaw fruit juices, combine, add pectin and bring to a full rolling boil, stirring constantly.
· Add sugar and bring to a full boil over high heat; boil again for 1 minute. Remove from heat and alternately skim and stir for 5 minutes.

• Pour into hot glasses or jars. Cover with paraffin at once or adjust lids on jars and process in boiling water bath (212°F.) 5 minutes. Remove from canner and complete seals unless closures are self-sealing type. Makes 8 to 9 half pints.

WINTER APPLE JELLY

Makes wonderful glaze when spread over baking ham for last half hour

1	qt. bottled or canned apple juice
5	drops (about) red food color
1	pkg. powdered fruit pectin
5½	c. sugar

• Combine juice, color and pectin in large saucepan; bring to a full boil.
• Add sugar; stir until dissolved. Return to boil; boil 2 minutes.
• Remove from heat; skim. Pour into hot glasses or jars. Cover with paraffin at once or adjust lids on jars and process in boiling water bath (212°F.) 5 minutes. Remove from canner and complete seals unless closures are self-sealing type. Makes about 7 half pints.

VARIATIONS

CINNAMON/APPLE: Add ⅓ c. red cinnamon candies with sugar, omitting food color.

CRANBERRY/APPLE: Use equal parts bottled cranberry juice cocktail and apple juice, omitting food color.

SPICE MINTED APPLE: Substitute green for red food color and add to apple juice; tie 1 tblsp. whole cloves in muslin bag; add to juice with pectin. Remove after cooking; add ½ tsp. peppermint extract.

GERANIUM: Lay a washed rose-geranium leaf in each jar before pouring in the hot jelly mixture.

GRAPE: Use bottled grape juice for apple juice.

GRAPEFRUIT/LEMON: Use unsweetened canned grapefruit juice for apple juice; add juice of 2 lemons and about 10 drops yellow food color.

CRANBERRY: Use bottled cranberry juice cocktail for apple juice.

LAYERED JELLIES: Make one color at a time; fill jars or glasses part way; skim. Let set 4 hours or longer before adding the next color. Try layers of red, green and yellow—Cinnamon/Apple, Spice Minted Apple and Grapefruit/Lemon jellies—or your own color and flavor combinations.

Give Homemade Jelly at Christmas

When you're wondering what to give your good neighbors and friends for Christmas remembrances, freshly made jelly is an excellent choice. Make it with canned or frozen fruit juices and trim glasses or jars with ribbons and fancy wrappings.

A FARM JOURNAL reader gave Orange Jelly one yuletide season. She poured the cheerful-as-sunshine jelly into individual juice glasses and gave a glass, trimmed with holly, to every family member.

ORANGE JELLY

For extra glamor, wrap in festive paper and tie with holiday ribbons

2   c. water
1   pkg. powdered fruit pectin
3 ½ c. sugar
1   (6 oz.) can frozen orange
     juice concentrate, thawed

• Mix water and pectin in saucepan; bring quickly to full rolling boil; boil hard 1 minute; add sugar and concentrate; stir until dissolved (don't boil).
• Remove from heat; pour into hot glasses or jars. Cover with paraffin at once or adjust lids on jars and process in boiling water bath (212°F.) 5 minutes. Remove from canner and complete seals unless closures are self-sealing type. Makes 5 half pints.

VARIATIONS

TANGERINE JELLY: Substitute frozen tangerine juice for orange.

PINEAPPLE JELLY: Substitute pineapple juice for orange.

CINNAMON JELLY

A red beauty—right for Christmas, but good for breakfast any day

1   qt. bottled or canned apple
     juice
1   pkg. powdered fruit pectin
4 ½ c. sugar
1   or 2 tblsp. red cinnamon
     candies

• Combine juice and pectin in large saucepan. Bring to full rolling boil.
• Add sugar and candies; stirring constantly, return to boil. Boil 2 minutes. Remove from heat. Let boiling subside and skim.
• Pour into hot glasses or jars. Cover with paraffin at once or adjust lids on jars and process in boiling water bath (212°F.) 5 minutes. Remove from canner and complete seals unless closures are self-sealing type. Makes 7 half pints.

MARJORAM JELLY

Gourmet special: Serve with meats— it's tangy, crystal clear, tasty

2   tblsp. marjoram leaves
1   c. boiling water
⅓   c. lemon juice
3   c. sugar
½   c. liquid fruit pectin

• Combine marjoram and water. Let stand 15 minutes. Strain through fine mesh cheesecloth. Measure liquid and add water to make 1 c.
• Strain lemon juice through cheesecloth. Combine lemon juice, sugar and herb liquid in a saucepan. Place over high heat. Bring to a boil; stir

in pectin. Stirring constantly, bring to a full boil. Boil ½ minute. Remove from heat. Skim. Pour into hot glasses or jars. Cover with paraffin at once or adjust lids on jars and process in boiling water bath (212°F.) 5 minutes. Remove from canner and complete seals unless closures are self-sealing type. Makes 3 half pints.

PLUM JELLY

Melt a little jelly, thin with hot water and use to baste the ham loaf

4   c. juice (4 lbs. red plums)
1   c. water
6½   c. sugar
½   bottle liquid fruit pectin

· Wash plums. Add water and cook until soft. Strain through jelly bag. Measure juice; add sugar and mix well. Bring to a boil, stirring constantly. Stir in pectin and bring to a full rolling boil.
· Boil hard for 1 minute, stirring constantly. Remove from heat; skim. Pour into hot glasses or jars. Cover with paraffin at once or adjust lids on jars and process in boiling water bath (212°F.) 5 minutes. Remove from canner and complete seals unless closures are self-sealing type. Makes 4 pints.

RHUBARB JELLY

Pink-red and just right with veal. Use it often to garnish desserts

3½   c. rhubarb juice (about 3 lbs. fresh rhubarb)
7   c. sugar
1   bottle liquid fruit pectin

· Cut unpeeled red rhubarb stalks into 1" lengths. Grind. Place in jelly bag and squeeze out juice.
· Measure 3½ c. juice. Place in large kettle. Add sugar, mix well. Put over heat and bring to a boil, stirring constantly. Stir in pectin.
· Bring to a rolling boil; boil hard 1 minute, stirring constantly. Remove from heat, skim off foam.
· Ladle into hot glasses or jars. Cover with paraffin at once or adjust lids on jars and process in boiling water bath (212°F.) 5 minutes. Remove from canner and complete seals unless closures are self-sealing type. Makes about 10 half pints.

VARIATION

RHUBARB/STRAWBERRY JELLY: Follow recipe for Rhubarb Jelly but use 1½ lbs. rhubarb and 1½ qts. ripe strawberries, 6 c. sugar. Grind rhubarb, crush berries and mix. Put in jelly bag and squeeze out juice.

RUBY JELLY

Reflects the glow of jewels—a top favorite of all taste-testers

1   qt. loganberries
1½   qts. red raspberries
1   pkg. powdered fruit pectin
5½   c. sugar

· Crush fully ripe berries and place in jelly bag. Squeeze out juice.
· Measure 4 c. juice into large saucepan. Stir in pectin; bring to boil.
· Add sugar and return to a full rolling boil, stirring constantly. Boil 1 minute. Remove from heat and skim.
· Pour into hot glasses or jars. Cover with paraffin at once or adjust lids on jars and process in boiling water bath

(212°F.) 5 minutes. Remove from canner and complete seals unless closures are self-sealing type. Makes 3½ pints.

APRICOT JAM

Like sunshine on the breakfast table —has a rich, tangy-sweet taste

3   c. diced apricots
¼   c. lemon juice
7   c. sugar
½   bottle liquid fruit pectin

• Mix apricots, lemon juice and sugar. Boil until apricots are soft. Remove from heat; stir in pectin. Stir and skim for 5 minutes.
• Pour into hot jars. Adjust lids at once and process in boiling water bath (212°F.) 5 minutes. Remove from canner and complete seals unless closures are self-sealing type. Makes 3½ pints.

BLUEBERRY/RASPBERRY JAM

"My mother gave me this recipe— her mother used it," a reader said

1   pt. blueberries
1   qt. red raspberries
7   c. sugar
1   bottle liquid fruit pectin

• Crush berries; measure 4 c. (if necessary, add water to make 4 c.).
• Add sugar, mix well. Heat to full rolling boil; boil hard 1 minute, stirring constantly. Remove from heat; stir in pectin; skim.
• Ladle into hot jars. Adjust lids at once and process in boiling water bath (212°F.) 5 minutes. Remove from canner and complete seals unless

closures are self-sealing type. Makes 10 half pints.

BLUEBARB JAM

The union of blueberries and rhubarb is a miracle flavor-blend

3   c. finely cut rhubarb
3   c. crushed blueberries
7   c. sugar
1   bottle liquid fruit pectin

• Combine rhubarb and blueberries in large saucepan, add sugar; mix.
• Place over high heat; bring to full, rolling boil and boil hard 1 minute, stirring constantly. Remove from heat, add pectin. Stir and skim for 5 minutes. Ladle into hot jars. Adjust lids at once and process in boiling water bath (212°F.) 5 minutes. Remove from canner and complete seals unless closures are self-sealing type. Makes about 9 half pints.

Note: This recipe was tested with fesh rhubarb and unsweetened, frozen blueberries.

PEACHY PEAR JAM

Guaranteed to add pleasing variety to your collection of sweet spreads

3 ½   c. mashed peaches and
        pears
6 ½   c. sugar
Juice of 2 lemons
½   tsp. ground cinnamon
½   tsp. ground nutmeg
½   bottle liquid fruit pectin

• Mix all ingredients, except pectin.
• Place over high heat and bring to a full rolling boil. Boil hard for 1 minute, stirring constantly.

• Remove from heat; stir in pectin. Skim. Stir and skim for 5 minutes. • Pour into hot jars. Adjust lids at once and process in boiling water bath (212°F.) 5 minutes. Remove from canner and complete seals unless closures are self-sealing type. Makes 4 pints.

Longer-cook Jams

This is the traditional or standard method. Mix from ¾ to 1 c. sugar with 1 c. soft fruit, like peaches and apricots, finely chopped, or berries, crushed, and heat the mixture slowly, stirring constantly, until the sugar dissolves. When the mixture comes to a boil, boil rapidly until smooth and thick. Test for the jellying point or doneness by the tests for jelly (see Longer-cook Jellies, this chapter). Skim, ladle into hot jars and process in boiling water bath (212°F.).

STRAWBERRY JAM

This old-time sweet never loses its appeal—an all-American favorite

8   c. strawberries
Lemon juice (optional)
6   c. sugar

• Wash, drain, hull and crush berries. If they are very ripe and sweet, add 1 tblsp. lemon juice to every cup of crushed berries.
• Add sugar and cook slowly, stirring constantly until sugar dissolves. Bring quickly to a boil and boil rapidly until the jellying point is reached.
• Pour or ladle hot jam into hot jars. Adjust lids at once and process in boiling water bath (212°F.) 5 minutes. Remove from canner and complete seals unless closures are self-sealing type. Makes 6 half pints.

APPLE/RASPBERRY JAM

The woman who shares this recipe says: "A delight to make and eat"

9   c. sugar
2   c. water
6   c. finely chopped tart apples
     (about 2 lbs.)
3   c. red raspberries, washed
     and drained

• Combine sugar and water; boil until mixture spins a thread.
• Stir in apples and boil 2 minutes. Add raspberries and boil 20 minutes longer, stirring often.
• Pour into hot jars. Adjust lids at once and process in boiling water bath (212°F.) 5 minutes. Remove from canner and complete seals unless closures are self-sealing type. Makes 5 pints.

APRICOT/BLACK RASPBERRY JAM

One of the tastiest ways to preserve summer's bounty in glasses

Sugar
2   qts. blackcaps (black
     raspberries, about 7 c.)
4   qts. fresh apricots, diced

• Add sugar equal in weight to fruit. Mix. Boil to consistency desired.
• Ladle into hot jars. Adjust lids at once and process in boiling water

bath (212°F.) 5 minutes. Remove from canner and complete seals unless closures are self-sealing type. Makes 10 pints.

APRICOT/PINEAPPLE JAM

Pure gold—extend your pleasure by giving a glass of it to a friend

4 c. diced apricots
4 c. sugar
1 (1 lb. 4 oz.) can crushed
   pineapple

· Mix apricots and sugar. Boil for 20 minutes. Add drained pineapple. Let come to a boil again.
· Ladle into hot jars. Adjust lids at once and process in boiling water bath (212°F.) 5 minutes. Remove from canner and complete seals unless closures are self-sealing type. Makes 3 pints.

FRENCH APRICOT JAM

An old French recipe—crack a few pits and cook the kernels with fruit

5 c. sugar
3 lbs. (24 to 30) apricots,
   peeled, pitted and chopped

· Pour 2 c. sugar over apricots; let stand 8 hours.
· Add remaining sugar; boil gently until thick (mash with spoon while mixture cooks). Remove from heat; skim.
· Ladle into hot jars. Adjust lids at once and process in boiling water bath (212°F.) 5 minutes. Remove from canner and complete seals unless closures are self-sealing type. Makes 6 half pints.

GREEN BLUFF STRAWBERRY JAM

Perfect for topping vanilla ice cream and also good on homemade bread

2 ½ c. sugar
½ c. water
1 qt. fresh strawberries (measure
   after washing and hulling)

· Mix 2 c. sugar and ½ c. water in large kettle. Boil until the soft crack stage (290°F.).
· Quickly add all strawberries at once. They will sear and sizzle, but lift edges with a fork gently and juice and melted sugar will soon appear. When boiling begins again, cook steadily and gently 10 minutes.
· Add the remaining ½ c. sugar and boil 5 minutes longer.
· Pour into a shallow pan and let stand in cool place overnight.
· In the morning, bring to a boil and ladle into hot jars. Adjust lids at once and process in boiling water bath (212°F.) 5 minutes. Remove from canner and complete seals unless closures are self-sealing type. Makes about 4 half pints.

APRICOT/ORANGE JAM

Tasty winter-made specialty with nice flavor and color blends

1 lb. dried apricots
2 unpeeled oranges
2 (1 lb. 4 oz.) cans crushed
   pineapple
8 c. sugar

· Soak apricots overnight; cook until soft. Put apricots and unpeeled oranges (cut in quarters, seeds discarded) through food chopper.

• Mix all fruit and sugar; cook 20 to 25 minutes. Pour into hot jars. Adjust lids at once and process in boiling water bath (212°F.) 5 minutes. Remove from canner and complete seals unless closures are self-sealing type. Makes 6 pints.

CHERRY/LOGANBERRY JAM

Full-fruit flavors—favorite recipe of Michigan cherry grower's family

2   lbs. tart red or light cherries
       (5 ½ c. stemmed and pitted)
7   c. sugar
2   lbs. loganberries (7 c.)

• Pit cherries and cover with 2 c. sugar. Add berries and cover with 2 c. sugar. Allow to stand 1 hour.
• Add remaining sugar to mixed fruits. Cook to desired consistency.
• Pour into hot jars. Adjust lids at once and process in boiling water bath (212°F.) 5 minutes. Remove from canner and complete seals unless closures are self-sealing type. Makes 4½ pints.

SWEET CHERRY/BERRY JAM

Gladdens the top of baked custard, French toast, waffles, ice cream

4   c. pitted, sweet red cherries
4   c. red or black raspberries
8   c. sugar

• Cut cherries in halves or grind very coarsely. Cover, heat slowly. Simmer 5 to 7 minutes until skins are slightly softened.
• Add raspberries (if using black ones —use plump, large berries; not small seedy ones). Add sugar. Stir gently.

Cook briskly about 15 minutes (218°F.). Do not cook over 20 minutes.
• Pour into hot jars. Adjust lids at once and process in boiling water bath (212°F.) 5 minutes. Remove from canner and complete seals unless closures are self-sealing type. Makes 11 to 12 half pints.

TRI-CHERRY JAM

Recipe from a Michigan farm woman. Delicious served on ice cream

2   c. light sweet cherries
2   c. dark sweet cherries
2   c. tart red cherries
6   c. sugar
Juice of 1 lemon

• Pit and measure cherries. Grind coarsely. Simmer about 5 minutes to soften skins. Add sugar and juice.
• Cook until thickened, 15 to 20 minutes (218°F.). Do not cook more than 20 minutes.
• Pour into hot jars. Adjust lids at once and process in boiling water bath (212°F.) 5 minutes. Remove from canner and complete seals unless closures are self-sealing type. Makes 8 to 9 half pints.

CURRANT JAM

If you don't mind the seeds, you'll like this; if you do mind, make jelly

5 ¼   c. stemmed currants
4 ½   c. sugar
3   tblsp. lemon juice

• Heat crushed currants until some juice forms. Add the sugar; stir until dissolved. Add the lemon juice.
• Bring to a boil, shaking pan in circular motion for a time.
• Boil until of jelly-like consistency, stirring constantly.
• Ladle into hot jars. Adjust lids at once and process in boiling water bath (212°F.) 5 minutes. Remove from canner and complete seals unless closures are self-sealing type. Makes 5 half pints.

ORANGE/FIG JAM

You can use either white or dark figs

3½   c. peeled, chopped figs
2   c. sugar
1   large orange
¼   c. water
3   tblsp. lemon juice

• To figs, add sugar.
• Cut orange peel very fine with scissors. (There should be about ⅓ c.) Cook peel in water until tender.
• Chop orange pulp, discarding seeds, and add it and peel to figs. Cook slowly until thick, about 30 minutes, stirring frequently.
• Add lemon juice. Remove from heat and ladle into hot jars. Adjust lids at once and process in boiling water bath (212°F.) 5 minutes. Remove from canner and complete seals unless closures are self-sealing type. Makes 3 to 4 half pints.

Note: Use ¼ c. lemon juice with dark figs.

GOOSEBERRY JAM

Excellent with meats. Use ripe berries for the most attractive color

2   qts. gooseberries (1 qt. ground)
4   c. sugar
Juice of 1 lemon

• Remove both ends from the gooseberries. Wash. Grind with a medium-coarse blade of food chopper.
• Combine ingredients in wide kettle.
• Cook until mixture clings to the wooden spoon, showing it has begun to thicken. Stir constantly.
• Ladle into hot jars. Adjust lids at once and process in boiling water bath (212°F.) 5 minutes. Remove from canner and complete seals unless closures are self-sealing type. Makes 4 half pints.

Note: Half-ripe or ripe berries may be used. With half-ripe or green berries, omit lemon juice.

PEACH/APPLE JAM

A good cook's company special

2   c. chopped peaches
2   c. chopped apples
3   tblsp. lemon juice
2   tsp. grated lemon peel
3½   c. sugar

• Combine ingredients; mix well. Cook slowly until thick and transparent, about 1 hour, stirring often.
• Ladle into hot jars. Adjust lids at once and process in boiling water bath (212°F.) 5 minutes. Remove from canner, complete seals unless closures are self-sealing type. Makes 2 pints.

PEACH/APRICOT JAM

Thick, tangy and richly golden

1 lb. peaches
2 lbs. apricots
Sugar

• Peel and slice fruits. Combine, and measure (should be about 6 c.). Add 1 c. sugar for each cup fruit (amount of sugar depends on tartness of fruits —¾ to 1 c.). Let stand 2 hours to bring out juices.
• Simmer gently until thick, about 20 minutes, stirring often.
• Ladle into hot jars. Adjust lids at once and process in boiling water bath (212°F.) 5 minutes. Remove from canner and complete seals unless closures are self-sealing type. Makes 7 half pints.

PEACH/PLUM JAM

The blending of two fruits, pointed up with lemon, is the flavor secret

4 c. peaches (about 3 lbs.)
5 c. red plums
8 c. sugar
1 lemon, very thinly sliced

• Peel and pit peaches. Pit plums. Cut fruits in small pieces or chop. Measure into large kettle.
• Add sugar and lemon slices (seeds discarded) and stir to mix well.
• Boil rapidly, stirring, until jellying point is reached, or until thick.
• Remove from heat; skim and stir alternately for 5 minutes.
• Ladle into hot jars. Adjust lids at once and process in boiling water bath (212°F.) 5 minutes. Remove from canner and complete seals unless closures are self-sealing type. Makes 12 half pints.

PEACH/PINEAPPLE JAM

Three fruits mingle their flavors—this is excellent with ham

12 large peaches, peeled
1   orange, juice and grated peel
1   (8¼ oz.) can crushed
     pineapple (1 c.)
9   c. sugar

• Mash the peaches.
• Mix all ingredients and cook rapidly 30 minutes, or to desired consistency.
• Pour into hot jars. Adjust lids at once and process in boiling water bath (212°F.) 5 minutes. Remove from canner and complete seals unless closures are self-sealing type. Makes 4 pints.

ORIENTAL PEAR JAM

You'll like what ginger does to pears —serve with chicken or pork

8 medium pears
1 (8¼ oz.) can crushed
    pineapple (1 c.)
4 c. sugar
1 (4 oz.) pkg. crystallized
    ginger, diced

• Peel and core pears, and put through food chopper.
• Mix all ingredients and cook approximately 30 minutes; stir often.
• Pour into hot jars. Adjust lids at once and process in boiling water bath

(212°F.) 5 minutes. Remove from canner and complete seals unless closures are self-sealing type. Makes 2½ pints.

Note: Amount of ginger may be reduced for less pronounced spicing.

RASPBERRY/PEAR JAM

Invented by a farm woman who says: "Perfect filling for jelly rolls"

2 ½   lbs. pears (10 medium)
5   c. sugar
Juice of 1 lemon
1   pt. frozen red raspberries

• Peel and core pears and put through food chopper.
• Cook pears, sugar and lemon juice for 20 minutes. Add raspberries and cook until thick and transparent.
• Pour into hot jars. Adjust lids at once and process in boiling water bath (212°F.) 5 minutes. Remove from canner and complete seals unless closures are self-sealing type. Makes 3 pints.

RED PLUM JAM

A deep red jam with a slightly tart taste. Excellent with meats

5   lbs. red plums (about 11 ¼ c. pitted and chopped)
½   c. water
Sugar

• Cook plums in water until soft. Put through food mill. Add sugar, 1½ c. to each cup plum purée.
• Boil rapidly to jelly stage, approximately 10 minutes.

• Ladle into hot jars. Adjust lids at once and process in boiling water bath (212°F.) 5 minutes. Remove from canner and complete seals unless closures are self-sealing type. Makes 6 pints.

CRUSHED RASPBERRY JAM

For variety, make with black or wild raspberries—extra-delicious

1   c. crushed red raspberries
4   c. diced rhubarb, scalded
5   c. sugar

• Combine raspberries, rhubarb and 2½ c. sugar in saucepan.
• Bring to a boil and cook for 3 minutes, stirring constantly. Add remaining sugar and boil 5 minutes.
• Pour into hot jars. Adjust lids at once and process in boiling water bath (212°F.) 5 minutes. Remove from canner and complete seals unless closures are self-sealing type. Makes 5 half pints.

WHIPPED RASPBERRY JAM

Simple to make, good to eat—no wonder busy women vote for it

6   c. red raspberries
6   c. sugar

• Mash berries in saucepan and stir in sugar. Cook slowly until sugar dissolves. Bring quickly to a boil and boil 3 minutes, stirring constantly.

• Remove from heat and beat with a wire whip or rotary beater 6 minutes.
• Pour into hot jars. Adjust lids at once and process in boiling water bath (212°F.) 5 minutes. Remove from canner and complete seals unless closures are self-sealing type. Makes 5 half pints.

RED RASPBERRY/APRICOT JAM

An interesting way to use the last of the year's dried apricots

1 ½ c. dried apricots
1   c. water
9   c. fresh red raspberries
6   c. sugar
½   tsp. salt

• Simmer apricots with water for 15 minutes. Add raspberries, sugar and salt. Cook rapidly for 15 minutes, or until of desired consistency.
• Ladle into hot jars. Adjust lids at once and process in boiling water bath (212°F.) 5 minutes. Remove from canner and complete seals unless closures are self-sealing type. Makes 5 pints.

RED RASPBERRY/PLUM JAM

Colorful medley of two red-ripe fruits

4 lbs. tart red plums, pitted
     (9 c.)
4 c. red raspberries (1 lb.)
Sugar

• Grind together plums and raspberries, using medium blade of food chopper. Measure pulp and for each cup of pulp, use 1 c. of sugar.
• Bring to a boil, stirring often; boil about 20 minutes or until jellying

point is reached. (The riper the fruit, the longer the cooking time needed.)
• Pour into hot jars. Adjust lids at once and process in boiling water bath (212°F.) 5 minutes. Remove from canner and complete seals unless closures are self-sealing type. Makes about 5 pints.

STRAWBERRY/RHUBARB JAM

Coat sponge cake slices with jam and sprinkle with confectioners sugar

3 c. strawberries
3 c. diced rhubarb
6 c. sugar

• Mash strawberries. Cut rhubarb into ½″ pieces. Combine and mix. Add 4 c. sugar; bring to a rolling boil and boil 4 minutes.
• Add 2 c. sugar and boil 4 minutes.
• Pour into hot jars. Adjust lids at once and process in boiling water bath (212°F.) 5 minutes. Remove from canner and complete seals unless closures are self-sealing type. Makes 2½ pints.

TRIPLE FRUIT JAM

Three fruits blend in this pretty red delicacy that wins praise

9 c. sugar
2 c. water
5 c. chopped Transparent or
     other early apples (about
     2 lbs.)
2 (8 ¼ oz.) cans crushed
     pineapple, drained
4 c. red raspberries, washed and
     drained

• Combine sugar and water; boil until mixture spins a thread.
• Add apples, pineapple and raspberries and boil until thick, about 20 to 30 minutes, stirring often.
• Pour into hot jars. Adjust lids at once and process in boiling water bath (212°F.) 5 minutes. Remove from canner and complete seals unless closures are self-sealing type. Makes 5 pints.

PLUM/RASPBERRY JAM

A favorite in short-grass Kansas country

3 lbs. prune plums, ground (5 c.)
5 c. sugar
1 (10 oz.) pkg. frozen red
    raspberries

• Put ripe, firm plums through food chopper using medium blade.
• Combine plums and sugar in a 5- or 6-qt. pan. Add raspberries. Mix.
• Bring to a boil; reduce heat and simmer until thick, about 40 minutes. Stir occasionally. Pour into hot jars. Adjust lids at once and process in boiling water bath (212°F.) 5 minutes. Remove from canner and complete seals unless closures are self-sealing type. Makes 8 half pints.

LET YOUR PEARS RIPEN

The generous Alabama farm woman who sent this favorite recipe wrote: "I use firm, ripe Kieffer pears to make this honey-colored, plantation spread —as typical of the South as honeysuckles climbing on the back porch. We pick the fruit when it becomes slightly yellow and wrap it in paper.

In two weeks, or possibly three, it will be mellowed, full-flavored and ready to can." The pears in the recipes that follow are the Bartlett variety, unless otherwise specified.

PEAR HONEY

You are sure to like the honey with lemons added, but try all three kinds

5 lbs. Kieffer pears
10 c. sugar
2 (8¼ oz.) cans crushed
    pineapple

• Peel pears, remove hard core and discard. Put pears through food chopper, using coarse blade.
• Combine pears, sugar and pineapple; cook until the mixture is thick and pears are clear.
• Pour into hot jars. Adjust lids at once and process in boiling water bath (212°F.) 5 minutes. Remove from canner and complete seals unless closures are self-sealing type. Makes 7 pints.

VARIATIONS

LEMON/PEAR HONEY: At the beginning of the cooking period, add 1 c. lemon juice or 2 lemons very thinly sliced, seeds discarded.

AMBROSIA PEAR HONEY: Add ½ c. shredded coconut when cooked.

LIME/PEAR HONEY

Rivals the gift of bees—the tasty medley of three fruit flavors

3 lbs. pears (about 12 medium)

1 (8¼ oz.) can crushed
      pineapple
1 lime, juice and grated peel
5 c. sugar

• Peel and core pears and put through food chopper.
• Mix all ingredients and cook approximately 20 minutes; stir often.
• Pour into hot jars. Adjust lids at once and process in boiling water bath (212°F.) 5 minutes. Remove from canner and complete seals unless closures are self-sealing type. Makes 3 pints.

REBA'S PEAR HONEY

Honey-colored if cooked no longer than necessary for right consistency

4 c. peeled, crushed pears
3 c. sugar
¼ tsp. salt
1 lemon, ground

• Combine all ingredients and cook in a heavy pan, stirring occasionally, for about 15 minutes or until of spreading consistency.
• Pour into hot jars. Adjust lids at

once and process in boiling water bath (212°F.) 5 minutes. Remove from canner and complete seals unless closures are self-sealing type. Makes 2½ pints.

VARIATION

ORANGE/PEAR HONEY: Use 1 orange, ground, instead of lemon.

PEACH HONEY

Try it on grapefruit or toast—makes winter breakfast taste like spring

1   large orange
12 large peaches, peeled
Sugar

• Put orange, including peel, and peaches through the food chopper.
• Measure the mixture and add an equal amount of sugar.
• Cook until of desired consistency, approximately 20 minutes.
• Pour into hot jars. Adjust lids at once and process in boiling water bath (212°F.) 5 minutes. Remove from canner and complete seals unless closures are self-sealing type. Makes 5 pints.

Longer-cook Jellies

Many people prefer the flavor of jelly made the traditional way. Grandmother knew that tart apples, tart blackberries, crab apples, cranberries, red currants, gooseberries, Concord grapes, lemons, loganberries, May haws, muscadines and many varieties of tart plums were good jelly makers. Her rule, which still holds, was:

Use slightly underripe fruits or at least ¼ underripe and ¾ ripe. She used the poor jelly makers for jams, marmalades and preserves—apricots, figs, peaches, pears, pomegranates, prunes, raspberries, strawberries, ripe apples, tart cherries, elderberries, grapefruit, loquats and oranges.

If she was in an adventuresome

mood, she mixed equal parts of juices from a poor jelly-making fruit and a good one, like apples or plums. Sometimes her efforts paid off with tasty jelly. Often she was disappointed.

You will avoid failure if you find out how much pectin and acid the fruit contains. The same kind of fruit often varies in amounts of pectin and acid from one lot to another, owing to growing conditions, variety and maturity. Make the following "modern" tests.

Pectin Test: To 1 tsp. cooked juice add 1 tblsp. rubbing alcohol (70% alcohol). *Do not taste.* Stir the mixture slightly so that all the juice comes in contact with the alcohol. Juice rich in pectin will form a gelatinous mass that you can pick up with a fork. Juice low in pectin will form only a few pieces of gelatinous material. If the test indicates the juice is low in pectin, it is best to add pectin before making jelly with it. To 1 c. fruit juice, add 1 tblsp. liquid or liquefied powdered pectin (directions follow). Use 1 tsp. of this juice to again make the pectin test. Repeat the additions and pectin tests until you obtain a strong pectin test. Keep track of the measurement of pectin added so you can add the same amount for each cup of juice. The amount of sugar to add depends on the pectin in the juice.

To Liquefy Powdered Fruit Pectin: Empty contents of a box of pectin into a small saucepan. Add ½ c. water. Bring the mixture to a boil and boil 1 minute, stirring constantly. Pour into a 1-c. measure and fill with cold water. Stir to mix thoroughly.

Acid Test: Compare, by tasting, the tartness of the fruit juice with 1 tsp. lemon juice mixed with 3 tblsp. water and 2 tsp. sugar. If the fruit juice is not as tart as the diluted lemon juice, add 1 tblsp. lemon juice to every cup of fruit juice.

Amount of Sugar: The quantity of sugar depends on the amount of pectin and acid in the juice. A general rule is to use ¾ to 1 c. sugar to 1 c. juice. When the juice contains only a moderate amount of pectin, use ⅔ to ¾ c. sugar to 1 c. juice. (Too much sugar results in syrup, not jelly.)

To Make Jelly: Cook 4 to 6 c. juice at a time in a large kettle (big enough to hold 4 to 5 times the amount of juice to be cooked to provide room for expansion). Measure carefully the juice and pectin, if you use it, and start to heat. When juice comes to a boil, add the sugar and stir until it dissolves. Boil rapidly. Do not overcook because you will lose fruit flavor and color and destroy the jellying power of the pectin.

Tests for Jellying Point: (1) You can use a candy, deep-fat or jelly thermometer. The *jellying point for your altitude* may be determined in this way: Boil some water before you start to make the jelly. Note the temperature at which it boils; then add 8°F. to get temperature of finished jelly.

(2) Grandmother used the spoon test. Many women find it a good idea to test jelly this way in addition to using the thermometer. Dip a metal spoon into boiling juice mixture and

hold it at least 12" above the kettle, out of the steam, and let the liquid run off the sides. As it is reaching the jellying point, the jelly will run off in two drops. When it reaches the jellying point, the drops slide together and drop off the spoon in a sheet. At this stage, remove jelly from heat at once.

(3) Put some jelly on a small plate and set it in the refrigerator, removing the kettle from the heat. If the jelly in the refrigerator jells in a few minutes, it is cooked enough.

To Skim Jelly: Skim after cooking. Allow the jelly to stand a minute after it is removed from the heat. This permits the film to form. Then circle the top of the hot jelly with a spoon gathering up the film. Or if you prefer, pour the jelly through a strainer. If you add ½ to 1 tsp. butter to the juice before boiling, it tends to prevent the jelly from boiling over and it greatly reduces the amount of film.

Ladle the jelly into hot glasses or jars. Cover with paraffin at once. Or if using half-pint jars, fill to within ¼" of top. Quickly remove any foam, wipe sealing edge, adjust self-seal lid and process 5 minutes in boiling water bath. Four cups of juice and 3 c. of sugar make 1½ pints of jelly.

APPLE/GERANIUM JELLY

Gourmet shops report splendid sales of this old-fashioned delicacy

6   c. apple juice (about 5 lbs.
      apples)
4   c. sugar
12 rose geranium leaves

• Prepare juice by removing stem and blossom ends of tart, red apples. Slice and put in kettle with water, barely to cover. Cook until very tender. Turn into jelly bag, let juice drip into bowl.
• Measure 6 c. juice into large kettle; bring quickly to a boil. Add sugar, stirring until dissolved. Boil rapidly until jellying point is reached.
• Quickly place 2 small (or 1 large) rose geranium leaves in each hot jar. Skim jelly and pour into hot glasses or jars. Cover with paraffin at once. Or adjust lids on jars and process in boiling water bath (212°F.) 5 minutes. Remove from canner and complete seals unless closures are self-sealing type. Makes 6 half pints.

Note: If apples are not tart, test juice for pectin before making jelly.

VARIATION

Mint Jelly: Omit geranium leaves. Delicately tint jelly just before pouring into jars with green food color; add ½ tsp. peppermint extract.

CRAB APPLE JELLY

Spread between the folds of a puffed-up omelet, or use to glaze baked ham

5   lbs. crab apples
8   c. water
Sugar
1   tsp. vanilla (optional)

• Remove stem and blossom ends from washed crab apples, cut in halves and place in large kettle. (Red fruit makes the most colorful jelly.) Add water and cook until fruit is very soft, about 10 minutes.

• Strain mixture through jelly bag, but do not squeeze or force juice through bag.

• Measure juice. You should have about 7 c. Stir in ¾ c. sugar for every cup of juice. Bring to a boil quickly and cook rapidly until jellying point is reached.

• Skim off foam, stir in vanilla and pour into hot glasses or jars. Cover with paraffin at once. Or adjust lids on jars and process in boiling water bath (212°F.) 5 minutes. Remove from canner and complete seals unless closures are self-sealing type. Makes about 4 half pints.

Note: The amount of jelly depends on the juiciness of the fruit.

RED CURRANT JELLY

Bright, red gem on shelf or table—it's tart enough to accompany meats

2 ½   qts. red currants
1   c. water
4   c. sugar

• Sort, wash and crush currants without removing stems. Place in kettle, add water, bring quickly to a boil over high heat. Lower heat, simmer 10 minutes. Let drip through jelly bag.

• Measure juice. There should be 4 c. Stir in sugar. Boil until jellying point is reached.

• Remove from heat; skim off foam quickly. Pour at once into hot glasses or jars. Cover with paraffin at once. Or adjust lids on jars and process in boiling water bath (212°F.) 5 minutes. Remove from canner and complete seals unless closures are self-sealing type. Makes about 4 half pints.

TWO-STEP GRAPE JELLY

Make it this way and you'll not find crystals in the amethyst

3 ½   lbs. Concord grapes
½   c. water

• Select ¼ underripe and ¾ ripe grapes. Wash and remove stems. Place in kettle, crush, add water, cover and bring quickly to a boil.

• Lower heat and simmer 10 minutes. Let juice drip through jelly bag.

• Cover juice and let stand in a *cool place overnight.* Strain through two thicknesses of damp cheesecloth to remove crystals.

Second Step

4   c. grape juice
3   c. sugar

• Pour juice into large kettle; stir in sugar. Boil over high heat until jellying point is reached.

• Remove from heat; skim off foam quickly. Pour at once into hot glasses or jars. Cover with paraffin at once. Or adjust lids on jars and process in boiling water bath (212°F.) 5 minutes. Remove from canner and complete seals unless closures are self-sealing type. Makes about 4 half pints or 5 (6 oz.) glasses.

PLUM AND ORANGE JELLY

Beat jelly and add to mayonnaise for fruit salads—¼ jelly to ¾ dressing. For company meals, thin it with a touch of heavy cream, whipped

5   lbs. red plums
6   large oranges, peeled and
    sliced

1 lemon, sliced
Sugar

• Wash plums and cover with water. Add oranges and lemon. Cook until skin and pits of plums separate from pulp. Strain through jelly bag. Boil juice for 20 minutes.

• Add 3½ c. sugar for each 4 c. juice. Boil rapidly to jellying point.

• Remove from heat; skim, pour into hot glasses or jars. Cover with paraffin at once. Or adjust lids on jars and process in boiling water bath (212°F.) 5 minutes. Remove from canner and complete seals unless closures are self-sealing type. Makes 7 pints.

"What Went Wrong with My Jelly?"

Many questions about jelly troubles have come to the Food Editors of FARM JOURNAL. Here are questions asked frequently, and our answers:

Q. My jelly did not set; it is thick and sticky. What caused the trouble?

A. You used too much sugar or cooked the mixture too slowly and too long. Or there was not enough acid or pectin in the fruit juice.

Q. Why is my jelly soft?

A. Chances are it was not cooked enough. You may have used too much juice and too little sugar. Or there was not enough acid in the juice. Soft jelly also occurs when you make too big a batch of jelly at a time.

Q. Why does jelly "weep"?

A. The causes are too much acid in the juice, or storage of jelly in a place too warm or with widely fluctuating temperatures. Very rapid jellying also causes "weeping." This occurs when the fruit is too green.

Q. Why is jelly cloudy?

A. Cloudiness results when jelly is poured too slowly into jars or glasses, when the mixture stands too long before pouring and when the juice is not strained properly and some of the fruit pulp remains.

Q. Some of the jelly I made is tough. Why?

A. The mixture was cooked too long before it reached the jellying point, a result of using too little sugar.

Q. One batch of jelly I made is gummy. What mistake was made?

A. The jelly mixture was overcooked.

Q. A few jars and glasses of jelly are dark at the top. Why?

A. It was stored in a place too warm or the seal was imperfect.

Q. Why do crystals form in jelly?

A. Too much sugar, lack of acid or pectin, or overcooking often result in crystals. In the case of grape jelly, the difficulty may be caused by using fruit that is too ripe, failure to let the juice stand overnight before making the jelly or stirring up the sediment when pouring the juice into the kettle for cooking. Crystals forming at top of opened glass are due to evaporation.

Q. Some of my prized red jellies have turned brown. What did I do?

A. The jelly was stored in a place with too much light. Or perhaps the storage place was too warm.

Q. Why does jelly ferment?

A. The containers were not sterilized properly or the storage place was too warm or damp. Perhaps the seal was not airtight.

Q. What causes mold on jelly?

A. The storage place was damp, the seal was imperfect or the containers were not properly sterilized. Mold is not harmful. If it is slight, remove it and use the jelly, providing the flavor is not affected.

CURRANT JELLY SAUCE

Try this with venison

1 ½ c. currant jelly
¾   tsp. dry mustard

· Melt jelly over low heat. Stir until smooth. Add mustard, mixing well. Makes 8 servings.

AN IOWA FARMER'S JELLY SAUCE: Add 3 tblsp. prepared horse-radish to Currant Jelly Sauce and serve with pork. Makes 8 to 10 servings.

APPLE JELLY SAUCE

Makes baked ham something special

1 ½ c. apple or crab apple
     jelly
2   whole cloves

· Melt jelly with cloves over low heat. Stir until smooth. Remove cloves. Serve warm. Makes 8 servings.

MINTED ORANGE SAUCE

Perfect with lamb roast or chops

1 ½ c. mint jelly
1 ½ tsp. grated orange peel

· Melt jelly over low heat. Stir until smooth. Mix in orange peel. Serve warm. Makes 8 servings.

Putting Up Preserves

Good preserves are made from whole small fruits, like strawberries and cherries, or uniform large pieces of larger fruits, like peaches and pears. When cooked, the fruit is tender and clear; it retains its shape, natural flavor and color. The consistency of the syrup varies from that of honey to a semijelly.

The problem is to keep the fruit plump and distributed through the syrup. The solutions are (1) to let soft fruits stand with the sugar added until the juice starts to flow, and then cook; (2) and to precook hard fruit until barely tender in a little

water before adding the sugar.

The method used in making preserves differs somewhat with different fruits.

You need to stir some preserves gently and frequently for 5 minutes after removing them from the heat, skimming them at the same time. Then cover them and let stand several hours or better still, overnight. Next morning, heat them. When they come to a boil, cook them 2 minutes. Then seal them in hot jars. Or pack the cold preserves into hot jars, adjust the lids as the manufacturer directs and process at the simmering point in a water bath for 20 minutes.

If you live in a warm climate and have no cool place to store preserves, or if you have trouble with canned foods keeping, it is best to process preserves in a boiling water bath.

It is desirable to cook small quantities at a time. And if you cook preserves rapidly once they come to a boil, they will retain their color, flavor and good texture. You need to stir them frequently as they cook, to prevent scorching.

The proportion of sugar to use depends on how sweet the fruit is. For tart fruits, use 1 pound sugar to 1 pound of fruit; for sweeter fruits, ¾ pound sugar to 1 pound fruit. (One pound of sugar measures approximately 2 cups. The weight of fruits varies, but a rule of thumb is: 1 pound of prepared fruit measures about 3 cups. It's best to weigh for accuracy.)

APPLE PRESERVES

For those who like sweets—inexpensive if you grow your own apples

2   c. sugar
1   c. hot water
4   c. apples, peeled and cored

· Combine sugar and water in a saucepan. Bring to a boil, stirring constantly until when tested it will form a hard ball in cold water.
· Stir in apples and simmer until they are transparent, stirring constantly.
· Ladle into hot jars. Adjust lids at once and process in boiling water bath (212°F.) 5 minutes. Remove from canner and complete seals un-

less closures are self-sealing type. Makes 3 pints.

Note: This recipe was tested with Winesap apples.

CANTALOUPE PRESERVES

A farm cook captures sunshine in jars—ribbons at fairs with this recipe

2   lbs. firm, ripe cantaloupe
1 ¾ lbs. sugar (4 c.)
Juice of 1 lemon

· Peel cantaloupe and cut in thin slices 1″ long. Mix sugar and cantaloupe; let stand overnight.
· Add lemon juice; cook until clear. Pour into hot jars. Adjust lids at once and process in boiling water bath (212°F.) 5 minutes. Remove from canner and complete seals unless closures are self-sealing type. Makes about 2 pints.

CHERRY/PLUM PRESERVES

Beautiful burgundy-red preserves

10   red plums, pitted
4   c. stemmed, halved and
         pitted Bing cherries
1   c. water
Sugar
½   tsp. salt
1   pkg. powdered fruit pectin

· Combine fruits, add water; bring to slow boil. Simmer 3 minutes. Remove from heat; measure.
· Add amount of sugar equal to cooked fruit; mix well. Add salt and pectin; stir until dissolved.

• Boil rapidly 2 minutes, stirring constantly. Remove from heat and skim.
• Ladle into hot jars. Adjust lids at once and process in boiling water bath (212°F.) 5 minutes. Remove from canner and complete seals unless closures are self-sealing type. Makes 9 half pints.

FIG/LEMON PRESERVES

Ginger spices the fruit delightfully

6   qts. figs, peeled
6   qts. boiling water
8   c. sugar
3   qts. water
3   lemons, thinly sliced
4   tblsp. sliced preserved ginger

• Wash and stem figs. Pour boiling water over, let stand 15 minutes.
• Drain and rinse figs in clear, cold water. Drain again.
• Combine sugar and 3 qts. water; bring to a boil; add lemon slices (seeds discarded) and ginger; boil rapidly 10 minutes. Skim. Lemon slices may be removed.
• Add figs, a few at a time, to the syrup, so as not to stop the boiling. Cook rapidly until transparent.
• Lift figs out of syrup and place in a shallow pan. Boil syrup down until thick as honey. Pour over figs and let stand overnight.
• In the morning, bring to a boil. Pack into hot jars. Adjust lids at once and process in boiling water bath (212°F.) 5 minutes. Remove from canner and complete seals unless closures are self-sealing type. Makes about 5 pints.

SESAME FIG PRESERVES

Toasted sesame seeds add new touch

1½   lbs. peeled firm ripe figs
3½   c. sugar
2   c. water
4   lemon slices, seeds discarded
2   tblsp. toasted sesame seeds

• Prepare figs; weigh after peeling.
• Combine sugar, water and lemon slices in preserving kettle. Cook about 20 minutes. Drop figs carefully into syrup and cook until clear, about 30 minutes.
• Pack figs, lemon slices and sesame seeds into hot jars. Cook syrup to thickness desired and pour over fruit. Adjust lids at once and process in boiling water bath (212°F.) 5 minutes. Remove from canner and complete seals unless closures are self-sealing type. Makes 4 half pints.

Note: Toast sesame seeds in moderate oven (350°F.) about 20 minutes.

GROUND CHERRY PRESERVES

Rather thin in consistency but very rewarding in taste

6   c. husked ground cherries (husk tomatoes)
1   c. water
8   c. sugar
¼   c. lemon juice (about 2 lemons)
1½   c. light corn syrup

• Put the prepared fruit in a large kettle. Add water. Bring to a boil and simmer for 10 minutes. Add sugar, lemon juice and syrup.

• Bring to a boil again and simmer 30 minutes. Remove from heat and let cool overnight.

• Next morning, heat to boiling, pour into hot jars. Adjust lids at once and process in boiling water bath (212°F.) 5 minutes. Remove from canner and complete seals unless closures are self-sealing type. Makes 8 half pints.

Note: If thicker preserves are desired, the boiling mixture may again be cooled overnight, heated to boiling and canned the second morning.

KUMQUAT PRESERVES

Serve these sunny preserves to complement duck, other fowl or pork

1	qt. kumquats
2	c. sugar
3	c. water
1 ½	c. light corn syrup

• Wash kumquats and make ½″ slits in one side of each kumquat. Simmer fruit gently in a little water about 10 minutes to tenderize skins. Drain.

• Combine sugar and water; bring to a boil and boil 5 minutes. Add kumquats and bring to a boil. Remove from heat, set aside overnight.

• Next morning, add ½ c. corn syrup to kumquats and bring to a boil. Remove from heat and let stand overnight the second time. Repeat the process two more times, adding corn syrup, bringing to a boil, removing from heat and letting stand overnight. The last morning, heat to a boil, ladle into hot jars. Adjust lids

at once and process in boiling water bath (212°F.) 5 minutes. Remove from canner and complete seals unless closures are self-sealing type. Makes 2 pints.

PEACH PRESERVES

Heat and blend ¼ c. butter and ½ c. preserves to dress up waffles

1 ½	qts. peaches, diced
1	orange, diced, and grated peel
Juice of 2 lemons	
1	c. chopped maraschino cherries
6	c. sugar

• Mix all ingredients and cook until of desired consistency.

• Pour into hot jars. Adjust lids at once and process in boiling water bath (212°F.) 5 minutes. Remove from canner and complete seals unless closures are self-sealing type. Makes 3½ pints.

STRAWBERRY PRESERVES

An heirloom recipe for a great national favorite—colorful and luscious

4	c. hulled strawberries
3	c. sugar

• Add sugar to berries and let stand 10 minutes or until juices start to flow. (Some cooks like to cover them and leave in the refrigerator overnight.)

• Put berry-sugar mixture in a 4-qt. kettle and bring them to a boil, stirring constantly until sugar dissolves. Cook until berries are tender, about 3 minutes. Let stand overnight.

• Next morning bring preserves to a

boil and boil 1 minute. Cover the preserves, remove from heat and let stand 2 minutes. Stir gently about 5 minutes, skimming if necessary.

· Pour or ladle into hot jars. Adjust lids at once and process in boiling water bath (212°F.) 5 minutes. Remove from canner and complete seals unless closures are self-sealing type. Makes 3 half pints.

ROSY STRAWBERRY PRESERVES

Cook a batch daily while getting lunch during the strawberry season

1   qt. halved strawberries
4   c. sugar
1   tblsp. vinegar or lemon juice

· Combine strawberries and sugar. Stir lightly and let stand 1 hour in flat bottomed shallow pan.
· Bring to a boil and cook 10 minutes, stirring constantly.
· Add vinegar; boil 3 minutes longer.
· Remove from heat, cover and let stand 24 hours.
· Bring to a boil and ladle into hot jars. Adjust lids at once and process in boiling water bath (212°F.) 5 minutes. Remove from canner and complete seals unless closures are self-sealing type. Makes 2 pints.

SUN-COOKED PRESERVES

The South's abundant sunshine and plentiful kitchen help, plus the superior flavor of the preserves, made these delicacies popular there in antebellum days. They were adopted by cooks in all areas where the sun is generous.

Today few homemakers make these preserves because many hours elapse between the berry patch and filled jars on the cupboard shelf. As one woman says, "You have to keep them on your mind two whole days." But there are gourmets who hold that the sweet is too good to give up and claim they can taste the sunshine.

SUNSHINE STRAWBERRY PRESERVES

Elegant, delicious—worth making if you have the time and sunshine

2   tblsp. lemon juice
4   c. hulled strawberries (1 qt.)
4   c. sugar

· Combine all ingredients. Heat slowly to boiling point and cook rapidly 8 to 10 minutes, stirring constantly.
· Pour berry mixture into platters or shallow containers. Cover with glass or plastic wrap, prop cover up a little to permit evaporation.
· Set in sunshine, stirring or turning occasionally. Bring into the kitchen at night. At the end of two (or three) days, the preserves will be thick enough. Heat until simmering.
· Pack into hot jars. Adjust lids at once and process in boiling water bath (212°F.) 5 minutes. Remove from canner and complete seals unless closures are self-sealing type. Makes about 4 half pints.

VARIATIONS

RED RASPBERRY PRESERVES: Substitute red raspberries for the strawberries.

CHERRY PRESERVES: Substitute dark, pitted cherries for strawberries.

RED RASPBERRY PRESERVES

A state fair champion. Spoon it on vanilla ice cream for a treat

4 c. whole red raspberries
4 c. sugar
Juice of 1 lemon

• Place raspberries in kettle with sugar and lemon. Bring slowly to a boil over low heat, *shaking* all the while. *Do not stir.* Continue shaking and boil for 5 minutes.
• Remove from heat. Cover; let stand several hours or overnight. Heat and pour into hot jars. Adjust lids at once and process in boiling water bath (212°F.) 5 minutes. Remove from canner and complete seals unless closures are self-sealing type. Makes 7 pints.

RIPE TOMATO PRESERVES

An inexpensive sweet for hearty farm eaters if you grow your tomatoes

2 lbs. tomatoes
4 c. sugar

2 lemons, thinly sliced
½ tsp. salt
½ tsp. whole cloves
½ tsp. whole allspice
1 stick cinnamon
½ tsp. ground ginger

• Scald, skin and weigh small firm red or yellow tomatoes. (If larger than small hen egg, cut in halves or quarters.)
• Cover with sugar and let stand overnight in a cool place.
• Next morning, drain off juice; add lemon (seeds discarded), salt and spices, tied loosely in clean, thin white cloth, to the juice. Boil 10 minutes.
• Add tomatoes and cook, stirring frequently until they are clear and syrup fairly thick. Remove spices. Pour into hot jars. Adjust lids at once and process in boiling water bath (212°F.) 5 minutes. Remove from canner and complete seals unless closures are self-sealing type. Makes 1½ pints.

VARIATIONS

PINEAPPLE/TOMATO PRESERVES: Add with tomatoes 1 c. pineapple tidbits. Makes 2 pints.

TOMATO CONSERVE: With tomatoes add 1 c. light raisins. Makes 2 pints.

Special Occasion Conserves

Conserves look like jams and they have the same consistency. But they are made with a combination of fruits.

Often nuts and/or raisins are added. They are favored especially for meat and poultry accompaniments.

APRICOT/ALMOND CONSERVE

Pots of gold on the shelf. Especially good with chicken or pork

3   oranges
Water
1   (4¾ oz.) pkg. shelled almonds
5   lbs. apricots (40 to 50)
10   c. sugar

• Peel oranges. Cover peel with cold water and bring to a boil. Boil 3 or 4 minutes. Pour off water. Remove white from peel and from oranges.
• Blanch almonds and remove brown skins. Dice apricots and oranges, discarding seeds. Grind orange peel and nuts; mix with fruit. Add sugar.
• Cook rapidly for 45 minutes or until desired thickness. Pour into hot jars. Adjust lids at once and process in boiling water bath (212°F.) 5 minutes. Remove from canner and complete seals unless closures are self-sealing type. Makes 6½ pints.

Note: To blanch almonds, cover with cold water and bring slowly to a rolling boil. Drain; slip off skins by pressing between forefinger and thumb.

SWEET APPLE CONSERVE

Delightful in filled cookies and equally fine on hot biscuits

4   c. sweet apples, peeled and chopped (1½ lbs.)
2   c. sugar
2   c. raisins
Peel of 1 orange
Juice of 2 oranges
Peel of 1 lemon
Juice of 1 lemon
½   c. nuts (optional)

• Combine all ingredients, except nuts, in a large saucepan. Cook slowly until thick, about 45 minutes. Add nuts.
• Pour into hot jars. Adjust lids at once and process in boiling water bath (212°F.) 5 minutes. Remove from canner and complete seals unless closures are self-sealing type. Makes 4 half pints.

CANTALOUPE/PEACH CONSERVE

Two summer friends, peaches and melon, unite to give winter pleasure

4   c. chopped peeled cantaloupe
4   c. chopped peeled peaches
6   c. sugar
¼   c. lemon juice
½   tsp. ground nutmeg
¼   tsp. salt
1   tsp. grated lemon peel
½   c. chopped walnuts (optional)

• Combine cantaloupe and peaches.
• Simmer 20 minutes, stirring until there is enough liquid to prevent fruit from sticking.
• Add sugar and lemon juice. Boil until thick. Add nutmeg, salt, lemon peel and nuts; boil 3 minutes.
• Ladle into hot jars. Adjust lids at once and process in boiling water bath (212°F.) 5 minutes. Remove from canner and complete seals unless closures are self-sealing type. Makes 4 to 5 half pints.

Note: Substitute orange peel for the lemon peel. Papaya may be used instead of cantaloupe.

CHERRY CONSERVE

*Whole cherries add texture and flavor
—try this favorite with ham*

6	c. pitted, tart cherries
2	c. black raspberries
2 ⅔	c. sugar

• Combine all ingredients in saucepan
and cook until thick, about 20 minutes, stirring often.
• Pour into hot jars. Adjust lids at
once and process in boiling water
bath (212°F.) 5 minutes. Remove
from canner and complete seals unless closures are self-sealing type.
Makes 2 pints.

BING CHERRY CONSERVE

*Thanks to the Idaho homemaker for
her recipe for this gourmet special*

1 ¾	lbs. Bing cherries, halved and pitted
1	qt. loganberries
2	slices pineapple, diced
12	apricots, cut fine
½	lemon, juice and grated peel
½	orange, juice only
Sugar equal to weight of combined fruits	

• Place all fruits and juices in a large
kettle. Bring to a boil and cook until
cherries are tender. Add sugar. Boil
for 10 minutes.
• Ladle into hot jars. Adjust lids at
once and process in boiling water
bath (212°F.) 5 minutes. Remove
from canner and complete seals unless closures are self-sealing type.
Makes 6 pints.

CRANBERRY/APPLE CONSERVE

*Winter holiday special that's fine for
Christmas giving and eating*

3	c. cranberries
5	apples
1	orange
1	lemon
1	(1 lb. 4 oz.) can crushed pineapple (2 ½ c.)
1	pkg. powdered fruit pectin
5 ½	c. sugar
1	(2 oz.) pkg. almonds, slivered

• Discard soft cranberries. Quarter
and core unpeeled apples. Put through
food chopper, using medium blade.
• Extract orange and lemon juice;
discard seeds. Grind orange and lemon
peels, using fine blade.
• Combine ground cranberries, apples,
orange, lemon and pineapple in kettle.
Bring to a boil.
• Add pectin and bring to a boil.
• Add sugar, stirring constantly; bring
to a boil and boil hard 1 minute.
• Remove from heat; stir and skim
for 5 minutes. Add almonds.
• Pour into hot jars. Adjust lids at
once and process in boiling water
bath (212°F.) 5 minutes. Remove
from canner and complete seals unless closures are self-sealing type.
Makes 9 half pints.

FIG/CITRUS CONSERVE

*California hostesses keep a few jars
handy for fast-fix guest meals*

5	lbs. figs
Water	
10	c. sugar

2   lemons, coarsely ground
4   oranges, coarsely ground
2   tsp. ground ginger

• Cover figs with a small quantity of water and boil until liquid is tan. Drain and reserve about 2 c. liquid. Mix with sugar, stir and heat to make a heavy syrup.
• Combine figs, sugar syrup, lemon and orange fruit pulp. Simmer gently about 1½ hours, stirring frequently. Skim foam from time to time.
• Add ginger, mixing well. Pour into hot jars. Adjust lids at once and process in boiling water bath (212°F.) 5 minutes. Remove from canner and complete seals unless closures are self-sealing type. Makes about 5 pints.

Note: Four tblsp. finely chopped nuts may be added with the ginger.

GOOSEBERRY CONSERVE

The reader who shares this recipe gathers the berries in the woods

2   qts. gooseberries (4 c. ground)
3 ½   c. sugar
1   lb. candy orange slices
½   c. walnuts, cut

• Stem gooseberries with scissors or sharp knife. Wash carefully, grind.
• Bring to a boil. Add the sugar, stirring constantly.
• Bring again to a boil. Add the candy orange slices, cut in eighths. Stir constantly until mixture begins to thicken to desired consistency. Remove from heat, skim and stir; add walnuts.
• Ladle into hot jars. Adjust lids at once and process in boiling water bath (212°F.) 5 minutes. Remove

from canner and complete seals unless closures are self-sealing type. Makes 6 half pints.

Note: Slivered almonds may be used instead of walnuts.

GRAPE CONSERVE

Harmonious mingling of orange and grape flavors with rich raisin taste

8   c. stemmed Concord grapes (about 5 lbs.)
¼   c. water
2   oranges
1   c. seeded raisins
6   c. sugar
¼   tsp. salt
1   c. walnuts, chopped

• Slip skins from washed grapes. Put skins in large kettle, pulp in a small one. Add water to skins and simmer gently 20 minutes. Cook pulp until soft enough to loosen seeds. Put pulp through food mill or sieve to remove seeds; mix with skins.
• Peel oranges, remove white membrane; cut in thin slices (discard seeds), peel in fine slivers. Mix orange slices and peel, raisins and sugar into grape mixture. Bring to a brisk boil and cook until conserve is thick (until jellying point is reached). Stir in salt and nuts. Bring to a boil and pour into hot jars. Adjust lids at once and process in boiling water bath (212°F.) 5 minutes. Remove from canner and complete seals unless closures are self-sealing type. Makes 10 half pints.

Note: You can use pecans or blanched almonds instead of walnuts.

PLUM/CRAB APPLE CONSERVE

Try this tasty tri-flavored special

2	c. diced crab apples
⅔	c. crushed pineapple
1	qt. pitted red plums
5 ½	c. sugar
⅓	c. shredded almonds

• Dice unpeeled, cored, firm yet ripe crab apples in about ¼″ cubes. Add them and drained pineapple to the plums. Heat the mixture to a boil.
• Add sugar, stirring constantly. Cook to the desired consistency, stirring constantly. Remove from heat, stir and skim; add almonds.
• Pour into hot jars. Adjust lids at once and process in boiling water bath (212°F.) 5 minutes. Remove from canner and complete seals unless closures are self-sealing type. Makes 7 half pints.

PLUM AND PEACH CONSERVE

Fruits complement each other—the flavor contrasts make the difference

3	c. ground sweet plums (Italian prunes)
3	c. mashed peaches
6	c. sugar
2	medium oranges (juice from both, grated peel from one)

• Combine ingredients; cook about 25 minutes, or to desired consistency.
• Pour into hot jars. Adjust lids at once and process in boiling water bath (212°F.) 5 minutes. Remove from canner and complete seals unless closures are self-sealing type. Makes 4 pints.

RAISIN CONSERVE

Keep a few jars on hand to team with ham—a splendid combination

1	(15 oz.) pkg. seedless raisins (4 c.)
2 ½	c. water
½	c. lemon juice (4 lemons)
½	c. finely chopped walnuts
1	pkg. powdered fruit pectin
4	c. sugar

• Combine raisins, water and lemon juice. Cover and let stand overnight or at least 4 hours.
• Bring mixture to a boil and simmer, covered, 30 minutes, stirring often.
• Drain raisins, reserving juice. Put raisins through food chopper or chop them very fine.
• Measure 4 c. raisins and juice into a large kettle. Add nuts and pectin. Place over high heat and cook, stirring, until mixture comes to a hard boil. Stir in sugar. Bring to a full rolling boil; boil hard 1 minute.
• Remove from heat and skim off foam. Stir and skim 5 minutes to cool slightly and prevent floating fruit.
• Ladle quickly into hot jars. Adjust lids at once and process in boiling water bath (212°F.) 5 minutes. Remove from canner and complete seals unless closures are self-sealing type. Makes about 7 half pints.

RHUBARB/ORANGE CONSERVE

Quickly made with strawberry-red rhubarb and candy . . . very colorful

5	c. red rhubarb
1	lb. candy orange slices
3	c. sugar

· Dice washed rhubarb (not skinned) into ⅓" cubes.

· Cut candy slices into eighths, cutting the long way first, using scissors. (Dip the scissors in cold water to prevent sticking.)

· Mix rhubarb and sugar in a wide saucepan. Stir constantly over high heat. When the mixture begins to boil, add the orange pieces. Continue boiling and stirring until the mixture thickens to a jelly-like consistency.

· Ladle into hot jars. Adjust lids at once and process in boiling water bath (212°F.) 5 minutes. Remove from canner and complete seals unless closures are self-sealing type. Makes 6 half pints.

RASPBERRY/APPLE CONSERVE

More summer apples than you need for pies? Then try this good jam

9   c. sugar
2   c. water
6   c. Transparent or other early
    apples, diced
3   c. red raspberries

· Boil sugar and water until it spins a thread. Add apples; cook 2 minutes.

· Add raspberries; cook 10 minutes.

· Ladle into hot jars. Adjust lids at once and process in boiling water bath (212°F.) 5 minutes. Remove from canner and complete seals unless closures are self-sealing type. Makes 3½ pints.

RHUBARB/APRICOT CONSERVE

If you have frozen rhubarb, you can make this spread on wintry days

1   (12 oz.) pkg. dried apricots
2   c. water
1   qt. rhubarb, diced
5   c. sugar
⅓   c. slivered almonds

· Wash the dried apricots carefully. Cut with scissors into small pieces. Add water and soak about 2 hours.

· Combine rhubarb and apricots and cook 10 minutes, stirring constantly.

· Add sugar gradually, stirring to mix. Continue cooking until of jam-like consistency. (This will take about 20 minutes of careful stirring.) Add almonds.

· Ladle into hot jars. Adjust lids at once and process in boiling water bath (212°F.) 5 minutes. Remove from canner and complete seals unless closures are self-sealing type. Makes 6 pints.

FOUR-FRUIT CONSERVE

Buffet supper special. Adds color and a taste surprise that wins praise

1   qt. sweet cherries (2¾ c.
    stemmed and pitted)
1   qt. strawberries (3½ c.)
1   large orange, peeled and
    diced
2   c. drained, crushed
    pineapple
7   c. sugar
¼   c. chopped walnuts
    (optional)

· Combine all ingredients, except nuts, in large saucepan. Stir until sugar is dissolved.

· Cook over low heat, stirring frequently, until mixture sheets from spoon. Stir and skim. Add nuts.

· Pour into hot jars. Adjust lids at

once and process in boiling water bath (212°F.) 5 minutes. Remove from canner and complete seals unless closures are self-sealing type. Makes 4 pints.

STRAWBERRY/CHERRY CONSERVE

Bright as strawberries plus cherries and twice as good as either alone

1	lb. Bing cherries (2 ½ c. pitted)
2	c. sliced strawberries
3	c. sugar
¼	c. lemon juice
¼	tsp. almond extract

• Combine cherries, strawberries and sugar and cook over low heat, shaking pan until sugar is dissolved. Increase heat and boil 8 minutes, stirring occasionally.

• Add lemon juice and almond extract and boil 3 to 5 minutes or until jellying point is reached. Stir and skim.

• Pour into hot jars. Adjust lids at once and process in boiling water bath (212°F.) 5 minutes. Remove from canner and complete seals unless closures are self-sealing type. Makes 2 pints.

GREEN TOMATO CONSERVE

Loaded with that marvelous old-fashioned flavor—a treasured recipe

2	lemons
1 ½	c. water
16	green tomatoes, parboiled
1	(2″) stick cinnamon
½	tsp. whole cloves
1	tblsp. mixed pickling spices
2	c. diced peeled tart apples
3	c. sugar

• Peel lemons lengthwise. Cut peel into sliver-thin pieces. Cook peel in water for 30 minutes.

• Parboil tomatoes for 5 minutes. Chop coarsely.

• Tie spices in clean, thin white cloth.

• Add apples, tomatoes, sugar and spices to cooked lemon peel. Bring to full boil and boil 20 minutes, stirring often. Remove spices. Reduce heat to simmer and cook 20 minutes, stirring often.

• Cut peeled lemons into very thin slices; discard seeds. Add to mixture and cook 20 minutes, stirring often.

• Pour into hot jars. Adjust lids at once and process in boiling water bath (212°F.) 5 minutes. Remove from canner and complete seals unless closures are self-sealing type. Makes 7 pints.

YOUNGBERRY CONSERVE

Crunchy texture and fruity flavors unite to make this distinctive

3	large oranges
4	c. crushed youngberries (about 2 qts.)
7 ½	c. sugar
½	bottle liquid fruit pectin
1	c. finely chopped walnuts

• Grate ¼ c. peel from oranges; then squeeze ½ c. juice. Remove any remaining peel from oranges.

• Cut up peeled oranges; combine with berries, grated orange peel and juice and sugar in a large saucepan. Place over high heat and bring to a full, rolling boil, stirring constantly. Boil hard 1 minute. Remove from heat and stir in liquid pectin. Skim, if necessary. Add nuts.

· Pour into hot jars. Adjust lids at once and process in boiling water bath (212°F.) 5 minutes. Remove from canner and complete seals unless closures are self-sealing type. Makes 4 pints.

Old-fashioned Fruit Butters

Grandmother made fruit butters for two important reasons that are just as valid today: (1) they taste exceptionally good and (2) they make use of the sound parts of windfalls or culls. Among the favorite fruits for butters are apples, apricots, grapes, peaches, pears, plums, quinces, guavas and combinations of fruits.

HOW TO PREPARE FRUITS FOR BUTTERS

Cook fruits until soft, stirring constantly.

APPLES: Peel and slice or quarter. Cook in an equal amount of water, cider, half water and half cider or Concord grape juice.

APRICOTS: Remove pits; peel if desired, crush fruit and cook in its own juice. (Grated orange peel makes a delightful seasoning.)

GRAPES: Crush and cook in own juice.

GUAVAS: Remove blossom and stem ends. Peel if skins are tough or blemished. Slice, put through food mill.

PEACHES: Scald and remove skins if desired. Pit, crush fruit and cook in its own juice.

PEARS: Remove stems, but do not core or peel. Quarter or slice. Cook in half as much water as fruit. Add 3 tblsp. lemon juice to each gallon fruit pulp.

PLUMS: Halve or quarter, remove pits and cook in their own juice.

QUINCES: Remove blossom ends, but do not core or peel. Cut in small pieces. Cook with half as much water as fruit.

FRUIT COMBINATIONS: Use equal parts of apples and quinces or apples and plums.

Put cooked fruit through food mill or colander. For a superior, smooth butter, sieve the pulp to remove fibrous material.

ADDITIONS TO FRUIT PULP

Sugar: Use white or brown sugar. Brown sugar darkens the light fruits; it gives a pronounced flavor to bland ones. The amount of sugar to add depends on personal tastes, but the general rule is half as much sugar as pulp.
Salt: Add ¼ to ½ tsp. for every gallon of fruit butter.
Spices: Usually ground spices are added, although some people prefer to omit them. About 1 tsp. ground

cinnamon and ½ tsp. each ground ginger and ground allspice to 1 gal. of butter is a good proportion. Whole spices tied loosely in clean, thin white cloth may be substituted for ground spices in making light-colored fruit butters. Ginger is an especially tasty spice with pears. Also, adding 3 tblsp. lemon juice to 1 gallon of fruit pulp steps up the flavor.

COOKING FRUIT BUTTERS

1. Measure the pulp and sugar into a large kettle; add the salt. Boil rapidly, stirring constantly to prevent scorching. As the butter becomes thick, lower heat to reduce spattering.

2. Add spices and lemon juice.

3. Continue cooking until butter is thick enough almost to flake off the spoon, or as Grandmother used to say: "Until it is thick enough to spread." Another test for consistency is to pour a tablespoon of the hot butter onto a chilled plate—if no rim of liquid forms around the edge of the butter, it is ready for canning.

4. Pour into hot jars. Adjust lids at once and process in boiling water bath (212°F.) 5 to 10 minutes. Remove from canner and complete seals unless closures are self-sealing type.

20-MINUTE APPLE BUTTER

Candy tints and spices—vinegar points up the apple flavor

3   qts. canned applesauce
10 c. sugar
½   c. vinegar
1   c. red cinnamon candies

• Combine all ingredients in saucepan and cook until candies dissolve and mixture is thick, 20 to 25 minutes.

• Pour into hot jars. Adjust lids at once and process in boiling water bath (212°F.) 5 minutes. Remove from canner and complete seals unless closures are self-sealing type. Makes 6 pints.

LEMON/APPLE BUTTER

Brings a change to an old-time spread —lemon takes the place of spices

4   lbs. apples (about 12 medium)
2   c. sugar
Grated peel of 1 lemon

• Wash apples and cut in eighths.

• Cook in small amount of water until tender, then put through colander.

• Add sugar and grated lemon peel; cook until thick.

• Pour into hot jars. Adjust lids at once and process in boiling water bath (212°F.) 5 minutes. Remove from canner and complete seals unless closures are self-sealing type. Makes 4 pints.

Note: Jonathan apples were used by our testers, but you may use others.

RHUBARB BUTTER

Kind to the pocketbook, exquisite rosy-red color, on the tart side

6   c. cut-up rhubarb
½   c. water
2½ c. sugar
4   drops red food color

• Cut rhubarb in 1″ lengths. Add water. Blend in blender. This should make 3 c. of pulp.

• Heat to a boil; mix in sugar. Cook, stirring, until mixture is consistency of fruit butter. Add food color.

• Ladle into hot jars. Adjust lids at once and process in boiling water bath (212°F.) 5 minutes. Remove from canner and complete seals unless closures are self-sealing type. Makes 3 half pints.

GRAPE/APPLE BUTTER

Apples, grape juice and brown sugar make a dark butter with rich taste

2   lbs. apples
1½   c. grape juice
7½   c. brown sugar, firmly packed
½   tsp. butter
½   bottle liquid fruit pectin
½   tsp. ground cinnamon

• Wash and remove stems from apples. Do not core. Dice finely into large kettle.

• Add grape juice; simmer 15 minutes or until tender.

• Sieve mixture. Measure 5 c., adding more grape juice if needed, and return to kettle. Add sugar and butter. Bring to rolling boil; boil 1 minute. Remove from heat.

• Add pectin and cinnamon. Stir frequently for 5 minutes.

• Ladle into hot jars. Adjust lids at once and process in boiling water bath (212°F.) 5 minutes. Remove from canner and complete seals unless closures are self-sealing type. Makes 4 pints.

Note: Winesap apples were used in testing this recipe.

ALMOND/CRAB APPLE BUTTER

A Minnesota State Fair winner—the almond taste is subtle

4   qts. crab apples
Water
3   c. sugar
½   tsp. almond extract
2   drops red food color (optional)

• Quarter crab apples. Cover with cold water. Bring to a boil; simmer until tender. Put through colander or food mill. You should have 4 c. pulp.

• Put pulp in a shallow kettle; add sugar. Boil rapidly, stirring constantly. As butter becomes thick, reduce heat to prevent spattering.

• Add almond extract and color. Continue cooking until butter is thick.

• Ladle into hot jars. Adjust lids at once and process in boiling water bath (212°F.) 5 minutes. Remove from canner and complete seals unless closures are self-sealing type. Makes 8 half pints.

Note: Some crab apples are red enough to make addition of food color unnecessary.

VARIATION

SPICED CRAB APPLE BUTTER: Omit almond extract and add ¼ tsp. each, ground cinnamon and nutmeg.

TOMATO BUTTER

Many children walked fast to Grandmother's to spread this on bread

5   qts. ground ripe tomatoes
3   medium onions, ground
1   pt. vinegar
3   c. brown sugar, firmly packed

2 c. sugar
1 tsp. ground cinnamon
1 tsp. ground cloves
1 tsp. ground allspice
1 tblsp. salt

• Peel and grind tomatoes and onions.
• Combine vinegar, sugars, spices and salt in heavy saucepan; bring to a boil.
• Add the vegetables and simmer over low heat until thick, stirring frequently to prevent sticking. Or cook in a moderate oven (350°F.); stir occasionally to prevent a crust forming.

• Ladle hot mixture into hot jars. Adjust lids at once and process in boiling water bath (212°F.) 5 minutes. Remove from canner and complete seals unless closures are self-sealing type. Makes about 5 pints.

APPLE/PEAR BUTTER: A FARM JOURNAL reader's favorite spread is fruit butter made with equal parts of pear and apple pulp, spiced and sweetened to taste. The fruit blend is delicious.

Cheerful Marmalades

Speak of marmalades and almost everyone mentally conjures up oranges. Citrus fruits play an important role in this sweet, but many other fruits, like cherries, apples and pears, make delicious marmalades too. They look like jams, but they contain thin fruit slices or ground (through the coarse blade of the food chopper) or diced fruit distributed through clear, translucent jelly.

ute, stirring constantly over entire bottom of kettle.
• Remove from heat. Stir in pectin; skim. Pour into hot jars. Adjust lids at once and process in boiling water bath (212°F.) 5 minutes. Remove from canner and complete seals unless closures are self-sealing type. Makes 4½ pints.

Note: Marmalade may be made without pectin. If so, use only 3 c. sugar.

CRANBERRY/BANANA MARMALADE

Spring a breakfast surprise—gives buttered toast a festive taste

4 c. cranberries
1 c. water
6 medium bananas, mashed
     (about 2 c.)
7 c. sugar
1 bottle liquid fruit pectin

• Wash cranberries; add water. Simmer in covered kettle for 10 minutes.
• Add bananas and sugar; mix well. Bring to full rolling boil. Boil 1 min-

GROUND CHERRY MARMALADE

Lovely yellow color, crystal clear and delicate, yet rich in flavor

3 c. husked ground cherries
     (husk tomatoes)
2 c. cooked pears, drained and
     diced finely
¾ c. water
½ c. drained, crushed pineapple
¼ c. lemon juice (2 lemons)
7 c. sugar
½ bottle liquid fruit pectin

• Husk and wash the ground cherries. Combine with pears and water; simmer 25 minutes.

• Add pineapple, lemon juice and sugar; bring quickly to full rolling boil. Add pectin; boil rapidly 3 minutes.

• Remove from heat and alternately skim and stir for 3 minutes.

• Pour into hot jars. Adjust lids at once and process in boiling water bath (212°F.) 5 minutes. Remove from canner and complete seals unless closures are self-sealing type. Makes 7 half pints.

HONEYED MARMALADE TOPPING

Just right on hot pancakes and waffles—good on all hot breads

1   c. orange marmalade
½   c. honey

• Combine marmalade and honey in small saucepan. Bring to a boil over low heat, stirring constantly. Serve hot. Makes about 1⅓ cups.

GOOSEBERRY/ORANGE MARMALADE

Gives a special flavor boost to lamb

2   large oranges
½   c. water
1½   qts. gooseberries
1   pkg. powdered fruit pectin
7   c. sugar

• Peel oranges; shave off and discard about half of white part of peel. Slice remaining peel fine and place in saucepan with water. Cover and cook for 10 minutes or until peel is tender.

• Chop fruit pulp (discard seeds) and add to peel. Cook 10 minutes longer.

• Grind gooseberries and combine with orange mixture. Measure 5½ c. into large saucepan. Add water, if necessary, to make up volume.

• Stir in pectin and bring to a boil; boil 1 minute.

• Stir in sugar and return to a full rolling boil; boil 1 minute.

• Pour into hot jars. Adjust lids at once and process in boiling water bath (212°F.) 5 minutes. Remove from canner and complete seals unless closures are self-sealing type. Makes 4 pints.

LEMON MARMALADE

Team with toast or fruit bread and tea—your guests will like it

2   c. thinly sliced lemon
6   c. water
4½   c. sugar

• Combine lemon slices (seeds discarded) and water in large preserving kettle. Cook rapidly until tender, about 20 minutes; stir occasionally.

• Drain and measure liquid; add enough water to make 6 cups. Add with sugar to lemons, mixing well. For a more delicate flavor, divide mixture in half and cook separately.

• Boil rapidly, stirring frequently about 15 to 20 minutes, or until jellying point is reached. Stir and skim for a few minutes.

• Pour into hot jars. Adjust lids at once and process in boiling water bath (212°F.) 5 minutes. Remove from canner and complete seals unless closures are self-sealing type. Makes 2 pints.

ORANGE MARMALADE

Spread a thin layer on your pumpkin pie and top with whipped cream

4   oranges
2   lemons
Water
Sugar

• Wash unpeeled fruit and slice very thin. Remove seeds and cores.
• Measure the sliced fruit and for each cup add 3 c. cold water; let stand 24 hours.
• Heat mixture to boiling; boil 15 minutes and again let stand 24 hours.
• On the third day, measure 3 c. of the mixture into a large saucepan; add 3 c. sugar and boil rapidly, stirring frequently, about 20 minutes or to the jellying point. Stir and skim a few minutes to prevent floating.
• Pour into hot jars. Adjust lids at once and process in boiling water bath (212°F.) 5 minutes. Remove from canner and complete seals unless closures are self-sealing type.
• Repeat in 3-c. batches until all has been used. Cooking in small amounts gives a more delicate marmalade. Makes about 5 pints.

PINEAPPLE/CARROT MARMALADE

Make this spun-gold spread in spring when fruit closet supplies are low

4   lbs. carrots, peeled
3   lemons
1   (1 lb. 4 oz.) can crushed
        pineapple (2 c.)
4   c. sugar
1   c. orange juice

• Put carrots and seeded but unpeeled lemons through food chopper.

Add remaining ingredients; cook until clear, stirring occasionally.
• Pour into hot jars. Adjust lids at once and process in boiling water bath (212°F.) 5 minutes. Remove from canner and complete seals unless closures are self-sealing type. Makes 4½ pints.

TOMATO/CITRUS MARMALADE

Beautiful color and taste and a compliment-catcher when served

4   qts. ripe tomatoes, peeled
Sugar
2   lemons
3   oranges
½   oz. stick cinnamon
¼   oz. whole cloves

• Cut tomatoes into small pieces. Drain off half the juice. Weigh tomatoes; add equal amount of sugar.
• Slice lemons and oranges very thin and cut slices into quarters; discard seeds. Add with spices, which have been tied loosely in clean, thin white cloth, to tomatoes and sugar. Cook rapidly, stirring frequently, until mixture reaches the jellying point.
• Remove spices. Pour immediately into hot jars. Adjust lids at once and process in boiling water bath (212°F.) 5 minutes. Remove from canner and complete seals unless closures are self-sealing type. Makes 6 pints.

Note: For best results use a large shallow kettle and never cook more than the above amount at one time.

FRUIT/TOMATO MARMALADE

Let this brighten your next potluck or buffet supper—colorful and tasty

6   tart apples, peeled and cored
12   peaches, peeled and pitted
2   large ripe tomatoes, peeled
4   oranges, seeded
Sugar

• Chop apples, peaches and tomatoes. Put oranges through food chopper.

Combine fruits; measure.

• Bring to full boil; reduce heat, cook 10 minutes. For each cup of fruit, as measured before boiling, add ¾ c. sugar; stir well. Cook 45 minutes, or until thick, stirring often.

• Ladle into hot jars. Adjust lids at once and process in boiling water bath (212°F.) 5 minutes. Remove from canner and complete seals unless closures are self-sealing type. Makes about 6 half pints.

The Gourmet Corner

When you visit department stores in metropolitan cities, you usually find a Gourmet Food Corner. And you also pass exclusive gourmet food shops in big urban centers. On the shelves of many of these luxury markets are rows of jellies, jams, marmalades, preserves and relishes. These specialties of good cooks, many of them from country kitchens, have high—even exorbitant—price marks. Yet they move from shelves to tables throughout the whole year.

A charming homemaker, who lives on a Mississippi plantation, has a gourmet shelf in her own cupboard. She says she's ready to add, in the twinkling of an eye, a sprightly, flavorful note to meals on days her husband brings business guests to dinner.

We borrowed from her the idea of having a gourmet section in this chapter. These recipes rate high with our taste-testers. Their inclusion in this exclusive place signifies they are worth a good price, if you want to sell them, and that they'll win compliments from people who taste them.

BLUSHING PEACH JAM

Follow recipe with loving care for a beauty with that luscious Melba taste

2   c. crushed, peeled and pitted peaches (about 1 ½ lbs.)
¼   c. lemon juice
2   c. red raspberries
7   c. sugar
1   bottle liquid fruit pectin
Few drops almond extract

• To the crushed peaches add 2 tblsp. lemon juice. Let stand.

• Crush berries and add remaining 2 tblsp. lemon juice.

• Combine peaches and raspberries with sugar in heavy kettle; mix well, and bring to a full rolling boil, stirring constantly. Boil 1 minute, remove from heat and add pectin.

• Stir and skim for several minutes to prevent fruit floating. Add extract.

• Pour into hot jars. Adjust lids at once and process in boiling water bath (212°F.) 5 minutes. Remove from canner and complete seals unless closures are self-sealing type. Makes 4 half pints.

THREE-BERRY JAM

An extra-delicious spread that captures the taste of summer

3 c. red raspberries
3 c. youngberries
3 c. loganberries
1 pkg. powdered fruit pectin
7 c. sugar

· Crush berries, one layer at a time; measure 5 c. into large saucepan.
· Stir in pectin. Place over high heat and bring to a hard boil, stirring.
· Add sugar and stir until mixture comes to a full rolling boil; boil hard 1 minute. Skim off foam with spoon and pour into hot jars. Adjust lids at once and process in boiling water bath (212°F.) 5 minutes. Remove from canner and complete seals unless closures are self-sealing type. Makes 4 pints.

BLACKBERRY/LEMON JAM

The lemon masks some of the strong berry taste. Adds a tang to meals

2 lemons, seeded and coarsely ground or chopped
1½ c. water
6 c. blackberries
7 c. sugar

· Combine lemons and water and cook for 20 minutes.
· Add berries and sugar and continue cooking 20 minutes, or until thickened.
· Pour into hot jars. Adjust lids at once and process in boiling water bath (212°F.) 5 minutes. Remove from canner and complete seals unless closures are self-sealing type. Makes 4 pints.

AMBROSIAL JAM

For special guests on festive occasions —lovely color, mingled flavors

8 peaches, peeled and pitted
3 large oranges, seeded
Pulp of 1 peeled medium cantaloupe
1 lemon
1 (8¼ oz.) can crushed pineapple (1 c.)
Sugar

· Chop all ingredients fine, putting oranges through food chopper, and combine. Add ¾ c. sugar for every cup of fruit. Let stand overnight.
· Next morning, gently cook mixture for 1 hour, stirring frequently.
· Pour into hot jars. Adjust lids at once and process in boiling water bath (212°F.) 5 minutes. Remove from canner and complete seals unless closures are self-sealing type. Makes about 8 pints.

Note: You can add 6 maraschino cherries, drained and sliced thin, just before removing jam from heat.

RUBY PRESERVE

A gem from a Montana kitchen

Sugar
1 qt. strawberries
1 qt. red raspberries
1½ lbs. pitted stemmed cherries
¼ c. lemon juice

· Add sugar equal in weight to all fruits. Mix. Boil for 25 minutes.
· Add lemon juice and boil 2 minutes.
· Pour into hot jars. Adjust lids at once and process in boiling water

bath (212°F.) 5 minutes. Remove from canner and complete seals unless closures are self-sealing type. Makes 6½ pints.

AUTUMN CHERRY CONSERVE

Five fruits blend their flavors with ground cherries in this golden treat

¾   c. ripe ground cherries (husk tomatoes)
1   (13¼ oz.) can crushed pineapple (1⅔ c.)
Juice of ½ lemon
Grated peel and juice of 1 orange
5   medium apples, finely diced
1   c. cranberries
1   pkg. powdered fruit pectin
4½ c. sugar

· Hull, wash and prick ground cherries. Combine with pineapple, lemon juice, grated orange peel and juice and apples. Add cranberries.
· Bring to a boil, add pectin and stir while bringing to a boil.
· Add sugar, stirring constantly. Bring to a full rolling boil over high heat; boil hard 1 minute, stirring constantly.
· Remove from heat; skim and stir alternately for 5 minutes.
· Pour into hot jars. Adjust lids at once and process in boiling water bath (212°F.) 5 minutes. Remove from canner and complete seals unless closures are self-sealing type. Makes 5 to 6 half pints.

CURRANTS LUSCIOUS

Luscious to look at—luscious to eat

1   qt. red currants
Sugar

1   qt. loganberries
1   pt. strawberries
1   lb. black cherries, pitted (about 2¾ c.)
1   pt. red raspberries

· Wash currants (not necessary to remove stems); mash slightly to start juice; cook slowly until currants look white. Drain in jelly bag. Add 1 c. sugar to each cup of juice.
· Weigh remaining fruits and add 2 c. sugar for each pound of fruits. Pour sweetened currant juice over fruits and sugar and let stand overnight.
· Boil rapidly for 15 minutes. Ladle into hot jars. Adjust lids at once and process in boiling water bath (212°F.) 5 minutes. Remove from canner and complete seals unless closures are self-sealing type. Makes 6½ pints.

AMBER MARMALADE

"The best of all citrus marmalades," says the contributor of this recipe

1   grapefruit
1   orange
1   lemon
Sugar

· Wash unpeeled fruit and slice very thin. Remove seeds and cores.
· Measure the sliced fruit and for each cup add 3 c. cold water; let stand 24 hours.
· Heat mixture to boiling; boil 15 minutes and again let stand 24 hours.
· On the third day, measure 3 c. of the mixture into a large saucepan, add 3 c. sugar and boil rapidly, stirring frequently about 20 minutes or until the jellying point is reached. Stir and skim a few minutes to prevent floating.

• Pour into hot jars. Adjust lids at once and process in boiling water bath (212°F.) 5 minutes. Remove from canner and complete seals un-less closures are self-sealing type. • Repeat in 3-c. batches until all has been used. Makes about 5 pints.

Wild Blackberry Topping

In many city gourmet shops, you see high-priced dessert toppings that look like jams. And that is exactly what they are, only you cook them a shorter time and they are thinner in consistency than regular jams. Perhaps none of these luscious fruity toppings for desserts is more famed than the one made from Washington's wild blackberries.

A Yakima County, Washington, home economist, who tested some of the jam, jelly and other fruit recipes in this cookbook, wrote: "Every summer I make a trip to the west side of the Cascade Mountains to pick wild blackberries. Wild Blackberry Sundae Topping is a specialty at our house. Members of my club would be disappointed if I did not serve it on vanilla ice cream when they meet with me. It's so easy to make. The seeds in the berries are so small that you do not have to strain them out."

WILD BLACKBERRY SUNDAE TOPPING

One of the best-tasting sauces on ice cream that you'll ever encounter

1 qt. wild blackberries
1 c. sugar

• Cook blackberries 5 minutes. Mash while cooking. Add sugar and cook until slightly thickened.
• Ladle into hot jars. Adjust lids at once and process in boiling water bath (212°F.) 5 minutes. Remove from canner and complete seals unless closures are self-sealing type. Makes 3½ cups.

Sweet Berry Temptations

You never will taste more delicious strawberry preserves than those you make with this recipe. The excellent canner, famed in her county for these preserves, specifies that you must follow the recipe to the letter. The *timing is especially important.*

You will notice the first cup of berries cooks 16 minutes, the last, 4.

Red raspberries also make a superior preserve. Fragile as they are, some of the berries remain whole.

CARDINAL STRAWBERRY PRESERVES

Juicy-ripe berries keep their plumpness in the glossy syrup

1 c. crushed strawberries
1 qt. whole berries
4 c. sugar

· Place crushed berries in an 8-qt. heavy kettle. Divide whole berries into three equal parts.
· Add 1 c. sugar to crushed berries. Cook, stirring constantly until sugar dissolves and mixture comes to a boil. When bubbles start to appear around side of kettle, start counting time and boil exactly 4 minutes.
· Add one third of whole berries and 1 c. sugar, stirring until sugar dissolves. When boiling starts, count time and boil exactly 4 minutes.
· Add the second third of the whole berries and 1 c. sugar, stirring until the sugar dissolves; boil 4 minutes.
· Add the last third of the berries and 1 c. sugar and boil exactly 4 minutes. Stir gently to prevent scorching. Use care not to break berries.
· Remove from heat, skim and pour preserves into a flat glass utensil (like a large cake pan) and let stand 10 to 12 hours, giving fruit a chance to plump.
· Ladle into hot jars. Adjust lids at once and process in boiling water bath (212°F.) 5 minutes. Remove from canner and complete seals unless closures are self-sealing type. Makes about 4 half pints.

VARIATION

GOURMET RED RASPBERRY PRESERVES: Substitute red raspberries for strawberries.

Wild Fruit Specialties

Summer in the country finds good cooks and children coming home from the woods, mountains and pastures with buckets and baskets full of wild fruits. What marvelous fruity spreads are put up the next day! Here is a sampling of these treats.

BLACKBERRY/HUCKLEBERRY JAM

Cook some of the jam less—it's thinner, wonderful on vanilla ice cream

6 c. wild blackberries
¼ c. water
1 c. huckleberries
7 c. sugar
½ bottle liquid fruit pectin

· Wash and pick over blackberries. Crush. Combine with water in saucepan. Bring to a boil and simmer, covered, 5 minutes.
· Force mixture through coarse sieve or food mill.
· Wash and sort over huckleberries, leaving in green ones. Add to blackberry pulp; measure 4 cups (add water if necessary to make full amount).
· Combine fruit and pulp with sugar in very large saucepan, mixing well. Heat to full rolling boil; boil hard 1 minute, stirring constantly. Remove from heat; stir in pectin; skim.
· Pour into hot jars. Adjust lids at once and process in boiling water bath (212°F.) 5 minutes. Remove

from canner and complete seals unless closures are self-sealing type. Makes 10 half pints.

VARIATION

BLACKBERRY/BLUEBERRY JAM: Substitute blueberries for huckleberries.

WILD BLACKBERRY/PLUM BUTTER

Taste and you'll know why it's good to have wild berries grow nearby

1	qt. wild blackberries
2	lbs. tart plums
½	c. water
7½	c. sugar
½	bottle liquid fruit pectin

• Wash and pick over berries. Pit plums but do not peel. Cut in small pieces. Combine fruit and water in saucepan. Bring to a boil and simmer, covered, 5 minutes.

• Force mixture through coarse sieve or food mill to remove seeds. Measure 4½ c. pulp into a very large saucepan. If necessary, add water to make full amount.

• Add sugar, mix well. Heat to full rolling boil; boil hard 1 minute, stirring constantly. Remove from heat; stir in pectin; skim.

• Pour into hot jars. Adjust lids at once and process in boiling water bath (212°F.) 5 minutes. Remove from canner and complete seals unless closures are self-sealing type. Makes 8 half pints.

Bittersweet Cherries

Chokecherry jelly and butter have a bittersweet flavor that many country people relish. But some families prefer to let the birds have the bright red cherries! One farm cook explains it this way: "If you like game, you usually enjoy wild cherry spreads. We think they are a perfect accent for wild duck dinners."

Use fully ripe chokecherries to prepare the juice for jelly making. Stem about 3½ lbs. cherries and place in a large kettle with 3 c. water. Cover and cook 15 minutes. Place in jelly bag and squeeze out the juice.

CHOKECHERRY JELLY

Wild cherry jelly—serve it proudly, for few hostesses can

3	c. chokecherry juice
6½	c. sugar
1	bottle liquid fruit pectin
¼	tsp. almond extract (optional)

• Pour juice into large kettle. Add sugar and stir to mix.

• Place over high heat and bring to a boil, stirring constantly. Stir in pectin, bring to a full rolling boil and boil hard 1 minute, stirring constantly.

• Remove from heat and stir and skim for 5 minutes. Add extract. Pour into hot glasses or jars. Cover with paraffin at once. Or adjust lids on jars and process in boiling water bath (212°F.) 5 minutes. Remove from canner and complete seals unless closures are self-sealing type. Makes about 9 half pints.

Note: Almond extract gives a stronger cherry taste.

CHOKECHERRY SYRUP: Sometimes a Colorado farm homemaker omits pectin when making chokecherry jelly. "Of course, it doesn't jell," she says, "but you have a wonderful table syrup to serve on pancakes."

CHOKECHERRY/APPLE BUTTER

A favorite with grownups who had it on their tables in childhood

4   c. apple pulp
2   c. chokecherry pulp
5   c. sugar
½   tsp. almond extract

• Prepare pulp of both fruits first by putting cooked fruit (unsweetened) through a sieve or food mill.
• Heat to a boil, stirring carefully.
• Add sugar. Stir constantly until it just begins to thicken.
• Add extract and blend. Ladle into hot jars. Adjust lids at once and process in boiling water bath (212°F.) 5 minutes. Remove from canner and complete seals unless closures are self-sealing type. Makes 8 half pints.

ELDERBERRY JELLY

Something different and delicious to serve with game. Grandpa's delight

3 ½   c. elderberry juice (about
        3 ½ lbs. ripe berries)
Apple juice (optional)
½   c. fresh lemon juice, strained
7 ½   c. sugar
1   pkg. powdered fruit pectin

• Prepare elderberries by removing large stems. Place in large kettle; crush. Cover and simmer about 15 minutes. Strain through jelly bag.
• Measure juice. If you do not have quite enough, add apple juice. Add lemon juice and pour into kettle.
• Heat, adding sugar, and bring to a boil, stirring constantly.
• Add pectin. Bring to a full rolling boil and boil hard 1 minute.
• Remove from heat, skim off foam and pour into hot glasses or jars. Cover with paraffin at once. Or adjust lids on jars and process in boiling water bath (212°F.) 5 minutes. Remove from canner and complete seals unless closures are self-sealing type. Makes about 5 half pints.

New England Favorite

One of our Massachusetts readers gave us her Beach Plum Jelly recipe with the following comment: "Our family thinks this red jelly has few equals. We gather the tiny fruit from bushes that grow in the sand along the ocean. It has such interesting individual traits. Although the bushes bloom every spring, they bear fruit only once in three years.

"When ripe, the fruit has a tough skin like wild grapes, but its shape and pulp is more like that of a miniature plum. The refreshing taste is suggestive of wild cherries—a touch of bitterness that makes the jelly wonderful to serve with chicken and meats. And like many women near the ocean, I sell homemade Beach Plum Jelly at my roadside stand. Tourists who come to New England to see our colored foliage in autumn are good customers."

BEACH PLUM JELLY

Sparkling red jelly that tastes more nearly like wild cherries than plums

4   c. beach plum juice
4   c. sugar

• Use red beach plums (not ripe); cover them with water and bring to a boil. Drain and discard water. Pour on more hot water, not quite enough to cover. Cook until plums are soft.
• Drip juice through jelly bag. Measure and add an equal amount of sugar. Boil over high heat until jellying point is reached.
• Remove from heat; skim at once. Pour or ladle into hot glasses or jars. Cover with paraffin at once. Or adjust lids on jars and process in boiling water bath (212°F.) 5 minutes. Remove from canner and complete seals unless closures are self-sealing type. Makes 3 to 4 half pints.

PLUM BUTTER

It's "plum good" and makes a tasty, bright topping for vanilla ice cream

3¾   qts. pitted wild plums
Water
2¾   c. sugar

• Cover plums with water and boil until skins are tender. Put through a sieve. Makes 3⅓ c. pulp.
• Bring to a boil; add sugar, stirring as you do. Boil until jelly-like consistency, stirring constantly.
• Pour into hot jars. Adjust lids at once and process in boiling water bath (212°F.) 5 minutes. Remove from canner and complete seals unless closures are self-sealing type. Makes 4 half pints.

Note: "Tame" plums may be used instead of the wild fruit.

VARIATION

Spicy Plum Butter: For a spicy butter, add ground cinnamon, ½ tsp. to 3 c. pulp.

PLUM/PINEAPPLE CONSERVE

Serve when your club meets—it will be the talk of the afternoon

5   c. pitted wild plums
Grated peel of 1 orange
1   tsp. powdered ascorbic acid
1   (13¼ oz.) can crushed pineapple, drained
1   pkg. powdered fruit pectin
5   c. sugar
⅓   c. shredded almonds (optional)

• To plums, add orange peel, ascorbic acid and pineapple. Heat to boiling and add pectin, stirring constantly. Heat to a boil; add sugar, stirring.
• Bring to a full rolling boil, stirring constantly. Boil hard 1 minute.
• Remove from heat; skim and stir alternately 5 minutes. Stir in nuts.
• Pour into hot jars. Adjust lids at

once and process in boiling water bath (212°F.) 5 minutes. Remove from canner and complete seals unless closures are self-sealing type.

Makes 8 half pints.

Note: "Tame" plums may be used if wild ones are not available.

Minnesota Farm Woman's Wild Grape Butter

FIRST DAY

· Choose one beautiful, blue October day after the first light frost.
· Add a dear friend and go to your favorite haunt—be it the woods or railroad right-of-way where the wild grapes flourish.
· Leisurely pick your baskets full, stopping to enjoy the glory of autumn's coloring.
· Catch a glimpse and hear the honking of the wild geese as they fly in formation overhead.
· Listen to the chickadee as he flits near you, and to the wild ducks as they try to flee the hunters.
· As you work, remember the days when you and your brothers and sisters used to pick grapes along fence rows on the way to Grandpa's.
· Remember, too, the days when you took your own little children to the woods and gave them nature lessons (indelible to them now), as you all sauntered along, crunching leaves beneath your feet and with a song in your heart.
· Smell the tinge of horsemint and faint suggestion of smoke in the air.
· Think of the future of your forests.
· Pick a colorful bunch of bittersweet to send to that faraway sister who gave you some of your first lessons in art appreciation.
· Return home before the corn pickers do and set a colorful table, centered with autumn leaves and fresh vegetables right from your garden.
· Remember Psalm 19 as you work, and pray for continued peace.

SECOND DAY

· In the morning, cut the heavy stem ends from grape bunches and pull out the thistle or milkweed down. Wash grapes. Then follow this recipe.

WILD GRAPE BUTTER

Here's another recipe that will make the game supper special

6 qts. stemmed wild grapes
Water
4 qts. apples
4 c. sugar

· Cover grapes with water, bring to a boil and simmer 20 minutes. Drain. Save juice for jelly.
· Place the grape pulp in a bag made of loosely woven cheesecloth or marquisette. Return to the kettle (in the bag—to keep the grape seeds out of the apples and to get the flavor from the grape pulp). Add apples which have been quartered, but not peeled.

Cover with water. Bring to a boil; simmer 20 minutes. Drain. Save juice for Wild Grape Jelly (recipe follows).
• Discard the bag with grape seeds in it. Put the remaining apple pulp through a sieve. It should measure 5 c.
• Place in kettle, add the sugar and heat to boiling, stirring constantly. Cook to desired consistency.
• Pour into hot jars. Adjust lids at once and process in boiling water bath (212°F.) 5 minutes. Remove from canner and complete seals unless closures are self-sealing type. Makes 4 half pints.

WILD GRAPE JELLY

Well worth the effort of picking, an ideal escort for wild game

Juice of 1 lemon
6   c. wild grape juice
1   pkg. powdered fruit pectin
7½ c. sugar

• Add the strained lemon juice to the grape juice; heat to boiling.
• Add the pectin and again bring to a boil. Stir in the sugar.
• Bring to a rolling boil, boil hard for 1 minute, stirring constantly. Remove from heat; skim.
• Pour into hot glasses or jars. Cover with paraffin at once. Or adjust lids on jars and process in boiling water bath (212°F.) 5 minutes. Remove

from canner and complete seals unless closures are self-sealing type. Makes 6 half pints.

Note: Use grape and grape-apple juices saved from Wild Grape Butter.

SPICED MULBERRY JAM

Cinnamon and lemon blend temptingly with the wild mulberry taste

1   qt. prepared mulberries
3   c. sugar
¼   c. lemon juice
½   tsp. ground cinnamon

• Stem mulberries (mixture of ripe and green) and cover with cold salted water. Use ¼ c. salt to 1 qt. water. Let stand 5 minutes. Drain. Rinse in cold water three times.
• Crush berries. Add sugar, lemon juice and cinnamon; cook slowly, stirring, until the sugar dissolves. Boil rapidly, stirring constantly to prevent scorching, until jellying point is reached.
• Remove from heat; skim and stir alternately for 5 minutes.
• Ladle into hot jars. Adjust lids at once and process in boiling water bath (212°F.) 5 minutes. Remove from canner and complete seals unless closures are self-sealing type. Makes about 3 half pints.

OLD-FASHIONED MULBERRY JAM: Use cider vinegar for the lemon juice.

CHAPTER 10

FRUIT JUICES TO CAN AND FREEZE

Directions for Extracting Juices from Fruits and Berries, Canning and Freezing · How to Store Canned Juices · Blending Juices · Serving Frozen Juices · Recipes for Tomato Juice Cocktail, Frozen Grape Purée, Grape Pie, Grape Aspic, Berry Table Syrups and Grape Syrup

Perhaps the popularity of frozen, canned and bottled fruit juices women buy in supermarkets gave them the inspiration to supplement with juices put up in their country kitchens. The appetite for them is so great! And when berry and fruit crops are bountiful, juices are another good way to store them.

Look in any country fruit closet and you'll be almost sure to find jars filled with red tomato juice and purple grape juice. But this is just the beginning. This chapter gives easy-to-follow directions for canning and freezing apple, apricot, peach, berry, cherry and citrus fruit juices.

There are fascinating ways to use luscious juices. Start the day by chilling them for breakfast. Make fresh-tasting jelly from them when the spirit moves you. Tint and flavor cake frostings with them. Combine water and fruit juice for the liquid in making gelatin salads and desserts. Make table syrups to serve hot on pancakes and waffles, cold on ice cream and pudding. Pep up fruit cocktails for extra-tasty meal starters and add the juices to fruit compotes for desserts. Serve iced, plain or blended, in glasses or, spiced and heated, in tea cups for refreshments. Pass cookies from the freezer with refreshing fruit juice drinks when you entertain.

You'll want to try Limelight Banana Crush and Starlight Three-Fruit Punch, frozen, when you fill the punch bowl. Both are wonderful to sip and they're frozen so you need add little or no ice. And don't miss the recipes from country cooks using juices as ingredients.

Festive Fruit Juices
THEY KEEP THE RIPE FRUIT TASTE

Fruit juices are festive in country homes because they show up on special occasions—they set the stage for pleasant visiting. One country cook calls them "hostess helpers." They often start her company meals. She gets the juice (or blended juices) ready to pour and puts it in the refrigerator. When guests arrive, her husband and children do the serving in the living room while she puts the finishing touches on the food.

Another farm woman says her family enjoys sipping juices with friends around the calendar—in summer while they sit outdoors under the stars, indoors when eating popcorn in the winter. And a third homemaker writes she likes best to cook with fruit and tomato juices—especially to use them in molded salads.

No matter how you want to use them, you'll find that this chapter's directions lead to fresh-tasting juices that keep their attractive colors. They came to us, in the main, from California ranch homemakers, many of whom are wives of orchard and citrus grove owners. Some of these FARM JOURNAL readers say their County Extension Home Economist taught them how to handle fruits and tomatoes to make the best juices. We give instructions in considerable detail to insure top quality results for you.

For success in canning and freezing fruit juices (1) *avoid overheating* them. If you boil them, or cook them longer than necessary below the boiling point, the flavor changes. (2) *Chill the heated juices quickly.*

Equipment to Use: Choose stainless steel, glass, plastic or unchipped enamelware utensils. You may use aluminum; the juice in them heats more rapidly, but sometimes the acids pit the metal, making it unattractive.

Canning Jars: Sterilize standard glass canning jars by boiling them in water to cover. Keep them in water just below the boiling point until you fill them.

Canning Jar Lids: Scald the jar lids as manufacturer directs. If you have no directions, scald just before using.

Freezer Containers: Use plastic containers or standard glass canning or freezing jars that you can seal tightly.

To Prepare Fruits: It is best to heat some fruits and berries for easier juice extraction and to deepen juice color. (See directions for Extracting Fruit Juices that follow.) The heat also inactivates the enzymes, resulting in juices of good quality. Among the fruits to heat before extracting the juice are apricots, berries, red cherries, red grapes, Concord grapes, peaches, plums and rhubarb. Do not heat apples, light cherries, grapefruit, white grapes, lemons or oranges.

Use sound, ripe fruit; sort and wash it. Crush or grind it, using coarse blade of food chopper, to obtain the most juice. Closely woven cloth bags, muslin or canvas, are best for draining the juice. You will obtain clear juice if you press the bag only lightly.

Straining Juice: Strain all juices, except citrus, through 3 or 4 thicknesses of cheesecloth that has been washed and rinsed. Unwashed cloth may give an undesirable flavor.

Adding Sugar: Often juices do not need sweetening, but if you add sugar, stir the juice until the sugar dissolves thoroughly. Then you are ready to process the juice.

Processing the Juice for Freezing: There are two methods. Choose the one you prefer, but the juice will keep more fresh fruit taste if you use the Double Boiler Method. This is especially true of citrus fruit juices. You will need a thermometer to determine correct temperatures.

1. *Double Boiler Method:* Use a large double boiler and fill the top pan about two thirds full of juice. (You can improvise a double boiler with two pans, one smaller than the other.) Bring the water in the lower pan to a boil. Pour the juice into the top pan and place it over the boiling water. Insert thermometer in juice. Stir the juice as it heats to the simmering point (190°F.). Remove double boiler from the heat, but do not set it on a cold surface.

2. *Direct Heat Method:* Juices heated this way will have more of a cooked flavor. You need not use a thermometer, but you will have better results if you do. Bring the juice to the simmering point (190°F.) over direct heat. If you have an asbestos pad, put it under the pan. Stir the juice while it heats. The next step is to freeze it.

Freezing Prepared Juice: Chill the heated juice in the refrigerator or by packing ice cubes around it. Pour into standard glass canning jars, leaving head space for expansion. This varies from ½″ for pint and 1″ for quart jars with wide mouth and no shoulder to 1½″ for both pint and quart jars with wide mouth and shoulder and 1½″ for pint and 2″ for quart jars with small top and shoulder. Most fruit juices will keep about 8 months; citrus juices 3 to 4 months.

Canning Prepared Juice: Take the jars, one at a time, from the hot water and fill to within ½″ from the top with the juice heated to the simmering point (about 190°F.). Adjust lids. Process in boiling water bath (212°F.) 10 minutes. Remove jars from canner and complete seals unless closures are the self-sealing type.

Storing: Cool jars, wipe them dry and put them in a cool, dry place. The cooler the storage place, the better the juice will retain its fresh flavor and vitamins. If the storage closet is not dark, either wrap bottles and jars with brown paper or store them in cardboard cartons. If the juices are stored in a warmer place, they should not spoil if they were properly prepared, but they will lose flavor, color and vitamins in storage above 70°F.

Select the reddest crab apples you can find to make Rosy Crab Apple Pie (recipe, page 122). This old-fashioned dessert will have rich color, luscious flavor. Make and freeze; or bake, freeze and reheat.

Treat both your family and friends with venison from the freezer: (top, left) hearty Venison Steak Casserole, Meatballs in Sauce, Venison Herb Roast and Venison-Noodle Medley (recipes start on page 64).

Layered Jelly with its mingled fruit flavors and beautiful colors makes wonderful Christmas gifts (recipe, page 177). Guests will admire the color array when the sparkling jelly shimmers in the serving dish.

You can fill your cupboard shelves with these luscious jams, jellies and other spreads (recipes in Chapter 9). Taste-testers selected these recipes from thousands of farm favorites.

Extracting Fruit Juices

APPLES: Wash fruit, put through food chopper, using coarsest blade. Do not heat. Squeeze juice through strong, clean cloth bag; strain. Add no sugar.

APRICOTS, NECTARINES AND PEACHES: Use firm ripe fruit, wash and remove stems. Drop fruit into boiling water, 1″ deep in kettle and boil until tender. Put through colander to remove skins and pits. Strain pulp and juice. Mix equal parts pulp with a thin syrup (1 c. sugar to 4 c. water) or with an equal amount of orange or grapefuit juice.

BERRIES: Wash and crush well-ripened blackberries, boysenberries, loganberries, red or black raspberries or youngberries. Heat to 175°F. Drain and squeeze through a cloth or bag; strain. If you wish to sweeten juice, add 1 c. sugar to 9 c. juice.

STRAWBERRIES: Wash, hull and crush. Heat to 175°F. Drain and squeeze through a cloth bag; strain; add 1 c. sugar to 3 c. juice. If blended with other berry juice, add 1 c. sugar to 9 c. juice.

CHERRIES, RED: Wash, stem, pit and put sweet or tart red cherries through food chopper, or chop. Heat to 160°F. Drain and squeeze through a cloth bag; strain. If you wish to sweeten juice more, add 1 c. sugar to 9 c. juice.

CHERRIES, LIGHT: Wash, stem and pit cherries. Put through food chopper. Do not heat. Drain and squeeze through a bag; strain. Sweeten like red cherries if desired.

CITRUS FRUITS: Have oranges, lemons or grapefruit at room temperature. Navel oranges are not recommended for juice to can or bottle, but if you use them, cut out the navel end before reaming. Ream fruits with any type of reamer you like except the press type; avoid pressing oil from peel and do not try to remove all the pulp. Strain juice through colander. Do not heat juice or add sugar.

RED GRAPES: Wash, remove large stems. Put 1 qt. grapes into cheese-cloth bag and immerse in 1 gal. rapidly boiling water ½ minute. Crush fruit and let stand 10 minutes, stirring occasionally. Do not reheat. Drain and squeeze juice through a cloth bag. Strain. Do not add sugar.

CONCORD GRAPES: Wash and stem ripe grapes; crush fruit and heat to 140 to 145°F., or until fruit is soft. Drain and squeeze through a cloth bag; strain. Let juice stand 6 to 8 hours, or overnight, to allow crystals to settle to bottom. Carefully pour off clear juice. Add ¼ c. sugar for each qt. juice; mix well. Heat juice rapidly to steaming hot (190°F.) in upper part of double boiler. To can, pour into hot quart jars; adjust lids and process 5 minutes in a simmering water bath (190°F.). Remove jars from canner and complete seals unless closures are the self-sealing type.

To freeze, pour into containers, cool, seal, label, date and freeze.

WHITE GRAPES: Wash and stem ripe grapes; crush fruit, or put through food mill, but do not crush seeds. Do not heat. Drain and squeeze through a cloth bag; strain. Do not add sugar.

PLUMS: Use firm, rich-flavored, well-colored plums. Wash, crush, and add 1 qt. water to each 2 lbs. plums. Heat at about 180°F. until fruit is soft. Drain and squeeze juice through cloth bag and strain. Add 1 c. sugar to 1 qt. juice, if you want sweet juice.

RHUBARB: Use red varieties. Wash stalks, cut into 4" lengths. Add 2 qts. water to 10 lbs. rhubarb. Heat until water starts to boil. Drain and squeeze juice through cloth bag. Strain. Add 1 c. sugar to 2 qts. juice.

TO SERVE FROZEN JUICES

Thaw them, covered, in their containers in the refrigerator, at room temperature or under running cold water. Shake the container occasionally to hasten the thawing. When thawed, stir before serving. The juice that thaws first contains a large share of soluble solids and if served, it may be too rich, the remainder too diluted.

TO BLEND JUICES

Delightful flavors may be obtained by mixing different kinds of fruit juices before freezing. Apricot, peach or nectarine purées are delicious mixed with orange or grapefruit juice. The different citrus juices or pineapple juice and apricot or grapefruit juice may be blended with pleasing results. Equal parts of black and red raspberry juices, apple-plum, apple-cherry and apple-raspberry are other tasty blends. You can experiment and make your own blends. Many women believe these blended juices taste best when mixed before freezing.

Putting Up Tomato Juice

Tomato juice may be canned or frozen. Because this fruit-vegetable contains less acid than fruits, you need to process it in a boiling water bath when canning it. Fortunately, tomatoes can withstand heat without developing an undesirable flavor—more so than the fruits, with the exception of apricots. Here are the steps:

1. Use only sound, red-ripe tomatoes. Wash, peel and core and cut them into small pieces.

2. Cook at once and quickly until soft to inactivate the enzymes that may change the color and consistency and destroy vitamin C.

3. Put them through a fine sieve or food mill to remove seeds. (You may extract the juice from uncooked tomatoes if you prefer.)

4. Heat the extracted, strained juice at once to the simmering point (204°F.). Salt to taste; most people like 1 tsp. salt to 1 qt. tomatoes.

5. Pour the simmering hot juice into clean hot jars to within ¼" from top; adjust the lids, process in boiling water bath (212°F.) 10 minutes.

Water Bath: Use a deep kettle with

rack and lid. The rack should have openings and allow jars to stand without danger of tilting. It should be raised ½″ from bottom of kettle. The kettle should be deep enough to hold water to cover the jars 1 to 2″ above tops.

The jars should not touch one another or the sides of the kettle. Heat the water before putting in the jars of hot juice. If necessary, add more hot water to keep the water 1 to 2″ above tops of jars.

When you have put in the jars, bring the water quickly to the boiling point. Start counting the processing time when the water boils again.

Remove the jars from boiling water and tighten seals if lids are not the self-sealing type. Cool, leaving space between jars for air circulation. Do not set on a cold surface or in a draft.

Note: Some varieties of today's tomatoes contain less acid than those grown a few years ago. Their juices may require longer processing time.

6. To freeze, quickly pour the heated juice into freezer containers, leaving 1″ head space for quart containers with wide tops, 1½″ for those with narrow tops. Cool and freeze.

TOMATO JUICE COCKTAIL

You can freeze or can it

2   qts. tomato juice, freshly extracted
3   tsp. salt
2   tsp. grated celery
1   tsp. prepared horse-radish
3   tblsp. lemon juice
⅛   tsp. Worcestershire sauce
1   tsp. onion juice

· Add seasonings to tomato juice.
· Freeze or can like Tomato Juice. Makes about 2 quarts.

STARLIGHT THREE-FRUIT PUNCH

Pull stems of dainty, tiny flowers through thin lemon and orange slices —float them on the punch

2   (6 oz.) cans frozen orange juice concentrate, thawed
2   (6 oz.) cans frozen lemon juice concentrate, thawed
6   c. water
1   (46 oz.) can pineapple juice
1   c. sugar
2   (12 oz.) bottles ginger ale, chilled

· Combine concentrates, add water and pineapple juice; stir in sugar. Makes 4 quarts.
· To freeze, ladle into wide-topped freezer containers, leaving 1″ head space. Cover tightly and freeze. Recommended storage time: Up to 1 month.
· To serve, partially thaw juice mixture at room temperature, about 5 hours. Place in punch bowl. Stir with fork to break up chunks of ice. Add ginger ale. Makes about 30 servings in punch cups.

LIMELIGHT BANANA CRUSH

Easy mix-in-the-glasses drink will take spotlight when you serve it

4   c. sugar
6   c. water
1   (46 oz.) can pineapple juice
2   (12 oz.) cans frozen orange juice concentrate, thawed

1 (12 oz.) can frozen lemonade
    concentrate, thawed
5 bananas
Ginger ale

· To freeze, dissolve sugar in water. Add juices. Peel and mash bananas; put through food mill. Stir into juice. Ladle into wide-topped freezer containers, leaving 1" head space. Cover tightly; freeze. Makes 6 quarts.

Recommended storage time: Up to 1 month.
· To serve, thaw Banana Crush in refrigerator to mush consistency, about 4 hours; half fill glasses with mixture. Fill with chilled ginger ale; stir. You will get 8 (12 oz.) glasses from 1½ qts. Banana Crush.

Note: Add fresh strawberry slices, when available, for color.

Enjoy Concord Grapes in Winter

Nothing makes a country cook consider her freezer an enchanting helper more than a few jars of purple Concord grapes in it when winter breezes whip around the corner of the house. Stop when you take a jar of Grape Purée out to make a splendid special occasion dessert and think about the good neighbor down the road—the one who does you so many favors. What could be a more acceptable gift for her at Christmas time than Frozen Grape Purée, a remembrance of summer? Why not take along a couple of good recipes for using the deep purple mixture—Grape Aspic or Fluffy Grape Pie, for instance?

FROZEN GRAPE PURÉE

Wash and stem Concord grapes. In large kettle, heat grapes 8 to 10 minutes at low temperature (not over 145°F.) to loosen skins. *Do not boil.* Put through food mill or wide-mesh strainer. Discard skins and seeds. Pour purée into jars, leaving ½ to 1" head space; seal, label, date and freeze. Recommended storage time: 6 to 8 months.

Note: Purée may develop gritty texture after long freezer storage. This disappears when heated slightly.

FLUFFY GRAPE PIE

Top-favorite winter pie in Erie County, New York, where people grow and know how to use Concords

Baked 9" pie shell
1   c. Grape Purée, thawed
      enough to measure
¼   c. water
1   (3 oz.) pkg. lemon flavor
      gelatin
¾   c. sugar
1½ c. heavy cream, whipped

· Bring Grape Purée and water just to a boil; stir in gelatin until dissolved. Add sugar; mix well; chill until mixture mounds when dropped from spoon, stirring occasionally.
· Beat until fluffy; fold in whipped cream. Pour into pie shell. Refrigerate at least 2 hours or overnight. Serve with thin layer of whipped cream.

GRAPE ASPIC

Serve it with baked ham or turkey for that important winter buffet

2   tblsp. unflavored gelatin
½   c. orange juice
¼   c. lemon juice
½   c. sugar
½   tsp. salt
2   c. Grape Purée
1   c. water
2   whole sticks cinnamon
4   whole cloves

• Sprinkle gelatin over mixture of orange and lemon juices to soften.
• Mix remaining ingredients; heat 15 minutes; do not boil. Then bring just to a boil; add gelatin, stir to dissolve.
• Pour into individual ring molds; refrigerate until set.
• To serve, unmold on lettuce; fill centers with seeded Tokay grape halves, mandarin oranges, drained, and grapefruit sections. Pass salad dressing separately. Makes 6 servings.

DELAWARE APPLE/LIME CREAM

Lime fans like to find this frosty treat in their dessert glasses

1½ c. apple juice or cider
1   (3 oz.) pkg. lime flavor
        gelatin
½   c. applesauce
½   c. heavy cream, whipped

• Heat apple juice to boiling. Pour gelatin into a deep mixing bowl. Pour hot apple juice over it and stir to dissolve gelatin. Place bowl in pan containing ice water to cool quickly.
• When gelatin starts to thicken, beat it with an electric or rotary beater until thick and fluffy. Fold applesauce and whipped cream into gelatin mixture. Pour into a 1-qt. container. Chill 4 hours. Spoon into dessert glasses. until firm. Makes 8 servings.
• To freeze, wrap with aluminum foil or plastic wrap; label, date and freeze. Recommended storage time: Up to 1 month.
• To serve, thaw in refrigerator 3 to

Tasty Table Syrups

Pour boysenberry syrup on a stack of hot, buttered pancakes; strawberry syrup on vanilla ice cream. Visitors to the Pacific Northwest from other areas admire the luscious berry syrups country women often take from their fruit closets or freezers to serve on waffles, pancakes and ice cream—and in punches. "We really like them the way Easterners like maple syrup," an Oregon homemaker says. "We don't have maple groves, but we do have wonderful strawberries, blackberries, boysenberries, red raspberries, blue-

berries. All make good syrups. Sometimes we blend two or more berries, always including at least one that's tart."

Berry syrups are so delicious and colorful that they are worthy of adoption by country cooks in every state. Gourmet shops in big cities enjoy excellent fruit syrup sales—and pleasing profits. You can make them in your kitchen by directions developed by the Cooperative Extension Service, Oregon State University.

HOW TO MAKE BERRY SYRUPS

1. Start by making a test batch to check the syrup's consistency when cool. Berries vary greatly from one season to another in acid and pectin. If your syrup is too thick, let the rest of the juice stand in the refrigerator overnight. That will destroy some of the pectin, and syrup made will be thinner. If it is too thin, add corn syrup (see note following recipe for Western Berry Syrup).

2. Place 10 unscented white facial tissues in 2 qts. boiling water. Let stand 1 minute. It filters and clarifies the juice and keeps the jelly bag from clogging. Break the tissues into small pieces with two forks to make a cellulose pulp. Pour the cellulose into a strainer. Shake, but do not press to remove excess water. Makes 1 cup cellulose pulp.

3. Wash table-ripe berries; cap or stem if necessary. Don't use underripe fruit—its pectin may jell the syrup. Crush berries with a potato masher.

4. For every 3 c. crushed berries or fruit, add 1 c. cellulose pulp. Stir well and heat just to a boil, stirring constantly to prevent sticking. If fruit remains firm, simmer 1 or 2 minutes longer, but don't overcook or you'll destroy fresh fruit flavors.

5. Pour hot fruit into jelly bag or several thicknesses of cheesecloth in a strainer or colander. Let juice drip into bowl. When cool enough to handle, twist the bag or press against the side of the colander to extract juice. Discard dry pulp. Use the basic recipe to make syrup.

WESTERN BERRY SYRUP

Use raspberries, strawberries, boysenberries or any other berries you have

1 ¼   c. prepared berry juice
1 ¾   c. sugar

• Combine juice and sugar in a large, heavy kettle. Bring to a full rolling boil; boil 1 minute. Count the time after the mixture comes to a boil that you cannot stir down. Remove from heat and skim off foam. Don't boil too long or the syrup may jell.
• Pour into clean, hot jars. Adjust lids. Process in boiling water bath (212°F.) 10 minutes.
• Remove jars from canner and complete seals unless closures are self-sealing type. Makes 1 pint.
   Store in a cool, *dark* place. If you prefer, leave head space in the jars and freeze instead of processing in boiling water bath. Once syrup is opened, keep in refrigerator. If the syrup jells when you open it, stir vigorously or place the jar in a pan of warm water, heat until jell dissolves.

Note: For a more tart syrup, add 1 tblsp. lemon juice. For a thicker syrup, use 1½ c. sugar and ¼ c. light corn syrup instead of 1¾ c. sugar.

ROYAL GRAPE SYRUP

You can use unsweetened canned or frozen grape juice concentrate, diluted with 2 parts water to 1 part frozen juice concentrate, instead of the Grape Purée in the recipe for Grape Table Syrup. And you can freeze or can it like Western Berry Syrup.

GRAPE TABLE SYRUP

Serve with pancakes, biscuits or over ice cream or vanilla pudding

1 ¼   c. Grape Purée (see Index)
1 ½   c. sugar
¼   c. corn syrup
1   tblsp. lemon juice

· Combine ingredients in heavy pan; bring to a rolling boil; boil 1 minute, counting time after mixture comes to a boil that cannot be stirred down.
· Remove from heat; skim off foam. Pour into containers. Cool; cover and store in refrigerator. Makes 1 pint.

CHAPTER 11

FRUITS AND VEGETABLES

How to Prevent Fruits from Darkening When Canned · Sweetening Canned Fruits · Altitude Adjustments for Canning · Methods for Canning Fruits, Rhubarb, Tomatoes, Tomato Purée, Vegetables · Salad and Dessert Pears, Apple/Plum Sauce, Tinted Green Grapes, Pear Mincemeat, Peach Macaroons, Hominy, Vegetable Soup Mixture, Directions for Making Vegetable/Beef Stew, Green Tomato Mincemeat and Sun-dried Corn

When plenty spills from almost every vine and bush in the garden, home canning swings into high gear in country kitchens. Green and yellow beans so crisp they snap between your fingers—and tomatoes, plump and heavy with ripeness, are the two favorite vegetables for home canning. Or as FARM JOURNAL readers say: "We like them better canned than frozen."

Baskets of blushing peaches and tart-sweet plums and summer apples show up in farm kitchens in midsummer. And peaches, beans and tomatoes make the "big three" in country home canning. Farm families like peaches canned and frozen—"they taste so different."

Mothers and children often pick vegetables in early morning before the sun heats them. While the cook fixes them for processing, clean glass jars wait in the electric dishwasher or in a pan of hot water. Shiny, new lids are on the counter top; the canner is ready. Before sundown, rows of filled jars record the accomplishments of a busy day.

"Sometimes in the rush of summer," a farm woman confesses, "I swear I'll never again look at a seed catalog. Then maybe we won't plant so much. But when I get tasty, economical meals all winter using lots of food from fruit closet and freezer, I change my mind. I realize that summer's work pays off in dollars and cents and better meals—that it gives me free time the other three seasons."

Read the up-to-date methods for canning fruits and vegetables in this chapter. And don't experiment. Canning is a science and failure to heed the rules brings waste and disappointment.

Firm-Ripe Fruits, Tomatoes
ROUND THEM UP IN JARS FOR WINTER

Farmers say they can tell what week it is in their neighborhoods, any time between spring and frost, by stepping into country kitchens. They tell how to do it—first sniff the aroma of the fruit or berries heating for canning. Then look in bowls or baskets on the counter top. By that time you'll know whether it's cherries, peaches or plums, or some other fruit that's ripe.

And ripe—firm-ripe—it should be for canning. At this stage of maturity fruits reach their flavor peak; yet they hold their shape when processed.

Home-canned fruits never were so beautiful as they are today. The use of color protectors to prevent darkening has something to do with it. And so do the simplified, exact methods of canning. Look for them in this chapter.

Fruit Canning Tips

TO PREVENT DARKENING

When Peeling: Some fruits, like apples, pears and peaches, darken quickly after peeling. Drop them into a *salt-vinegar water* (2 tblsp. each salt and vinegar added to 1 gal. cold water). Do not let them stand in this solution more than 20 minutes. If you exceed 15 minutes, rinse in cold water.

When Packing in Jars: Add a color protector to peaches, pears, apricots, applesauce and plums to keep their bright colors and prevent darkening fruit at top of jars. Add ½ tsp. powdered ascorbic acid (available at drugstores) to 1 qt. fruit (¼ tsp. to 1 pt.)

just before processing. Or use your favorite ascorbic acid mixture, following directions on the package label.

TO SWEETEN FRUITS FOR CANNING

SUGAR SYRUPS

	Sugar Cups	Water Cups	Yield Cups
Thin	2	4	5
Medium	3	4	5½
Heavy	4¾	4	6½

Boil sugar and water together 5 minutes. Skim if necessary. Fruit juice may be substituted for all or part of the water. To extract juice, heat crushed fruit to simmering point (185 to 210°F.) over low heat. Strain through jelly bag. You will need from ¾ to 1 c. syrup for each qt. fruit.

SUGAR

For juicy fruit packed hot, add about ½ c. cane or beet sugar to each qt. ripe fruit. Omit syrup. Heat to simmering point (185 to 210°F.) over low heat. Pack fruit in the juice that cooks out.

CORN SYRUP AND HONEY

You may use light corn syrup or mild-flavored honey to replace half the sugar in canning fruits.

UNSWEETENED FRUITS

You may can fruits without sweetening them, either in water, in their own juices or in extracted fruit juices. Process the same as fruits with syrup.

MAKE ALTITUDE ADJUSTMENTS

The processing times in this book for foods canned by boiling water bath are for altitudes less than 1000 feet above sea level. When processing food for 20 minutes or less, increase processing time 1 minute for every 1000 feet increase in altitude, 2 minutes for foods processed more than 20 minutes. The pressures given in this book for processing food in steam pressure canners are for altitudes less than 2000 feet above sea level. In higher altitudes increase processing time ½ pound for every 1000 feet increase in altitude.

To Can Fruits and Tomatoes

APPLES: Wash, peel, core and quarter or slice apples. Drop them into salt-vinegar water (2 tblsp. each salt and vinegar to 1 gal. water) to prevent darkening. Lift out, rinse and boil in thin syrup or water for 5 minutes. *Hot Pack Only:* Pack hot fruit to within ½″ of jar top. Cover with hot thin syrup or water, leaving ½″ head space. Adjust lids. Process in boiling water bath (212°F.).

Pint jars   15 minutes
Quart jars   20 minutes

Remove jars from canner and complete seals unless closures are self-sealing type.

APPLESAUCE: Make applesauce, sweetened or unsweetened. Heat to simmering (185 to 210°F.). Stir to prevent sticking.
Hot Pack Only: Pack hot applesauce to ½″ of jar top. Adjust lids. Process in boiling water bath (212°F.).
Pint jars   10 minutes
Quart jars   10 minutes

Remove jars from canner and complete seals unless closures are self-sealing type.

APRICOTS: Use firm, not overripe fruit. Can unpeeled or peeled, whole or cut in halves and pitted. To peel, plunge whole apricots into boiling water for 1 minute, then into cold water. *Raw Pack:* Some varieties of apricots hold their shape better raw-packed than hot-packed. If halved, pack in overlapping layers. If whole, pack close. Pack hot jars and cover with boiling medium syrup to 1½" of jar top. Adjust lids. Process in boiling water bath (212°F.).

Pint jars   25 minutes
Quart jars   30 minutes

Remove jars from canner and complete seals unless closures are self-sealing type.

Hot Pack: Prepare apricots as directed for raw pack. Bring to a boil in medium syrup and cook through gently (about 1 to 3 minutes). Pack hot jars with hot fruit and cover with hot medium syrup, leaving ½" head space. Adjust lids. Process in boiling water bath (212°F.).

Pint jars   20 minutes
Quart jars   25 minutes

Remove jars from canner and complete seals unless closures are self-sealing type.

BERRIES (EXCEPT STRAWBERRIES)

Soft: Blackberries
        Dewberries
        Loganberries
        Raspberries
Firm: Blueberries
        Currants
        Elderberries
        Gooseberries (see instructions)
        Huckleberries

PREPARATION OF SOFT BERRIES:
Use fully ripe berries. Wash with a spray or in water and lift carefully

from water, cap and stem, if necessary. Drain. Work with small amounts at a time (1 to 2 qts.).

Raw Pack: Pack hot jars with raw berries. Shake down several times while filling jar to pack berries tightly without crushing. Cover with boiling medium syrup, leaving 1 to 1½" head space. Adjust lids. Process in boiling water bath (212°F.).

Pint jars   10 minutes
Quart jars   15 minutes

Remove jars from canner and complete seals unless closures are self-sealing type.

Hot Pack: Not recommended for soft berries.

PREPARATION OF FIRM BERRIES:
Wash and drain as for soft berries. Add ½ c. sugar to each qt. fruit. Cover pan and bring to boil. Shake pan to prevent berries from sticking.

Blueberries should be blanched. Blueberries and huckleberries require neither sugar nor liquid. Put 2 or 3 qts. in a square of cheesecloth, hold cloth by the gathered corners and dip berries into boiling water for 15 to 30 seconds. When juice spots appear on cloth, remove and cool. This method gives a more attractive pack with less liquid, but ½ c. sugar may be added to each quart.

Raw Pack: Not recommended for firm berries, except blueberries. (Prepare blueberries as directed for soft berry raw pack.)

Hot Pack: Pack berries and juice to within ½" of jar top. Adjust lids. Process in boiling water bath (212°F.).

Pint jars   10 minutes
Quart jars   15 minutes

Remove jars from canner and com-

plete seals unless closures are self-sealing type.

CHERRIES, SWEET OR TART: Stem, wash and remove pits, if desired. (Pie cherries should always have pits removed and may be canned in water instead of syrup.) If cherries are left whole, prick skins to prevent splitting. *Raw Pack:* Pack hot jars, shaking cherries down several times while filling, for a firm pack. Cover with boiling heavy syrup for tart cherries, thin syrup for sweet cherries. Leave 1 to 1½" head space. Adjust lids. Process in boiling water bath (212°F.).

Pint jars	20 minutes
Quart jars	25 minutes

Remove jars from canner and complete seals unless closures are self-sealing type.
Hot Pack: Prepare cherries as directed for raw pack. Add ½ c. sugar to each qt. fruit. Add a little water to prevent sticking while heating to simmering (185 to 210°F.). Ladle into hot jars, leaving ½" head space. Adjust lids. Process in boiling water bath (212°F.).

Pint jars	10 minutes
Quart jars	15 minutes

Remove jars from canner and complete seals unless closures are self-sealing type.

CHERRIES, SURINAM: Use sound, ripe, freshly picked cherries. Wash and pit. Precook 2 minutes and use the water from the precooking to make a medium syrup.
Hot Pack Only: Pack cherries in hot jars, shake down and cover with boiling syrup. Leave ½" head space. Adjust lids. Process in boiling water bath (212°F.).

Pint jars	12 minutes
Quart jars	16 minutes

Remove jars from canner and complete seals unless closures are self-sealing type.

FIGS: Sort and wash firm, ripe, freshly picked figs. Bring to a boil in hot water. Let stand in hot water 3 to 4 minutes. Drain.
Hot Pack Only: Pack hot in hot jars. Add 1 tblsp. lemon juice to each qt. and cover with hot medium syrup, leaving ½" head space. Adjust lids. Process in boiling water bath (212°F.).

Pint jars	90 minutes
Quart jars	90 minutes

Remove jars from canner and complete seals unless closures are self-sealing type.

FRUIT PURÉES: Use sound, ripe fruit. Wash and remove pits if necessary. Cut large fruit in pieces. Simmer until soft, adding a little water to prevent sticking. Put through a food mill or strainer. Add sugar to taste. Heat again to simmering (185 to 210°F.). *Hot Pack Only:* Pack hot to within ½" from jar top. Adjust lids. Process in boiling water bath (212°F.).

Pint jars	10 minutes
Quart jars	10 minutes

Remove jars from canner and complete seals unless closures are self-sealing type.

GOOSEBERRIES: Wash and drain. Snip off stem and blossom ends with scissors. Flavor will be enhanced if each berry is pricked with a fork.
Hot Pack Only: Work with 1 qt. berries at a time. Add to 3 c. boiling medium or thick syrup for 15 to 30 sec-

onds. Drain in a colander until several quarts are ready. Pack closely in hot jars, shaking down to insure close pack. Cover with boiling syrup in which gooseberries were heated. Leave ½" head space. Adjust lids. Process in boiling water bath (212°F.).

Pint jars   15 minutes
Quart jars   20 minutes

Remove jars from canner and complete seals unless closures are self-sealing type.

GRAPEFRUIT: Wash and peel thoroughly ripened fruit. With a sharp knife cut a slice from both ends of the grapefruit, cutting into the flesh. Remove the remainder of the peel and the white membrane by cutting from one end to the other in wide strips. Use a paring knife or spatula to separate the segments. Discard seeds.
Raw Pack Only: Pack segments firmly into hot jars. Add light syrup heated to simmering point (185 to 210°F.), leaving 1 to 1½" head space. Adjust lids. Process in water bath at simmering (190°F.) to retain the most flavor.

Pint jars   30 minutes
Quart jars   35 minutes

Remove jars from canner and complete seals unless closures are self-sealing type.

GUAVAS, SHELLS: Wash, remove stem and blossom and peel. Remove seeds with a spoon.
Hot Pack Only: Drop shells into a medium syrup and cook 2 to 3 minutes. Pack in overlapping layers, adding 1 to 2 tblsp. syrup with each layer. Adjust lids. Process in boiling water bath (212°F.).

Pint jars   16 minutes
Quart jars   20 minutes

Remove jars from canner and complete seals unless closures are self-sealing type.

LOQUATS, WHOLE: Wash, rinse and drain freshly gathered fruit. Remove stem and blossom end. Peel and remove seeds, if desired.
Hot Pack Only: Cook 2 to 4 minutes in medium syrup and pack hot in hot containers, leaving ½" head space. Adjust lids. Process in boiling water bath (212°F.).

Pint jars   15 minutes
Quart jars   20 minutes

Remove jars from canner and complete seals unless closures are self-sealing type.

MANGOES, GREEN: Pick before any color appears and peel as directed for ripe mangoes.
Raw Pack Only: Let stand for 2 minutes in hot medium syrup before packing in hot jars. Cover with boiling syrup, leaving 1 to 1½" head space. Adjust lids. Process in boiling water bath (212°F.).

Pint jars   15 minutes
Quart jars   20 minutes

Remove jars from canner and complete seals unless closures are self-sealing type.

MANGOES, RIPE: Use firm fruit only. Wash and peel from stem to blossom end. Slice, place in hot thin syrup and let stand 1 to 2 minutes.
Raw Pack Only: Pack into hot jars. Boil syrup down 5 to 8 minutes; strain while hot over the raw fruit, leaving 1 to 1½" head space. Adjust lids. Process in boiling water bath (212°F.).

Pint jars   15 minutes
Quart jars   20 minutes

Remove jars from canner and complete seals unless closures are self-sealing type.

NECTARINES: Prepare and process using directions for peaches.

PAPAYAS, GREEN: Wash and peel. *Hot Pack Only:* Prepare syrup consisting of 3½ c. sugar, 1 c. vinegar, 1 c. water, ½ oz. ginger root and 2 tblsp. cracked cinnamon sticks. Bring to a boil; strain. Precook green papayas 4 minutes; pour the spiced syrup over and bring to a boil. Pack hot in hot jars and cover with syrup, leaving ½" head space. Adjust lids. Process in boiling water bath (212°F.).

Pint jars   15 minutes
Quart jars   20 minutes

Remove jars from canner and complete seals unless closures are self-sealing type.

PAPAYAS, RIPE: Choose ripe but firm fruit. Wash, cut and remove seed. Make a medium syrup; after cooling, add juice of one lemon or lime. *Hot Pack Only:* Slice fruit; add to the cooled syrup, bringing slowly to a boil. Cook approximately 3 minutes and pack hot in hot jars, adding hot syrup to cover. Leave ½" head space. Adjust lids. Process in boiling water bath (212°F.).

Pint jars   15 minutes
Quart jars   20 minutes

Remove jars from canner and complete seals unless closures are self-sealing type.

PEACHES: Use ripe, firm peaches.

Wash. Dip into boiling water for about ½ minute, plunge into cold water and slip off skins. Cut peaches in half and remove pits. Slice if desired. To keep from darkening, drop them into a gallon of salt-vinegar water (2 tblsp. each salt and vinegar to 1 gal. water). Drain before heating or packing raw.

Raw Pack: Pack raw fruit (halves) cut side down, edges overlapping, into hot jars. Cover with boiling medium syrup, leaving 1 to 1½" head space. Adjust lids. Process in boiling water bath (212°F.).

Pint jars   25 minutes
Quart jars   30 minutes

Remove jars from canner and complete seals unless closures are self-sealing type.

Hot Pack: Prepare as directed for raw pack. Heat in hot syrup. Or if peaches are very juicy, omit syrup and add ½ c. sugar for each qt. fruit. Heat gently, then pack hot jars with hot fruit and juice which has cooked out, leaving ½" head space. Adjust lids. Process in boiling water bath (212°F.).

Pint jars   20 minutes
Quart jars   25 minutes

Remove jars from canner and complete seals unless closures are self-sealing type.

PEARS: Use pears ripened after picking. Can them while still firm. Wash, peel, cut in lengthwise halves or quarters and core. A half-teaspoon measuring spoon and paring knife do a good coring job. Work quickly to prevent darkening or drop into salt-vinegar water (2 tblsp. each salt and vinegar to 1 gal. water); drain before using.

Hot Pack: Boil pears 3 to 5 minutes in thin or medium syrup. Pack hot, with cups down, to within ½" of jar top. Add hot syrup, leaving ½" head space. (If desired, add 1 tsp. lemon juice to each qt.) Adjust lids. Process in boiling water bath (212°F.).

Pint jars	25 minutes
Quart jars	30 minutes

Remove jars from canner and complete seals unless closures are self-sealing type.

Note: Pears may be packed raw (without precooking) if they are ripe enough to be quite soft. Pack jars with pears and add syrup to within 1½" of jar top. Adjust lids and follow processing directions for hot pack. Most canners consider pears precooked before canning superior to those canned by the raw pack.

PINEAPPLE: Choose sound, ripe fruit. Wash pineapple, slice, peel and remove eyes and core from each slice. Leave slices whole or cut in pieces. *Hot Pack Only:* Boil pineapple 5 to 10 minutes in medium syrup. Pack hot in hot jars and cover with syrup, leaving ½" head space. Adjust lids. Process in boiling water bath (212°F.).

Pint jars	20 minutes
Quart jars	20 minutes

Remove jars from canner and complete seals unless closures are self-sealing type.

PLUMS: Choose ripe, firm fruit just beginning to soften. Greengage and other meaty plums are best for canning. The juicy varieties mush easily. Wash and drain plums. Prick skins with a needle if plums are to be canned whole. This does not prevent skins from splitting, but helps prevent the fruit from bursting. The freestone variety may be cut in half and pitted. *Raw Pack:* Pack gently but closely in jar. Cover with boiling syrup, heavy for tart plums, medium for sweet ones. Leave 1 to 1½" head space. Adjust lids. Process in boiling water bath (212°F.).

Pint jars	20 minutes
Quart jars	25 minutes

Remove jars from canner and complete seals unless closures are self-sealing type.

Hot Pack: Prepare as directed for raw pack. Heat fruit in boiling medium syrup. Or if plums are juicy, add ½ c. sugar to each qt., using no syrup. Pack hot fruit to within ½" of jar top and cover with boiling syrup. Leave ½" head space. Adjust lids. Process in boiling water bath (212°F.).

Pint jars	20 minutes
Quart jars	25 minutes

Remove jars from canner and complete seals unless closures are self-sealing type.

PRUNES, FRESH: Wash. Leave whole if small size or cut in halves and pit. Prick skins to help prevent cracking. Peel if skin is tough. *Raw Pack:* Pack in hot jars. Cover with boiling medium syrup, leaving 1 to 1½" head space Adjust lids. Process in boiling water bath (212°F.).

Pint jars	20 minutes
Quart jars	20 minutes

Remove jars from canner and complete seals unless closures are self-sealing type.

Hot Pack: Prepare as directed for raw pack. Heat plums to boiling in syrup or juice and pack hot in hot jars. Cover with boiling liquid, leaving ½" head space. Adjust lids. Process in boiling water bath (212°F.).

Pint jars   15 minutes
Quart jars   15 minutes

Remove jars from canner and complete seals unless closures are self-sealing type.

RHUBARB: Wash tender, young stalks and cut into ½" pieces.
Raw Pack: Pack tightly in hot jars and pour boiling heavy syrup to within 1 to 1½" of jar top. Rotate jar between hands to remove air bubbles. Adjust lids. Process in boiling water bath (212°F.).

Pint jars   10 minutes
Quart jars   10 minutes

Remove jars from canner and complete seals unless closures are self-sealing type.
Hot Pack: Prepare as directed for raw pack. Add ½ c. sugar to each qt. rhubarb. Let stand to draw out juice. After juice appears, place rhubarb in pan on top of range and simmer. Or put rhubarb in the oven until it is hot and juicy. Fill jars carefully to prevent mushing, leaving ½" head space. Adjust lids. Process in boiling water bath (212°F.).

Pint jars   10 minutes
Quart jars   10 minutes

Remove jars from canner and complete seals unless closures are self-sealing type.

STRAWBERRIES: Not recommended for canning. Usually the result is not a good product. Plan to freeze them, if possible, or make jam and preserves.

TOMATOES: Select sound, ripe tomatoes. Wash. Dip into boiling water ½ minute or until skins crack; dip quickly into cold water. Cut out stem ends, remove cores and slip off skins.
Raw Pack: Leave tomatoes whole or cut in halves or quarters. Pack in jars, pressing down gently after each two tomatoes are added, to release juice and fill spaces. Add no water or liquid to cut tomatoes; tomato juice made of imperfect, ripe fruit may be added to whole tomatoes, rotating jars to remove air bubbles. Leave ½" head space. Add ½ tsp. salt to pints, 1 tsp. to quarts. Adjust lids. Process in boiling water bath (212°F.).

Pint jars   35 minutes
Quart jars   45 minutes

Remove jars from canner and complete seals unless closures are self-sealing type.
Hot Pack: Prepare as directed for raw pack. Cut tomatoes in quarters or halves. Put in kettle and bring to a boil. Stir gently to prevent sticking, but use care not to make tomatoes mushy. Fill hot jars with boiling hot tomatoes to within ½" of jar top. Add ½ tsp. salt to pints, 1 tsp. to quarts. Adjust lids. Process in boiling water bath (212°F.).

Pint jars   10 minutes
Quart jars   10 minutes

Remove jars from canner and complete seals unless closures are self-sealing type.

Note: Many tomatoes today contain less acid than those in our gardens a few years ago. This is one reason more canned tomatoes spoil today. Be sure *never to use the open kettle method our grandmothers handled successfully* in their canning operations. The addition of 1 tsp. lemon juice, vinegar or ascorbic acid powder to every quart of tomatoes does provide acid; some taste-testers find they can detect added tartness. Research is under way to solve the problem of canning tomatoes. In the meantime, play safe and ask your County Extension Office what the recommendation is for your state. And be sure not to cut short the processing period. You may want to stay on the generous side in the timing.

TOMATO PURÉE, SEASONED: Choose firm ripe tomatoes. Prepare about 4 qts. at a time.
Hot Pack Only: Wash, chop and simmer tomatoes until soft. Prepare seasoning mixture as follows: Chop 3 onions, 3 branches celery and 3 sweet red or green peppers. Simmer in boiling water until soft. Add to tomatoes and put through a sieve. Add ½ tsp. each of salt and sugar for each pint of pulp. Reheat to the boiling point. Mixture should be thick. Ladle into hot jars, leaving ½″ head space. Adjust lids. Process in boiling water bath (212°F.).

Pint jars   35 minutes

Remove jars from canner and complete seals unless closures are self-sealing type.

Slick Canning Tricks

If you like to experiment in canning, try these fruit specials of three farm women.

SALAD AND DESSERT PEARS: "I like to can pear halves in canned unsweetened pineapple juice instead of syrup. When chilled, they are delicious for salad or dessert. . . . Sometimes I can large, top quality pears, cut in lengthwise halves and cored, without peeling. They are especially pretty if you put a maraschino cherry in the center of each pear half before packing into jars. Add syrup and process as usual. I serve these pears for salad and I also slice and add them to fruit compotes. . . . I can small pear halves in syrup tinted red, pink or green. They come in handy for garnishing."

APPLE/PLUM SAUCE: "When I have both apples and plums, I combine equal amounts of chopped, pitted plums and sliced, unpeeled apples. I cook the mixture until the fruits are soft and put it through the food mill. When sweetened to taste, I can the fruit combination like applesauce."

TINTED GREEN GRAPES: "I often can slightly underripe seedless green grapes in tinted medium syrup. After washing and stemming the grapes, I bring them to a boil in hot syrup tinted red, green or pink, pack the mixture in hot pint jars and process 15 minutes in a water bath. Chilled, they are attractive and delicious in fruit salads and cocktails."

OLD-TIME PEAR MINCEMEAT

New-time cooks win praise on pies made with Grandma's pear mincemeat

7	lbs. ripe Bartlett pears
1	lemon
2	(1 lb.) pkgs. seedless raisins
6¾	c. sugar
1	c. vinegar
1	tblsp. ground cloves
1	tblsp. ground cinnamon
1	tblsp. ground nutmeg
1	tblsp. ground allspice
1	tsp. ground ginger

• Core and quarter pears. Quarter lemon, removing seeds. Put pears, lemon and raisins through chopper.

• Combine remaining ingredients in large kettle. Add chopped fruit mixture. Bring to a boil over medium heat; simmer 40 minutes.

• Pack at once in hot pint jars, leaving ½" head space. Adjust lids. Process in boiling water bath (212°F.) 25 minutes.

• Remove jars from canner and complete seals unless closures are self-sealing type. Makes 9 pints.

PEACHY THRIFT DESSERT

Farm women are talented in making good use of foods in their cupboards—and breadboxes. A good example of their thrift and imagination is the way they combine canned peaches and bread crumbs.

PEACH MACAROONS

Homely dessert that is distinctive and taste-rewarding—pretty, too

1	egg white, stiffly beaten
¼	c. light corn syrup
½	c. brown sugar, firmly packed
2	c. coarse bread crumbs
16	canned peach halves

• Slowly combine egg white and corn syrup; beat until blended. Add brown sugar and bread crumbs.

• Place 2 tblsp. meringue mixture in center of each peach half. Arrange in baking pan.

• Bake in moderate oven (350°F.) 20 minutes. Serve warm. Makes 16.

Prize-winning Recipes

A Kansas woman, who proudly comes home from state and county fairs every year with many First Premiums on food she cans, shares several of her winning recipes.

FRUIT COCKTAIL

• Select firm but ripe pineapples, pears and peaches; cut into chunks. Precook separately in medium syrup (1 c.

sugar to 2 c. water) 3 to 5 minutes, or until limp. Precook whole seedless white grapes the same way.

• Simmer red maraschino cherries in water 5 minutes to prevent bleeding; drain. Leave whole.

• Fill hot pint jars to within ½" of top with equal amounts of fruit, except cherries (use 3 per pint).

• Cover with strained hot syrup, leaving ½" head space. Adjust lids. Process in boiling water bath (212°F.) 20 minutes. Remove jars from canner and complete seals unless closures are self-sealing type. Cool out of drafts.

PRIZE PEACH HALVES

• Wash, rinse and drain firm, ripe peaches. Place in wire basket or cheesecloth bag and dip in boiling water, then in cold. Peel and pit.
• Drop halves into mixture of 2 tblsp. salt, 2 tblsp. vinegar and 1 gal. water. Rinse. Cook peaches in heavy syrup (1 c. sugar to 1 c. water) until limp.
• Pack in hot quart jars in over-lapping layers, cavity side down. Cover to within ½″ of top with the strained syrup. Adjust lids. Process in boiling water bath (212°F.) 20 minutes. Remove jars from canner and complete seals unless closures are self-sealing.

WILD PLUMS

• Wash and stem firm, medium-ripe wild plums. Prick the skins and pack cold in hot quart jars to the top.

• Cover with hot heavy syrup (1 c. sugar to 1 c. water) and let sit 5 minutes. Drain off syrup; strain and reheat to boiling. The plums will have shrunk to shoulder of jar.
• Cover plums with boiling syrup, leaving 1 to 1½″ head space. Adjust lids; process 20 minutes in boiling water bath (212°F.). Remove jars from canner and complete seals unless closures are self-sealing type.

FANCY PACK WHOLE TOMATOES

• Scald small, firm, red tomatoes; remove skins and cores, being careful not to break seed pockets. Pack in hot pint jars.
• Pour boiling water to top of jars; let sit 2 minutes, then pour off water. Repeat process with boiling water four more times, last time adding ½ tsp. salt to each pint and filling to neck of jar with boiling water. Adjust lids. Process 35 minutes in boiling water bath (212°F.) for pints. Remove jars from canner and complete seals unless closures are self-sealing type.

Peak-of-the-Season Vegetables
HURRY THEM FROM GARDEN INTO CANS

If you have a pressure canner and a bountiful garden, you have the first two requirements of a good vegetable canner. Add the knowledge of up-to-date methods and the will to follow them—then you have what it takes

to put up prize winners. Your family will have better meals at a lower cost.

This chapter contains the latest approved canning methods for vegetables, arranged alphabetically. Read directions before you pick the succulent peas or tender asparagus to can. You'll be well informed for the job at hand and pleased with the results you get. Don't miss the tricks a Connecticut homemaker uses to win ribbons and money at fairs.

Vegetable Canning Tips

Salt: The addition of salt is optional. It flavors vegetables but may be added when you serve them. If you use salt in canning, add it after you pack food in jars.

Altitude Adjustments: For each 1000 feet above sea level, add ½ pound pressure.

To Can Vegetables

ARTICHOKES, GLOBE: Wash and trim small artichokes from 1¼ to 2″ in length. Prepare a vinegar-water solution (¾ c. vinegar to 1 gal. water). *Hot Pack Only:* Precook artichokes 5 minutes in vinegar solution. Drain and pack hot in hot jars, being careful to not overfill. Prepare a brine by adding ¾ c. vinegar (or lemon juice) and 3 tblsp. salt to 1 gal. water. Pour boiling hot over artichokes to within ½″ of top of either pint or quart jars. Adjust lids. Process in pressure canner at 10 pounds pressure (240°F.).

Pint jars   25 minutes
Quart jars   25 minutes

Remove jars from canner and complete seals unless closures are self-sealing type.

ASPARAGUS: Choose young, fresh asparagus. Wash, trim bracts (scales) and tough ends and wash once again. Cut into 1″ pieces, or in lengths ¾″ shorter than jar and pack in bundles. *Raw Pack:* Pack asparagus very tightly to within ½″ of jar top. Add salt (½ tsp. to pints; 1 tsp. to quarts).

Cover to within ½″ of top with boiling water. Adjust lids. Process in pressure canner at 10 pounds pressure (240°F.).

Pint jars   25 minutes
Quart jars   30 minutes

Remove jars from canner and complete seals unless closures are self-sealing type.

Hot Pack: Precook to wilt asparagus in boiling water from 1 to 3 minutes. Plunge quickly into cold water. Pack hot and very loosely to within ½″ of jar top. Add salt (½ tsp. to pints; 1 tsp. to quarts) and cover with boiling hot cooking liquid (or plain boiling water), leaving ½″ head space. Adjust lids. Process in pressure canner at 10 pounds pressure (240°F.).

Pint jars   25 minutes
Quart jars   30 minutes

Remove jars from canner and complete seals unless closures are self-sealing type.

BEANS, FRESH LIMA: Choose only young, tender beans for canning. *Hot Pack:* Shell beans and cover with boiling water; bring to boil. Pack loosely to within 1″ of jar top. Add salt (½ tsp. to pints; 1 tsp. to quarts). Fill jars with boiling water, leaving 1" head space. Adjust lids. Process in pressure canner at 10 pounds pressure (240°F.).

Pint jars 40 minutes
Quart jars 50 minutes

Remove jars from canner and complete seals unless closures are self-sealing type.

BEANS, SNAP: Wash beans, trim and string. Cut into 1" pieces or leave whole. (If whole, pack standing on end in jars.)

Raw Pack: Pack tightly to within ½" of jar top. Add salt (½ tsp. to pints; 1 tsp. to quarts). Fill with boiling water to cover to within ½" of jar top. Adjust lids. Process in pressure canner at 10 pounds pressure (240°F.).

Pint jars 20 minutes
Quart jars 25 minutes

Remove jars from canner and complete seals unless closures are self-sealing type.

Hot Pack: Prepare as directed for raw pack. Cover with boiling water and boil for 5 minutes. Pack hot beans loosely to within ½" of jar top. Add salt (½ tsp. to pints; 1 tsp. to quarts). Cover with fresh boiling water or use the liquid in which beans were precooked, leaving ½" head space. Adjust lids. Process in pressure canner at 10 pounds pressure (240°F.).

Pint jars 20 minutes
Quart jars 25 minutes

Remove jars from canner and complete seals unless closures are self-sealing type.

BEETS: Remove beet tops except for 1 to 2" of stem; leave roots on. Wash and sort to uniform size to insure even cooking. Cover beets with boiling water; boil 15 to 25 minutes; dip in cold water and slip skins, roots and stems. Baby beets (diameter under 2") may be left whole, but larger ones should be cubed in ½" pieces or sliced. Large slices should be quartered or halved.

Raw Pack: Not recommended.

Hot Pack: Pack hot beets to within ½" of jar top. Add salt (½ tsp. to pints; 1 tsp. to quarts). Cover with boiling water to which 1 to 2 tblsp. vinegar, depending on jar size, has been added to retain color. Leave ½" head space. Adjust lids. Process in pressure canner at 10 pounds pressure (240°F.).

Pint jars 30 minutes
Quart jars 35 minutes

Remove jars from canner and complete seals unless closures are self-sealing type.

CARROTS: Use only young, tender carrots. Wash, scrape or peel. Slice, dice or, leave very small carrots whole.

Raw Pack: Pack tightly to within 1" of jar top. Add salt (½ tsp. to pints; 1 tsp. to quarts). Cover with boiling water to within ½" of jar top. Adjust lids. Process in pressure canner at 10 pounds pressure (240°F.).

Pint jars 25 minutes
Quart jars 30 minutes

Remove jars from canner and complete seals unless closures are self-sealing type.

Hot Pack: Prepare as directed for raw pack. Cover with boiling water and bring to boil. Pack hot carrots to within ½" of jar top. Add salt (½ tsp. to pints; 1 tsp. to quarts). Cover with boiling hot cooking water, leaving ½" head space. Adjust lids. Process in pressure canner at 10 pounds pressure (240°F.).

Pint jars   25 minutes
Quart jars   30 minutes

Remove jars from canner and complete seals unless closures are self-sealing type.

CELERY: Wash and slice or cut into asparagus-style lengths.
Raw Pack: Pack loosely to within ½" of jar top. Add salt (½ tsp. to pints; 1 tsp. to quarts). Cover with boiling water, leaving ½" head space. Adjust lids. Process in pressure canner at 10 pounds pressure (240°F.).

Pint jars   30 minutes
Quart jars   30 minutes

Remove jars from canner and complete seals unless closures are self-sealing type.
Hot Pack: Prepare as directed for raw pack. Precook 1 to 3 minutes. Pack hot into hot jars and add salt (½ tsp. to pints; 1 tsp. to quarts). Cover with boiling liquid retained from precooking, adding boiling water, if needed, to fill jars to within ½" of top of either pint or quart jars. Adjust lids. Process in pressure canner at 10 pounds pressure (240°F.).

Pint jars   35 minutes
Quart jars   35 minutes

Remove jars from canner and complete seals unless closures are self-sealing type.

CELERY AND TOMATOES: Prepare celery as directed for raw pack, but chop it. Wash, core, peel and chop tomatoes.
Hot Pack Only: Use equal parts of the two vegetables and boil, without water added, for 5 minutes. Fill jars to within ½" of jar top. Adjust lids. Process in pressure canner at 10 pounds pressure (240°F.).

Pint jars   35 minutes
Quart jars   35 minutes

Remove jars from canner and complete seals unless closures are self-sealing type.

CORN, CREAM STYLE: Harvest in small quantities (2 to 3 doz. ears at a time), if convenient. *Immediately prepare for processing.* Cut ends from ears, peel off husks and silk. Trim blemishes from ears. Cut kernels from cob about ⅔ the depth of the kernels. Scrape cob to remove the remaining corn, but not any of the cob. Use pint jars only.
Raw Pack: Fill to within 1" of jar top, being careful not to shake or pack down. Add ½ tsp. salt to each pint and fill with boiling water, leaving ½" head space. Adjust lids. Process in pressure canner at 10 pounds pressure (240°F.).

Pint jars   95 minutes

Remove jars from canner and complete seals unless closures are self-sealing type.
Hot Pack: Prepare as directed for raw pack. Add 1 pt. boiling water to each quart of prepared corn and heat to boiling. Pack hot corn into pint jars to within 1" of jar top. Add ½ tsp. salt to each pint jar. Adjust lids. Process in pressure canner at 10 pounds pressure (240°F.).

Pint jars   85 minutes

Remove jars from canner and com-

plete seals unless closures are self-sealing type.

CORN, WHOLE KERNEL: Prepare as directed for hot pack cream-style corn, but do not scrape the cob. Use only the whole kernels.
Hot Pack: Add 1 pt. boiling water to each qt. of prepared corn and heat to boiling. Pack corn in jars to within 1" of jar top and cover with hot cooking liquid. Leave 1" head space. Add salt (½ tsp. to pints; 1 tsp. to quarts). Adjust lids. Process in pressure canner at 10 pounds pressure (240°F.).
Pint jars   55 minutes
Quart jars   85 minutes.
Remove jars from canner and complete seals unless closures are self-sealing type.

HOMINY: Shell 2 qts. dry white or yellow field corn. Make a solution of 8 qts. water and 2 oz. lye in an enameled pan or iron kettle. Add the dry corn to this brine and boil hard for 30 minutes, or until hulls come loose. Let stand for about 20 minutes, then rinse corn thoroughly with several hot water rinses, followed by cold water rinses to cool the corn sufficiently for handling and to remove all of the lye. Work hominy, using your hands, to remove dark kernel tips. The corn and the tips are more easily separated if placed in a coarse sieve and floated off by water.

Next, add about 1" of water to cover hominy and boil for 5 minutes; change water. Repeat four times. Then cook the corn kernels about 30 to 45 minutes (or until soft) and drain. Makes about 6 quarts.
Hot Pack: Fill jars with hot hominy

to within ½" of jar top. Add salt (½ tsp. to pints; 1 tsp. to quarts). Fill with boiling water, leaving ½" head space. Adjust lids. Process in pressure canner at 10 pounds pressure (240°F.).
Pint jars   60 minutes
Quart jars   70 minutes
Remove jars from canner and complete seals unless closures are self-sealing type.

MUSHROOMS: Soak fresh mushrooms in cold water for 10 minutes before washing, to remove all the soil. Trim stem ends and remove discolored portions. Rinse well through several changes of cold water. Leave small mushrooms whole; cut larger ones in halves or quarters. Proceed with any of the three following methods: (1) steam for 4 minutes, (2) heat gently for 15 minutes in a covered saucepan with no liquid added, or (3) cover with boiling water and boil for 2 to 3 minutes.
Hot Pack Only: Pack hot mushrooms to within ½" of jar top in half-pint or pint jars only. Add ¼ tsp. salt and $\frac{1}{16}$ tsp. crystalline ascorbic acid to each half pint; ½ tsp. salt and ⅛ tsp. ascorbic acid to pints. Add boiling water or boiling hot cooking liquid to mushrooms, leaving ½" head space. Adjust lids. Process in pressure canner at 10 pounds pressure (240°F.).
Half-pint jars   30 minutes
Pint jars   30 minutes
Remove jars from canner and complete seals unless closures are self-sealing type.

OKRA: Wash and trim only tender pods, being careful not to remove the "cap" unless okra will be used for soup. For soup, slice across pods in ½ to 1″ lengths. Cook in boiling water for 1 minute. If canning whole, do not cut into the pod.

Hot Pack Only: Pack hot okra in jar, leaving ½″ at top. Add salt (½ tsp. to pints; 1 tsp. to quarts). Cover with boiling water, leaving ½″ head space. Adjust lids. Process in pressure canner at 10 pounds pressure (240°F.).

Pint jars	25 minutes
Quart jars	40 minutes

Remove jars from canner and complete seals unless closures are self-sealing type.

OKRA AND TOMATOES: Prepare okra as directed for that vegetable. Leave small pods whole, or cut in 1″ lengths. Combine with peeled, quartered tomatoes. Add salt (½ tsp. to pints; 1 tsp. to quarts). Heat to boiling.

Hot Pack Only: Pack hot seasoned vegetables in either pint or quart jars, leaving ½″ head space. Adjust lids. Process in pressure canner at 10 pounds pressure (240°F.).

Pint jars	25 minutes
Quart jars	35 minutes

Remove jars from canner and complete seals unless closures are self-sealing type.

PEAS, FRESH BLACK-EYED (Cowpeas, Black-eyed Beans): Shell and wash, discarding the too-mature peas.

Raw Pack: Pack raw peas loosely in jars to within 1½″ of top of pints; 2″ for quarts. Add salt (½ tsp. to pints; 1 tsp. to quarts.). Cover peas with boiling water, leaving ½″ head space. Adjust lids. Process in pressure canner at 10 pounds pressure (240°F.).

Pint jars	35 minutes
Quart jars	40 minutes

Remove jars from canner and complete seals unless closures are self-sealing type.

Hot Pack: Prepare as directed for raw pack; cover with boiling water. Bring to a rolling boil; drain. Pack hot vegetable, being careful not to shake down, to within 1¼″ from top of pint jars; 1½″ for quarts. Add salt (½ tsp. to pints; 1 tsp. to quarts). Cover with boiling water, leaving ½ to 1″ head space. Adjust lids. Process in pressure canner at 10 pounds pressure (240°F.).

Pint jars	35 minutes
Quart jars	40 minutes

Remove jars from canner and complete seals unless closures are self-sealing type.

PEAS, FRESH GREEN: Harvest at the best stage for eating. Can immediately after picking to assure sweet-flavored freshness.

Raw Pack: Fill jars with fresh peas, shelled and washed, being careful not to press down, to within 1″ of jar top. Add salt (½ tsp. to pints; 1 tsp. to quarts). Pour boiling water over to cover, leaving 1″ head space. Adjust lids. Process in pressure canner at 10 pounds pressure (240°F.).

Pint jars	40 minutes
Quart jars	40 minutes

Remove jars from canner and complete seals unless closures are self-sealing type.

Hot Pack: Prepare as directed for raw pack. Cover with boiling water and bring to a boil. Pack hot peas gently and loosely to within 1″ of jar top. Add salt (½ tsp. to pints; 1 tsp. to quarts). Cover with boiling water or liquid in which peas were precooked, leaving 1″ head space. Adjust lids. Process in pressure canner at 10 pounds pressure (240°F.).

Pint jars	40 minutes
Quart jars	40 minutes

Remove jars from canner and complete seals unless closures are self-sealing type.

PEPPERS—BELL, GREEN AND RED: Wash, remove stem, core inside partitions, remove seeds.

To peel: cook in hot water 3 minutes or until skins will slip easily. Or heat in a hot oven (450°F.) 8 to 10 minutes until skins blister and crack. Do not let burn. Remove skins with slender knife blade. Chill peppers immediately in cold water.

Raw Pack: Not recommended.

Hot Pack: Flatten peppers and pack carefully in horizontal layers. Fill hot jars to within ½″ from top; cover with boiling water to within ½″ of jar top. Add ½ tsp. salt and ½ tblsp. lemon juice (or 1 tblsp. vinegar instead of lemon juice) to pints; 1 tsp. salt and 1 tblsp. lemon juice to quarts (2 tblsp. vinegar if substituted for lemon juice). Vinegar and lemon juice improve flavor. Adjust lids. Process in pressure canner at *5 pounds pressure.* High pressure injures both the texture and the flavor.

Pint jars	50 minutes
Quart jars	60 minutes

Remove jars from canner and complete seals unless closures are self-sealing type.

POTATOES, NEW: Wash, scrape and rinse small freshly dug new potatoes. Boil 10 minutes in water; drain.

Hot Pack Only: Pack hot to within ½″ of jar top. Add salt (½ tsp. to pints; 1 tsp. to quarts). Cover with fresh boiling water. Leave ½″ head space. Adjust lids. Process in pressure canner at 10 pounds pressure (240°F.).

Pint jars	30 minutes
Quart jars	40 minutes

Remove jars from canner and complete seals unless closures are self-sealing type.

POTATOES, SWEET: Wash and sort for size. Boil or steam 20 to 30 minutes to facilitate slipping the skins. Cut in uniform pieces if large or leave smaller ones whole.

Dry Pack: Pack hot sweet potatoes tightly, pressing gently to fill air spaces to within 1″ of jar top. Do not add salt or liquid. Adjust lids. Process in pressure canner at 10 pounds pressure (240°F.).

Pint jars	65 minutes
Quart jars	95 minutes

Remove jars from canner and complete seals unless closures are self-sealing type.

Wet Pack: Prepare as directed for dry pack. Pack hot sweet potatoes to within 1″ of jar top. Add salt (½ tsp. to pints; 1 tsp. to quarts). Cover with either boiling water or medium syrup, as you prefer. Leave 1″ head space. Adjust lids. Process in pressure canner at 10 pounds pressure (240°F.).

Pint jars	55 minutes
Quart jars	90 minutes

Remove jars from canner and complete seals unless closures are self-sealing type.

PUMPKIN, OR MATURE WINTER
SQUASH: Wash, remove seeds, scrape
out fibrous material and peel. Cut into
1″ cubes or strips. Place in a tightly
covered kettle with just enough water
to cover; bring to a boil.

Raw Pack: Not recommended.

Hot Pack: Pack hot pumpkin or
squash, in strips or cubed, in hot jars
to within ½″ of jar top. Add salt (½
tsp. to pints; 1 tsp. to quarts). Cover
with hot cooking liquid, leaving ½″
head space. Adjust lids. Process in
pressure canner at 10 pounds pressure
(240°F.).

Pint jars   55 minutes
Quart jars   90 minutes

Remove jars from canner and complete seals unless closures are self-
sealing type.

PUMPKIN, STRAINED: Wash, remove
seeds and scrape fibrous material
from flesh. Cut in cubes or strips.
Steam (as directed for regular pumpkin) 25 minutes or until tender.
Scrape flesh from rind and put
through colander or food mill. Simmer pulp until heated through, stirring
to prevent sticking.

Hot Pack Only: Pack hot pulp in hot
jars to within ½″ of jar top. Add no
liquid or salt to strained pumpkin. Adjust lids. Process in pressure canner at
10 pounds pressure (240°F.).

Pint jars   65 minutes
Quart jars   80 minutes

Remove jars from canner and complete seals unless closures are self-
sealing type.

SPINACH AND OTHER GREENS: Pick
fresh, tender spinach and wash thoroughly. Cut out tough stems and mid-
ribs. Put about 2½ pounds spinach in

a cheesecloth bag and steam until
well wilted (about 10 minutes).

Hot Pack Only: Pack loosely, while
hot, to within ½″ of jar top. Add salt
(¼ tsp. to pints; ½ tsp. to quarts).
Cover with boiling water. Leave ½″
head space. Adjust lids. Process in
pressure canner at 10 pounds pressure
(240°F.).

Pint jars   70 minutes
Quart jars   90 minutes

Remove jars from canner and complete seals unless closures are self-
sealing type.

SQUASH, BANANA: Prepare as directed
for Strained Pumpkin.

SQUASH, SUMMER: Wash, trim ends,
remove any imperfect portions, but
do not peel. Cut uniform pieces, quarters, halves or ½″ slices.

Raw Pack: Pack tightly to within 1″
of jar top. Add salt (½ tsp. to pints;
1 tsp. to quarts). Fill jar with boiling
water to within ½″ of top. Adjust
lids. Process in pressure canner at 10
pounds pressure (240°F.).

Pint jars   25 minutes
Quart jars   30 minutes

Remove jars from canner and complete seals unless closures are self-
sealing type.

Hot Pack: Prepare as directed for
raw pack. Add water to cover squash
and bring to a boil. Pack hot squash
loosely to within ½″ of jar top. Add
salt (½ tsp. to pints; 1 tsp. to quarts).
Pour boiling hot cooking liquid over
squash, leaving ½″ head space. Adjust lids. Process in pressure canner at
10 pounds pressure (240°F.).

Pint jars   30 minutes
Quart jars   40 minutes

Remove jars from canner and com-

plete seals unless closures are self-sealing type.

SQUASH, WINTER (see Pumpkin)

TURNIPS: Prepare as directed for carrots. Process in pressure canner at 10 pounds pressure (240°F.). The time for *pint* jars is 5 minutes longer than for carrots.

Pint jars   30 minutes
Quart jars   30 minutes

Remove jars from canner and complete seals unless closures are self-sealing type.

VEGETABLE SOUP MIXTURE: Any mixture of vegetables may be used. Prepare them as directed in previous instructions for canning each individually. Combine vegetables and boil 5 minutes with water to cover. Peeled, cut-up tomatoes may be used for part of the liquid.
Hot Pack Only: Pour hot vegetable mixture into jars. Cover with boiling liquid. If enough tomatoes are used, no additional water will be necessary. Add salt (½ tsp. to pints; 1 tsp. to quarts). Leave ½" head space. Adjust

lids. Process in pressure canner at 10 pounds pressure (240°F.).

Pint jars   60 minutes
Quart jars   70 minutes

Remove jars from canner and complete seals unless closures are self-sealing type.

VEGETABLE/BEEF STEW: Cube and combine the following ingredients:

2   qts. stewing beef (1½" cubes)
2   qts. potatoes (½" cubes)
2   qts. carrots (½" cubes)
3   c. celery (¼" pieces)
1¾ qts. small whole onions (1" or less in diameter)

Raw Pack Only: Pack jars loosely with meat-vegetable mixture to within 1" from top. Add salt (½ tsp. to pints; 1 tsp. to quarts). Do not add liquid. Adjust lids. Process in pressure canner at 10 pounds pressure (240°F.).

Pint jars   60 minutes
Quart jars   75 minutes

Remove jars from canner and complete seals unless closures are self-sealing type.

Three Vegetable Specialties

GREEN TOMATO MINCEMEAT

Makes downright delicious pies—the best way to salvage green tomatoes

6   lbs. green tomatoes
2   lbs. tart apples
2   c. raisins
4   c. brown sugar, firmly packed
2   c. strong coffee
1   lemon (grated peel and juice)
2   tsp. grated orange peel
½   c. vinegar
1   tsp. salt
1   tsp. ground nutmeg
1   tsp. ground allspice

· Core and quarter tomatoes and apples; put through food chopper with raisins. Combine all ingredients in large saucepan. Simmer 2 hours, stirring frequently.

• Pack at once in hot pint jars; leave 1″ head space. Adjust lids. Process in boiling water bath (212°F.) 25 minutes.

• Remove jars from canner and complete seals unless closures are self-sealing type. Makes about 10 pints.

Note: You can freeze this mincemeat if you have space in your freezer.

FANCY PACK GREEN BEANS

Suggestion from a canning champion

• Select uniform size young green beans. Wash; remove ends and cut into uniform lengths the height of pint jar to the shoulder. Pack raw into hot jars, standing beans on end, filling jar firmly tight so beans stay in place. Add ½ tsp. salt per pint.

• Cover with boiling water to within ½″ of top. Adjust lids. Process in pressure canner 20 minutes at 10 pounds. Remove jars from canner and complete seals unless closures are self-sealing type.

SUN-DRIED SWEET CORN

Sometimes when you remember how good sun-dried corn tasted in Thanksgiving dinners and other winter meals, you feel the urge to make a supply. Here's the way to do it.

Choose a day when the sun is hot.

Remove the husks and silks from ears of sweet corn. Drop them into boiling salted water and cook 5 minutes or until the milk in the kernels sets. Remove corn and cool enough to handle.

Cut kernels from cobs, spread them in a single layer in a shallow pan. Cover with a clean cloth.

Set the pan in direct sunlight until the kernels dry thoroughly, bringing them in the house at night. It will take at least 2 days of warm sunshine for the drying.

Store the dried corn at room temperature in clean, covered jars. It will remain in good condition up to 6 months.

HOW TO COOK DRIED CORN

Rinse the corn with cold water, drain and cover with cold water. Let it stand overnight. Next day, cook in boiling water, salted to taste, until the kernels are tender. It will take about 30 minutes.

Drain cooked corn and season with cream, butter, pepper and, if needed, salt. Serve piping hot. If your family enjoys the hominy-like flavor, you will plan to dry more corn next year.

CHAPTER 12

MEAT, POULTRY AND GAME

Methods for Canning Beef, Veal, Pork, Lamb, Big Game, Ground Beef, Sausage, Chickens, Recipes for Blue Ribbon Mincemeat and State-of-the-Union Mincemeat · Turkey, Other Poultry, Giblets, Rabbits

You'd think from the freezers and lockers full of meat that freezing has just about replaced meat and poultry canning on farms. But not quite! Good country cooks say there's a place in their kitchens for both the frozen and canned. "I can step to the cupboard, take a couple of jars of home-canned beef or chicken off the shelf and put them on to heat," says a farm woman. "It's an old farm custom," she adds, "and my salvation when I look out the window and see a car driving in near mealtime."

Canned meat and chicken also provide a change of pace from frozen and cured meats, homemakers say. And they take no thawing time. Meats and poultry in jars are invaluable when freezer and locker space vanishes. But clever cooks also plan to keep jars of meat and chicken on hand just to please the people at the table with their old-fashioned taste.

Most cooks have pet ways (but few recipes) for dressing up canned meats and chicken—often heirloom methods their grandmothers and mothers used. One woman puts chicken on to heat while she cooks noodles in chicken broth she canned. She combines them to serve. Another home-maker heats canned beef, adds barbecue sauce and spoons it over fluffy rice or toasted buns. Two hearty main dishes for 30-minute dinners!

A Kansas farmer and his wife, when driving to Colorado for a family reunion, took along 52 quarts of canned beef to make cooking easier and more economical in their rented cottage. They also wanted to treat their grown children, now scattered in homes of their own, to what-mother-used-to-make. Their reward—many compliments.

Off-the-Shelf Meats
HANDY WHEN TIME IS SHORT

Canned meats and poultry are favorite convenience foods in country kitchens. Cooks feel calm with them in the cupboard—it's like having money in the bank to fall back on in time of need. You can fix them for the table in jig-time. And they become individual when the cook adds her own dash of seasoning.

"At our house, we especially like sandwiches made with canned beef or chicken," one FARM JOURNAL reader wrote. "With a touch of salad dressing and chopped pickles or olives mixed in, I often serve them to guests —also to the family. Sometimes I toast them. And always the fillings are generous. They go over big."

This chapter contains the up-to-date methods for canning meat. They will lead you to success if you follow them—also to many surprisingly good, hurry-up meals. So get out the pressure canner and other canning equipment when you have a surplus of meat, poultry or game that you want to put away for future use.

Remember to make altitude adjustment (see page 234 in Chapter 11).

How to Can Meats and Large Game

Follow these steps for canning beef, veal, pork, lamb and big game, like venison and elk:

1. Select clean, fresh meat that has been well bled. Chill immediately after slaughtering until all the animal heat is gone. Can or hold several days at 40°F. or lower. You will find chilled meat easier to handle. If you can avoid it, do not freeze meat before canning. It will not be of the best quality if you do. In case you must can frozen meat, do not thaw it. Cut it with a saw or a stout, sharp knife. Put pieces in boiling water until soft enough to pack into jars.

2. Do not wash meat. Wipe it off with a damp cloth before cutting. Washing draws out the juices.

3. Cut meat in pieces that slip easily into jars. Cut across the grain when possible. Bone the larger pieces. Cut off most of the fat. Select cuts you use for roasts, steaks and chops for canning in large pieces. Can the smaller, less tender cuts for use in stews and casserole dishes. Use bones to make broth for canning or soup stock.

4. Put 1 tsp. salt in each clean quart jar, ½ tsp. salt in each pint jar to season (optional—such a small amount does not help preserve the meat).

5. Use hot pack or raw pack.

Hot Pack: Put meat in a large shallow pan. Add a little water to prevent sticking. Cover and heat until pink color is about gone from center of meat (medium done). Stir occasionally so meat will heat evenly.

Pack hot meat loosely in clean hot jars. Add meat juices or broth (about 2 tblsp. per pint jar, 4 tblsp. per quart jar). The liquid should not cover the meat. (More juices cook out during the processing and grease in them might reach the lids and prevent a good seal.) Leave 1" head space. Wipe off sealing edge of jar.

Raw Pack: Pack raw, lean meat loosely in jars; leave 1" head space. Add no liquid. Wipe off sealing edge.

6. Adjust lids on jars. Process at once in a pressure canner at 10 pounds pressure (240°F.).

Pint jars   75 minutes
Quart jars   90 minutes

Remove jars from canner and complete seals unless closures are self-sealing type.

CANNING GROUND MEAT

1. Select and grind small pieces of meat or meat from the less tender cuts. Make certain all the meat is fresh. Keep it cold. Discard any pieces of questionable freshness. Don't use chunks of fat.

2. Add 1 tsp. salt to each pound of ground meat. Mix well.

3. Form meat into fairly thin, small patties that can be packed into glass jars without breaking.

4. Put meat patties into cooking pan and precook in a moderate oven (350°F.) until medium done. The red color should be almost gone from center of patties.

5. Pack hot patties into clean hot jars, leaving 1" head space.

6. Skim fat from drippings and do not use in canning.

7. Cover meat patties with juices, adding hot water if needed. Leave about 1" head space in jars.

8. Work out air bubbles with knife. If necessary, add more liquid to cover meat. Again leave 1" head space.

9. Adjust lids on jars.

10. Process at once in a pressure canner at 10 pounds pressure (240°F.).

Pint jars   75 minutes.
Quart jars   90 minutes

Remove jars from canner and complete seals unless closures are self-sealing type.

Ready-to-Go Hamburger Sauce Mix

You'll find that jars of home-canned Hamburger Sauce Mix will come in handy. With them in the cupboard and buns or bread in the freezer, you have the makings for wonderful, quick main dishes. Unlike frozen ground beef, this canned mix is ready for instant use.

The recipe came to us from a California ranch kitchen. When the rancher took off on a camping trip in the wilderness, he took along jars of meat and spaghetti sauce lovingly canned by his wife. He returned home with a few leftover jars of the sauce. Soon the ranch cook began to use them in making a variety of dishes that her family liked and praised.

She started to experiment with the sauce and the Hamburger Sauce Mix is the result. She finds that canning a mildly seasoned sauce gives her a better chance to vary the dishes in which she uses it. And she says that adding the herbs and spices after the canning gives the sauce better flavors. Here is her recipe for the mix plus five California-type dishes to make with it.

HAMBURGER SAUCE MIX

Good between toasted buns—or use in many substantial, tasty dishes

2   lbs. lean ground beef
2   large onions, chopped (3 c.)
2   (6 oz.) cans tomato paste
1⅓ c. water
2   tsp. salt
½   tsp. pepper

• Cook beef and onions in large container until meat browns. Pour off fat.
• Add remaining ingredients, bring to a boil and simmer 5 minutes.
• Pack at once into hot pint jars. Adjust lids. Process in pressure canner at 10 pounds pressure (240°F.).
Pint jars   75 minutes
   Remove jars from canner and complete seals unless closures are self-sealing type. Makes about 3 pints.

Note: If you have large enough kettles, double the recipe and precook mix in two of them. Process quarts 90 minutes.

PIZZABURGERS

All taste-testers made the same comments—delicious and satisfying

1   pt. Hamburger Sauce Mix
1   tsp. orégano leaves
6   to 8 buns
6   to 8 slices sharp process
     cheese

• Blend Hamburger Sauce Mix and orégano. Heat.
• Spoon between hot, buttered buns. Put a slice of cheese in every bun. Serve at once. Makes 6 to 8.

CHILI AND BEANS

From start to finish, this dish takes 20 minutes of your time

1   pt. Hamburger Sauce Mix
½   c. tomato juice or water
1   (15½ oz.) can kidney beans
1   tblsp. chili powder
½   tsp. cumin seed (optional)
2   cloves garlic

• Combine Hamburger Sauce Mix, tomato juice, kidney beans, chili powder and cumin seed. Place garlic cloves on toothpicks; add to mixture. Simmer 15 minutes. Remove garlic. Makes 4 servings.

Note: Chili and beans are a hot dish. Decrease chili powder if you like a milder seasoning.

TAMALE AND CHILI BAKE

Serve this easy South-of-the-Border dish with pineapple salad

1   pt. Hamburger Sauce Mix
½   c. water
1   tblsp. chili powder
1   clove garlic
2   (15 oz.) cans tamales
¼   lb. sliced sharp process cheese

• Combine Hamburger Sauce Mix, water and chili powder. Place garlic on a toothpick and add to mixture. Bring to a boil and simmer 5 minutes. Remove garlic.
• Unwrap tamales and place in a greased 2-qt. casserole. Top first with Hamburger Sauce Mix, then cheese.
• Bake in moderate oven (350°F.) until bubbling hot, about 30 minutes. Makes 6 servings.

HURRY-UP SPAGHETTI

You can fix a wonderful spaghetti supper in half an hour

1	pt. Hamburger Sauce Mix
1	c. tomato juice
1	tsp. basil leaves
1	tsp. parsley flakes
½	tsp. orégano leaves
¼	tsp. salt
2	cloves garlic
1	(12 oz.) pkg. spaghetti, cooked
Cheese	

• Combine Hamburger Sauce Mix, tomato juice, herbs and salt. Stick a toothpick through garlic cloves; add to mixture. Simmer, covered, 15 minutes. Remove garlic.

• Place hot, drained spaghetti in serving dish. Pour sauce mixture over spaghetti. Sprinkle with grated Parmesan cheese or other hard cheese. Serve at once. Makes 4 servings.

BEST-EVER PIZZA

Tasty version of the popular American-style pizza. Seasoning is mild

1	(13¾ oz.) pkg. hot roll mix
1	pt. Hamburger Sauce Mix
1	tsp. orégano leaves
1	c. shredded Mozzarella cheese

• Prepare dough from hot roll mix by package directions, but omit rising. Divide dough in half. Roll on lightly floured surface to make two 14" circles.

• Place on ungreased baking sheets; turn up edges to form 13" circles.

• Combine Hamburger Sauce Mix and orégano. Spread on dough circles.

• Bake in very hot oven (450°F.) 10 minutes; remove from oven and top with cheese. Bake about 10 minutes longer or until crust is done. Serve at once. Makes 2 pizzas.

CANNING PORK SAUSAGE

Use your favorite sausage recipe (or see recipe in chapter on Curing Meat, Poultry, Fish), omitting the sage. It often gives canned sausage a bitter taste. Use a light hand with other herbs, spices, onion and garlic because flavors change in processing and storage. You may wish to add more seasoning when you heat the sausage for serving. Use ¾ lean meat to ¼ fat to make the best sausage. Process like ground meat.

CANNING SOUP STOCK

If you use the bones of beef or chicken to make broth, skim off the fat and remove all pieces of bone, but do not strain out bits of meat or sediment. Fill the hot jars with the hot liquid, leaving 1" head space. Process like ground meat.

BLUE RIBBON MINCEMEAT

Farm homemaker won first place with this at Colorado State Fair

6	c. ground beef
12	c. chopped apples
6	c. seedless raisins
1	c. apple cider
1	tblsp. ground cinnamon

1   tblsp. ground allspice
1   tblsp. ground nutmeg
3½   c. sugar

- Cook beef well, but do not brown.
- Put meat and apples through food chopper, using medium blade.
- Combine all ingredients in large kettle. Simmer 30 minutes.
- Pack at once in hot pint jars. Adjust lids. Process in pressure canner 60 minutes at 10 pounds pressure (240°F.).
- Remove jars from canner and complete seals unless closures are self-sealing type. Makes 8 pints.

STATE-OF-THE-UNION MINCEMEAT

Old recipe from Alaska where bear meat used to substitute for beef

3   lbs. lean beef
1   qt. water
1   c. chopped dates
1   c. washed suet, finely chopped
3½   lbs. apples
1   lb. seedless raisins

1   lb. white raisins
4   c. orange marmalade
2   qts. apple cider
2   tblsp. ground cinnamon
1   tsp. ground cloves
1   tsp. ground nutmeg
3   tblsp. salt

- Simmer beef in water until tender (add more water if needed). Drain. Trim away bone and gristle. Put meat through food chopper, using medium blade.
- Combine all ingredients in large kettle. Mix well. Bring to a boil; reduce heat, simmer 1½ hours; stir often.
- Pour at once into hot pint jars. Adjust lids. Process in pressure canner 60 minutes at 10 pounds pressure (240°F.).
- Remove jars from canner and complete seals unless closures are self-sealing type. Makes about 10 pints. Store in cool, dark place.

Note: Takes time to make, but this recipe, adapted by a California homemaker from the Alaska favorite, is rich in blended fruit flavors.

How to Can Poultry and Small Game

Follow these steps for canning chicken, turkey and other kinds of poultry.

1. Can only healthy, plump chickens. (Can the giblets separately.) The texture and flavor of young birds, when canned, is not so good as that of mature ones.

2. Starve chickens 18 hours before killing. Be sure they bleed freely; otherwise the meat will have a reddish color.

3. Remove feathers, chill chickens under running water or in pans of ice water. When chilled, remove from water, dry and singe. Wash thoroughly and dry with a clean, damp cloth. Dress as for table use, dividing into 3 groups—meaty pieces, bony pieces and giblets.

4. Make broth with the bony pieces. (You will need to add it or hot water to chicken in jars.) Cover them with cold water and simmer until the meat

is tender. Strip meat from bones. You may can the little pieces for chicken à la king, creamed chicken and sandwiches. Skim fat from broth.

5. Use either hot pack or raw pack to can chicken.

Hot Pack, with Bone: Bone the breast and saw drumsticks off short. Leave the bones in the other meaty pieces, like second joints. Trim off large pieces of fat. Heat broth (see Step 4) and pour over raw chicken pieces to cover and cook until meat is medium done, or until almost no pink color shows at center of pieces. Stir occasionally to heat meat evenly.

If salt is desired, put 1 tsp. in each clean quart jar for seasoning. Then pack hot second joints and drumsticks in hot jars; place with skin next to the glass. Fit breasts in the center and add smaller pieces where needed. Leave 1″ head space.

Cover meat with hot broth, using from ½ to ¾ c. to each quart jar. Leave 1″ head space.

Process in pressure canner at 10 pounds pressure (240°F.).

Pint jars   65 minutes
Quart jars   75 minutes

Remove jars from canner and complete seals unless closures are self-sealing type.

Hot Pack, without Bone: Follow preceding directions for hot pack, with bone, but remove bone, not skin, from meaty pieces before or after cooking.

Process at once in pressure canner at 10 pounds pressure (240°F.).

Pint jars   75 minutes
Quart jars   90 minutes

Remove jars from canner and complete seals unless closures are self-sealing type.

Raw Pack, with Bone: Prepare chicken as for hot pack, with bone, but do not precook. Pack raw meaty pieces into clean jars the same way.

Set open jars in a large kettle with warm water extending to about 2″ below rims of jars. Cover container and heat at a slow boil until meat is steaming hot, about 75 minutes. You can test the temperature with a thermometer. The meat is ready to process when the center of the jar registers 175°F.

Remove jars, adjust lids.

Process at once in pressure canner at 10 pounds pressure (240°F.).

Pint jars   65 minutes
Quart jars   75 minutes

Remove jars from canner and complete seals unless closures are self-sealing type.

Raw Pack, without Bone: Follow directions for raw pack, with bone, only remove bone from meaty pieces before packing into jars.

Process at once in pressure canner at 10 pounds pressure (240°F.).

Pint jars   75 minutes
Quart jars   90 minutes

Remove jars from canner and complete seals unless closures are self-sealing type.

SAFETY PRECAUTION: When using any home-canned meat or chicken, turn it out of jar, add a little water if needed, *cover and boil 20 minutes before tasting or adding other ingredients.* If meat has an off-odor during or after heating, discard it. Burn or bury it so the spoiled food will not be eaten by animals.

HOW TO CAN GIBLETS

It is best to can the liver separately from the gizzards and hearts.

1. Put hearts and gizzards or the livers in saucepan. Cover with broth made from bony pieces, or hot water. Cover and precook until medium done, stirring occasionally.

2. Add salt for seasoning, if desired, ½ tsp. to a pint jar.

3. Pack giblets hot. Leave about 1" head space. Add 2 or 3 tblsp. hot broth or water.

4. Work out air bubbles with a knife. Be sure to leave 1" head space.

5. Adjust lids.

6. Process at once in pressure canner at 10 pounds pressure (240°F.). Pint jars   75 minutes

Remove jars from canner and complete seals unless closures are self-sealing type.

HOW TO CAN RABBITS

Skin rabbits, remove entrails and cut out the waxy glands under the front legs where they join the body. Wash the carcass in salty water; cut in pieces. Can like chicken.

HOW TO CAN GAME BIRDS

Cut birds in pieces suitable for canning. Follow, as far as possible, the directions for canning chicken.

HOW MUCH WILL IT MAKE?

For a quart jar allow about:
  Beef (untrimmed)
    round, 3 to 3½ lbs.
    rump, 5 to 5½ lbs.
  Pork (untrimmed)
    loin, 5 to 5½ lbs.
  Chicken (dressed, undrawn)
    with bone, 4½ to 5½ lbs.
    without bone, 7 to 8 lbs.

CHAPTER 13

PICKLES

Pickling Methods, Ingredients and Equipment · How to Store Pickles · Recipes for Dill, Whole Sweet, Sliced, Chunk and Mixed Cucumber Pickles · Dilled Beans and Okra · Beet, Zucchini and Onion Pickles · Corn Relish · Green Tomato Pickles · Pepper Pickles and Relishes · Brine-Cured Cucumbers · Glass-Jar and Stone-Jar Sauerkraut

When green vines, sprawling on the earth, yield basketfuls of crisp cucumbers . . . when dill heads turn green-gold on their feathery stalks, country cooks know it's pickling time. They also know that hours to make pickles are hard to come by. But sure that the effort, crowded into a busy schedule, will pay off next winter, they tackle it. Nothing, they say, gives meals a color and flavor lift more economically and delightfully than sours —the name Pennsylvania Dutch women gave to pickles.

We asked FARM JOURNAL readers for their best pickle recipes. Thousands of these treasures came to our Countryside Test Kitchens in friendly response. We started reading and sorting, moved on to cooking and canning and wound up taste-testing months later when flavors were blended and mellowed.

In the meantime, we shipped hundreds of recipes to homemaking home economists to try in their kitchens. When their reports and samples came back, we added them to ours and selected the recipes for this chapter— typical representatives of choice pickles farm women make.

You will note that the pickle recipes divide into two main groups— quick-process and long brine-cured. About 99% of the reader recipes are for the fast-fix kind. Reason—they take less time, yet are delicious. And there are fewer variables. We also give directions for making pickles by the long brining method because some farm families prefer them.

Don't overlook the directions for making sauerkraut—glass-jar and stone-jar. And when you have looked at all the recipes for cucumber and other vegetable pickles in this chapter, turn to the fruit relishes and pickles, the sweet-sours, featured in superior recipes in the next chapter.

The Tempting Sours
THEY BOOST FINE FLAVORS IN MEALS

When a farm woman goes to the garden daily to look at the cucumber vines, she's daydreaming. She sees jars filled with all kinds of pickles on her fruit closet shelves . . . imagines how at Christmas she will tie ribbons on some prized jars and nest them in baskets for gifts. And she can almost hear guests around her table repeat: Please pass the pickles!

Indeed pickle making flourishes today in country kitchens. Cooks can the old-time greats—piccalilli, chow-chow, India relish, icicle pickles and others with fanciful names. But they use new rather than heirloom recipes (or adaptations of the old) because ingredients have changed. Now the acid content of vinegar is standardized in a way it couldn't be in homemade vinegars. Grandmother's pickle recipes called for the kind of vinegar she made—strong or weak— and your neighbor's grandmother may have made vinegar of a different strength.

No group of homemakers can match the zeal of the pickle makers. When FARM JOURNAL prints a pickle recipe, many readers write the Food Department about how wonderful their pickles look and taste. Other homemakers ask what they did wrong to cause their pickles to spoil. There

should be fewer such letters from now on, because research just recently completed by USDA home economists has thrown some light on the sometimes puzzling pickle spoilage. They now recommend that all pickles and relishes be processed in a boiling water bath (212°F.) a short time. In open-kettle canning there is always danger of spoilage organisms entering the food when it is transferred from kettle to jar. The processing destroys such organisms, and inactivates enzymes that may cause undesirable changes in flavor, color and texture. Also, yeasts and molds, harmless in themselves, may start to grow in a jar of unprocessed pickles and reduce the acid content. In the resulting low-acid product, botulinum spores, if present, could grow and produce a deadly poison (before thought possible only in nonacid foods). Processing destroys such yeasts and molds. So, to help you have more successful pickles, we have included new short-processing times in all our recipes here.

Some other factors affecting success with pickles are:

Storage—it is better to keep them in a cool dry place than warm and humid.

Varieties—there are special cucumber varieties best for pickling.

Timing—it really pays to hurry cucumbers from vines into jars.

You can't be too careful about making sure the pickles have a *tight seal*. If you have trouble getting airtight seals, process filled jars in a boiling water bath 10 to 15 minutes.

Good pickle makers *cover the pickles in the jar with vinegar solution.*

Meet the Pickle Families

Pickles divide into two important families—those made by (1) the quick-process and (2) the brine-cure. Most women now use the quick-process to save time and work. In this method you cook the vegetable or fruit in vinegar to preserve it.

In the brine-cure, you hold vegetables in brine about 4 weeks. Then you soak them in water to remove surplus salt, and add vinegar, sugar and spices to make pickles. Homemakers who champion this procedure find it easier to put the cucumbers down in brine when bringing them from the garden in summer. Then they make pickles as needed and on days when they are not so rushed. Many experts agree that often these pickles are more nearly crisp and better-tasting. But many quick-process pickles are delicious.

Regardless of what kind of pickles you choose to make, there are rules to heed for success. So start your pickling by reading.

START WITH RIGHT INGREDIENTS

1. Use fresh vegetables as soon as possible after you pick them. If you cannot make the pickles within an hour or two, store them without washing in the refrigerator. *Do not use cucumbers that have been picked more than 24 hours.* Use top-quality fruits, slightly underripe. These firm fruits will hold their shape better and have a better texture when pickled.

2. Use vegetables (and fruits) free of blemishes. Sort for size and degree of maturity. Immature cucumbers make the best pickles. *It pays to use the varieties of cucumbers grown for pickling.* You can find seeds for these more easily in seed catalogs than in seed stores. Ask your County Extension Home Economist which varieties to grow.

3. *Thoroughly wash* all vegetables and fruits to remove the dirt that otherwise may start bacterial action. *Be sure all the blossoms are removed from cucumbers.* They contain an enzyme that may cause spoilage.

4. Use a clear vinegar of 4 to 6% acid content (look on bottle label for acid content). Do not use homemade vinegar because its acid content varies greatly; often it is too weak to prevent spoilage or strong enough to cause shriveling. A white distilled vinegar gives pickles the best color and should always be used with the light fruits and vegetables. Cider vinegar may darken the pickles, but some cooks use it for its flavor and aroma.

5. *Pure granulated salt (sack or bag salt) is best for pickle making; granulated flake salt is recommended for brining cucumber pickles. Pure granulated salt is used in the recipes in this cookbook that do not designate a different type of salt.* Table salt may be used in pickles that are not brined, but it contains chemicals that prevent lumping and often is iodized. These chemicals may cause cloudiness and darkening.

6. Use fresh spices for the best flavors. Leftover, old spices often give pickles a musty taste. Whole spices help produce pickles of superior color. Tie them in clean, thin white cloth and *remove them before canning.* Left in the jar, they may darken pickles and cause an off-flavor.

7. Use beet or cane sugar. Some recipes call for brown sugar for added flavor in products where the darker color is not objectionable.

8. Water containing iron may darken pickles. In areas where hard water is chemically treated, boil it, let it cool and then remove the film.

USE RIGHT EQUIPMENT

Pickling Kettle: Use an aluminum, unchipped enamelware, glass, or stainless steel kettle large enough to prevent food boiling over. Copper utensils often give pickles an unusual green color; iron darkens them. Acid and salt may react with galvanized utensils to form a poisonous substance.

Canning Jars: Select glass jars, carefully avoiding those that are cracked or chipped. Pint and half-pint jars are a good choice for pickles and relishes processed in a hot water bath.

Lids: There are many types of lids and closures. *Be sure to follow the manufacturer's directions for sterilizing and sealing them.*

Container for Brining: Use a stone jar or crock, washing it in soapy water, rinsing thoroughly and scalding. You will need a clean, thin, white cloth, a scalded, heavy plate that just fits inside the crock or a round board (not resinous wood like pine), cut the right size and coated with paraffin. Clean stones or bricks covered with paraffin will weight the cucumbers down in the brine. *Do not use limestone* for a weight.

Convenient · Tools: A long-handled wooden spoon, wide-mouthed funnel and household scale will make the work easier.

PROCESS PICKLES ACCURATELY

To Prepare Jars: Wash jars in hot soapy water, rinse well or wash them in the electric dishwasher. If the pickles are not to be processed, sterilize the jars. (Sterilize funnel along with jars.) Follow manufacturer's directions for preparing lids.

To Sterilize Jars: Cover washed jars with warm water in a large kettle. Cover and bring to a boil. Boil 20 minutes. Remove one at a time from hot water when ready to fill.

To Fill Jars: Fill jars to be sealed hot to within ⅛″ from top with boiling hot pickles and liquid and wipe off any spill. *Fill one jar and seal at a time; keep unpacked pickles at simmering until used. (Be sure liquid covers food.)* Seal. If glass lid is used, invert for 3 minutes.

To process pickles, fill hot jars to

within ½″ of top. Cover with liquid. Wipe off any spill. Place lids on jars, following manufacturer's directions. Process in boiling water bath by placing jars on a rack in a deep container. Cover 2″ over the top with boiling water. Bring water quickly back to boiling. Start to count time; boil gently and steadily for time recommended. *See page 234 for Altitude Adjustments.*

Remove jars, one at a time, from water bath and seal glass jars; do not disturb self-seal lids. Leave metal rings on until jars have cooled.

Cool jars, well separated, on a rack or folded towel away from drafts or cool surfaces.

STORE PICKLES PROPERLY

Check all the seals. (Jars that are not sealed should be refrigerated and used.) Label and store in a cool, dark, dry place. Make certain that the liquid in the jars covers the fruits and vegetables during storage and when opened. Keep opened jars refrigerated.

Discard, without tasting, any pickles that have a bad odor, appear moldy, mushy or gassy when opened.

QUICK-PROCESS PICKLES

FARM JOURNAL readers like quick pickling methods. Almost all of their recipes in this chapter skip brining or cut it down from weeks (long cure) to a few hours. Vinegar plays an important part in up-to-date pickling. Country cooks depend on its standardized strength (acid content) not only to flavor the pickles but to preserve them.

Before you use these pickle recipes look at the label on your vinegar bottle to make certain the acid content is between 4 to 6%. Don't use homemade vinegar or any other kind of unknown strength.

Tangy Dill Pickles

Some farm people believe food for picnics, church suppers and community feasts is not complete without plenty of cool, crunchy dill pickles. And some farmers hold that there's nothing they'd rather sit down to on a blowy, autumn day, when they come cold and hungry to dinner, than a deep brown pot roast or stew with a big bowl of dill pickles nearby.

FRESH-PACK DILLS

Speedy, new way to make crisp dills

17	to 18 lbs. (3 to 5″) cucumbers
1 ½	c. salt
2	gals. water
6	c. vinegar
¾	c. salt
¼	c. sugar
9	c. water
2	tblsp. whole pickling spices

Dill heads, fresh or dried
Whole mustard seeds

• Wash cucumbers; cover with brine made by adding 1½ c. salt to 2 gals. water. Let stand overnight. Drain.

· Combine vinegar, ¾ c. salt, sugar, 9 c. water and pickling spices, tied loosely in clean, thin white cloth. Heat to boiling.

· Pack cucumbers into hot quart jars. Add 3 dill heads and 2 tsp. mustard seeds to each jar. Pour boiling vinegar mixture, spice bag removed, over cucumbers to within ½″ of jar tops. Adjust lids. Process in boiling water bath (212°F.) 20 minutes.

· Remove jars from canner and complete seals unless closures are self-sealing type. Makes 7 quarts.

SWEET DILLS

Tote these to community suppers if you enjoy bouquets for your cooking. At home, serve them with hamburgers

4½ qts. dill-size cucumbers
2 large onions
18 heads dill
6 c. vinegar
6 c. sugar
¾ c. salt
1½ tsp. celery seeds
1½ tsp. mustard seeds

· Slice cucumbers and onions.

· Put 1 head dill and 2 thin slices onion into each clean hot jar. Fill jars with cucumber slices; shake jar to pack.

· To make syrup, combine vinegar, sugar, salt, celery seeds and mustard seeds; heat to boiling. Pour over cucumber slices.

· Add 1 head dill and 1 slice onion at top of jar; adjust lids at once. Process in boiling water bath (212°F.) 5 minutes. Remove jars from canner and complete seals unless closures are self-sealing type. Makes 9 pints.

DILL MARINADE: Soak slices of fresh cucumbers or onions or cooked beets 2 hours in the spicy brine from a jar of dill pickles. Drain and use in salads or as a relish. The vegetables will have an appetizing dill flavor.

DILL PICKLES

Dill seeds do the seasoning

4 lbs. (4″) pickling cucumbers
6 tblsp. salt
3 c. vinegar
3 c. water
1 c. dill seeds
21 peppercorns

· Wash cucumbers; cut in lengthwise halves. Combine salt, vinegar and water. Heat to boiling.

· Pack cucumbers into clean hot pint jars. Add about 2 tblsp. dill seeds and 3 peppercorns to each jar. Fill with the pickling syrup to within ½″ of jar top. Immediately adjust lids. Process in boiling water bath (212°F.) 15 minutes.

· Remove jars from canner and complete seals unless closures are self-sealing type. Makes 7 pints.

KOSHER DILLS: Add 14 garlic cloves, split in halves, to salt, water and vinegar mixture. Heat to boil; remove garlic. Put 4 halves into each jar.

EASY SWEET DILLS

Use some of your dill pickles to make these on a leisurely winter day

2 qts. dill pickles, sliced (8 to 10 pickles)

4   cloves garlic, crushed
     (optional)
2 ⅓ c. vinegar
2   tblsp. whole allspice
1   tblsp. whole black pepper
4   c. white sugar
1   c. brown sugar, firmly packed

• Drain dill pickles.
• Make a pickling syrup of garlic,
vinegar, spices and sugars. Simmer 5
minutes. Add pickles; heat to a boil.
• Pack in hot jars; adjust lids at once.
Process in boiling water bath (212°F.)
5 minutes. Remove jars from canner
and complete seals unless closures are
the self-sealing type. Makes 2 quarts.

EXTRA-GOOD SWEET DILL PICKLES

Short on cooking time; long on flavor

6   cucumbers
Ice water
Onion slices or clove garlic
Dill, fresh or dried
1   c. sugar
1   c. water
1   pt. vinegar
⅓   c. salt

• Soak whole cucumbers in ice water
3 to 4 hours. Drain. Slice or cut in
strips. Place in hot pint jars along
with onions and a generous amount
of dill.
• Combine sugar, water, vinegar and
salt; bring to boil. Pour over pickles
to within ½″ from jar top. Adjust
lids at once. Process in boiling water
bath (212°F.) 20 minutes (start to
count the processing time as soon as
hot jars are placed into the actively
boiling water). Remove jars from can-

ner and complete seals unless closures
are self-sealing. Makes 3 pints.

CRISP DILLED BEANS

Chill thoroughly and serve for supper

2   lbs. small tender green beans
1   tsp. red pepper
4   cloves garlic
4   large heads dill
2   c. water
¼   c. salt
1   pt. vinegar

• Stem green beans and pack uniformly in hot jars.
• To each pint, add ¼ tsp. red pepper, 1 clove garlic and 1 head dill.
• Heat together water, salt and vinegar. Bring to boil; pour over beans.
Adjust lids at once. Process in boiling
water bath (212°F.) 5 minutes. Remove jars from canner and complete
seals unless closures are the self-sealing type. Makes 4 pints.

DILLED OKRA

Unusual and amazingly good

3   lbs. young okra, uncut
Celery leaves
Cloves garlic
Large heads and stems dill
1   qt. water
1   pt. vinegar
½   c. salt

• Pack scrubbed okra into hot pint
jars with a few celery leaves, 1 clove
garlic and 1 head and stem dill for
each jar.
• Make brine of water, vinegar and
salt; heat to boiling. Pour over okra;

adjust lids at once. Process in boiling water bath (212°F.) 5 minutes. Remove jars from canner and complete seals unless closures are the self-sealing type. Let stand 3 to 4 weeks. Makes 6 pints.

Whole Sweet Pickles

The expert pickle maker who shares the following recipe considers it the best one she ever used to make small sweet pickles. She uses white vinegar. You will see some of the pickles she sent us in a color picture in this book —they tasted wonderful. Several other homemakers sent this recipe with words of praise. All of them live in northern parts of the country.

But some excellent cooks had failures making pickles this way. So the recipe is controversial. Certainly, it would be wise to try it in cooler weather. And all directions must be followed carefully. We give the recipe, both favored by enthusiastic champions and decried by women whose pickles were not successful. Want to try your luck?

WHOLE SWEET PICKLES

Be sure to use freshly picked cucumbers for these party pickles

1	gal. small (2″) cucumbers
Boiling water	
⅓	c. salt
1 ½	gals. water
1	qt. vinegar
1	c. water
8	c. sugar
¼	c. mixed pickling spices

• Wash cucumbers carefully, using care not to bruise skins. Make certain all blossoms are removed. Place in a clean, scalded crock. Cover with boiling water; be sure water covers all the cucumbers. Drain and cover with fresh boiling water every day for 5 more days.

• On the 7th day, cover drained cucumbers with weak brine made by adding the salt to 1½ gals. water.

• On the 8th day, make a syrup by boiling the vinegar, 1 c. water, sugar and spices, loosely tied in clean, thin white cloth, 20 minutes.

• Pierce each drained cucumber with a long needle or cut off the end of each to permit syrup to penetrate.

• Pack the cucumbers in hot jars; pour the boiling syrup over them, discarding spice bag. Make certain hot syrup covers cucumbers. Adjust lids at once. Process in boiling water bath (212°F.) 5 minutes. Remove jars from canner and complete seals unless closures are the self-sealing type. Makes about 8 pints.

Note: Usually the seal will be made if the syrup is boiling hot when poured over cucumbers packed in hot jars. A sure way is to process them in simmering hot water bath 10 minutes.

Iowa Sweet Pickles

Among the prized pickle recipes we give you in this cookbook is this favorite from an Iowa County Extension Home Economist. She says: "When you make these pickles, you will find that you spend only a few minutes every day for the two weeks."

She suggests the points to heed—use commercially bottled cider vinegar with 5% acid content on label and accurate measurements, using a medicine dropper, purchased from the drugstore, to add exact amounts of oils of cinnamon and cloves.

EXPERT'S SWEET PICKLES

Crisp, sweet-tart and less work to make than you think

75 (3 to 3½") cucumbers (1 peck)
2   c. coarse pickling salt
Water
Powdered alum
10 c. sugar
5   c. vinegar
18 drops oil of cinnamon
18 drops oil of cloves
2   tblsp. celery seeds

• Place cucumbers in a stone jar, glass or enameled container. Combine salt and 1 gal. water. Bring to a boil and pour over cucumbers. Cover with a plate; weight down. Brine must cover cucumbers. Let stand 8 days, but stir the cucumbers every day to discourage formation of film. (You can use your hand.)

• On the 8th day, empty cucumbers into large container and wash thoroughly with cold water. Cut them lengthwise or into chunks and return to container.

• In the meantime, bring 1 gal. fresh water, with 1 tblsp. powdered alum added, to a boil. Pour boiling hot over cucumbers. Weight down.

• On the 9th day, pour off the alum solution. Drain cucumbers. Bring 1 gal. fresh water with 1 tblsp. alum added, to a boil. Pour over cucumbers; weight down.

• On the 10th day, repeat procedure for 8th and 9th days.

• On the 11th day, pour off alum solution. Drain cucumbers thoroughly. (Put them in the sink and let them drain while you wash jars.) Put pickles back in container.

• Combine sugar, vinegar, oils of cinnamon and cloves, measured with a medicine dropper, and celery seeds. Bring to a boil and pour over the cucumbers. Weight down.

• On the 12th day, drain syrup from cucumbers. Bring syrup to a boil and pour over cucumbers. Weight down.

• On the 13th day, drain off syrup, bring to a boil and pour over cucumbers. Weight down.

• On the 14th day, pack cucumbers in hot glass jars. Bring syrup to a boil; pour over cucumbers to cover.

• Adjust lids at once. Process in boiling water bath (212°F.) 5 minutes. Remove jars from canner and complete seals unless closures are the self-sealing type. Makes 12 to 14 pints.

14-DAY SWEET PICKLES

Adaptation of an heirloom recipe long treasured in country kitchens

3½   qts. (2″) pickling cucumbers
1   c. coarse pickling salt
2   qts. boiling water
½   tsp. powdered alum
5   c. vinegar
3   c. sugar
1½   tsp. celery seeds
4   (2″) sticks cinnamon
1½   c. sugar

• Wash cucumbers carefully; cut in lengthwise halves and place in stone crock, glass, pottery or enamel-lined (unchipped) pan.

• Prepare brine by dissolving salt in boiling water; pour over cucumbers. Weight cucumbers down with a plate almost as large as the crock and lay a stone or paraffined brick (not marble or limestone) on plate to keep cucumbers under the brine. Let stand 1 week.

• On the 8th day, drain; pour 2 qts. fresh boiling water over cucumbers. Let stand 24 hours.

• On the 9th day, drain; pour 2 qts. fresh boiling water mixed with alum over cucumbers. Let stand 24 hours.

• On the 10th day, drain; pour 2 qts. fresh boiling water over cucumbers. Let stand 24 hours.

• The next day, drain. Combine vinegar, 3 c. sugar, celery seeds and cinnamon; heat to boiling point and pour over cucumbers.

• For the next 3 days, drain, retaining liquid. Reheat this liquid each morning, adding ½ c. sugar each time. After the last heating, on the 14th day, pack pickles into hot pint jars. Remove cinnamon sticks; pour boiling hot liquid over pickles; adjust lids at once. Process in boiling water bath (212°F.) 5 minutes. Remove jars from canner and complete seals unless closures are the self-sealing type. Makes 5 to 6 pints.

Sliced Cucumber Pickles

Pickles with sandwiches once were the rule. Now it's often pickles in sandwiches. Country cooks find it convenient to have jars of pickle slices to tuck into sandwiches and to add to other foods. And certainly the spices and other seasonings have an easier time penetrating small pieces.

Some of the recipes that follow call for thin slices, others for thick slices and chunks. Some are sweet and some are sweet-sour. But in all of them you see signs of an imaginative cook behind scenes.

SWEET PICKLE SLICES

Take time to fix, but superior flavor and green color make it worth while

4   qts. unpeeled cucumber
      slices, ⅛″ thick
6   c. vinegar
3   tblsp. salt
1   tblsp. mustard seeds
3¼   c. sugar
2¼   tsp. celery seeds
1   tblsp. whole allspice

• In covered kettle simmer cucumber slices in 4 c. vinegar with salt, mustard seeds, and ¼ c. sugar for about 15 minutes, or until slices turn slightly yellow. Do not overcook. Drain; discard cooking liquid. Spoon slices into hot, sterilized jars.

• Bring to a boil 2 c. vinegar, 3 c. sugar, celery seeds and whole allspice. Pour over pickles. Adjust lids at once. Process in boiling water bath (212°F.) 5 minutes. Remove jars from canner and complete seals unless closures are the self-sealing type. Makes 5 pints.

CRISP-AS-ICE CUCUMBER SLICES

Always get compliments . . . crisp—good in sandwiches, with roast beef

½	c. salt
4	qts. thinly sliced cucumbers
8	onions, thinly sliced
2	green peppers, seeded and cut in strips
4	c. sugar
1½	tsp. ground turmeric
½	tsp. ground cloves
3½	tsp. mustard seeds
4½	c. vinegar

• Sprinkle salt over the sliced vegetables; mix; empty tray of ice cubes in center. Let stand 3 hours.

• Combine sugar, spices and vinegar; heat to boiling.

• Drain vegetables thoroughly. Pour hot syrup over them; heat over low temperature to scalding. Do not allow to boil. Stir often to prevent scorching.

• Ladle into hot jars; adjust lids at once. Process in boiling water bath (212°F.) 5 minutes. Remove jars from canner and complete seals unless closures are the self-sealing type. Makes 5½ pints.

OLIVE OIL PICKLES

If you like salty pickles, try these

24	medium cucumbers, thinly sliced
1	c. salt
1	qt. vinegar
½	c. olive oil
¼	c. sugar
¼	c. mustard seeds
¼	c. celery seeds

• Peel and slice cucumbers; layer salt and cucumbers; let stand overnight; drain. Rinse well with cold water.

• Combine vinegar, olive oil, sugar and spices; boil 1 minute. Add cucumbers; simmer until cucumbers change color. Pack boiling hot into hot jars; adjust lids at once. Process in boiling water bath (212°F.) 5 minutes. Remove jars from canner and complete seals unless closures are self-sealing type. Makes 5½ pints.

CUCUMBER PICKLES

Color and taste exceptionally good

6	large cucumbers, thinly sliced
6	large onions, sliced
½	c. salt
1	lb. brown sugar
1	qt. vinegar
½	tsp. ground turmeric
½	tsp. white mustard seeds
1	tsp. celery seeds

• Combine cucumbers and onions; sprinkle with salt. Let stand overnight.

• Drain; rinse with cold water. Drain.

• Combine sugar, vinegar and spices; add vegetables; cook 15 to 30 minutes.

• Pack in hot jars; adjust lids at once. Process in boiling water bath (212°F.) 5 minutes. Remove jars from canner and complete seals unless closures are the self-sealing type. Makes 5 pints.

CINNAMON CUCUMBER RINGS

Tint them red and green for your Christmas holiday relish tray

2	gals. large green cucumbers
2	c. salt
8 ½	qts. water
7	c. vinegar
1	tblsp. powdered alum
1	tsp. food color
12	c. sugar
4	sticks cinnamon

• Cut unpeeled cucumbers in thirds crosswise; remove seeds. Slice in ½" rings (should be 2 gals.). Add salt and 8 qts. water; let stand 5 days. Drain.

• Combine 1 c. vinegar, alum and food color in kettle. Add cucumber rings and water to cover. Simmer 2 hours. (Or divide rings in two parts; simmer one with ½ tsp. red food color, the other with ½ tsp. green color added.)

• Drain. Make a syrup by bringing to boil 6 c. vinegar, 2 c. water, sugar and cinnamon. Pour over rings; let stand overnight. Drain; reheat syrup and pour over rings. Repeat for 3 days. On 3rd day, pack rings in hot jars. Pour in boiling syrup; adjust lids at once. Process in boiling water bath (212°F.) 5 minutes. Remove jars from canner and complete seals unless closures are the self-sealing type. Makes 9 pints.

ICICLE PICKLES

The color of these sweet pickles is exceptionally good—so is the taste

4	qts. (3") cucumbers
2	c. salt
1	gal. boiling water
1 ½	tblsp. powdered alum
2 ½	qts. vinegar
5	lbs. sugar
2	tblsp. whole allspice

• Cut cucumbers in quarters, lengthwise. Dissolve salt in boiling water; pour over cucumbers in crock; weight down with plate; let stand 1 week.

• Drain; add 1 gal. fresh boiling water; let stand 24 hours; drain. Add alum to 1 gal. fresh boiling water; pour over pickles; let stand 24 hours; drain.

• To make syrup, combine vinegar, sugar and allspice; heat to boiling and boil 20 minutes. Pour over cucumbers in crock. Let stand 3 days.

• Pack pickles in hot jars; reheat syrup to boiling; boil 10 minutes; pour over pickles. Adjust lids at once. Process in boiling water bath (212°F.) 5 minutes. Remove jars from canner and complete seals unless closures are the self-sealing type. Makes 5 pints.

CURRY PICKLES

Curry powder gives different flavor but does not predominate the taste. Fine with veal, pork and chicken

6	large cucumbers, peeled
10	medium onions
2	large sweet red peppers
½	c. salt
1	pt. vinegar

1   c. water
4   c. sugar
3   tblsp. mixed pickling spices
2   tblsp. celery salt
1   tsp. curry powder

• Slice vegetables thin; sprinkle with salt and add cold water to cover; let stand overnight. Drain.
• Add vinegar, water, sugar, pickling spices tied in loose, thin white cloth, and celery salt. Heat to boil; cook 15 to 30 minutes; add curry powder.
• Ladle into hot jars; adjust lids at once. Process in boiling water bath (212°F.) 5 minutes. Remove jars from canner and complete seals unless closures are the self-sealing type. Makes 6½ pints.

BREAD AND BUTTER PICKLES

Bread and butter pickles are a must in country cupboards. Some good cooks always keep a jar of them in the refrigerator to serve icy cold on the spur of the moment. These family favorites are equally at home in everyday and company meals. For a sandwich go-with, they rate high. And what tastes better at a picnic than these old-fashioned pickles, chilled?

Countless recipes for this kind of relish are treasured across country. The following one comes to us from Oregon; it is highly recommended.

BEST-EVER BREAD-AND-BUTTERS

The ice cubes help keep the thin cucumber slices from breaking

4   qts. sliced cucumbers (40 to
       50)
½   c. salt

2   qts. sliced onions
1   qt. vinegar
4   c. sugar
1   tblsp. celery seeds
2   tblsp. mustard seeds
1   tblsp. ground ginger
1   tsp. ground turmeric (optional)
½   tsp. white pepper (optional)

• Gently stir salt into thinly sliced cucumbers. Cover with ice cubes; let stand 2 or 3 hours or until cucumbers are crisp and cold. Add more ice if it melts. Drain; add onions.
• Mix remaining ingredients; bring quickly to a boil, boil 10 minutes.
• Add cucumber and onion slices and bring to boiling point. Pack loosely at once in hot jars; adjust lids. Process in boiling water bath (212°F.) 15 minutes. Remove jars from canner and complete seals unless closures are self-sealing type. Makes 8 pints.

CELERY/CUCUMBER PICKLES

Wonderful with cold cuts

6   large cucumbers
Ice water
Celery
Onions
1   qt. vinegar
1   c. sugar
½   c. water
⅓   c. salt

• Soak cucumbers in ice water 5 hours. Cut each cucumber lengthwise into 5 strips. Pack closely in 3 hot quart jars, with 3 branches celery and 3 slices onion in each. Drain juice.
• Bring vinegar, sugar, water and salt to rapid boil. Pour over pickles in

jars; adjust lids at once. Process in boiling water bath (212°F.) 5 minutes. Remove jars from canner and complete seals unless closures are the self-sealing type. Makes 3 quarts.

PICKLES AND ONIONS

Old-fashioned, country-fresh flavor

8   (4") cucumbers, cut in 1" chunks
¾   lb. small white onions
Vinegar
Water
5   tsp. salt
2   c. sugar
1   pt. vinegar

· Cover cucumbers and onions (2½ c. large onion slices may be used) with equal parts of vinegar and water; bring to boil. Remove immediately from vinegar water; discard liquid.
· Fill hot jars with pickles and onions. Add 1 tsp. salt to each half-pint jar. Combine sugar and 2 c. vinegar; boil 2 minutes. Pour over pickles. Adjust lids at once. Process in boiling water bath (212°F.) 5 minutes. Remove jars from canner and complete seals unless closures are the self-sealing type. Makes 5 half pints.

CRISP PICKLES

Easy to make—but they take 10 days

10   medium cucumbers
Boiling water
8   c. sugar
1   qt. vinegar
5   tblsp. salt
2   tblsp. mixed whole pickling
     spices
2   tsp. celery seeds

· Cover cucumbers with boiling water. Let stand overnight. Drain. Repeat process for 4 successive days (add fresh boiling water, let stand overnight and drain).
· On the 6th morning, slice cucumbers into ¼ to ½" slices.
· To make syrup, combine sugar, vinegar, salt and spices loosely tied in clean, thin white cloth; heat to boil. Pour over slices. Let stand overnight.
· The next morning, drain the vinegar syrup, reheat to boiling and again pour over the cucumber slices. Repeat this process 3 more days.
· On the 10th day, pack slices in one hot jar at a time. Bring syrup to a boil; remove spices. Pour hot syrup over slices in jars one at a time, leaving ½" head space; adjust lids on each jar at once. Process in boiling water bath (212°F.) 5 minutes. Remove jars from canner and complete seals unless closures are the self-sealing type. Makes 5 pints.

Yellow-Ripe Cucumber Pickles

Grandmother knew what to do with those big cucumbers that ripened under the leaves before she saw them. She turned them into relishes to please her family and friends. She made firm, spicy, transparent pickles with them. And many old-fashioned country cooks considered them perfect for chicken dinners—along with fluffy mashed potatoes and gravy.

Today's farm cooks treasure and use updated versions of their grandmothers' recipes or of heirlooms, borrowed from their neighbors. Every summer they fill jars with tempting pickles to use in the frosty days ahead. Here are a few recipes they prize.

SPICY RIPE CUCUMBER PICKLES

Perfect with chicken pie. The trick— long, slow cooking that retains cucumbers' delightful crispness

12   large ripe cucumbers
½   c. salt
Water
4   tsp. powdered alum
4   c. sugar
1   pt. vinegar
2   tblsp. whole cloves
2   tblsp. stick cinnamon

· Peel, remove seeds and cut cucumbers in quarters lengthwise. Sprinkle with salt and cover with water. Let stand overnight. Drain.
· Cover with 3 qts. fresh water; add alum. Gradually heat to boiling. Let stand on very low heat 2 hours; drain; chill in ice water; drain.
· Combine sugar, vinegar and spices loosely tied in clean, thin white cloth; heat to boiling. Add cucumbers; cook 15 minutes, or until cucumbers appear transparent. Remove to bowl; pour hot syrup over.
· Repeat process 3 successive mornings, heating spice bag with syrup.
· The last morning, heat syrup, remove spice bag. Fill hot jars with cucumbers and boiling syrup, leaving ½" head space; adjust lids at once. Process in boiling water bath (212°F.) 5 minutes. Remove jars from canner

and complete seals unless closures are the self-sealing type. Makes 5 pints.

CHEERFUL SWEET PICKLES

Especially tasty with pork chops or roast. Chop pickles, mix with cream cheese for dark bread sandwiches

9   ripe cucumbers (9 c., cubed)
½   c. salt
3½   qts. water
3½   c. sugar
1   pt. vinegar
1   tsp. whole cloves
2   sticks cinnamon
1   (4 oz.) jar red maraschino
        cherries and juice
2   tsp. red food color

· Peel, seed and cut cucumbers into cubes; sprinkle with salt; cover with water. Let stand overnight.
· In the morning, heat to boiling; drain. Combine sugar, vinegar and spices loosely tied in clean, thin white cloth; heat to boiling. Pour over cucumbers. Let stand overnight.
· Next morning, heat to boiling; then simmer until cucumbers are tender. (Do not overcook.) Add cherries, juice and red food color.
· Ladle into hot jars; adjust lids at once. Process in boiling water bath (212°F.) 5 minutes. Remove jars from canner and complete seals unless closures are the self-sealing type. Makes 4 pints.

YELLOW CUCUMBER PICKLES

Chunks of vegetables make these special—perfect with baked beans

12   large ripe cucumbers
12   large white onions

12 large branches celery
½ c. salt
3 c. sugar
1 qt. vinegar
2 tblsp. mustard seeds
1 c. prepared mustard

· Peel cucumbers; scrape out seeds. Cut cucumbers, onions and celery in small cubes. Sprinkle with salt; let stand 2 hours. Rinse well with cold water; drain.

· Add sugar, vinegar, mustard seeds and prepared mustard. Bring all to a boil; stir to prevent scorching.

· Ladle into hot jars; adjust lids at once. Process in boiling water bath (212°F.) 5 minutes. Remove jars from canner and complete seals unless closures are the self-sealing type. Makes 11 pints.

RIPE CUCUMBER RELISH

Favorite in Maine's North Country

8 large ripe cucumbers
2 c. chopped onion

½ c. salt
2 tblsp. flour
2 c. sugar
1 tsp. celery seeds
1 tsp. mustard seeds
1 tblsp. dry mustard
2 tsp. ground turmeric
1 pt. vinegar

· Peel, remove seeds and cut cucumbers in 1" squares. Add onion. Sprinkle with salt and let stand overnight. Drain. Rinse well.

· To make sauce, combine remaining ingredients. Heat to boiling; stir frequently to make a smooth sauce.

· Add vegetables to the sauce. Cook over low heat 1 hour, or until vegetables are transparent.

· Ladle into hot jars; adjust lids at once. Process in boiling water bath (212°F.) 5 minutes. Remove jars from canner and complete seals unless closures are the self-sealing type. Makes 4 pints.

Farmhouse Pickle Relish

The busy home economist who shares this recipe, often dices the vegetables in the evening. She combines the cucumbers, onions and salt in one utensil and the celery and peppers in another. She refrigerates them overnight and next morning leaves the celery and peppers in the refrigerator while the cucumber-onion mixture drains over the sink.

You can use sweet green peppers. The flavor is good, but the relish is not so colorful as with red peppers.

GOLDEN CUCUMBER RELISH

You couldn't serve your company a relish that would get more praise

12 large ripe cucumbers
12 onions (2" in diameter)
¾ c. salt
2 large stalks celery, diced
6 large sweet peppers, diced
1 qt. vinegar
4 c. sugar
2 tblsp. mustard seeds

• Peel cucumbers, scoop out and discard seeds and centers; dice pulp into ¼" cubes. Dice peeled onions in cubes of same size. Add the salt, mix well, cover and let stand 10 to 12 hours. Drain in a white cloth until dry.

• Dice celery (whole stalks) and pepers in ¼" cubes.

• Combine vinegar, sugar and mustard seeds in large enameled kettle, add the four vegetables and cook over low heat until the mixture is thick and the cucumbers are golden in color.

• Ladle into hot jars; adjust lids at once. Process in boiling water bath (212°F.) 5 minutes. Remove jars from canner and complete seals unless closures are the self-sealing type. Makes 6 pints.

Mixed Pickles Galore

Mixed pickles, like crazy quilts and hit-and-miss rag rugs, use up scraps —often the tag ends of garden vegetables. These pickles have a tremendous following in the country. Farm women praise the marvelous blended flavors of many vegetables and seasonings—they consider them a potpourri of summer's best.

It's a rare country fruit closet that does not have rows of jars filled with these sweet-sour-spicy pickles. We give our readers credit for the recipes.

CHOWCHOW

Old-fashioned special that today's children like on hot dogs

1	medium head cabbage, chopped (2 qts.)
6	medium onions, chopped
6	green peppers, coarsely chopped
6	sweet red peppers, coarsely chopped
1	qt. chopped green tomatoes
¼	c. coarse salt
2	tblsp. prepared mustard
6	c. vinegar

2½	c. sugar
1½	tsp. ground turmeric
1	tsp. ground ginger
2	tblsp. mustard seeds
1	tblsp. mixed whole pickling spices

• Combine vegetables and mix with salt. Cover, let stand overnight; drain.

• Mix mustard with a little vinegar in kettle; add remaining vinegar, sugar and spices. Simmer 20 minutes. Add vegetables; simmer 10 minutes. Continue simmering while packing one hot jar at a time. Fill to within ⅛" from jar top. Make sure liquid covers vegetables. Adjust lid on each jar at once. Process in boiling water bath (212°F.) 5 minutes. Remove jars from canner and complete seals unless closures are self-sealing. Makes 6 to 8 pints.

Note: Use this relish within 6 months.

CHRISTMAS PICKLES

Make a splendid holiday gift

10	diced peeled ripe cucumbers
½	c. salt

3   large red sweet peppers,
       seeded and cut in strips
3   large sweet green peppers,
       seeded and cut in strips
4   c. diced celery
2   medium onions, diced
5   c. sugar
1   qt. vinegar
2   tsp. mustard seeds
1   c. water

· Sprinkle cucumbers with salt; let stand overnight. Drain well.
· Add remaining vegetables, sugar, vinegar, mustard seeds and water. Heat to boiling; reduce heat; cook slowly until cucumbers look transparent. (Do not overcook.)
· Ladle into hot jars; adjust lids at once. Process in boiling water bath (212°F.) 5 minutes. Remove jars from canner and complete seals unless closures are self-sealing. Makes 8½ pints.

ORANGE/CUCUMBER PICKLES

An exceptional recipe

2   qts. chopped peeled
       cucumbers
⅔   c. chopped green peppers
⅔   c. chopped sweet red peppers
2   tblsp. salt
¼   c. cold water
1½   oranges
1   c. vinegar
1   c. brown sugar, firmly packed
½   tsp. mustard seeds
½   tsp. celery seeds

· Combine cucumbers and peppers; add salt and water, let stand overnight. In the morning, drain vegeta-

bles and discard liquid.
· Squeeze most of juice from oranges and use for some other purpose; discard seeds. Grind pulp and peel.
· Combine all ingredients and bring to a boil; boil 15 to 30 minutes.
· Pack in hot jars; adjust lids at once. Process in boiling water bath (212°F.) 5 minutes. Remove jars from canner and complete seals unless closures are the self-sealing type. About 3 pints.

HOMEMADE CUCUMBER PICKLES

Three-in-one recipe used every year by an expert pickle maker

6   lbs. (3 to 5″) pickling
       cucumbers, sliced
⅔   c. chopped green pepper
1½   c. chopped celery
6   medium onions, peeled and
       sliced
¼   c. prepared mustard
4⅔   c. vinegar
½   c. salt
3½   c. sugar
2   tblsp. mustard seeds
½   tsp. ground turmeric
½   tsp. whole cloves
3   tblsp. celery seeds
1½   tsp. powdered alum

· Wash and prepare vegetables.
· Blend mustard with a little vinegar; add remaining vinegar, salt, sugar, spices and alum. Cover and heat to boiling.
· Add vegetables. Cover and bring to a boil; simmer while packing each jar.
· Pack into hot jars; adjust lids at once. Process in boiling water bath

(212°F.) 15 minutes. Remove jars from canner and complete seals unless closures are the self-sealing type. Makes 9 pints.

VARIATIONS

MIXED PICKLES: Instead of sliced cucumbers, use 4 lbs. (3 to 4") pickling onions, quartered; 2 c. (½") carrot slices; 2 c. small cauliflower flowerets; 2 c. chopped sweet red peppers and 1 qt. (1½") celery slices. Alum may be omitted.

GHERKINS: Substitute an equal amount of 2" whole gherkins for the cucumbers, cut in chunks; 24 small sliced 3 to 5" pickling cucumbers.

MIXED GARDEN PICKLES

Open a jar when you have last-minute extras to feed—improves whole meal

5   cucumbers, 5 to 6" long
2   medium green peppers
1   c. cauliflower flowerets
¼   lb. fresh green beans
8   small white onions
2   c. salt
1   qt. vinegar
2   tblsp. mixed pickling spices

• Score cucumber peel with fork but do not peel. Cut into quarters lengthwise and then into ¾" chunks.
• Seed peppers, cut into ¾" pieces.
• Cut cauliflower into 1" pieces.
• Cut beans into 1" lengths.
• Combine all vegetables and mix in salt. Let stand 24 hours. Drain brine from vegetables and discard.
• Heat vinegar and spices; add vegetables and simmer until tender, about 15 minutes.

• Place in hot jars; adjust lids at once. Process in boiling water bath (212°F.) 15 minutes. Remove jars from canner and complete seals unless closures are the self-sealing type. Makes 4 pints.

MIXED PICKLE RELISH

You'll be glad to have this medley of vegetables when winter arrives

2   c. cut-up peeled carrots
2   c. lima beans
2   c. cauliflower flowerets
2   c. sweet corn
4   c. small cucumbers
2   c. small onions, peeled
2   c. cut-up green beans
1   branch celery, chopped
6   sweet peppers, coarsely
        chopped
2   c. sugar
¼   c. white mustard seeds
2½   tsp. salt
½   tsp. ground turmeric
Vinegar

• Boil vegetables until tender; then add other ingredients, adding enough vinegar to cover.
• Boil 15 minutes. Ladle into hot jars; adjust lids at once. Process in boiling water bath (212°F.) 15 minutes. Remove jars from canner and complete seals unless closures are the self-sealing type. Makes 10 pints.

TOMATO RELISH

Just what you've wanted to serve with meat and cheese sandwiches

8   qts. ripe tomatoes, peeled
6   large onions, peeled

4   sweet green peppers, cored
2   c. cut-up celery
1   qt. vinegar
3   c. brown sugar, firmly packed
⅓   c. salt
¼   c. mustard seeds
3½   tblsp. ground cinnamon

• Chop tomatoes coarsely. Put other vegetables through coarse blade of food chopper.
• Combine all ingredients and cook slowly, stirring occasionally, 2 hours or until mixture is thick and clear.
• Ladle into hot jars; adjust lids at once. Process in boiling water bath (212°F.) 5 minutes. Remove jars from canner and complete seals unless closures are the self-sealing type. Makes about 14 pints.

1000-ISLAND PICKLES

A Sunday-dinner pickle from a Wyoming ranch home. Good with game

8   large cucumbers
1   large head cauliflower
2   large onions
2   sweet green peppers
1   sweet red pepper
½   c. salt
1   tblsp. mustard seeds
1   tblsp. celery seeds
6   tblsp. dry mustard
1   tblsp. ground turmeric
6   c. sugar
¾   c. flour
2⅔   c. water
5   c. hot vinegar

• Chop cucumbers and cauliflower, peeled onions and peppers, first discarding seeds. Mix salt with vegetables and let stand 1 hour. Drain liquid.

• Mix spices, sugar and flour in large kettle; moisten with water. Add hot vinegar and drained vegetables. Cook 20 to 30 minutes.
• Pack in hot jars; adjust lids at once. Process in boiling water bath (212°F.) 15 minutes. Remove jars from canner and complete seals unless closures are the self-sealing type. Makes 10 pints.

CRISP MUSTARD PICKLES

Secret of these pickles is the sauce

6   medium cucumbers, chopped
2   c. chopped onion
3   sweet red peppers, chopped
1   medium head cauliflower, cut up
1   qt. small pickling onions
1   c. salt
4   c. sugar
1   qt. vinegar
¾   c. flour
¼   c. dry mustard
1½   tsp. ground turmeric
1   tblsp. celery salt

• Layer vegetables and salt in bowl; cover with cold water. Let stand overnight. Drain; rinse with cold water.
• To make sauce, combine sugar and vinegar; heat to boiling. Mix remaining ingredients; add some of vinegar mixture, cooled; mix and add to boiling mixture; stir well.
• Add drained vegetables; cook 15 to 30 minutes.
• Pack in hot jars; adjust lids at once. Process in boiling water bath (212°F.) 15 minutes. Remove jars from canner and complete seals unless closures are the self-sealing type. Makes 6½ pints.

MIXED PICKLES

An excellent way to put the garden in jars for use in winter meals

1   qt. chopped cucumbers
1   qt. chopped onion
6   sweet green peppers, chopped
1   sweet red pepper, chopped
1   qt. small pickling onions
1   qt. small cucumbers, whole
1   head cauliflower, cut in small
      pieces
¾   c. salt
8   c. brown sugar, firmly packed
2   qts. vinegar
1   tblsp. mustard seeds
2 ¼   tsp. celery seeds

2   tblsp. ground turmeric
⅔   c. flour

• Combine vegetables. Sprinkle with salt; cover with cold water; let stand overnight.
• Drain. To make sauce, combine sugar and vinegar. Mix spices and flour; moisten with vinegar solution; return to sauce.
• Heat to boiling; stir constantly for a smooth sauce. Add vegetables. Cook 15 to 30 minutes.
• Ladle into hot jars; adjust lids at once. Process in boiling water bath (212°F.) 5 minutes. Remove jars from canner and complete seals unless closures are the self-sealing type. Makes 12 pints.

Rancher's Favorite Relish

The Western homemaker who shares the following recipe says: "My husband tells our friends that I put everything except the kitchen sink in this relish. But he always adds that it's his favorite dish from the garden.

"Autumn comes early to our mountain country; so in September when I see the aspens yellow at higher elevations, I start cutting up the last vegetables, stirring and cooking them with vinegar and sugar."

END-OF-GARDEN RELISH

No one ever discovered a better relish

1   c. sliced cucumbers
1   c. chopped sweet pepper
1   c. sliced onions (thin)
1   c. chopped cabbage
Salt water
1   c. cut green beans
1   c. cut yellow string beans

1   c. lima beans
1   c. raw carrots, scraped and
      finely cut
1   tblsp. celery seeds
1   c. chopped raw celery
2   tblsp. mustard seeds
1   pt. vinegar
2   c. sugar
2   tblsp. ground turmeric

• Soak cucumbers, pepper, onions and cabbage in salt water (½ c. salt to 2 qts. water) overnight. Drain.
• Prepare and cook the remaining ingredients. Add the raw, soaked vegetables to the cooked vegetables and boil all together for 15 to 30 minutes.
• Ladle into hot jars; adjust lids at once. Process in boiling water bath (212°F.) 15 to 20 minutes. Remove jars from canner and complete seals unless closures are the self-sealing type. Makes 6 to 7 pints.

Garden Special Pickles

More cucumbers end up in pickle jars than all the other vegetables put together. But few country women let summer slip into autumn without putting up pickled beets. They add a flash of red color to meals and contribute a likable sweet-sharp flavor.

Some of the other garden vegetables, like corn and zucchini, when pickled, also contribute tasty morsels to meals. Do try the recipes that follow. You're bound to like them.

PICKLED BEETS

Slice beets with corrugated cutter to give them a fancy look

24	small beets
1	c. cooking liquid
1	pt. vinegar
1¼	c. sugar
2	tblsp. salt
6	whole cloves
1	(3″) stick cinnamon
3	medium onions, sliced

· Remove beet tops, leaving roots and 1″ stems. Cover with boiling water; cook until tender. Drain, reserving 1 c. cooking liquid. Remove skins; slice.
· Combine cooking liquid, vinegar, sugar and salt. Add spices tied in thin white cloth. Heat to boiling.
· Add beets and onions. Simmer 5 minutes. Remove spice bag. Continue simmering while quickly packing beets and onions into one hot pint jar at a time. Fill to within ½″ of jar top. Adjust lids. Process in boiling water bath (212°F.) 30 minutes.
· Remove jars from canner and complete seals unless closures are self-sealing type. Makes 4 pints.

ITALIAN PICKLES

In California, where zucchini grows extensively and good cooks prize it highly, "bread and butter" pickles are made from the squash. The ranch woman who sent this recipe obtained it from her County Extension Home Economist.

SLICED ZUCCHINI PICKLES

Make sandwiches taste better

1	qt. vinegar
2	c. sugar
½	c. salt
2	tsp. celery seeds
2	tsp. ground turmeric
1	tsp. dry mustard
4	qts. sliced, unpeeled zucchini
1	qt. onions, sliced

· Bring vinegar, sugar, salt and spices to a boil; pour over zucchini and onions and let stand 1 hour.
· Bring to a boil; cook 3 minutes.
· Pack in hot jars; adjust lids at once. Process in boiling water bath (212°F.) 5 minutes. Remove jars from canner and complete seals unless closures are the self-sealing type. Makes 6 to 7 pints.

VARIATION

DILLED ZUCCHINI PICKLES: Substitute 2 tsp. dill seeds for turmeric.

PICKLED ONIONS

Quick and easy version of tedious-to-fix old-fashioned pickled onions

4	qts. small onions
1	c. salt
¼	c. mixed pickling spices
2	qts. vinegar
2	c. sugar

• Peel onions. Add salt and let stand overnight.
• In the morning, put in colander and rinse thoroughly with cold water to remove all salt. Drain.
• Tie spices loosely in clean, thin white cloth; boil 10 minutes with vinegar and sugar. Discard spices.
• Pack onions into hot jars. Pour boiling hot vinegar mixture over. Adjust lids at once. Process in boiling water bath (212°F.) 5 minutes. Remove jars from canner and complete seals unless closures are the self-sealing type. Makes 8 pints.

BEET RELISH

Adds a spot of color to the plate

3	c. drained finely chopped or ground canned beets
1	c. vinegar
6½	c. sugar
2	tsp. prepared horse-radish
¼	tsp. ground cinnamon
¼	tsp. ground cloves
¼	tsp. ground allspice
1	bottle liquid fruit pectin

• Measure beets into a very large saucepan. Add vinegar, sugar, horse-radish and spices, mixing well.

• Bring to a full rolling boil over high heat and boil hard 1 minute, stirring constantly. Remove from heat and stir in liquid pectin at once. Skim.
• Ladle into hot jars; adjust lids at once. Process in boiling water bath (212°F.) 15 minutes. Remove jars from canner and complete seals unless closures are the self-sealing type. Makes about 8 half pints.

MINTED ONION RINGS

Delicious with lamb or veal—you may wish to use more mint

1	qt. vinegar
¼	c. sugar
2	c. fresh mint leaves, or ¼ c. dried mint flakes
Few	drops green food color
4	c. sliced peeled onions
4	pimientos, thinly sliced

• Combine vinegar, sugar and mint, tied in clean, thin white cloth, in saucepan. Heat gently 10 minutes; remove from heat.
• Stir in food color. Add onions and pimientos; heat to boiling. Remove mint. Pour into clean, hot jars; adjust lids at once. Process in boiling water bath (212°F.) 5 minutes. Remove jars from canner and complete seals unless closures are the self-sealing type. Makes 4 half pints.

VARIATION

PEPPER ONION RINGS: Use 4 sweet red peppers, sliced, for pimientos.

IOWA CORN RELISH

Young, tender corn at its flavor peak makes the best-tasting relish

20	ears sweet corn (2 ½ qts. kernels cut from cobs)
1	c. chopped green pepper
1	c. chopped sweet red pepper
1 ¼	c. chopped onion
1	c. chopped celery
1 ½	c. sugar
1 ½	tblsp. mustard seeds
1	tblsp. salt
1	tsp. celery seeds
½	tsp. ground turmeric

2 ⅔	c. vinegar
2	c. water

• Boil corn 5 minutes. Plunge into cold water. Cut kernels from cobs; measure. Combine all ingredients; simmer 20 minutes.

• Pack into clean, hot pint jars, leaving 1″ head space. Make certain vinegar solution covers vegetables. Adjust lids. Process in boiling water bath (212°F.) 15 to 20 minutes.

• Remove jars from canner and complete seals unless closures are self-sealing type. Makes 6 to 7 pints.

Green Tomato Pickles

When shorter days are noticeable and the sumac leaves start to look like red flames, farm women know the last of the year's pickle making is at hand. Baskets filled with green tomatoes come to the kitchen for the cook's magic that turns them into pickles.

Recipes for different kinds of green tomato pickles appear in this cookbook. All of them are from country cooks who rate them tops.

GREEN TOMATO PICKLES

Pickles are spicy and sharp with a sweet tang—brown sugar adds flavor

2	qts. sliced green tomatoes
3	tblsp. salt
2	c. vinegar
⅔	c. dark brown sugar, firmly packed
1	c. sugar

3	tblsp. mustard seeds
½	tsp. celery seeds
1	tsp. ground turmeric
3	c. sliced onions
2	large, sweet red peppers, chopped
1	hot green or red pepper, chopped

• Mix tomatoes and salt. Let stand about 12 hours. Drain.

• Heat vinegar, sugars and spices to a boil; add sliced onions and boil gently 5 minutes. Add the drained tomatoes and peppers; bring slowly to a boil. Simmer 5 minutes, stirring occasionally with a wooden spoon.

• Pack into hot jars. Be sure syrup covers vegetables. Adjust lids at once. Process in boiling water bath (212°F.) 5 minutes. Remove jars from canner and complete seals unless closures are self-sealing. Makes 9 half pints.

INDIAN PICKLE

A chopped pickle that's been made in one family for three generations

4	lbs. green tomatoes
4	lbs. ripe tomatoes, peeled
3	medium onions, peeled
3	sweet red peppers, seeded
3	green peppers, seeded
1	large cucumber
7	c. chopped celery
⅔	c. salt
3	pts. vinegar
3	lbs. brown sugar
1	tsp. dry mustard
1	tsp. white pepper

• Chop coarsely all the vegetables. Sprinkle with salt and let stand 12 hours or overnight.

• In the morning, drain well, discard liquid and add remaining ingredients.

• Bring to a boil and simmer slowly about 30 minutes, stirring occasionally. Pour into hot jars; adjust lids at once. Process in boiling water bath (212°F.) 5 minutes. Remove jars from canner and complete seals unless closures are the self-sealing type. Makes about 6 pints.

BEST-EVER PICCALILLI

Tastes like the relish Grandma used to make, and that means extra-good

22	medium-size green tomatoes, quartered
1	pt. small onions
6	green peppers, quartered lengthwise
6	sweet red peppers, quartered
1½	qts. vinegar
3½	c. sugar
¼	c. salt

1½	tsp. ground allspice
1½	tsp. ground cinnamon
4	tsp. celery seeds
½	c. mustard seeds

• Wash vegetables; put through food chopper, using medium blade. Drain.

• Place vegetables in a large kettle; add 1 qt. vinegar. Boil 30 minutes, stirring frequently. Drain and discard liquid. Return vegetables to kettle and add remaining vinegar, sugar, salt and spices. Simmer 3 minutes. Keep mixture simmering while packing jars.

• Pack into one hot jar at a time. Fill to within ½" of jar top. Adjust lid on each jar at once. Process in boiling water bath (212°F.) 5 minutes. Remove jars from canner and complete seals unless closures are the self-sealing type. Makes 6 to 7 pints.

RUMMAGE PICKLE

An old-time pickle to make of garden odds and ends when Jack Frost is due

2	qts. green tomatoes
1	small head cabbage
3	sweet green peppers
3	sweet red peppers
1	large ripe cucumber
3	large onions
1	qt. red tomatoes
6	c. celery
½	c. salt
1½	c. vinegar
1½	c. water
4	c. sugar
1	tsp. dry mustard

• Chop all vegetables first, discarding pepper seeds and peeling onions.

• Add salt and let stand overnight. In the morning, drain and discard liquid.

• Add vinegar, water, sugar and mustard to vegetables. Bring to a boil and simmer about 1 hour or until clear. • Pack into hot jars; adjust lids at once. Process in boiling water bath (212°F.) 5 minutes. Remove jars from canner and complete seals unless closures are the self-sealing type. Makes 14 pints.

GREEN TOMATO/PEPPER RELISH

A Nebraska farm woman gives jars of this for Christmas gifts every year

1	gal. green tomatoes
2	medium onions
4	large green peppers
2	large red peppers
½	c. salt
1	tsp. mixed pickling spices
3	c. vinegar
1	c. water
2	c. sugar

• Wash, chop and mix vegetables, peeling onions and discarding pepper seeds. Add salt and let stand for several hours or overnight. Drain liquid and discard.
• Tie spices in clean, thin white cloth; combine all ingredients and simmer 30 minutes.
• Ladle boiling hot mixture into hot jars; adjust lids at once. Process in boiling water bath (212°F.) 5 minutes. Remove jars from canner and complete seals unless closures are the self-sealing type. Makes 12 pints.

OLD-FASHIONED RAG PICKLES

Add to mayonnaise—serve with fish

2	qts. cucumbers
2	qts. green tomatoes

2	qts. cabbage
10	large onions, peeled
2	tsp. ground turmeric
2	tsp. celery seeds
2	tsp. dry mustard
2	tsp. salt
2	c. sugar
1	qt. vinegar

• Cut vegetables fine, combine, add remaining ingredients and boil 30 minutes, stirring occasionally.
• Pack in hot jars; adjust lids at once. Process in boiling water bath (212°F.) 5 minutes. Remove jars from canner and complete seals unless closures are self-sealing type. Makes 14 pints.

DANISH GREEN RELISH

Excellent with peanut butter sandwiches, baked beans and meats

30	green tomatoes
5	large onions
3	sweet red peppers
3	sweet green peppers
¼	c. salt
¼	c. dry mustard
1	tblsp. celery seeds
4	c. sugar
5	c. vinegar

• Grind tomatoes, peeled onions and seeded peppers in food chopper.
• Add salt and let stand overnight. Drain, discard liquid and add remaining ingredients to vegetables. Bring to a boil and simmer 15 to 30 minutes.
• Ladle into hot jars; adjust lids at once. Process in boiling water bath (212°F.) 5 minutes. Remove jars from canner and complete seals unless closures are self-sealing. Makes 6 pints.

Colorful Pickled Peppers

You may have trouble saying the Simple Simon tongue-twister about pickled peppers, but you won't have difficulty making relishes with the recipes that follow. Plump, meaty, sweet peppers, both red and green, are favorites for pickling. Perhaps their cheerful colors have something to do with their popularity, but their superior flavors have more to do with it. Many country cooks like to fix pepper relishes to serve during the holidays. In fact, they often call them Christmas relishes. Certainly their sharp flavor and gala colors fit beautifully into turkey and chicken dinners.

Hot peppers, prized so highly in the Southwest, sometimes wind up in peppy relishes. The example that follows, Hot Pepper Relish, won blue ribbons for a FARM JOURNAL reader at the New Mexico State Fair. And Pepper Slaw captured the same honors for an Eastern farm woman at the Connecticut State Fair.

Use fresh, tender, young peppers to make relishes with the best taste.

HOT PEPPER RELISH

Made with hot chili peppers; won first prize at New Mexico State Fair

18	red chili peppers
18	green chili peppers
15	onions
1	tblsp. salt
2½	c. vinegar
2½	c. sugar

• Put peppers, discarding seeds, and peeled onions through food chopper.
• Add salt; cover with boiling water. Let stand 10 minutes. Drain liquid and discard. Add vinegar and sugar to vegetables. Bring to a boil and simmer 20 minutes.
• Ladle into hot jars; adjust lids at once. Process in boiling water bath (212°F.) 5 minutes. Remove jars from canner and complete seals unless closures are the self-sealing type. Makes 6 pints.

PEPPER RELISH

All pepper relishes are best served within six months after being canned

12	sweet green peppers
12	sweet red peppers
12	small onions, peeled
	Boiling water
3	c. vinegar
1½	c. sugar
4	tsp. salt
2	tsp. celery seeds

• Put peppers, seeds discarded, and onions through food chopper. Add boiling water to cover; let stand 10 minutes. Drain and discard liquid. Add remaining ingredients to vegetables. Boil slowly for 15 minutes.
• Ladle into hot jars. Adjust lids at once. Process in boiling water bath (212°F.) 5 minutes. Remove jars from canner and complete seals unless closures are the self-sealing type. Makes 6 pints.

CABBAGE/PEPPER RELISH

One of the relishes women in the Ozarks serve with justified pride

2	medium heads cabbage
6	sweet green peppers
6	sweet red peppers
8	carrots, peeled
8	onions, peeled
½	c. salt
2	qts. vinegar
6	c. brown sugar, firmly packed
1	tblsp. celery seeds
1	tblsp. white mustard seeds

• Chop vegetables, discarding pepper seeds.

• Mix with salt and let stand 3 hours. Drain liquid from vegetables and discard. Boil vinegar, sugar and spices and while hot pour over chopped vegetables. Bring to a boil and cook 15 to 30 minutes; pack into hot jars. Adjust lids at once. Process in boiling water bath (212°F.) 15 minutes. Remove jars from canner and complete seals unless closures are the self-sealing type. Makes 14 pints.

CANADIAN PEPPER RELISH

A North-of-the-Border neighbor shares her favorite relish recipe with us

1	c. chopped sweet green peppers
1	c. chopped sweet red peppers
7	c. sugar
1½	c. vinegar
1	bottle liquid pectin

• Drain liquid from peppers. Place them in a large kettle with sugar and vinegar. Bring to a full rolling boil, stirring, and boil for 2 minutes. Remove from heat. Add pectin; skim.

• Ladle into hot jars; adjust lids at once. Process in boiling water bath (212°F.) 5 minutes. Remove jars from canner and complete seals unless closures are the self-sealing type. Makes 2½ pints.

SPICY PEPPER RELISH

From a North Carolina home where it rates tops among canned relishes

6	large sweet green peppers
3	large sweet red peppers
1	medium head cabbage
2	large onions, peeled
1	gal. green tomatoes
1	qt. vinegar
1	c. sugar
1	c. brown sugar, firmly packed
1	tsp. ground cinnamon
1	tsp. ground allspice
½	c. salt

• Chop or grind peppers, seeds discarded, cabbage, onions and tomatoes. Combine all ingredients in a large kettle and boil gently 30 minutes.

• Ladle into hot jars; adjust lids at once. Process in boiling water bath (212°F.) 5 minutes. Remove jars from canner and complete seals unless closures are the self-sealing type. Makes 12 pints.

FRENCH DRESDEN PICKLES

Keep a jar in the refrigerator to add a cool, spicy note to a meal

12	green peppers, seeded
12	sweet red peppers, seeded
3	small heads cabbage

Homemade pickles and relishes you'll be proud to serve: (starting top left) Water-melon Pickles, Crisp Mustard Pickles, Cinnamon Rings, Pepper Slaw and Sweet Cucumber Pickles (these recipes start on page 261).

We give a bountiful selection of choice pickle recipes from country kitchens—Pickles and Onions and Cheerful Sweet Pickles (recipes, pages 274, 275) represent the many great recipes in the pickle chapter.

Tangy Blender-made Ketchup (recipe, page 310) is a snap to make. It's only one of the ketchup recipes in this book. Can a supply of the red sauce when tomatoes are dead-ripe, to spice up winter meals.

Before frost visits your garden, gather up the last tomatoes and make Green Tomato Mincemeat (recipe, page 251). It cans and freezes beautifully, makes excellent pies. So does our Venison Mincemeat recipe.

8   large onions, peeled
1   c. salt
2   qts. vinegar
3   c. sugar
2   tblsp. white mustard seeds
2   tblsp. celery seeds

• Prepare vegetables and chop fine. Sprinkle with salt, let stand overnight.
• In the morning, drain thoroughly; discard liquid. Add remaining ingredients to vegetables and bring to a boil. Simmer 15 to 30 minutes; stir often.
• Pack into hot jars; adjust lids at once. Process in boiling water bath (212°F.) 5 minutes. Remove jars from canner and complete seals unless closures are the self-sealing type. Makes about 10 pints.

PEPPER SLAW

Takes the place of salad in a hurry-up sandwich-and-soup lunch

12   large sweet green
      peppers

12   large sweet red peppers
12   large onions
2   large heads cabbage
¼   c. salt
6   c. sugar
2½   tblsp. celery seeds
2½   tblsp. mustard seeds
Vinegar

• Discard pepper seeds. Chop peppers, onions and cabbage with coarse blade of food chopper.
• Add salt, mix and let stand overnight. In the morning drain off brine.
• Add sugar and spices and mix well. Cover with cold vinegar and bring to a boil; boil 15 to 30 minutes.
• Ladle into clean, hot jars; adjust lids at once. Process in boiling water bath (212°F.) 5 minutes. Remove jars from canner and complete seals unless closures are the self-sealing type. Makes 14 pints.

Brine-cured Pickles and Sauerkraut

Some farm women say success in brining cucumbers for 4 to 5 weeks (the long cure) is a matter of luck. They find it almost impossible to maintain the proper temperature (80 to 85°F.) during the curing—difficult to keep the strength of the brine under control. Other homemakers prefer to fix pickles this way and are pleased with results they get.

These steps to follow in curing cucumbers in brine are recommended by Extension Economists in Food Conservation, North Carolina State University:

1. Wash fresh cucumbers carefully, using care not to break the skins.

2. Weigh them; put them in a clean, scalded crock or stone jar. Cover with a *10% brine* made by dissolving 1 c. granulated flake or dairy salt in 2 qts. water. (Brine that will float an egg is approximately a 10% brine.)

3. Weight cucumbers down with a scalded heavy plate, placing a fruit jar filled with water or other weight on it. (See Use Right Equipment in this chapter.) Make sure cucumbers are well covered with brine.

4. Next morning, add 1 c. more salt

for each 5 lbs. cucumbers. This is necessary to *maintain the 10% brine*. Add the salt to the top of the plate so it will gradually be distributed. If added to the brine, it may sink to the bottom and make the brine there too strong.

5. Remove the film that forms as the fermentation takes place. If left on, it will destroy the acidity of the brine and result in spoilage.

6. At the end of a week and for 4 or 5 succeeding weeks, add ¼ c. salt for each 5 lbs. cucumbers. Place it on the plate each time.

7. Fermentation that causes bubbles should continue about 4 weeks. When it ceases, the cucumbers are cured. Add no more salt.

8. Cucumbers may be kept in this brine solution until made into pickles. Do not add more salt after they are cured.

9. The ideal temperature for brining vegetables is about 80 to 85°F.

Note: It is important to maintain the right strength of brine and the desirable temperature throughout the fermentation. Fresh cucumbers may be added to the brine during the curing provided enough salt is added to maintain a 10% brine (test with an egg). Weigh the cucumbers before adding them to determine how much salt to add.

TO PICKLE BRINED CUCUMBERS

Remove salt by soaking whole or sliced, cured cucumbers in cold water to cover 10 to 12 hours. The process may be shortened by changing the water often, using a large volume of water (3 to 4 times greater than the cucumbers) or by frequent stirring. The first step is to make Spiced Vinegar.

SPICED VINEGAR

1   gal. vinegar
Sugar
½   oz. whole allspice
½   oz. whole cloves
1   stick cinnamon
1   piece mace

• Bring vinegar, sugar and spices, tied in clean, thin white cloth, to a boil and simmer 15 minutes.
• Cool, cover and set aside for 3 weeks before removing spice bag.

Note: Use 2 c. sugar for sour pickles, 4 c. for less acid pickles and 10 c. for sweet pickles.

SWEET CUCUMBER PICKLES

Pack cucumbers, freshened by soaking in cold water as previously directed, in sterilized jars. Heat Spiced Vinegar (1 pt. to each qt. pickles) to boiling point. Pour over cucumbers and let them stand until the next day. Drain off vinegar; add sugar to it (½ c. for 2 c. vinegar). Bring to a boil and pour over cucumbers. Next day, drain cucumbers; add ½ c. sugar for every 2 c. vinegar drained from cucumbers. Heat drained vinegar and sugar, pour over cucumbers in hot quart jars. Adjust lids. Process in boiling water bath (212°F.) 20 minutes.

Remove jars from canner and complete seals unless closures are self-sealing type.

SOUR PICKLES

Use small cured and soaked cucumbers. To 6 qts. cucumbers, use 1 gal. Spiced Vinegar. If a sweeter pickle is desired, add 4 c. sugar. Bring to a boil. Add one fourth of cucumbers at a time. Repeat with other three portions. Let them boil 2 minutes, but not until soft. Place cucumbers in a large stone crock or glass jars as taken from the kettle. Cover with boiling vinegar. Seal jars or cover top of crock with thick paper, tied tightly to exclude air. Keep in cool place 6 weeks.

Pack pickles and their juices in quart jars. Adjust lids. Process in boiling water bath (212°F.) 20 minutes.

Remove jars from canner and complete seals unless closures are self-sealing type.

GRANDMOTHER USED GRAPE LEAVES

Look in old cookbooks and read the handwritten notes in them. You'll notice recipes in which Great-grandmother used grape leaves in making pickles. She believed they helped make good pickles. Some modern cooks scoff at the idea, but recent research indicates old-time pickle makers knew what they were doing.

Scientists today have discovered that grape leaves contain a substance that inhibits the development of the enzymes that cause cucumbers to soften in the brining. Of all the grapes studied, the Scuppernong variety, of the Muscadine family, a native American variety that originated in Tyrrell County, North Carolina, is especially rich in the substance that prevents cucumbers from softening.

If you want to follow the old-time method, wash grape leaves and layer them with the cucumbers in brine, discard them when you make pickles.

FERMENTED DILL PICKLES

Unsurpassable olive-green dills

20	lbs. (3½ to 5½") cucumbers
½	c. whole mixed pickling spices
2	to 3 bunches fresh dill
2	c. vinegar
1½	c. salt
2	gals. water
10	to 20 cloves garlic, peeled (optional)

• Cover cucumbers with cold water. Wash thoroughly, using a vegetable brush, handling gently to avoid bruising. Take care to remove any blossoms. Drain on rack or wipe dry.

• Place half the pickle spices and a layer of dill in a 5-gal. crock or stone jar. Fill with cucumbers to 3 or 4" from top of crock. Mix vinegar, salt and 2 gals. water and pour over the cucumbers. Place a layer of dill and remaining spices over the top of cucumbers. Add garlic.

• Cover with a heavy china or glass plate or lid that fits inside the crock and use a weight, such as a glass jar filled with water on top of the cover to keep cucumbers under the brine. Cover loosely with clean cloth. Keep pickles at room temperature and remove film daily when formed. Film may start forming in 3 to 5 days. Do not stir pickles around in jar but be sure they are completely covered with brine. If necessary, make additional brine, using original proportions.

· In about 3 weeks the cucumbers become olive-green and any white spots inside the fermented cucumbers will be eliminated by processing.

· Pack the pickles, along with some of the dill, into clean, hot jars; add garlic, if desired. Cover with boiling brine to ½" of top of jar. Adjust lids. Put jars into canner containing boiling water; be sure the water comes an inch or two over the jar tops. Cover the canner tightly and start to count the processing time. Continue heating and process for 15 minutes.

· Remove jars from canner immediately. Set jars on a wire rack several inches apart to cool. Complete seals unless closures are self-sealing type. Makes 9 to 10 quarts.

Note: Use of garlic gives dill pickles the flavor of those sold in delicatessens. The original brine is usually cloudy as a result of yeast development during the fermentation period. If this cloudiness is objectionable, fresh brine may be used to cover the pickles when packing them. Make it with the same proportions of vinegar, salt and water as in the original brine. The fermentation brine is generally preferred for added flavor; it should be strained and heated to boiling.

"What Went Wrong with My Pickles?"

Q. What makes my pickles soft and slippery?
A. They are spoiled and nothing will make them firm again. Here are some possible causes: (1) failing to remove blossom and stem ends from cucumbers and to wash them thoroughly; (2) using too weak vinegar, for cucumbers are low in acid; (3) cooking too long or at too high temperature or not heated enough to destroy organisms; (4) not covering pickles in jars with liquid or with brine in long-cure; (5) not sealing jars immediately when boiling hot pickling solution is added; (6) storing pickles in a place too warm; (7) insufficient salt.

Q. Why are my cucumber pickles hollow?
A. (1) Often this is due to growing conditions or the wrong variety of cucumbers (use pickling varieties). (2)

Or the cucumbers may have waited too long between gathering time and pickling. (3) A gaseous type of spoilage may have occurred.

Note: When making whole pickles, you can check the cucumbers that are hollow—usually they float in water.

Q. Why are my pickles shriveled and tough?
A. This occurs more frequently in very sweet or very sour pickles, and in whole ones rather than in chunks or slices. It is caused by (1) too strong vinegar solution or (2) too heavy syrup at beginning of cooking, (3) by not giving fruits a chance to plump up, (4) using too much salt, (5) cucumbers standing too long between the garden and pickling, or (6) overcooking or overprocessing.

Q. Why are my pickles dark?
A. The darkening may be due to corrosion of some metal utensils or jar lids, iron in water, use of ground rather than whole spices, or leaving spice bag in jars. Dark spots are caused by holding cucumbers too long after picking before pickling them.

Q. Why does the garlic clove in my pickles turn green?
A. The garlic was not dry enough.

Q. My pickles have a bitter flavor. What went wrong?
A. Among the possible causes: using cucumbers that had a very dry growing season; too much spice; packing whole spices with the pickles.

Homemade Sauerkraut

Country cooks often make sauerkraut when there's a surplus of cabbage. They find its sharp flavor adds a pleasing change of pace in winter meals. And it's a real country convenience food—ready to serve cold in salads or appetizers and to heat in a few minutes with frankfurters for a main dish. Many families prefer it hot alongside meats. Some FARM JOURNAL readers in Pennsylvania prefer sauerkraut with turkey to the New Englander's favorite, cranberry sauce.

Use pure granulated (sack salt) salt to make sauerkraut by the following directions and do measure it accurately. The cabbage will not ferment properly if you add too much salt.

GLASS-JAR SAUERKRAUT

If you have a big crop of cabbage, it is economical to cure it in brine—to make sauerkraut. The fermented vegetable serves as a "pickle" and brings variety to winter meals when fresh vegetables are not always abundant. Good country cooks like to serve it cold with a dash of celery or caraway seeds, a few chunks of chilled, drained canned pineapple or a little pineapple juice added, for an appetizer. They know that the sharpness of its flavor, when hot, depends on how long it is cooked. For the most tang and greatest crispness, they only heat it. They cook it longer for a milder flavor.

An easy way to make sauerkraut is to ferment the cabbage in glass fruit jars. Here are directions:

1. Remove and discard outer leaves from firm, matured heads of cabbage. Wash, drain, cut in halves or quarters and remove and discard cores.

2. Shred 5 lbs. cabbage at a time with a shredder or sharp knife. It should be no thicker than a dime.

3. Sprinkle 3½ tblsp. salt over shredded cabbage (5 lbs.) and mix thoroughly by hand.

4. Pack into clean glass jars, pressing cabbage down firmly with wooden spoon. Fill to within 1½ to 2" from jar top. Be sure juice covers cabbage. A quart jar holds about 2 lbs.

5. Wipe off jar top. Cover cabbage with pads of cheesecloth, edges tucked down against inside of jar. Hold cabbage down by crisscrossing two dry wood strips (some good kraut makers first coat the strips with melted paraffin) so they catch under the neck of

the jar. Wipe off jar, put on lids, but *do not seal tightly.*

6. Set filled jars in shallow pans or on folded newspapers—the brine may overflow during fermentation. *Keep at room temperature (70°F.) for top-quality sauerkraut.*

7. Skim film every few days if it forms. If directions have been followed carefully and correct temperature maintained, little or no film should form.

8. Keep cabbage covered with brine. If necessary add more weak brine made by dissolving 1½ tblsp. salt in 1 qt. water.

9. Let ferment about 10 days, or until liquid settles and bubbles no longer rise to the surface. Remove the cheesecloth and wood strips and add more weak brine if needed. (Some women fix 1 extra qt. cabbage for every 4 qts. to use in refilling jars when fermentation ends and shrinkage occurs.)

10. If sauerkraut is to be used soon, wipe mouths of jars and seal tightly; keep in a cool place. If it is to be stored longer than a few weeks, remove lids and set jars in a pan of cold water. Water should extend to shoulder of jars. Bring water slowly to a boil; then remove jars. Add boiling weak brine to sauerkraut, if needed to fill the jar to within ½″ from top. (To make brine, dissolve 1½ tblsp. salt in 1 qt. water.) Wipe off jar rims. Adjust lids. Process in boiling water bath (212°F.).

Quart jars   30 minutes

Remove jars from canner and complete seals unless closures are self-sealing type.

Note: For 20 to 25 lbs. cabbage, use ½ lb. salt. Makes 8 to 10 quarts.

NEW YORK AND WISCONSIN SAUERKRAUT TIPS

From good cooks in these two lake states, famed for excellent sauerkraut, we learned of these good ways to use sauerkraut.

SAUERKRAUT SANDWICH: Make a round, open-face hot dog sandwich. Slice the frankfurters to make "pennies" and arrange them around the outer edges of buns cut in crosswise halves. Put a spoonful of sauerkraut in center of each sandwich. Serve with knife and fork. Buns may be toasted and buttered, frankfurter slices heated in a little water and well drained.

SCALLOPED SAUERKRAUT: Scallop sauerkraut with Cheddar cheese slices.

SAUERKRAUT CARROT SALAD: Make a salad with chilled sauerkraut and shredded carrots.

STONE-JAR SAUERKRAUT

Prepare 40 to 50 lbs. cabbage as directed for Glass-Jar Sauerkraut. Shred and salt 5 lbs. cabbage at a time.

1. To 5 lbs. cabbage, add 3½ tblsp. salt. Mix thoroughly.

2. Pack firmly and evenly with a potato masher into a stone jar (or crock) that has been washed in soapy water, rinsed and scalded.

3. Repeat shredding and salting cabbage until jar is filled to within 5″ from top. Press firmly (do not pound) with masher to extract enough juice to cover cabbage by the time jar is filled. Keep cabbage covered with juice.

4. Cover with two or three layers of white, clean cloth, tucking edges down against inside of jar. On top, place a scalded, heavy plate that just fits inside the jar or a paraffined board. Weight it down with a fruit jar filled with water (or with a stone—not limestone—or paraffined brick), so that juice comes over plate.

5. Fermentation will begin the day following the packing. It works faster at high temperatures and the kraut is more likely to spoil at a high temperature. The best quality product is made at room temperature (70°F.).

6. Give the kraut daily care. Remove the film as it forms and wash and scald the cover cloth as often as necessary to remove mold and film.

7. When bubbling stops (in 2 or 3 weeks—or 4 weeks in cold weather), tap jar or crock gently. If no bubbles rise, fermentation has ended.

8. Pack into clean quart jars to within 1″ of top. Cover with sauerkraut juice. If you need more juice, add a weak brine (1½ tblsp. salt to 1 qt. water). Set jars in a pan of cold water. Water should extend to shoulder of jars. Bring water slowly to a boil; remove jars. Wipe off jar rims. Adjust lids. Process in boiling water bath (212°F.).

Quart jars   30 minutes

Remove jars from canner and complete seals unless closures are self-sealing type. Makes 15 to 18 quarts.

Note: If you eat sauerkraut often and will use your supply before winter ends, it will hold in the stone jar in a cold room (55°F. or lower).

SAUERKRAUT ANSWERS

Q. What makes sauerkraut turn pink?
A. The color is caused by certain kinds of yeast. They often grow when the salt is not evenly distributed, or when too much salt is used, and when the cabbage is too loosely packed in a crock or stone jar.

Q. What causes soft sauerkraut?
A. The salt content may be too low. High temperatures during curing also have a softening effect. Use of containers not cleaned thoroughly sometimes causes this, as does improper packing of cabbage which traps air.

Q. Why is sauerkraut sometimes slimy?
A. Certain bacteria are responsible and usually they flourish when not enough salt is used and the temperatures are too high.

Q. What makes sauerkraut darken at times?
A. Failure to clean the cabbage properly, uneven salting and a high curing temperature may be at fault.

Q. Is use of too much salt harmful?
A. Yes, it prevents fermentation.

Q. Can you prevent the formation of a white film?
A. The trick is to cover the sauerkraut and adjust the weights so very little kraut juice or kraut is exposed to the air. This treatment discourages the growth of this yeast.

CHAPTER 14

FRUIT PICKLES AND RELISHES

Recipes for Spiced Apples, Apricots, Cantaloupe, Cherries, Pickled
Crab Apples, Red Currants, Figs, Quinces, Peaches, Pears, Pine-
apple, Watermelon Rind · Fruit/Vegetable Relishes, Chili Sauces,
Ketchups · Fruit Chutneys

Halfway through summer, country kitchens begin to fill with the most
tantalizing of all food fragrances—fruits and tomatoes, spiced just right,
cooking in sugar-vinegar syrup. These pickles and relishes are the country cook's favorite meat and poultry go-withs.

In this chapter you will find old friends like golden peach and crisp
watermelon pickles that glorify chicken dinners. You will discover newer
gems: rosy crab apple pickles, and fresh pineapple slices, spiced and tinted
bright red and green—gala as Hawaiian leis.

You will see recipes for relish sauces, like ketchups made with dead-
ripe tomatoes, grapes, cranberries and gooseberries from the woods. And
for chutneys, like peach and apple, that taste so good with rice and poultry
dishes. Combination fruit and vegetable relishes also appear—Victory Relish contains peaches, pears, tomatoes, onions and sweet peppers. Recipes
for it have come to us from all parts of the country, along with praises.
Tomatoes often mix with fruits in this chapter's recipes.

Almost all the American fruits appear in the relish recipes that follow—
apples, apricots, peaches, pears, blueberries, quinces, figs, crab apples and
pineapples, to name the common ones.

This chapter also contains recipes for pickles and relishes to bring out
with game dinners, for country cooks know it takes these to make fowl and
game a real feast. Here are the sweet-sours to brighten meals when color,
other than the occasional streak of a cardinal beyond the window, leaves
the landscape. You will want to fix some to tote to community meals,
carry down the road to a laid-up neighbor and donate to food sales. Remember that all these recipes are specials from country kitchens.

Wonderful Sweet-Sours
FRUIT PICKLES, RELISHES GLAMORIZE MEALS

Country cooks depend greatly on spiced and pickled fruits to give meals a special color and flavor lift. They use all the A B C fruits, apricots, blueberries and cherries, on through the alphabet. Farm women prefer slightly underripe fruits for pickling —too green for freezing or canning.

In this chapter you will find choice recipes from Western ranches, Southern, New England and Midwestern kitchens—sweet-sour relishes that are conversation pieces at any party. Do try them. You'll enjoy what you make and will be justly proud to belong to the band of America's best cooks— farm women.

SPICED APPLE STICKS

A relish that's spiced just right— makes other foods taste better

12	peeled medium apples
3	qts. water
3	tblsp. vinegar
1	c. sugar
½	c. light corn syrup
1	c. vinegar
⅔	c. water
2	tsp. whole cloves
1 ½	sticks cinnamon

• Cut apples into eighths and cover with 3 qts. water and vinegar.
• Combine all other ingredients in kettle. Bring slowly to a boil.
• Add well-drained apples, cover and boil 3 minutes, stirring occasionally.
• Pack apple sticks in hot jars; cover with liquid. Adjust lids. Process in

boiling water bath (212°F.) 15 minutes.
• Remove jars from canner and complete seals unless closures are self-sealing type. Makes 4 pints.

SPICED APPLE PIECES

You'll like this sweet if you enjoy apple and ginger flavors blended

6	sliced peeled apples
4	c. sugar
2 ½	c. water
1	tblsp. crushed dried ginger root

• Add apples to syrup made by combining sugar and water and bringing to a boil. Boil 3 minutes, cool.
• Cook gently until apples are transparent. Pack into hot jars.
• Tie ginger root in clean, thin white cloth; add to syrup and boil, stirring constantly until jellying point is reached. Pour syrup over apples. Adjust lids. Process in boiling water bath (212°F.) 5 minutes. Remove jars from canner and complete seals unless closures are the self-sealing type. Makes 6 half pints.

OLD-FASHIONED GINGER APPLES

Grandmother's rule will work for you —use really tart apples

4   c. chopped peeled tart apples
Juice of 1 lemon
Peel of 1 lemon, grated

2 c. light brown sugar, firmly
       packed
2 c. water
5 pieces dried ginger root

· Mix apples, lemon juice and peel.
· Combine sugar, water and ginger root in a saucepan and bring to a boil; boil 15 minutes.
· Add apple mixture. Cook over low heat 2 hours, stirring often, until thick and dark. Remove ginger root.
· Ladle into hot jars. Adjust lids at once. Process in boiling water bath (212°F.) 5 minutes. Remove jars from canner and complete seals unless closures are the self-sealing type. Makes 3½ pints.

Note: Hold a week before using.

CINNAMON APPLE RINGS

Candy does the spicing and tinting—glamorous relish to serve with pork

18 tart apples
6 c. sugar
3 c. water
1 (9 oz.) pkg. red cinnamon
       candies
3 drops red food color

· Cut cored, peeled apples in rings.
· Combine sugar, water, cinnamon candies and food color. Bring to a boil; boil 3 minutes.
· Add apples to syrup; cook until transparent.
· Pack in hot jars. Cover with syrup. Adjust lids. Process in boiling water bath (212°F.) 25 minutes.
· Remove jars from canner and complete seals unless closures are self-sealing type. Makes 4 pints.

Note: Drop rings in slightly salted water before cooking to keep them from discoloring. We tested this recipe with Jonathan apples, but other tart varieties may be used.

CALIFORNIA FRUIT PICKLE

To make fruit pickles a popular California way, use small, firm, barely ripe peaches, pears or apricots. Peel peaches. You may peel pears if you like; do not peel apricots. Use half brown and half white sugars or all white or all brown. The quantities of sugar in the following recipe may be reduced if you like more tartness.

CALIFORNIA APRICOT PICKLE

Juicy fruit, spice and everything nice

4 qts. apricots
Whole cloves
4 c. sugar
4 c. brown sugar, firmly packed
1 qt. vinegar
6 (3") sticks cinnamon

· Stick each apricot with 2 or 4 cloves.
· Bring sugars, vinegar and cinnamon sticks (may be tied in cheesecloth) to a boil. Add 2 qts. apricots and simmer gently until soft. Remove fruit and repeat with remaining apricots.
· Remove cinnamon. Fill hot, sterilized jars with fruit to within ½" from top; pour on syrup, making certain it covers fruit. Adjust lids at once. Process in boiling water bath (212°F.) 20 minutes. Remove jars from canner and complete seals unless closures are the self-sealing type. Makes 6 pints.

PICKLING BLUEBERRIES

We received the following recipe for Spiced Blueberries from one of our readers with these comments: "My mother often served this sharp relish with game or with what she called 'heavy meats' like pork, beef and mutton. And when she did, the compliments went round and round the table.

"While I helped pick the berries with the hot sunshine on my back in the still north country, there was a fragrance of wintergreen when I stepped on the creeping plants. Thoughts of spiced berries made me fill my pail."

SPICED BLUEBERRIES

Ranks with blueberry pies, pancakes and muffins in appetite appeal

3 qts. blueberries
1 c. vinegar
1 c. sugar
2 tblsp. whole cloves

• Combine all ingredients in large kettle and bring to a boil. Simmer, stirring often until liquid begins to jell, about 20 to 25 minutes.
• Pour into hot jars; adjust lids at once. Process in boiling water bath (212°F.) 5 minutes. Remove jars from canner and complete seals unless closures are self-sealing. Makes 2 pints.

CANTALOUPE PICKLE

The perfect use of slightly underripe melon—tastes wonderful

1 medium underripe cantaloupe
1 qt. vinegar
2 c. water

1 tsp. ground mace
2 (3") sticks cinnamon
2 tblsp. ground cloves
4 c. sugar

• Peel cantaloupe and cut in 1" sections. Cut sections crosswise.
• Combine vinegar and water in kettle; bring to a boil; add spices.
• Place cantaloupe in a nonmetal container. Bring the vinegar water to a boil and pour over cantaloupe. Let stand overnight.
• In morning, drain cantaloupe; bring vinegar-water mixture to a boil. Add sugar and cantaloupe and cook until melon is transparent, about 1 hour.
• Pack hot pint jars with cantaloupe. Keep syrup boiling. Add syrup to jars to within ½" from top. Make certain it covers the melon. Adjust lids at once. Process in boiling water bath (212°F.) 5 minutes. Remove jars from canner and complete seals unless closures are the self-sealing type. Makes 2 pints.

Note: A medium syrup is desirable. If it is too thin, boil it longer. Keep the jars of cantaloupe pickles warm by setting them in a kettle of hot water until syrup is ready. You can use 2 c. white and 2 c. brown sugar instead of all white sugar.

PICKLED CHERRIES

If you like really tart relishes, pickled cherries are for you. Some cooks trim the stems slightly and leave these "handles" on the fruit. Wrap the jars of pickles in heavy brown paper when storing them in the fruit closet. It will protect their color.

PICKLED CHERRIES

Use the largest sweet cherries you can find to make this relish

2   qts. large cherries, stemmed
¼   c. sugar
2   doz. whole cloves
1   (3″) stick cinnamon
2   c. vinegar

• Wash cherries; but do not pit.
• Mix sugar, spices tied in clean, thin white cloth, and vinegar. Cook for 5 minutes.
• Add cherries, cook slowly until tender. Let stand overnight.
• In morning, remove spices. Drain syrup from cherries; pack them in clean, hot pint jars. Boil syrup rapidly until slightly thickened.
• Pour boiling hot over cherries; adjust lids at once. Process in boiling water bath (212°F.) 5 minutes. Remove jars from canner and complete seals unless closures are the self-sealing type. Makes 2½ pints.

CRAB APPLE PICKLE

No one has found a more colorful or tastier garnish for meat platters

4   lbs. crab apples
2½   c. vinegar
2   c. water
4   c. sugar
1   tblsp. whole cloves
3   (3″) sticks cinnamon
1   tsp. whole ginger

• Wash and remove blossom ends of crab apples; do not remove stems. Prick each apple in several places.
• Bring vinegar, water and sugar to a boil. Add spices tied in clean, thin white cloth.
• Cook half of the crab apples in the syrup for 2 minutes; remove. Repeat until all the crab apples are cooked. Pour syrup with spices over apples; let stand overnight.
• Remove spices. Pack apples in hot pint jars. Bring syrup to a boil. Pour over fruit.
• Adjust lids. Process in boiling water bath (212°F.) 30 minutes. Remove jars from canner and complete seals unless closures are self-sealing type. Makes 4 to 5 pints.

CHOPPED SPICED CRAB APPLES

Excellent with ham—you'll like these

6   lbs. crab apples
2   (15 oz.) pkgs. seedless raisins
2   oranges
1   pt. vinegar
2   lbs. brown sugar
2   tsp. ground cinnamon
½   tsp. ground cloves

• Wash, stem and remove blossom ends of crab apples; core and dice.
• Combine crab apples, raisins and oranges, peeled, diced, and seeded.
• Heat vinegar, sugar and spices; add apples, raisins and oranges.
• Cook until apples are soft.
• Ladle into hot jars; adjust lids at once. Process in boiling water bath (212°F.) 5 minutes. Remove jars from canner and complete seals unless closures are the self-sealing type. Makes 5½ pints.

SPICED CRANBERRIES

Vinegar and spices add zest and a change-of-pace to cranberry sauce

2	qts. cranberries (2 lbs.)
1⅓	c. vinegar
⅔	c. water
4	c. sugar
4	tsp. ground cinnamon
1	tsp. ground cloves

• Cook cranberries in syrup made by combining vinegar, water, sugar and spices. Bring to a boil; simmer, uncovered, 20 minutes.

• Continue simmering while quickly filling one hot jar at a time to within ½" from top. Make certain syrup covers fruit. Adjust lid on each hot jar at once. Process in boiling water bath (212°F.) 5 minutes. Remove jars from canner and complete seals unless closures are the self-sealing type. Makes 4 pints.

SPICED RED CURRANTS

Something special to serve with meat, turkey, chicken—try it also with ham

2½	qts. red currants
1	tsp. ground cloves
1	tsp. ground cinnamon
¼	c. water
¼	c. vinegar
7½	c. sugar
½	bottle liquid fruit pectin

• Wash and stem currants. Stir in spices, water and vinegar and bring to a boil, stirring constantly. Lower heat and continue cooking, covered, 10 minutes.

• Measure 4 c. currant mixture into a large kettle. Add sugar and mix well. Cook over high heat until mix-

ture reaches a full rolling boil; boil hard for 1 minute, stirring constantly.

• Remove from heat and stir in pectin at once. Stir and skim alternately for 5 minutes. Ladle into hot jars; adjust lids at once. Process in boiling water bath (212°F.) 5 minutes. Remove jars from canner and complete seals unless closures are the self-sealing type. Makes about 4 half pints.

PICKLED FIGS

The sweet-sour gives the figs an unusual new taste—excellent with meat

6	qts. figs (about 8 lbs.)
	Salt water
8	c. brown sugar, firmly packed
1	qt. vinegar
7	(3") sticks cinnamon
1	to 2 tsp. whole cloves

• Cover figs with salt water (1 tblsp. salt to 1 gal. water); bring to a boil; simmer 15 minutes.

• Combine sugar and vinegar; bring to a boil. Add the spices.

• Drain the figs and add to the boiling syrup. Simmer 1 hour.

• Pack into hot jars. Make certain figs are covered with syrup. Adjust lids at once. Process in boiling water bath (212°F.) 20 minutes. Remove jars from canner and complete seals unless closures are the self-sealing type. Makes 7 to 8 pints.

PRUNE PICKLE

These plump, spicy prunes are a real flavor boost with goose and duck

1	lb. dried prunes
1½	c. water

1   c. vinegar
12   whole cloves
4   sticks cinnamon
1   c. brown sugar, firmly packed

· Soak prunes in water to cover 1 hour. Drain; add enough water to liquid to make 1½ c.
· Place prunes in hot jars.
· Bring water, with 1 c. vinegar, cloves and cinnamon added, to a boil. Add sugar; boil 12 minutes. Pour over prunes in jars. Adjust lids at once. Process in boiling water bath (212°F.) 20 minutes. Remove jars from canner and complete seals unless closures are the self-sealing type. Makes 2 pints.

Note: Let the prunes stand at least a few weeks before using.

QUINCE PICKLE

Lovely apricot-peach color

8   quinces, peeled, cored and
       quartered
Whole cloves
2   oranges, sliced, seeds removed
6   c. sugar
2   c. vinegar
1   (3″) stick cinnamon
1   apple, peeled, cored, diced

· Cook quinces in a little water until tender; drain, reserving the liquid.
· Stick 2 cloves in each quince piece.
· Combine sliced oranges, sugar, vinegar, 1½ c. liquid from quinces (add water if measure is short), cinnamon and apple. Simmer over low heat 10 minutes. Add quince slices and simmer gently 30 minutes.

· Fill hot jars with fruit and pour on syrup to within ½″ from top. Make certain syrup covers fruit. Adjust lids immediately. Process in boiling water bath (212°F.) 20 minutes. Remove jars from canner and complete seals unless closures are the self-sealing type. Makes 6 pints.

SWEET QUINCE PICKLE

Different and delicious go-with for cold cuts, fowl, meats of all kinds

7   lbs. ripe, yellow quinces
8   c. sugar
2   c. vinegar
1   (3″) stick cinnamon
2   tblsp. mixed pickling spices
2   c. boiling water

· Cut fruit, cored but not peeled, in ⅓″ slices. Weigh. Simmer in a little water until tender. Drain and place in a crock, glass jars, pottery or enamel-lined pan with tight lid.
· Combine sugar, vinegar, spices and boiling water. Bring to a boil and boil 2 minutes. Immediately pour over the fruit. Make certain syrup covers fruit. Cover tightly and store in cool, dark place (or refrigerate if weather is warm) for 14 days. Use as needed. Makes 7 to 8 pints.

Note: Instead of placing cooked fruit in crock, you may heat and pack it into hot pint jars. Pour on boiling syrup to cover fruit; adjust lids at once. Process in boiling water bath (212°F.) 20 minutes (unless refrigerated). Remove jars from canner and complete seals unless closures are the self-sealing type.

PEACH PICKLE

Save syrup after eating pickles. Add to mayonnaise for fruit salads

4	lbs. peaches (about 16 medium)
1	tblsp. whole cloves
2	qts. water
2	tblsp. vinegar
4	c. sugar
1 ½	c. vinegar
¾	c. water
1	tsp. whole ginger
2	(3") sticks cinnamon

• Pour boiling water over peaches; let stand until skins slip off easily when dipped into cold water. Peel.

• Stick a clove in each peach. Pour on 2 qts. water with the 2 tblsp. vinegar added.

• Combine sugar, 1½ c. vinegar and ¾ c. water. Add ginger, remaining cloves and cinnamon tied in clean, thin white cloth. Bring to a boil; add drained peaches; cover, boil until tender, about 10 minutes. Let stand overnight.

• Drain, saving liquid; remove spices. Pack peaches into hot pint jars. Bring syrup to a boil and pour over peaches, leaving ½" head space. Make certain peaches are covered with syrup.

• Adjust lids. Process in boiling water bath (212°F.) 30 minutes.

• Remove jars from canner and complete seals unless closures are self-sealing type. Makes 4 to 5 pints.

PEAR PICKLES

Keep a few jars on your hostess shelf to spice up quick company meals

3 ½	lbs. ripe medium pears

1	qt. water
1	tblsp. vinegar
2 ½	c. sugar
1 ¼	c. vinegar
1	c. water
2	tsp. whole ginger
2	tblsp. whole cloves
7	(3") sticks cinnamon

• Wash, peel and core pears. Place at once in 1 qt. water with 1 tblsp. vinegar added.

• Combine sugar, 1¼ c. vinegar and 1 c. water; bring to a boil. Add spices tied in clean, thin white cloth. Cover; boil 5 minutes. Remove spices. Add pears and simmer 2 minutes. Pack pears in hot pint jars. Add syrup to within ½" from top of jar. Adjust lids. Process in boiling water bath (212°F.) 20 minutes.

• Remove jars from canner and complete seals unless closures are self-sealing type. Makes 3 to 4 pints.

GOURMET GINGER PEARS

A relish to serve with meats; a spread for hot biscuits and toast

4	lbs. fresh pears
⅓	c. finely chopped ginger root
¼	c. fresh lemon juice
5	c. sugar
2	tsp. grated lemon peel
¼	c. vinegar

• Wash, peel, quarter and core pears. (If extra-large, cut them into eighths.)

• Soak ginger in lemon juice while soaking pears.

• Add sugar to pears and mix well to coat each piece. Cover and let stand overnight or 6 to 8 hours.

• Stir lemon-soaked ginger into pears.

• Cook, uncovered, over medium-low heat until pears are tender and clear, about 1 hour, stirring frequently. (Cooking time depends upon ripeness of pears.) Add lemon peel and vinegar the last 5 minutes.

• Pack in hot, sterilized jars, filling to within ½" from top. Adjust lids at once. Process in boiling water bath (212°F.) 20 minutes. Remove jars from canner and complete seals unless closures are the self-sealing type. Makes 7 half pints.

PEAR RELISH

"Deep South" specialty

4	lbs. pears (Kieffer), finely chopped (about 4 c.)
6	medium white onions, finely chopped (about 4½ c.)
3	c. sugar
12	green peppers, finely chopped (about 5 c.)
3	to 5 small hot red or green peppers, finely chopped
3	c. vinegar
2	tblsp. salt
1½	tsp. celery seeds
Whole allspice (optional)	

• Combine all ingredients in large saucepan and bring to a boil. Simmer 30 to 40 minutes, stirring often.

• Ladle into hot jars; adjust lids at once. Process in boiling water bath (212°F.) 5 minutes. Remove jars from canner and complete seals unless closures are the self-sealing type. Makes 6 pints.

PINEAPPLE PICKLES

Good Hawaiian cooks tint the hot syrup red or green with food color

2	medium pineapples
1½	c. sugar
¾	c. water
⅓	c. vinegar
10	whole cloves
1	(3") stick cinnamon

• Cut pineapple in ¼" crosswise slices; peel and remove eyes. Cut slices into quarters; remove cores.

• Combine remaining ingredients and bring to a boil. Add pineapple; simmer 30 minutes. Continue simmering while packing fruit in one hot pint jar at a time, filling each jar with syrup to within ½" from top. Make certain liquid covers fruit. Adjust lids at once. Process in boiling water bath (212°F.) 20 minutes. Remove jars from canner and complete seals unless closures are the self-sealing type. Makes 2 pints.

Watermelon Pickles

"No matter how busy I am in summer, I always make time to put up watermelon and peach pickles," says a Georgia farm woman. "No relish adds more to chicken dinners than one of these favorites."

Through the years this superior cook has made watermelon pickles, she has accumulated knowledge that pickle makers can use. Here are her tips:

The rind of watermelon is better for pickling if the melon is not overripe and if not grown late in the season.

The pink flesh of the melon will not become crisp—leave only a very thin line of pink.

A 16-pound melon yields 5 to 6 pounds of rind. And 1 pound of rind measures 1 quart. One quart of rind makes 1 pint of pickles.

WATERMELON PICKLES

A perfect fried chicken go-with

Rind of 1 (20 lb.) watermelon
1 gal. cold water
2 tblsp. salt
2 c. vinegar
7 c. sugar
1 tblsp. whole cloves
2 or 3 sticks cinnamon

• Choose a melon with thick, firm rind. Trim off outer green skin and pink flesh, leaving a very thin line of pink. Stamp out rind with small cookie cutter or cut into neat squares.

• Soak overnight in brine made of 1 gal. cold water and 2 tblsp. salt. In morning, rinse in cold water and let stand in ice water for 1 hour.

• Drain; cover with boiling water and simmer until tender.

• Prepare syrup of vinegar, sugar and spices tied loosely in clean, thin white cloth. Add drained rind to boiling syrup. Cook gently until rind is clear and transparent. Remove spices. Put rind and syrup into a crock and let stand 24 hours or longer.

• Pack rind in hot pint jars and pour syrup, which has been brought to a boil, over the rind. Adjust lids at once. Process in boiling water bath (212°F.) 5 minutes. Remove jars

from canner and complete seals unless closures are the self-sealing type. Makes 6 pints.

3-DAY WATERMELON PICKLES

They're worth the effort

7 lbs. watermelon rind
Salt water
7 c. sugar
2 c. vinegar
½ tsp. oil of cloves
½ tsp. oil of cinnamon
Red food color (optional)

• Use rind from firm, preferably underripe melon; trim off dark green skin and pink section, leaving a very thin line of pink. Cut into 1″ cubes or circles with a small biscuit cutter or inside of doughnut cutter.

• Soak about 2 hours in salt water to cover (¼ c. salt to 1 qt. water). Drain; rinse, cover with cold water.

• Bring to boil; cook until tender, but not soft (about 10 minutes); drain.

• Combine sugar, vinegar and spices; heat to boiling. Add color if desired. Pour over rind in large glass or pottery bowl; let stand overnight at room temperature; cover with waxed paper.

• In the morning, drain off syrup; heat to boiling and pour back over rind. Let stand overnight.

• On third morning, heat rind in syrup; pack at once in hot jars; adjust lids. Process in boiling water bath (212°F.) 5 minutes. Remove jars from canner and complete seals unless closures are the self-sealing type. Makes 8 pints.

RELISH TRAY: Arrange alternate rows of watermelon pickles, celery hearts and carrot sticks. Or set a sherbet glass of sparkling jelly in center of tray, with watermelon pickles on one side, celery hearts on other.

ROSY WATERMELON PICKLES

A small bottle of maraschino cherries gives pickles a pretty rosy color

4	to 5 qts. watermelon rind
4	qts. water
3	tblsp. salt
3	c. vinegar
2	c. cold water
10	c. sugar
1	tblsp. whole cloves
3	sticks cinnamon
2	tsp. peppercorns
1	piece dried ginger root
½	c. maraschino cherries

· Trim outer green skin and pink flesh from melon leaving a thin line of pink. Cut into 1½ × 1 × ¾" pieces.

· Soak the melon in mixture of 4 qts. water and salt 24 hours. Drain.

· Cover melon pieces with boiling water and boil gently 1½ hours; drain and put melon into ice water until thoroughly chilled. Drain.

· Combine vinegar, 2 c. cold water, sugar and spices tied in clean, thin white cloth, and bring to a boil. Add rind; boil gently about 30 minutes; remove spices. Let stand 24 hours.

· Add maraschino cherries. Bring pickle mixture to a boil; pack in hot jars. Adjust lids at once. Process in boiling water bath (212°F.) 5 minutes. Remove jars from canner and complete seals unless closures are the self-sealing type. Makes 5 pints.

Note: Substitute ½ tsp. oil of cloves for whole cloves; ½ tsp. oil of cinnamon for stick cinnamon. If cherries fade in the jar, substitute a few from a new bottle before serving.

Fruit/Vegetable Relishes

Fruits and vegetables team together in many delightful relishes. None of them are more popular than Victory Relish. It goes by many names in various parts of the country. Some women call it a chutney, others a sauce. Its name is not important—taste is what counts. And just about everyone who samples, praises it and takes a second helping.

VICTORY RELISH

Relish has zip—cut down on spices if you prefer a milder taste

20	large peeled ripe tomatoes
8	pears, peeled and cored
8	peaches, peeled and pitted
6	large onions, peeled
2	sweet red peppers, cored
3	c. vinegar
4	c. sugar
2	tblsp. salt
4	oz. whole pickling spices

· Coarsely chop tomatoes; put pears, peaches, onions and peppers through the coarse blade of food chopper.

· Combine with vinegar, sugar, salt and the spices, which have been tied loosely in clean, thin white cloth.

Cook slowly, stirring occasionally, about 2 hours or until thick.

· Ladle into hot jars. Adjust lids at once. Process in boiling water bath (212°F.) 5 minutes. Remove jars from canner and complete seals unless closures are self-sealing type. Makes about 8 pints.

FRUITED VEGETABLE RELISH

Garden and orchard share honors in this prized relish—extra-good

12	large peeled ripe tomatoes
½	c. diced celery
1	large onion
1	sweet red pepper
1	sweet green pepper
5	peaches
3	pears
1	hot pepper
1	tblsp. mixed pickling spices
2½	c. sugar
1	tblsp. salt
1	c. vinegar

· Dice all vegetables, except hot pepper. Peel and dice peaches and pears.
· Tie pickling spices in clean, thin white cloth. Mix all ingredients. Cook slowly until thick (approximately 2 hours). Remove hot pepper and spices.
· Ladle into hot jars; adjust lids at once. Process in boiling water bath (212°F.) 5 minutes. Remove jars from canner and complete seals unless closures are self-sealing type. Makes 4½ pints.

INDIA RELISH

Good with hamburgers or in them

14	ripe tomatoes, peeled
12	tart apples, peeled
7	small onions, peeled
1	sweet red pepper, seeded
1	c. raisins
2	tsp. salt
1	c. sugar
2	c. vinegar

· Chop coarsely the tomatoes, apples, onions and pepper.
· Combine all ingredients and cook slowly, stirring occasionally, 1½ hours or until mixture is thick and clear.
· Ladle into hot jars; adjust lids at once. Process in boiling water bath (212°F.) 5 minutes. Remove jars from canner and complete seals unless closures are the self-sealing type. Makes about 7 pints.

TOMATO/APPLE RELISH

Apples and tomatoes are flavorful companions in this spicy treat

2	qts. chopped peeled ripe tomatoes
1	c. chopped white onion
1	c. sliced celery
2	c. diced tart apples
2	sweet green peppers, cored and chopped
2	sweet red peppers, cored and chopped
1½	c. vinegar
2¾	c. sugar
1	tblsp. salt
2	tblsp. white mustard seeds
½	tblsp. whole cloves
1	tblsp. whole cinnamon

· Combine ingredients; tie the spices loosely in clean, thin white cloth. Cook slowly, stirring occasionally, 2 hours or until mixture is thick and clear. Discard spices.

· Ladle into hot jars; adjust lids at once. Process in boiling water bath (212°F.) 5 minutes. Remove jars from canner and complete seals unless closures are the self-sealing type. Makes about 3 pints.

GOLDEN RELISH

Voted "very good" by taste-testers

4   c. chopped carrots
4   c. chopped celery
2   sweet green peppers, chopped
2   sweet red peppers, chopped
8   unpeeled apples, cored and chopped
2   lbs. sugar
2   c. vinegar
2   c. water
2   tsp. celery seeds
2   tblsp. coarse pickling salt

· Combine all ingredients; bring to a boil and simmer until carrots are tender, about 45 minutes.
· Pour into hot jars; adjust lids at once. Process in boiling water bath (212°F.) 5 minutes. Remove jars from canner and complete seals unless closures are the self-sealing type. Makes 6 pints.

Red Relish Sauces

Of all the relish sauces, chili sauce and ketchup have the widest circle of friends. Country cooks like to make them with ripe tomatoes so heavy that they are about to drop from the vines. Their full flavors produce marvelous sauces. A pair of recipes for each follows.

It's a good idea to wrap the filled jars with brown paper before putting them away. Excluding the light helps to retain their cheerful color.

EASTERN CHILI SAUCE

New Englanders like to serve this at their famed baked bean suppers

22   medium tomatoes
1 ½   c. vinegar
2   tsp. whole cloves
1   tsp. broken stick cinnamon
1   tsp. celery seeds
1   c. sugar
1   tblsp. chopped onion
½   tsp. ground red pepper
1   tblsp. salt

· Wash, peel and quarter tomatoes.
· Combine vinegar, cloves, cinnamon and celery seeds. Bring to a boil; remove from heat and let stand.
· Combine half of tomatoes with ½ c. sugar, onion and red pepper in large kettle. Boil 30 minutes, stirring frequently.
· Add remaining tomatoes and sugar to boiling tomato mixture. Boil vigorously 30 more minutes, stirring often. Strain vinegar and discard spices.
· Add spiced vinegar and salt to tomato mixture and cook, stirring constantly, about 15 minutes or until of desired consistency. Pour into hot jars; adjust lids at once. Process in boiling water bath (212°F.) 5 minutes. Remove jars from canner and complete seals unless closures are the self-sealing type. Makes 2 pints.

WESTERN CHILI SAUCE

Piquant relish to serve with meats

2 ½   qts. diced peeled ripe
        tomatoes
½   c. finely chopped green
        pepper
2   medium onions, finely chopped
1 ½   c. vinegar
⅓   c. sugar
2   tblsp. salt
1   or 2 hot chili peppers
2   tsp. ground cloves
2   tsp. ground cinnamon
2   tsp. ground allspice
2   tsp. grated nutmeg (optional)

• Combine all the ingredients. Heat gradually to boiling point; simmer 1 hour, or to desired consistency.
• Pour into hot jars; adjust lids at once. Process in boiling water bath (212°F.) 5 minutes. Remove jars from canner and complete seals unless closures are the self-sealing type. Makes about 2½ pints.

Note: You may wish to add more onion, and to use ½ c. sugar.

TOMATO KETCHUP

You can double recipe but cooking time may be longer, ketchup darker

32   medium tomatoes (8 lbs.)
1   c. sliced onions
¼   tsp. ground red pepper
1   c. vinegar
1 ½   tsp. whole cloves
1 ½   tsp. broken stick cinnamon
½   tsp. whole allspice
1   tsp. celery seeds

½   c. sugar
4   tsp. salt

• Cut washed tomatoes in quarters; combine with onions and red pepper. Cook, uncovered, 20 minutes, stirring occasionally.
• Combine vinegar and spices in kettle. Bring to a boil; remove from heat. Let stand.
• Put tomato mixture through food mill or sieve. Combine with sugar and cook, stirring frequently, until volume is reduced one half (about 1¼ hours).
• Strain vinegar to remove spices. Add salt to vinegar and stir into tomato mixture. Continue boiling, uncovered, until thick, stirring (about ½ hour).
• Pour into hot jars; adjust lids at once. Process in boiling water bath (212°F.) 10 minutes. Remove jars from canner and complete seals unless closures are the self-sealing type. Makes about 2 pints.

GRANDMOTHER'S SHIRLEY SAUCE

Unspiced, tangy sweet-sour—perfect teammate for beef

12   large tomatoes
2   large green peppers
2   large onions
2   c. sugar
2   c. vinegar
2   tblsp. salt

• Peel and cut up tomatoes; chop peppers and peeled onions.
• Combine ingredients; simmer 2 hours.
• Pack into hot jars; adjust lids at once. Process in boiling water bath (212°F.) 5 minutes. Remove jars from canner and complete seals unless closures are self-sealing. Makes 3 pints.

WESTERN GOURMET KETCHUP

A ranch hostess puts this up to pass at barbecues—it makes a hit

7	qts. tomato purée (18 lbs. tomatoes)
3	tblsp. salt
⅔	c. sugar
1	tblsp. paprika
¼	tsp. ground red pepper
1	tblsp. dry mustard
1	tblsp. peppercorns
1	tblsp. whole allspice
1	tblsp. mustard seeds
4	bay leaves
4	chili peppers (small hot peppers with pointed ends)
1	tblsp. basil leaves
2	c. vinegar

· Add all the ingredients, except the vinegar, to the tomato purée (tomatoes cooked until soft and put through a sieve). Spices should be tied loosely in clean, thin white cloth and mustard blended in a little tomato juice to prevent formation of lumps. Cook until thick, about 1½ hours.
· Add vinegar the last 10 minutes.
· Remove spices. Pour into hot jars; adjust lids at once. Process in boiling water bath (212°F.) 10 minutes. Remove jars from canner and complete seals unless closures are the self-sealing type. Makes 4 pints.

BLENDER-MADE KETCHUP

One Wisconsin country woman lets her blender chop the vegetables when she makes ketchup. She practically eliminates pot watching and stirring by cooking the tomato mixture in the oven. If you have an electric saucepan, oven roaster or a controlled surface unit or burner on your range, it also will cut out the necessity of constant watching and stirring.

BLENDER KETCHUP

Use dead-ripe tomatoes, white vinegar, and spices in thin white cloth

48	medium tomatoes (8 lbs.)
2	ripe sweet red peppers
2	sweet green peppers
4	onions
3	c. vinegar
3	c. sugar
3	tblsp. salt
3	tsp. dry mustard
½	tsp. ground red pepper
1½	tsp. whole allspice
1½	tsp. whole cloves
1½	tsp. broken stick cinnamon

· Quarter tomatoes; remove stem ends. Add peppers, seeded and cut in strips, and onions, peeled and quartered. Mix.
· Put vegetables in blender, filling three fourths full. Blend at high speed 4 seconds; pour into large kettle. Repeat until all vegetables are blended.
· Add vinegar, sugar, salt, dry mustard, red pepper and remaining spices, tied loosely in clean, thin white cloth. Simmer, uncovered, in slow oven (325°F.) or in electric saucepan until volume is reduced one half. Remove spices.
· Pour into hot jars. Adjust lids. Process in boiling water bath (212°F.) 10 minutes. Remove jars from canner and complete seals unless closures are the self-sealing type. Makes 5 pints.

VARIATION

BLENDER APPLE/TOMATO KETCHUP: Add 2 c. thick applesauce to the cooked ketchup and mix thoroughly.

KETCHUP WITHOUT BLENDER

Use same ingredients as in recipe above.

• Quarter tomatoes, peel onions and discard stems and seeds from peppers. Chop. Cook until tender, about 15 minutes. Put through food mill.

• Add remaining ingredients and simmer until you have half the amount you started with, or the consistency you like. The yield is less than if you use the blender. Recipe makes 3 pints.

VARIATION

APPLE/TOMATO KETCHUP: Add about 1 c. thick applesauce.

HOMEMADE FRUIT KETCHUP

Makes a good sandwich spread, but also use it like tomato ketchup

12	tart apples, cored and thinly sliced
2	medium onions, finely chopped
1	c. sugar
1	tsp. pepper
1	tsp. salt
1	tsp. dry mustard
1	tsp. ground cloves
1	tsp. ground cinnamon
¼	tsp. ground allspice
1 ½	c. vinegar
½	c. water

• Cook apples, covered with water, until tender. Put through sieve.

• Add remaining ingredients, cook over low heat, stirring often until thick, about 2½ hours.

• Pour into hot jars; adjust lids at once. Process in boiling water bath (212°F.) 10 minutes. Remove jars from canner and complete seals unless closures are the self-sealing type. Makes 5½ pints.

GOVERNOR'S SAUCE

Makes a pot roast meal special

14	lbs. tomatoes, slightly ripe
½	c. salt
1	medium head cabbage
6	large unpeeled red apples
6	large sweet green peppers
6	large sweet red peppers
6	c. sugar
1	qt. vinegar
1	(1 ½ oz.) pkg. mixed pickling spices

• Grind tomatoes; cover with ¼ c. salt; let stand 3 hours. Drain.

• Coarsely grind cabbage, apples and peppers. Add to tomatoes.

• Add ¼ c. salt, sugar, vinegar and pickling spices tied in clean, thin white cloth. Cook for 30 minutes; remove spices. Let stand overnight. Reheat to boiling point.

• Pour at once into hot jars; adjust lids at once. Process in boiling water bath (212°F.) 10 minutes. Remove jars from canner and complete seals unless closures are the self-sealing type. Makes about 12 pints.

GRAPE KETCHUP

Another relish that perks up meals

5	lbs. Concord grapes

½   c. water
5   c. sugar
2   c. vinegar
1   tsp. salt
½   c. mixed pickling spices

• Cover grapes with water; bring to a boil. Put through colander, sieve or food mill—should be 9 c. pulp. Stir in sugar, vinegar and salt.

• Tie spices in clean, thin white cloth; add to grape pulp. Cook slowly until thick, stirring occasionally. Remove spices. Pour into hot jars; adjust lids at once. Process in boiling water bath (212°F.) 5 minutes. Remove jars from canner and complete seals unless closures are the self-sealing type. Store in cool, dark place. Makes about 4 pints.

OLD-FASHIONED KETCHUP

"It tastes like the gooseberry ketchup Mother used to make," reports the farm homemaker who tested the following recipe for us. "And it has the same tantalizing aroma while cooking."

If you have wild gooseberries on your farm, use them almost ripe for this recipe. They give the ketchup some of their red color—make it so much more tempting, advises our tester. She adds: "We think the sauce tastes better made with the wild fruit than with cultivated berries."

Even if you gather your berries from the garden, you'll want to put up a few jars of the spicy relish to serve with pork and other meats. People who like the piquant gooseberry flavor will especially enjoy this country relish.

GOOSEBERRY KETCHUP

While this old-fashioned relish cooks, it has mincemeat's spicy aroma

2   qts. ripe gooseberries
2   qts. green gooseberries
2   c. sugar
2   c. vinegar
1   tblsp. ground cloves
1   tblsp. ground cinnamon
1   tblsp. ground allspice

• Mix all ingredients together. Bring to a boil and simmer until thick. Put through medium coarse sieve. If it is not thick enough, simmer until desired consistency. Pack at once in hot jars; adjust lids. Process in boiling water bath (212°F.) 5 minutes. Remove jars from canner and complete seals unless closures are the self-sealing type. Makes 4 half pints.

CRANBERRY KETCHUP

Quick to cook, beautiful color

4   lbs. cranberries
1   lb. onions, peeled
2   c. water
4   c. sugar
2   c. vinegar
1   tblsp. ground cloves
1   tblsp. ground cinnamon
1   tblsp. ground allspice
1   tblsp. salt
1   tsp. pepper

• Cook cranberries and onions in water until tender. Put through food mill.

• Add remaining ingredients, boil and stir until thick, about 8 minutes.

• Pour into hot jars. Adjust lids at once. Process in boiling water bath (212°F.) 5 minutes. Remove jars from canner and complete seals unless closures are self-sealing. Makes 5 pints.

CRANBERRY PICKLE SAUCE

Thick relish with fine flavor—it gets along famously with meats

4	c. cranberries
1⅓	c. sugar
½	c. vinegar
½	tsp. ground cinnamon
½	tsp. ground nutmeg
½	tsp. ground cloves

• Combine cranberries, sugar and vinegar; allow to come slowly to a boil. Cook until all cranberries burst.
• Add spices. Cook over low heat 15 minutes. Reduce heat to simmer the last 5 minutes. Pour into hot pint jar. Adjust lid at once. Process in boiling water bath (212°F.) 5 minutes. Remove jar from canner and complete seal unless closure is the self-sealing type. Makes 1 pint.

Country-Style Chutneys

You don't have to travel to India to enjoy chutneys. Country cooks make American versions of these highly spiced relishes from fruits they have—cranberries, for instance. Traditionally, you serve them with curried dishes—a splendid combination. But they're excellent with almost all chicken and rice combinations.

"When I hear the children at play rattling in autumn's fallen leaves," says a FARM JOURNAL reader, "I know it's time to make Apple/Tomato Chutney. We think it's tops with poultry and pork and I like to take it to covered dish suppers." Here is the recipe for it and several others.

APPLE/TOMATO CHUTNEY

A souvenir of autumn for Christmas giving—your friends will like it

12	large unpeeled apples
12	large peeled onions
12	large peeled tomatoes
3	c. sugar
4	c. vinegar
1	tsp. ground cinnamon
1	tsp. dry mustard
½	tsp. ground cloves
¼	tsp. pepper
¼	c. salt

• Wash and core apples; put through coarse blade of food chopper with onions; cut tomatoes in eighths.
• Put ingredients in a large kettle. Simmer slowly, stirring until thick.
• Ladle into hot jars; adjust lids at once. Process in boiling water bath (212°F.) 5 minutes. Remove jars from canner and complete seals unless closures are the self-sealing type. Makes about 10 pints.

APPLE CHUTNEY

Just right for chicken or game dinner

8	c. chopped peeled apples
2	c. seeded light raisins
Peel of 2 oranges, finely chopped	
4½	c. sugar
½	c. vinegar
⅓	tsp. ground cloves
1	c. chopped pecans (optional)

• Combine all ingredients, except nuts, in large saucepan. Bring to a rolling boil and reduce heat to simmer. Cook until apples are tender. Add pecans.
• Remove from heat and ladle into hot jars; adjust lids at once. Process in boiling water bath (212°F.) 5 minutes. Remove jars from canner

and complete seals unless closures are the self-sealing type. Makes 7½ pints.

HAWAIIAN CHUTNEY

Spicy-hot with sweet, fruity taste

1	(1 lb. 13 oz.) can crushed pineapple
4	c. chopped peeled apples
½	c. vinegar
½	c. light brown sugar, firmly packed
1	c. seeded light raisins
1½	tsp. salt
2	tblsp. candied ginger, finely chopped
2	medium cloves garlic, mashed
½	tsp. ground red pepper
½	tsp. ground cloves
½	tsp. ground cinnamon
½	c. slivered almonds (optional)

· Combine all ingredients except nuts.
· Cook over low heat, stirring often, for 30 minutes. Add almonds.
· Ladle into hot jars; adjust lids at once. Process in boiling water bath (212°F.) 5 minutes. Remove jars from canner and complete seals unless closures are the self-sealing type. Makes 6 half pints.

PEACH CHUTNEY

Complements rice and meat casseroles

4	qts. chopped peaches
1	c. chopped onions
1	clove garlic, chopped
1	pod hot pepper
1	c. raisins
1	qt. vinegar
2	tblsp. ground ginger

¼	c. mustard seeds
3	c. brown sugar, firmly packed
2	tsp. salt

· Mix ingredients, cook until thick.
· Pour into hot jars; adjust lids at once. Process in boiling water bath (212°F.) 5 minutes. Remove jars from canner and complete seals unless closures are the self-sealing type. Makes 8 pints.

PEACH/LIME CHUTNEY

Lime juice lends a distinctive tang. Good with cold meats, chicken, turkey, pork, also with rice casseroles

5	lbs. fresh peaches
½	lb. seeded raisins
½	lb. dates, chopped
1	lemon, quartered, thinly sliced
2	c. vinegar
¼	c. fresh lime juice
3	c. sugar
½	c. candied ginger, coarsely cut
½	c. nut meats (optional)

· Scald peaches in hot water for 30 seconds; dip in cold water; slip off skins. Dice peaches. Add raisins, dates, lemon, vinegar and lime juice.
· Cook mixture slowly until peaches are tender; stir to prevent scorching.
· Add sugar; cook over low heat until chutney has thickened, about 1½ hours. Stir in ginger (½ tsp. powdered ginger may be added for a stronger chutney). Add nut meats.
· Ladle chutney into hot jars; adjust lids at once. Process in boiling water bath (212°F.) 5 minutes. Remove jars from canner and complete seals unless closures are the self-sealing type. Makes 5 pints.

CHAPTER 15

CURING MEAT, POULTRY, FISH

Tips on Curing Meats · Sugar-Cured Ham and Bacon · Home-Cured Corned Beef · Smoked Chicken, Turkey, Fish · Recipes for Baked Ham, "Boiled" Ham, Glazes for Ham, Creamed Country Ham and Slick Tricks with Ham · Recipes for Making Sausage

When it's time to decorate the living room with holly and bring out glitter to hang on the Christmas tree, some farmers hang sugar-cured hams and bacon in the smokehouse. These early birds know that meat cured in November, December or January will be aging before spring arrives, bringing spoilage hazards from warm weather and insect pests.

These days, many other farmers have their meats custom-cured commercially. Still others freeze meats to bring out, thaw and cure when needed. But thousands of families still fix their hams and bacons and many of them do a good business selling country-style meats.

Ask the expert in home curing what he does to get good results and you'll find he follows rules. This chapter contains these rules and up-to-date directions based on research. One Kentucky farmer who cures excellent meat, explains his philosophy like this: "Curing is a race between salt and bacteria reaching the center of the meat. I try to help salt get there first."

This chapter also contains directions for making country-style sausage and corned beef, and for smoking poultry and fish.

People have different ideas on aging ham, depending largely on where they live. But just about everyone agrees that cured meats deserve priority in real country meals.

Sugar-Cured and Hickory-Smoked Meats
BEST CALL TO BREAKFAST

When a blizzard strikes in early morning and there are outdoor chores to do, about the happiest thing a farmer can face is a good country breakfast. With pan-fried ham, sizzling sausage cakes or ribbons of hickory-flavored bacon on the platter, the day gets off to a good start, regardless of the weather.

Tips on Curing Meats

The flavors of home-cured hams and bacon depend on a number of things. Temperature is of prime importance, not only chilling after slaughtering, before cutting the meat, but also during the curing and smoking. If the smokehouse goes much over 100°F., the heat destroys the enzymes in meat that develop the aging flavors so many people especially like.

Smoking does more than give flavor. It reduces insect damage; the fat does not become rancid so quickly. When smoked in stockinet covers, hams hold a better shape.

During the aging, the salt in hams and shoulders increases as the moisture content decreases. This increase helps to prevent spoilage in summer.

It is important to keep meats, when they come from the cure, in a *cool place several days to give the salt time to penetrate throughout.* Failure to do this is one of the main reasons for spoilage, especially of hams.

Salt does not penetrate until it dissolves in the moisture of the meat. Since the salt in the cure draws out the most moisture the first few days of curing, it is desirable to apply the Sugar-Cure Mixture to hams three times instead of rubbing it on once.

Salt provides the cure. *Sugar* adds flavor and helps to retard the hardening action of salt. *Saltpeter* brings out and retains the rich reddish color of meat that is so appealing in hams and shoulders and in that Southern delicacy, red-eye gravy. A lean meat-type hog makes the best cured meat.

Commercially prepared curing mixtures may be used. They may contain antioxidants to improve color and retard rancidity. They save the bother of mixing ingredients.

We give the following directions in detail. Do heed them for top-quality cured meats.

STEPS TO SUCCESS WITH SUGAR-CURE

Here are the directions for curing pork, recommended by North Carolina State University:

1. Chill meat quickly and keep it cold. If hogs are to be killed on farm, check the weather forecast; kill when your weatherman says: "Light frost tonight." Also keep it cold, 38 to 40°F., during the curing. Higher temperatures may cause spoilage; lower temperatures may interfere with the penetration of salt. If temperatures

fall below freezing for several days during the curing, add the same number of days to the curing time.

2. Weigh the meat and the ingredients for the Sugar-Cure Mixture. Salt is the most important one. Use exact amount of *medium granulated or flake salt* (often called bag or sack salt)— *do not use iodized salt.* Too little salt causes spoilage, while too much makes meat dry, hard and oversalty.

3. Allow enough curing time for the meat to absorb the salt.

4. Keep track of the curing time. If you cut it short, the meat may spoil. When it is too long, the meat loses quality.

5. Keep meat under refrigeration or let it hang in a cold place (38 to 45°F.) after curing to dry and to give the salt time to spread evenly through the meat.

SUGAR-CURE MIXTURE

8 lbs. medium granulated salt
3 lbs. white or light brown
      granulated sugar
3 oz. saltpeter

• Mix the ingredients, using care to distribute saltpeter evenly through the salt. *Use 1¼ to 1½ oz. of mix per pound of ham and ¾ to 1 oz. per pound of bacon.*

Dry Curing Hams and Shoulders: Rub on half the Sugar-Cure Mixture as soon as you cut the meat. You need not rub it a lot; just be sure the salt covers the surface. Use care not to break the outside membranes, or the hams may become hard and dry during aging. Pack some of mixture in

the shank end. Place meat in a clean box, barrel or stone jar, or use the shelf-curing method which follows. It gives the most even cure. On the third day, rub on half the remaining Sugar-Cure Mixture and repeat on the tenth day. Use care not to knock salt off ham. Treat shoulder cuts like ham.

Leave meat in the cure 2 days for each pound of meat, but never less than 25 days.

Dry Curing Bacon on Shelf: Rub the Sugar-Cure Mixture on pork sides at one time. Cover the bacon with the mixture, patting more of it on the thicker pieces of meat. Stack one upon another with skin side down. *Cure bacon 1½ days for each pound of meat or 7 days per 1″ of thickness.*

END OF CURING PERIOD

1. Remove cured meat from the dry pack. Brush the lighter cuts to remove excess salt. Hold them under refrigeration or in a *cold* place (36 to 45°F.) until heavier cuts are cured.

If you do not desire a smoky flavor, brush off any excess salt and hang the meat in a cold place at least a week; 3 weeks is better. If you wish to smoke the meat, soak the hams and shoulders in cold water from 1½ to 2 hours; bacon, 30 minutes. Put strong cord through ham and shoulder shanks and tie; hang from cord to dry in a cold place, at least a week, but 3 weeks is desirable.

Reinforce flank end of bacon with hardwood skewer or clean, galvanized wire to hold it square when hung by strong cord.

SMOKING HAMS AND BACON

2. Scrub the hung meat with a stiff brush and water so it will take a brighter color in smoking. Let it dry overnight to avoid streaking. A wet surface will not take on even color.

3. Hang the dry meat in the smoke-house so that no two pieces touch. Build under it a fire of any green hardwood, like hickory, oak, pecan or apple—or use corncobs or hardwood sawdust. Do not use resinous woods like pine and other evergreens.

The ideal temperature for the smokehouse is between 80 and 90°F. Open the ventilator to let the moisture escape. On the second day, close the ventilators and smoke meat until it has the color you like best, light or dark mahogany or chestnut brown. Usually two days of smoking is enough. Remember that a thin haze of smoke is as effective as a dense cloud. Use care not to overheat the meat.

STORING CURED MEATS

Cool the hams, shoulders and bacon: Sprinkle with black pepper, mixed with a little red pepper, if desired.

Pack meat in cotton bag: Put 6 to 7"

crumpled newspaper in the bottom of a clean, tightly woven cotton bag and add the meat. Stuff more paper loosely around the meat to hold it away from the bag. Do not pack the bag tightly. Tie the cloth bag securely to keep out insects. Hang by strings attached to meat. If bags are airtight, meats will spoil.

Hang smoked meats in a dry place to help control mold. Mold on hams and bacon makes them unattractive.

Aging: Hang the hams to age in a tight, cool, dry, well-ventilated room for at least 6 months. Shoulders should be used before 6 months. A good aging temperature is from 70 to 80°F. Below 45°F., little or no aging flavor develops. Many farmers keep their hams a year or longer. When a ham is a year old, it becomes an "old country ham." Hams over a year old tend to get hard and the fat may get rancid. Their flavor is more pronounced. Only heavy hams (over 25 lbs. at start of curing process) should be aged more than a year.

To stop aging, you can put the meat in cold storage, or cut, wrap and freeze it. For best flavor, do not keep ham, if frozen, longer than 3 months. Both treatments protect meat from insect and rodent damage.

Home-Cured Corned Beef

Combine home-cured corned beef with potatoes for the world's best hash. Top it with poached eggs, add a green vegetable and a fruit salad. Dinner is ready!

Fat animals make the best corned beef. Use the fatter cuts like the flank,

plate, chuck and rump. Remove all the bones so meat can be packed in even layers.

Cut meat in pieces about 6" square, uniformly thick. Cool meat and start the corning as soon as possible. Meat that is not really fresh may sour during the curing. Do not corn meat that is frozen.

1. Weigh meat. For each 100 lbs. allow 8 lbs. granulated salt (not iodized table salt).

2. Sprinkle a layer of salt ¼" deep in bottom of clean stone jar or wooden barrel.

3. Pack meat pieces as closely as possible, in a layer 5 to 6" thick.

4. Alternate layers of salt and meat, covering the top layer of meat with considerable salt.

5. Let the salted meat stand overnight.

6. In the morning, make a brine as follows: For 100 lbs. meat, use 4 lbs. sugar, 2 oz. baking soda, 4 oz. saltpeter. Dissolve in 1 gal. of lukewarm water. Add 3 gals. of cold water. Pour brine over meat.

7. Weight the meat down to keep it under the brine. Use a loose board cover with a weight on it. If any meat is not covered with brine, both the meat and the brine will spoil quickly.

8. Keep the meat in a cool place (under 45°F.), for the sugar in the brine has a tendency to ferment.

9. Keep the meat in the brine for 28 to 40 days to get a good cure.

10. Watch the brine closely for signs of spoilage. If it starts to appear ropy or stringy, remove the meat and wash vigorously with a stiff brush and warm water. Then repack, as previously, only use 6 lbs. of salt (instead of 8 lbs.) for the meat. Cover with new brine.

11. You can keep the beef in the brine until used. Or remove it, wash, drain and smoke, or can. (See chapter on Home Canning: Meat, Poultry and Game.)

Note: Beef corned in winter for use in summer is more likely to spoil in the spring than in any other season.

Smoked Chicken
THE WAY VIRGINIANS LIKE IT

These directions for smoking chickens were developed by the Poultry Husbandry Department, Virginia Polytechnic Institute:

1. Eviscerate chickens, wash thoroughly and cool to 38°F. Use your thermometer.

2. Dissolve 5 lbs. granulated salt, 5 lbs. sugar and 2 oz. saltpeter in 7 gals. water that has been boiled and cooled. Place in clean, scalded stone jar. Add approximately 25 lbs. chicken.

3. Let chickens remain in cure 1¼ days for every pound of chicken. Cure the chickens in a cool place (38°F.).

4. Remove birds from cure, wash in cool water (running water, if available) 30 minutes. Let birds drip dry.

5. Place chickens in stockinet and hang breast side down in smokehouse, 5 to 6' above source of smoke. Smoke 4 to 5 hours or until chickens reach the desired degree of brown color.

6. Roast the birds like fresh chicken; or cool, package and freeze for later use. Serve hot or cold.

Postscript: Hickory smoke gives the best flavor.

Smoked Turkey
THE WAY CALIFORNIA RANCHERS FIX IT

Turkeys, smoked by the following directions, have a decided, smokehouse flavor. They generally are enjoyed more for snacks and appetizers than for meat in a meal.

1. Cure the prepared turkeys in brine for 2 to 3 weeks before smoking. Remove feathers, viscera, crop, the entire neck and all superfluous tissues from inside pockets and cavities. Wash thoroughly. Remove the leg tendons to permit better penetration of the brine.

2. To make brine for 100 lbs. of turkeys, dressed weight, add to 18 gals. water: 25 lbs. salt, 12½ lbs. white or brown sugar, 12½ oz. saltpeter.

3. Place turkeys in a clean wood barrel (do not use metal container) and cover them with brine. Weight turkeys down to keep them from floating. Keep the temperature of the brine as near *38°F. as possible.* Leave them in the brine 1¼ days for each pound of bird, but not less than 2 weeks nor more than 3.

After the fourth day of curing, remove turkeys and thoroughly mix the solution. Repack the birds, interchanging the top and bottom turkeys. Repeat this process every 7 days during the curing.

Remove turkeys from brine and wash them thoroughly. Hang to drain in a cool place for 24 hours.

To smoke, hang turkeys by the drumsticks. Enlarge the openings at both ends slightly, propping them open for ventilation. Let birds hang without smoke for 6 hours in a warm place, 110°F. Then smoke them at a temperature of 110°F. for 20 hours or at 140°F. for 16 hours. The higher temperature gives more attractive color, but slightly increases shrinkage.

To store turkeys, hang them in a cool, dry place, with a temperature no higher than 68°F. They will keep from 1 to 2 weeks. If mold or yeast develops in the turkey cavity, swab it out with cotton saturated with 95% alcohol.

To cook turkeys, soak them in cold water 2 hours or longer, changing the water once. Roast them as you would fresh turkeys and serve hot or cold.

Wisconsin Smoked Fish
A TASTY WAY TO STORE THE CATCH

Many farm families have ardent fishermen who proudly bring home their catch. While most of the fish usually are enjoyed at once, or frozen, many people like the variety smoked fish adds to meals. Country cooks find their smoky flavor seasons many dishes delightfully. They add bits of the fish to scalloped potatoes and eggs, to scrambled eggs and potato salad, for instance. And on crackers, it makes a snack most men relish.

Equipment for Smoking Fish. If a smokehouse is not available, use a barrel with head removed. Remove about 1 foot from the lower end of one stave to permit stoking the fire in the pit below. If you do not have a barrel, use a cardboard carton about 30″ square and 48″ high. Remove one end from the carton; this makes the bottom of the improvised smokehouse. Unfasten the flaps on the opposite end so they can be folded back and used as a cover. You can strengthen them, if you find it necessary, by tacking ¾″ strips of wood vertically on the outside of each corner, and horizontally on the sides, top and bottom, to make it sturdy. On one side of the carton slash down 12″ in two places 10″ apart. By folding this piece up, you have an adjustable flap "door."

Prevent Fire. Control the ventilation and keep the fire covered to make smoke, not flames. Then the carton will not catch on fire. Keep door and top flaps closed during smoking, letting just enough air enter to keep the fire smoldering.

Suspend Rods in Barrel or Carton. Space iron or wooden rods across top of the "smokehouse" far enough apart that the fish do not touch when hung. Or use a rack of coarse wire instead of rods. If you place a tray of wire mesh below fish when hung, it will catch any that may fall off during smoking.

Make Wire Hooks. You can use 8 or 10″ gauge steel wire about 14″ long. Make a hook in the center of the wire large enough to slide over the rods. Bend the ends so fish will not slip off during smoking. Or use wire coat hangers; cut off the bottom cross wires, bend ends to form hooks.

Prepare Fish. Scale and dress fish, remove heads but leave collarbones attached. Wash thoroughly. Split fish to the back skin, but not through it. Cut large fish into steaks.

Place Fish in Brine. If fish are caught and cleaned in the evening for smoking the next day, let them stand in a brine overnight. As they are dressed, place them in a stone jar or an enameled container, in brine made of 1½ c. salt to 1 gal. water. When all the fish are dressed, remove them from the brine; drain. Lay them flat, flesh side up, in an enameled pan or crock (do not use metal) and salt each piece, using a salt shaker. Cover with waxed paper and store in the refrigerator or a very cold place overnight. In the morning, drain and rinse fish and let excess moisture drip off for 15 minutes before placing over fire.

If you catch and smoke the fish the same day, prepare them and place in a brine made of 4 c. salt to 1 gal. water. Leave in brine ½ to 1 hour, depending on size and thickness of fish. Remove from brine, rinse in cold, fresh water. Drain about 10 minutes and let hang in a breezy place about an hour. They are ready for smoking.

Fire for Smoking. Use oak, hickory, maple, alder, beech, apple, white birch or ash to make fire. Or use corncobs. Do not use wood containing resin. Cut wood pieces about 8″ long and 1″ in diameter. Sawdust burns slowly and makes a good smudge. Too much smoke overdoes the smoke flavor. Kindle the fire in pit under barrel or carton, using care to have it smoldering with smoke; do not let it flame. Stoke fire every half hour or as needed.

String Fish on Hooks. Thread them on wire just below the collarbone. This holds them flat and increases the capacity of the barrel or carton. It also makes for even smoking. Hang the hooks on the rods and space them evenly so that the fish do not touch.

Use Hot Smoke or Cold Smoke. Take your choice of methods.

Hot Smoke: Keep the temperature at the fish level at 100°F. for the first 4 or 5 hours of smoking. Hold your hand at the fish level. It should feel barely warm so the fish will dry slowly. Increase to about 180 to 200°F. for about an hour to cook fish. They are done when the backbone separates from the meat. Remove and cool—ready to eat.

Cold Smoke: Follow directions for Hot Smoke but do not use the high temperature at the end. These fish must be cooked before eating.

Store Properly: Keep fish in refrigerator or a cold place until used. Or wrap them and freeze.

Note: Some farmers use a barrel, set on the side of a hill, for the smokehouse. A stove pipe from a fire below carries the smoke. They remove both ends of the barrel and insert a wire shelf near the top; they cover the barrel top with burlap.

Note: To can smoked fish, process in pressure cooker at 10 pounds pressure (240°F.) 1 hour and 40 minutes.

Baked and Boiled Country Ham

To prepare for cooking: Wash and scrub ham with a stiff brush. Trim off dry, hard, dark edges. Cover with cold water and soak for 12 to 14 hours. You can skip the soaking with well-cured hams of good quality, but most homemakers prefer to soak them.

BAKED COUNTRY-STYLE HAM

1. Place the prepared ham, skin side up, on rack in open pan.
2. Bake uncovered (without adding water) in a slow oven (300°F.) until tender or until meat thermometer registers 170°F. Insert it in meat so bulb touches no bone or fat. Allow 25 to 30 minutes per pound for whole hams, 45 to 50 minutes per pound for butts.

3. Serve the ham, or remove the skin and glaze ham by directions that follow.

"BOILED" COUNTRY-STYLE HAM

1. Place prepared ham on rack in kettle and cover with boiling water. Add 1 tblsp. molasses or brown sugar to each quart water, if desired.
2. Simmer, *but do not boil,* until ham is tender and thermometer registers 160°F. Let ham cool in broth. It will finish cooking as it cools. Although the ham is cooked in simmering (not boiling) water, it is called "boiled ham."
3. When ham is cool, remove skin, chill and serve or add a glaze and bake 30 minutes.

GLAZING COUNTRY-STYLE HAM

1. Use sharp knife to remove skin from baked or "boiled" ham. Score in 1 or 2" squares down to meat surface.
2. Cover with glaze (see directions).
3. Stick long-stemmed clove into each square.
4. Bake in a moderate to hot oven (375 to 400°F.) 15 to 30 minutes or until surface is browned and glazed.

GLAZES FOR COUNTRY-STYLE HAM

HONEY/CHERRY: Baste ham while it bakes with strained honey, to which you have added chopped maraschino cherries or the cherry juice.

MUSTARD: Coat ham with thin layer of prepared mustard; sprinkle generously with brown sugar.

PEACH: Coat ham with brown sugar and baste with peach pickle juice (or spiced crab apple juice).

CIDER: Coat ham with brown sugar and baste with sweet cider.

PINEAPPLE: Mix 1 c. drained crushed pineapple and 1 c. brown sugar, firmly packed. Spread over ham. Baste often with syrup from canned pineapple.

BROWN SUGAR SYRUP: Baste ham while it bakes with syrup made by boiling 1 c. brown sugar, firmly packed, with ½ c. water 5 minutes.

MAPLE SYRUP: Baste ham with 2 c. maple syrup.

JELLY: Spread over ham 1 c. currant or apple jelly, cooked with 1 tblsp. cornstarch until clear.

ORANGE: Spread 1 c. orange marmalade over ham. Or spread over ham 1 c. brown sugar, firmly packed, and juice and grated peel of 1 orange, mixed. Garnish with orange slices.

CHERRY: Spread 1 c. sweet cherry preserves over ham.

CREAMED COUNTRY-STYLE HAM

For a farm feast, serve on hot corn sticks, biscuits, waffles or toast

1	tblsp. ham fat or butter
1	tblsp. chopped onion
2	c. chopped cooked lean ham
¼	c. flour
2½	c. milk

• Place fat in heavy frying pan, add onion and cook until onion is tender, not browned. Add ham, stir and heat.
• Add flour, stir and cook about 1 minute. Add milk, ½ c. at a time, stirring constantly. Cook 2 to 5 minutes until mixture is thick as heavy cream. Makes 4 servings.

Note: You can use scraps of cooked ham. The hock makes excellent creamed ham.

Slick Tricks with Ham

Almost all good country cooks have pet ways with cooked ham. Here are a few favorites from FARM JOURNAL readers. You'll want to try them.

WAFFLES: Sprinkle 2 tblsp. finely chopped ham on each waffle just before baking.

BISCUITS: When baking biscuits (2 c. flour), add ⅔ c. finely ground ham to the flour-fat mixture.

SALAD: Moisten 4 c. diced ham, ¾ c. chopped salted peanuts and 1½ c. diced celery, mixed, with salad dressing. Serve on crisp lettuce.

DEVILED EGGS: Add ½ c. finely ground ham to the mashed yolks of 6 hard-cooked eggs. Season with salad dressing and mustard pickle relish and heap in egg whites. Garnish with minced parsley or dust with paprika.

HAM IN POPOVERS: Fill hot popovers (recipe in Chapter 5) with Creamed Country-Style Ham (recipe above). A wonderful luncheon dish.

Sizzling Country Sausage

If your family approves of the sausage you make, treat your recipe like the treasure it is. While homemakers often disagree on sausage seasonings, almost everyone believes nothing tastes better on a cold morning than sausage with fried apples, scrambled eggs, pancakes or golden gravy and hot biscuits. Seasonings for this country special vary from one farm to another and in different areas. Southern cooks almost always add a generous dash of red pepper, for instance.

Choose the seasonings your family prefers or buy the ready-to-use blends on the market. But do grind *1 part fat to 3 parts lean pork to make sausage.* More fat makes it shrink when cooked and too rich—less gives hard patties that do not brown readily.

Combine the ingredients properly: either cut the pork in small pieces or put it through the chopper, using a coarse plate. Then spread it on a table or other flat surface and evenly sprinkle on the seasonings. Grind seasoned meat with a ⅛ or ³⁄₁₆″ plate.

When you feel adventurous and are not pleased with the way your sausage tastes, try different seasonings. You may want to make up a small batch first and test it on the family. Here are sausages that three excellent country cooks champion, along with three sausage tricks from farm kitchens.

GEORGIA SAUSAGE: To 25 lbs. ground pork add 1 c. salt, 3 tblsp. black pepper, ½ tblsp. ground red pepper and 3 tblsp. rubbed sage.

NORTH DAKOTA SAUSAGE: To 25 lbs. ground pork add 1 c. salt, 2 tblsp. rubbed sage, 2 tblsp. black pepper, 1 tsp. sweet marjoram leaves, 1 tblsp. sugar, 1 tsp. ground mace, 1 tsp. red pepper and 1 c. flour.

IOWA SAUSAGE: With 4 lbs. pork trimmings use 5 tsp. salt, 4 tsp. rubbed sage, 2 tsp. black pepper, ½ tsp. ground cloves or 1 tsp. ground nutmeg and 1 tsp. sugar. The country cook who champions this blend of seasonings warns that you may wish to omit the cloves or nutmeg.

Note: See the chapters on Freezing: Meat, Poultry, Fish and Game; Canning: Meat, Poultry and Game for directions for freezing and canning sausage.

Tricks with Sausage

BEEF PORK SAUSAGE: A Michigan country cook uses 1 lb. lean beef to every 3 lbs. pork for her sausage famous in her neighborhood. She especially recommends adding beef when the pork is fat.

HALF-AND-HALF SAUSAGE: Make North Dakota Sausage with equal parts of beef and pork. (Note that flour is sprinkled on with the seasonings.) Add a little cold water to make neat patties easily.

NO-CRUMBLE SAUSAGE: The secret of this, an Illinois farm woman says, is to add a little cold water to the sausage. She kneads it until the mixture becomes sticky and doughlike. Then she packs the sausage in a pan and chills it to slice for cooking. Slices hold their shape—do not crumble.

PENNSYLVANIA DUTCH SAUSAGE

A big family's favorite sausage recipe —note it contains brown sugar

20 lbs. fresh pork trimmings, cut into cubes
¾ c. salt
6 tblsp. black pepper
1 c. brown sugar, firmly packed

• Mix meat with seasonings before grinding; grind meat twice, using ⅛" hole plate.
• Attach stuffer spout; force enough sausage into spout to fill it and prevent air pockets; slip casing over spout; feed on as much casing as spout will hold.
• Stuff casings to desired length; then tie ends together with strong twine. Hang sausage to keep round shape.
• Smoke or freeze. Makes 20 pounds.

Note: If you like stuffed smoked sausage but don't have casings, you may be able to order them at the meat market or locker plant. Or, make cloth casings from cheesecloth, stitching about 12 by 1½".

Index

INDEX